The Protection of Civilians in Peacekeeping Operations

International Humanitarian Law Series

Editors-in-Chief

Professor Timothy L.H. McCormack

Editorial Advisory Board

VOLUME 71

The International Humanitarian Law Series is a series of monograhs and edited volumes which aims to promote scholarly analysis and discussion of both the theory and practice of the international legal regulation of armed conflict.

The series explores substantive issues of International Humanitarian Law, including:

- Protection for victims of armed conflict and regulation of the means and method of warfare
- Questions of application of the various legal regimes for the conduct of armed conflict
- Issues relating to the implementation of International Humanitarian Law obligations
- National and international approaches to the enforcement of the law and
- The interactions between International Humanitarian Law and other related areas of international law such as Human Rights, Refugee Law, Arms Control and Disarmament Law, and Intenational Criminal Law.

The titles published in this series are listed at *brill.com/ihul*

The Protection of Civilians in Peacekeeping Operations

A Legal Obligation

By

Tamer Morris

BRILL | NIJHOFF

LEIDEN | BOSTON

Cover illustration: Senegalese peacekeepers serving with the United Nations Organization Stabilization Mission in the Democratic Republic of the Congo (MONUSCO) prepare to go on patrol in the city of Goma on November 9, 2022. Since October 20, fighting has resumed between the Congolese army and the M23 (March 23 Movement), allegedly backed by the Rwandan army. In the two weeks prior to November 9, 2023, the M23 has doubled the size of the territory under its control, approaching 30 kilometers from Goma, the provincial capital of more than one million people that sits on the border with Rwanda. Alexis Huguet / AFP.

Library of Congress Cataloging-in-Publication Data

Names: Morris, Tamer, author.
Title: The protection of civilians in peacekeeping operations : a legal obligation / by Tamer Morris.
Description: Boston : Brill/Nijhoff, 2024. | Series: International humanitarian law series, 1389-6776 ; volume 71 | Includes bibliographical references and index. | Summary: "While the Security Council has been mandating peacekeepers to protect civilians since 1999, there is still contention on its legal meaning. Even though the concept of 'protection' can seem self-evident, as the concept of 'protection' is borrowed language, each body of law will perceive 'protection' through a different lens"– Provided by publisher.
Identifiers: LCCN 2024027457 (print) | LCCN 2024027458 (ebook) | ISBN 9789004707306 (hardback) | ISBN 9789004707313 (ebook)
Subjects: LCSH: War–Protection of civilians. | Peacekeeping forces (International law) | Responsibility to protect (International law)
Classification: LCC KZ6515 .M67 2024 (print) | LCC KZ6515 (ebook) | DDC 341.5/84–dc23/eng/20240627
LC record available at https://lccn.loc.gov/2024027457
LC ebook record available at https://lccn.loc.gov/2024027458

Typeface for the Latin, Greek, and Cyrillic scripts: "Brill". See and download: brill.com/brill-typeface.

ISSN 1389-6776
ISBN 978-90-04-70730-6 (hardback)
ISBN 978-90-04-70731-3 (e-book)
DOI 10.1163/9789004707313

This book is printed on acid-free paper and produced in a sustainable manner.

The Protection of Civilians in Peacekeeping Operations

A Legal Obligation

By

Tamer Morris

BRILL | NIJHOFF

LEIDEN | BOSTON

Cover illustration: Senegalese peacekeepers serving with the United Nations Organization Stabilization Mission in the Democratic Republic of the Congo (MONUSCO) prepare to go on patrol in the city of Goma on November 9, 2022. Since October 20, fighting has resumed between the Congolese army and the M23 (March 23 Movement), allegedly backed by the Rwandan army. In the two weeks prior to November 9, 2023, the M23 has doubled the size of the territory under its control, approaching 30 kilometers from Goma, the provincial capital of more than one million people that sits on the border with Rwanda. Alexis Huguet / AFP.

Library of Congress Cataloging-in-Publication Data

Names: Morris, Tamer, author.
Title: The protection of civilians in peacekeeping operations : a legal obligation / by Tamer Morris.
Description: Boston : Brill/Nijhoff, 2024. | Series: International humanitarian law series, 1389-6776 ; volume 71 | Includes bibliographical references and index. | Summary: "While the Security Council has been mandating peacekeepers to protect civilians since 1999, there is still contention on its legal meaning. Even though the concept of 'protection' can seem self-evident, as the concept of 'protection' is borrowed language, each body of law will perceive 'protection' through a different lens"– Provided by publisher.
Identifiers: LCCN 2024027457 (print) | LCCN 2024027458 (ebook) | ISBN 9789004707306 (hardback) | ISBN 9789004707313 (ebook)
Subjects: LCSH: War–Protection of civilians. | Peacekeeping forces (International law) | Responsibility to protect (International law)
Classification: LCC KZ6515 .M67 2024 (print) | LCC KZ6515 (ebook) | DDC 341.5/84–dc23/eng/20240627
LC record available at https://lccn.loc.gov/2024027457
LC ebook record available at https://lccn.loc.gov/2024027458

Typeface for the Latin, Greek, and Cyrillic scripts: "Brill". See and download: brill.com/brill-typeface.

ISSN 1389-6776
ISBN 978-90-04-70730-6 (hardback)
ISBN 978-90-04-70731-3 (e-book)
DOI 10.1163/9789004707313

This book is printed on acid-free paper and produced in a sustainable manner.

Contents

Acknowledgements

I would foremost like to acknowledge my gratefulness and thanks to my supervisors Professor Ben Saul and Professor Emily Crawford. They have made this project not only uncomplicated but extremely enjoyable. I would further like to thank them for their reassurance and their instrumental advice. I was privileged to have their guidance and be able to discuss the law with two magnificent minds.

I am very grateful for members of the UN Secretariat, Member States, UN researchers and the peacekeeping community for their consultation and involvement with this project. I would like to thank them for their time, encouragement and advice regarding my research.

A special thanks must be given to my family and friends. I cannot express how grateful I am for everyone listening to my endless discussions regarding my research. I thank them all for their support and encouragement, and not slapping me when I spoke too much.

Note on Previous Publications and Presentations

Some of this research has been published in earlier forms: "State Responsibility and Accountability in UN Peacekeeping: The Case of The Mothers of Srebrenica v. The Netherlands" (2022) 29 International Peacekeeping 204.

Introduction

Since the formation of the UN Mission in Sierra Leone (*UNAMSIL*) in 1999, the United Nations (*UN*) Security Council has mandated particular UN peace missions to use "all necessary means" to protect civilians under Chapter VII of the UN Charter. The mandate on protection of civilians originated as a response to the UN's failures in Rwanda and Srebrenica, particularly the 1999 report which concluded that the UN Assistance Mission for Rwanda (*UNAMIR*) had information of possible "extermination"[1] of the Tutsis in Kigali, but was informed by UN headquarters that no "action, including response to request for protection, should be taken by UNAMIR until clear guidance is received from Headquarters."[2] The inaction of the UN was accentuated with mass killings occurring the following year in Srebrenica, where "at least five written messages were sent on that day, expressing alarm about potential human rights abuses having been committed or that potentially might be committed."[3] The protection of civilians mandate marked the turning point in the Security Council's intention that peacekeepers were no longer to merely observe, but rather to use all avenues at their disposal to protect civilians under threat of physical violence.

Since its initial insertion, the Security Council has varied the language of the protection of civilians mandate to aggregate its capacity and forcefulness. Since 1999, the protection of civilians mandate has become a central theme of UN peacekeeping, becoming one of the primary motives for the deployment of new UN peace missions. Currently, UN peace missions in Mali, Democratic Republic of the Congo (*DRC*), South Sudan and the Central African Republic (*CAR*) are all mandated with the primary task to protect civilians.[4]

Although, protection of civilians is a central theme, there remains a divergence between what is mandated by the Security Council and genuine protection received by civilians in the field. Although the concept of protection pre-existed in a range of international instruments (particular international humanitarian law and international human rights law), such laws governing

1 United Nations Security Council, *Report of the Independant Inquiry into the Actions of the United Nations during the 1994 Genocide in Rwanda*, UN Doc S/1999/1257 at 10.

2 Ibid at 11.

3 United Nations General Assembly, *Report of the Secretary-General Pursuant to General Assembly Resolution 53/35: The Fall of Srebrenica*, 15 November 1999, UN Doc A/54/549 at paragraph 352.

4 A table of peacekeeping missions can be found in Appendix 2.

 | DOI:10.1163/9789004707313_002

the protection of civilians were not intended as a guidance to the deployment of peacekeepers.[5] The variance between Security Council resolutions and the practice by peacekeepers is commonly attributed to the absence of any guidelines or operational instruction to assist peacekeepers in implementing the ever-growing mandate.[6] Subsequently, the Security Council has been heavily criticised for inadequately managing the international community's expectation of the protection mandate, and for failing to provide adequate resources for peacekeepers to achieve their mandate.[7]

While protection of civilians is an ongoing discussion in the UN, there is still no consensus on the legal interpretation of the protection mandate conferred by the Security Council. Although peacekeepers' accountability and performance are prominent discussions within the UN and academic literature, it is unreasonable to demand a 'minimum' standard from UN peacekeepers when there is no clear legal framework on the obligation to protect.

This book seeks to clarify the legal framework of the protection of civilians mandate, by firstly identifying the legal character of Security Council's resolutions on the protection of civilians in UN peace missions; secondly, to whom the legal obligation is addressed; thirdly, the substantive content of any 'protection' obligations, chiefly by reference to international humanitarian law (*IHL*) and international human rights law (*IHRL*), as well as policy considerations; and fourthly, the availability of accountability and remedies for violations of the obligation to protect.

It will be maintained that the Security Council's mandate to protect civilians creates a legally binding obligation to protect. This obligation binds the UN, troop contributing countries (*TCCs*)/police contributing countries (*PCCs*) and host States of UN peace missions. Since the obligation is mandated by the Security Council, any interpretation of the obligation must be foremost discovered within the wording of the mandate, the Security Council's reports and guidance. As indicated by the Security Council, the content of the obligation to protect is found within existing laws, specifically IHL and IHRL. The obligation to protect is initiated with the deployment of peacekeepers, and so exists both in armed conflict and law enforcement situations. However, there are shortfalls within the existing legal framework that will need clarification from

5 United Nations Security Council, *Protection of Civilians in Armed Conflict, Security Council Report: Cross-Cutting Report, 2010 No. 3*, 29 October 2010 at 4.

6 Nicholas Lamp and Dana Trif, 'United Nations Peacekeeping Forces and the Protection of Civilians in Armed Conflict' 47 (2009) *Hertie School of Governance – Working papers* at 3.

7 Victoria K. Holt and Tobias C. Berkman, *The Impossible Mandate? Military Preparedness, the Responsibility to Protect and Modern Peace Operations* (The Stimson Center, 2006) at 86.

the Security Council, specifically regarding peacekeepers law enforcement undertakings, such as the detention of individuals. Further if the obligation is breached, the immunity of the UN will limit victims' legal avenues against the organisation. Although unlikely in practice, a TCC/PCC that is exerting control can be sanctioned by the Security Council for a breach under the UN Charter, or a claim by the host State against the TCC/PCC. However, liability can be sought by an individual victim against a TCC/PCC when they are exercising effective control, in a regional human rights court, as UN immunity does not cover a wrongful act of a State under the law.

To reach this conclusion, Chapter 1 of this book will demonstrate that the protection of civilians mandate is not merely an authority to use force, but rather a legal obligation to protect civilians. This obligation will bind the UN, TCCs/PCCs and the host States to ensure that the obligation is respected and fulfilled. Through an examination of the language of the Security Council's mandate on the protection of civilians it is determined that the mandate is drafted to create a positive legal obligation.

Once the legal obligation is observed, Chapter 2 will commence the discussion of content of the legal obligation to protect. Specifically, Chapter 2 will analyse the language of the Security Council and divide the content of the obligation into two categories – protection against the threat of physical violence, and human rights protection. It is concluded 'protection' under the obligation is the protection of legal rights of civilians, and therefore the content of the obligation must be found within existing international law structures. Although the obligation is divided into two categories, the emphasis of the Security Council is the protection against physical violence, as will be evidenced through their debates and resolutions.

Chapter 3 will scrutinise the obligation to protect against physical violence, specifically investigating the content of the obligation to protect recognised within IHL and IHRL. It is resolved that the content of the obligation is the protection of the 'civilian' status, and therefore the protection from direct and indiscriminate attacks, as well as protection from conflict-related violence. As peacekeepers cannot protect all civilians at all times, the obligation will be owed to civilians within their 'area of deployment', that is, within the vicinity of peacekeepers and UN base operations, as well as areas of patrol. In using force under the obligation to protect, peacekeepers are obliged in situations of armed conflict to ensure that all force is aligned with their obligations under IHL. The Security Council will still need to provide clarification on the interpretation of 'area of their deployment' as it will have a direct affect over the scope of the obligation.

Chapter 4 will continue to examine the obligation to protect against physical violence in regard to police enforcement activities under the obligation to protect. Chapter 4 will conclude that although peacekeepers are mandated to take all necessary measures, this does not give them the authority to detain individuals indefinitely, as this will be a violation of their human rights obligations. However, peacekeepers are confronted with a conflict between detaining individuals to protect civilians, and their observance of non-refoulement by not transferring individuals to local authorities. Therefore, as UN peace missions are currently limited in operational approaches other than detention, this conflict will need to be clarified or supplemented by the Security Council.

Chapter 5 will focus on the first major group identified by the Security Council for special attention by peacekeepers, that is women and children. It will be concluded that peacekeepers are to protect women from sexual and gender-based violence, however the content of the obligation is in association with conflict-related violence. Nevertheless, outside the detention of individuals, the Security Council needs to give guidance on what is expected by peacekeepers in order to protect women against conflict-related violence. Regarding the protection of children peacekeepers are to protect children from the recruitment into armed groups and the assistance of disarmament, demobilise and reintegration (*DDR*). Under their obligation stipulated in Chapter 3, peacekeepers must guarantee that all force follows the rules of proportionality and distinction. That is, when engaging with armed groups, UN peace missions must guarantee that women and children and not being targeted, even though they are 'members' of these groups. Moreover, UN peace missions are obliged to warrant that sufficient mechanisms are in place for all children detained as members of these groups.

Chapter 6 will focus on the second major group identified by the Security Council within the mandate to protect, that is, internally displaced individuals (*IDPs*). It will be concluded in Chapter 6 that peacekeepers are obliged to respect, protect and fulfil the human rights of all individuals under peacekeepers' control. Principally, IDPs in UN-controlled camps must have their rights guaranteed by UN peace missions. Outside the instances of effective control, UN peace missions are only obliged to monitor and report human rights violations to the UN.

Finally, Chapter 7 will look at the issue of accountability, and the legal ramifications of the obligation to protect. It will be determined that the UN as an organisation can be liable for a breach of obligation, however, due to their immunities before national courts there is no real legal avenue to be taken against the UN. Furthermore, international tribunals do not have jurisdiction to hold the UN accountable. As TCCs/PCCs, other international organisations and other States are involved in peacekeeping, all can be jointly responsible for the actions of peacekeepers, therefore, they can be held liable for the violations of international law. Moreover, it will be concluded that UN immunities does not extend to a State's breach of an obligation under the law when they are exercising effective control over their contingent.

1 The Evolution of the Protection of Civilians Mandate

In the aftermath of Rwanda and Srebrenica, the Canadian Mission to the UN, in their role as president of the Security Council, brought protection of civilians to the Security Council's agenda. In February 1999, the Security Council held their first open debate on protection of civilians in armed conflict,[8] which resulted in the Security Council adopting *Resolution 1261* in August 1999, on children in armed conflict. In the same month the Secretary-General submitted his bulletin on *Observance by UN forces of International Humanitarian Law* (the *Bulletin*),[9] in which the Secretary-General confirmed that IHL applies to all peace missions. Following *Resolution 1261*, the Secretary-General submitted his first report on the protection of civilians,[10] and the Security Council passed their first overarching resolution on protection of civilians, where they expressed their "willingness to consider how peacekeeping mandates might better address the negative impact of armed conflict on civilians."[11]

Ultimately, the protection of civilians debate reached its climax in October 1999, with the insertion of the protection mandate in the establishment of UNAMSIL in Sierra Leone. As UNAMSIL was the first mission to be created since February 1999, the insertion of the mandate was Security Council's attempt to take practical steps to ensure that peacekeepers are actively protecting civilians. Following the establishment of UNAMSIL, in 2000, the Security Council inserted the same mandate in the UN mission in the DRC.[12] In March 2000, Secretary-General Annan convened a high-level panel to review the current structures of UN peacekeeping to make recommendations. As a result of the

8 United Nations Security Council, *Overview of Security Council Meeting Records*, S/PV.3980 (1999).

9 United Nations, *Secretary-General's Bulletin: Observance by United Nations Forces of International Humanitarian Law*, UN Doc ST/SGB/1999/13.

10 United Nations Security Council, *Report of the Secretary-General to the Security Council on the Protection of Civilians in Armed Conflict*, UN Doc S/1999/957.

11 *United Nations Security Council Resolution 1265* (1999) at operational paragraph 11.

12 *United Nations Security Council Resolution 1291* (2000).

high-level panel, the Brahimi Report was submitted in August 2000. Within the Brahimi Report the protection of civilians was referred to as implied authorisation within UN peacekeeping:

> Indeed, peacekeepers – troops or police – who witness violence against civilians should be presumed to be authorized to stop it, within their means, in support of basic United Nations principles and, as stated in the report of the Independent Inquiry on Rwanda, consistent with "the perception and the expectation of protection created by [an operation's] very presence".[13]

Following the Brahimi Report on 31 October 2000 the Security Council passed the landmark *Resolution 1325* on women, peace and security. In the following year the first protection advisor was deployed to assist UNAMSIL.

In 2003, the Security Council expanded the protection of civilians mandate from its original formulae by mandating in the establishment of UN Mission in Liberia (*UNMIL*) to 'promote and protect' human rights.[14] Moreover, with the establishment of UNMIL the Security Council inserted specific references to the protection of women and children within the mandate.[15]

In 2004 Secretary-General Annan, submitted his report *A More Secure World: Our Shared Responsibility* to the General Assembly. Although the report only touched upon peacekeeping and the protection of civilians mandate, it is famous for explicitly mentioning the 'responsibility to protect' doctrine,[16] and confirmed that the distinction between peacekeeping and peace-enforcement is misleading, and no longer applies to modern peacekeeping.[17]

In 2006, the Secretary-General in his report *Overview of the Financing of the United Nations Peacekeeping Operations*,[18] the Secretary-General noted that Department of Peacekeeping Operations (*DPKO*) would be working on

---

13 United Nations, *Report of the Panel on United Nations Peace Operations of 21 August 2000*, UN Doc A/55/305 (Brahimi Report) at paragraph 62.

14 *United Nations Security Council Resolution 1509* (2003).

15 Ibid at operational paragraph 3(f).

16 United Nations General Assembly, *A More Secure World: Our Shared Responsibility, Report of the High-level Panel on Threats, Challenges and Change, 2 December 2004*, UN Doc A/59/565 at paragraph 36.

17 Ibid at paragraph 212.

18 United Nations General Assembly, *Overview of the Financing of the United Nations Peacekeeping Operations: Budget Performance for the Period from 1 July 2004 to 30 June 2005 and Budget for the Period from 1 July 2006 to 30 June 2007, Report of the Secretary-General, 24 February 2006*, UN Doc A/60/696 (*Peace Operations 2010*).

best strategies for peacekeeping missions. However, it took DPKO 2 years before submitting their guidelines. In March 2007, the Department of Field Support (*DFS*) was created to assist DPKO with their support of peacekeeping. In the same year, the Secretary-General submitted a report on strengthening the capacity of the UN to manage and sustain peace operations.[19] However, within his report protection of civilians was mentioned solely as a reference to the complexity of modern peacekeeping.[20] By July 2007, the Security Council established UN-African Union Hybrid Operation in Darfur (*UNAMID*) to protect civilians.

In 2008, DPKO published the *UN Peacekeeping Operations Principles and Guidelines*, better known as the Capstone Doctrine.[21] The Capstone Doctrine does not adequately discuss any operational guidance, nor does it barely touch upon the protection of civilians mandate. However, it does identify that:

> The protection of civilians requires concerted and coordinated action among the military, police and civilian components of a United Nations peacekeeping operation and must be main-streamed into the planning and conduct of its core activities. United Nations humanitarian agencies and non-governmental organization (NGO) partners also undertake a broad range of activities in support of the protection of civilians. Close coordination with these actors is, therefore, essential.[22]

However, the Capstone Doctrine did identify the importance of the 'promotion and protection' of human rights to peace missions, and that all "United Nations entities have a responsibility to ensure that human rights are promoted and protected by and within their field operations."[23]

In the same year, in *Resolution 1856* (2008) the Security Council inserted explicit language for the protection of internally displaced persons (*IDPs*) to the UN Mission in the DRC. In the following year, the Security Council in *Resolution 1888* and *1889* (2009) mandated the establishment of Women

19 United Nations General Assembly, *Comprehensive Report on Strengthening th Capacity of the United Nations to Manage and Sustain Peace Operations*, UN Doc A/61/858, 13 April 2007.

20 Ibid at paragraph 16.

21 United Nations Department of Peacekeeping Operations and Department of Field Support, *United Nations Peacekeeping Operations: Principles and Guidelines*, 2008 (*Capstone Doctrine*).

22 Ibid at 24.

23 Ibid at 27.

Protection Advisors and confirmed their intention to deploy them in UN peace missions.

In 2009, the UN Office for the Coordination of Humanitarian Affairs (*OCHA*) and DPKO commissioned an independent report on protection of civilians, which highlighted the lack of operational guidance to the mandate.[24] As a response, DPKO and DFS released the *Draft Operational Concept on Protection of Civilians*,[25] within the Operational Concept. The document identified that there was no common understanding of what 'protection' is, and also established the still-current three-tier understanding of protection:

- Tier 1: Protection through political process
- Tier 2: Providing protection from physical violence
- Tier 3: Establishing a protective environment[26]

Although DPKO/DFS mentioned that there is no hierarchy to the tiered system, within Security Resolutions there is still a focus on use of force, and protection from physical violence. Furthermore, the Operational Concept does not define a minimum standard of protection, nor does it attempt to interpret an obligation to protect.

In 2010, the Security Council established UN Organization Stabilization Mission in the DRC (*MONUSCO*), as the first peacekeeping mission deployed primarily for protection of civilians. Following their deployment in November 2010, MONUSCO in assistance with DRC government forces launched operation "Protection Shield" to neutralise armed groups in South Kivu. In the following year, the Security Council established the UN Mission in South Sudan (*UNMISS*) to primarily protect civilians.[27]

The protection of civilians regime changed directions, when in 2013, the Security Council established the Force Intervention Brigade (*FIB*) to 'neutralise' armed groups in the DRC.[28] Later that year, before the FIB was deployed, MONUSCO peacekeepers were killed in operations to push M24 out of Goma. In December 2013, outbreaks of violence in Juba, South Sudan, forced 30,000

24 Victoria K. Holt, Glyn Taylor and Max Kelly, 'Protecting Civilians in the Context of UN Peacekeeping Operations: Success, Setbacks and Remaining Challenges', *Independent study jointly commissioned by the Department of Peacekeeping Operations and the Office for the Coordination of Humanitarian Affairs* (2009).

25 United Nations Department of Peacekeeping Operations and Department of Field Support, *Draft DPKO/DFS Operational Concept on the Protection of Civilians in United Nations Peacekeeping Operations*, 2009 at paragraph 2 (*Draft Operational Concept*).

26 Ibid.

27 *United Nations Security Council Resolution 1999* (2011).

28 *United Nations Security Council Resolution 2098* (2013).

civilians to seek refuge in UN bases, spontaneously creating the protection of civilians sites (*PoC sites*).

In early 2014, the Security Council established the UN Multidimensional Integrated Stabilization Mission in CAR (*MINUSCA*) to primarily protect civilians, while in June 2014, the Security Council inserted the protection of civilians mandate in UN Multidimensional Integrated Stabilization Mission in Mali (*MINUSMA*). In that year, Secretary-General Ban-Ki Moon convened a High-level Panel to review UN peacekeeping. In 2015, the *Report of the High-level Independent Panel on Peace Operations on Uniting Our Strengths for Peace: Politics, Partnership and People* (*HIPPO Report*)[29] was submitted to the UN. The HIPPO Report identified that protection of civilians was a core function of UN peacekeeping, however "expectations and capability must converge."[30] Moreover, the HIPPO Report emphasised the use of force and that "[n]ew operating environments demand much greater clarity on when and how the United Nations and its partners will use force, under what conditions and with what principles."[31]

In July 2016, attacks in Juba in South Sudan overflowed to the Juba PoC site. Chinese peacekeepers abandoned their post resulting in the deaths of more than 20 civilians.[32] Moreover, UNMISS failed to respond to a request for assistance from a humanitarian camp, located 1.2 kilometres from UN base, which resulted in three humanitarian workers being sexually assaulted, five being physical beaten, and one killed.[33] In August 2016, the Security Council established the Regional Protection Force (*RPF*) to be deployed in Juba.[34]

In 2017, UN Police (*UNPOL*) published guidelines of the role of UNPOL in protection of civilians. In the guidelines it was identified that protection of civilians is a central theme of UNPOL's work. In the same year the UN-commissioned report by Santos Cruz (*Cruz Report*) was submitted focusing on protection of UN personnel, and how peacekeepers should be using more force to deal with armed groups.

In 2018 the Secretary-General launched the 'Action for Peacekeeping' (*A4P*) initiative to strengthen UN peacekeeping, by reconfirming shared

---

29 United Nations General Assembly and Security Council, *The Future of United Nations Peace Operations: Implementation of the Recommendations of the High-level Independent Panel on Peace Operations*, 17 June 2015, UN Doc A/70/357-S/2015/682 (*HIPPO Report*).

30 Ibid at paragraph 38(b).

31 Ibid at paragraph 38(c).

32 Executive Summary of the Independent Special Investigation into the Violence which Occured in Juba in 2016 and UNMISS Response.

33 Ibid.

34 *United Nations Security Council Resolution 2304* (2016).

commitments among Member States and regional organisations. In November 2018, 112 civilians were killed in attacks on Alindao IDP camp in CAR, as only 55 peacekeepers were deployed to protect the camp.

In 2019, the Secretary-General reformed the UN's peace and security pillar, by creating the Department of Peace Operations (*DPO*), which incorporated both DPKO and DFS. In 2020, DPO collates and releases *The Protection of Civilians in United Nations Peacekeeping Handbook* (*2020 Handbook*) and the *Handbook for United Nations Field Missions on Preventing and Responding to Conflict-Related Sexual Violence* (*CRSV Handbook*). Both Handbooks were to give practical guidance to UN contingents on implementing the protection of civilians mandate.

In December 2020, the Security Council unanimously adopted *Resolution 2559* to terminate the UNAMID mandate, and urged the Sudanese government to "fully and swiftly implement the National Plan for Civilian Protection (S/2020/429) and to protect civilians in Darfur."[35]

In March 2021, the Secretary-General announced Peacekeeping Plus (A4P+) a two-year implementation strategy for A4P that prioritises urgent challenges facing UN peacekeeping.

In July 2022 protests irrupted in the DRC against peacekeepers due to their inability to protect civilians. During the protests 36 civilians, including 4 UN peacekeepers, died.[36] Further, MONUSCO's spokesperson was expelled from the DRC for inappropriate comments. The climax was reached in February 2023 when MONUSCO peacekeepers fired into a crowd of civilians blocking their entrance, killing 8 civilians, and injuring 28.[37]

In June 2023, Mali's de facto government demanded the withdraw of the UN peace mission, deployed since 2013.[38] With the removal of consent, the Security Council mandated the withdraw of MINUSMA. On 20 July 2023, Secretary-General Guterres presented *A New Agenda for Peace*, which outlined his vision for multilateral efforts for peace and security. The New Agenda for Peace emphasised Regional approaches to peace operations, as "United Nations and regional peace operations can play important roles in this respect: mobilizing

35 *United Nations Security Council Resolution 2559* (2020).

36 Jason Burke, "Death toll reaches 36 in eastern DRC as protesters turn on UN peacekeepers", *The Guardian*, 5 August 2022.

37 "Eight civilians dead in clash with UN peacekeepers in east Congo -local govt", *Reuters*, 9 February 2023, https://www.reuters.com/world/africa/eight-civilians-dead-clash-with-un-peacekeepers-east-congo-local-govt-2023-02-08/.

38 "UN peacekeeping mission in Mali officially ends after 10 years", *Al Jazeera*, 11 December 2023.

collective action, promoting comprehensive approaches with strong civilian, police and development dimensions and – most importantly – pursuing political solutions and sustainable peace."[39] In December 2023, the DRC government demanded the accelerated withdraw of MONUSCO, contending that the UN mission as ineffective.[40]

Timeline of Events is summarised in Appendix 1.

2 Peacekeeping Structure and Deployment

In order to sufficiently assess the protection of civilians mandate, an understanding of peacekeeping structure is essential. Once the Security Council has mandated a UN peace mission, the command of the peacekeeping Mission is vested in the Secretary-General. The Secretary-General, in turn, appoints the Special Representative of the Secretary-General (*SRSG*) to serve as head of the Mission and is responsible for implementing the mandate.[41] Therefore, in practice, the SRSG is to interpret the Security Council's mandate into a strategic and operational guidance for the Mission. The SRSG reports to the Secretary-General through the Under-Secretary-General for Peace Operations and DPO.

Before peacekeepers are deployed, a Status of Forces Agreement (*SOFA*) is signed between the host State and the Mission. The SOFA sets out the rights and obligations of the host State and the Mission during deployment. The SOFA is negotiated by the DPO and the Permanent Mission of the host State to the UN.

The SRSG is assisted in the implementation of the mandate by the Force and Police Commanders, who are heads of command of the military and police components of the Mission respectively. However, on a tactical level both Force and Police commanders will rely on the TCC's and PCC's contingent commanders for reporting arrangements and disciplinary action.

When a Member State decides to contribute troops to a Mission, a Memorandum of Understanding (*MOU*) is signed between the UN and the Member State. The MOU is an agreement that sets out the administrative

39 United Nations, *Our Common Agenda Policy Brief 9: A New Agenda for Peace*, at 13.

40 "All UN peacekeepers to leave DR Congo by end of 2024", *Al Jazeera*, 13 January 2024, https://www.aljazeera.com/news/2024/1/13/un-says-all-peacekeepers-will-leave-dr-congo-by-end-of-2024#:~:text=The%20United%20Nations%20peacekeeping%20mission,by%20the%20end%20of%202024.

41 United Nations Department of Peacekeeping Operations, *Handbook on United Nations Multidimensional Peacekeeping Operations*, December 2003 at paragraph 9.

conditions that govern the contribution of troops. Further the MOU will outline the standards of conduct for the Member State contribution. Although there is a model MOU, each MOU is negotiated between the Department of Operational Support and the TCC/PCC.

The civilian components of peacekeeping do not follow a standard command and control structure across Missions.[42] Each Mission will vary in their civilian structure based on their mandate and the capabilities of the Mission. Therefore, civilian components determine their own internal reporting structures.

3 Methodology

This research analyses the language employed by the Security Council within the protection of civilians mandates, using a content analysis approach.[43] As UN peace missions are created by Security Council resolutions, the obligation and its content will be found within Security Council's syntax. Therefore, all UN Peacekeeping Security Council resolutions from 1999 were analysed to identify joint words, phrases and activities. Further this categorisation of the language must be compared against UN protection reports and the DPO's guidelines and manuals. Although academic literature has written on UN peacekeeping, the core research conducted on the protection of civilians mandate is UN documentation and reports. Further, a doctrinal approach is used to analyse the obligation to protect found in existing international law, in particular, to arrange and order existing laws into categories that applies directly to UN peacekeeping. This approach is utilised to identify gaps within the existing framework that will need clarification from the Security Council.

Further interviews were undertaken with the UN Secretariat, TCCs/PCCs, and Member States who are members of the Special Committee on Peace-Keeping Operations (C34). The interviews involved a grounded theory approach,[44] using open questioning in order to prompt responses from interviewees on a wide range of normative, practice-oriented and theoretical

42 United Nations Department of Peacekeeping Operations and Department of Field Support, *Policy: Authority, Command and Control in United Nations Peacekeeping Operations*, 15 February 2008 at paragraph 63.

43 Klaus Krippendorff, 'Content Analysis' in Neil J. Salkind (ed), *Encyclopedia of Reserach Design* (SAGE Publications, 2010).

44 Anselm Strauss and Juliet Cobin, 'Grounded Theory Methodology' in N Denzin and Y Lincoln (eds), *Strategies of Qualitative Inquiry* (SAGE Publications, 1998).

issues. The questions varied according to the interviewee and context and were developed in the light of the findings of the research as it progressed. A list of questions that was asked across the field can be found in Appendix 3. Further a qualitative empirical approach was undertaken with the data gathered from interviews and the reports prepared by the UN and non-government organisations, to determine the content of the obligation being practiced in the field.

This research is limited to analysis of UN peace missions primarily deployed under the protection of civilians mandate, that being, South Sudan, DRC, CAR and Mali, in the period from 2010.

CHAPTER 1

The Legal Obligation to Protect Civilians

Within recent UN discussions and open debates peacekeeping performance has become a featured focus.[1] Demands for accountability for peacekeeping failures are not only regarding peacekeepers' misconduct, but their failure to fulfil their mandate. Although the theme of accountability is prominent, there remains an absence of a framework to which peacekeepers can be held accountable.

While the Security Council has mandated peacekeepers to protect civilians since 1999, until recently, the peacekeeping literature has predominantly concentrated on the application of IHL and IHRL within UN missions. A large part of literature is focused on the application of IHL and the use of force; with the legal interpretation of the Security Council's mandate yet to be fully discussed. Although Wills has discussed a creation of a legal obligation,[2] the majority of work on protection of civilians is done outside academic literature by the UN and non-government organisations.

While some scholars have suggested that the protection mandate *could* place a positive obligation on peacekeepers to protect civilians,[3] it is suggested that this positive obligation is similar to that which is found in the Geneva Conventions, and so "this obligation applies to peacekeeping troops, even though they are not directly engaging in an armed conflict."[4] Wills, the foremost supporter of this positive obligation, contends that both IHL and IHRL 'require' peacekeepers to protect civilians in their "immediate care", and so they are "to take reasonable precautions, where feasible, to prevent attacks where these are clearly foreseeable."[5] Wills divides peacekeepers 'responsibility to protect' into

1 United Nations Security Council Resolution 2436 (2018).

2 Siobhán Wills, Protecting Civilians: The Obligations of Peacekeepers (Oxford University Press, 2009).

3 Scott Sheeran and Catherine Kent, 'Protection of Civilians, Responsibility to Protect, and Humanitarian Intervention' in Haidi Willmot et al (eds), *Protection of civilians* (Oxford University Press, 2016) 29 at 46; Hitoshi Nasu, 'Operationalizing the Responsibility to Protect in the Context of Civilian Protection by UN Peacekeepers' (2011) *18(4) International Peacekeeping* 364; Wills, above note 2.

4 Hitoshi Nasu, 'The Protection of Civilians from Violence and the Effects of Attacks in International Humanitarian Law' in David W Lovell and Igor Primoratz (eds), *Protecting Civilians During Violent Conflict: Theoretical and Practical Issues for the 21st Century* (Ashgate Publishing Limited, 2012) 65 at 69.

5 Wills, above note 2 at 266.

 | DOI:10.1163/9789004707313_003

three categories – "preventing attacks and abuse by their own troops; protecting people in their care from attacks and abuses by third-parties; and protecting the local population from attacks and abuse."[6]

Other commentators have suggested that by failing to protect civilians, peacekeepers are invariably failing their mandate, and thus are 'positively' obliged to protect civilians.[7] Nevertheless, this obligation is rarely seen as a legal obligation,[8] rather it is considered purely as a 'moral' obligation.[9] As Schütte explains, the language of the protection mandate does not imply a positive obligation, but "to be understood as a clarification and acknowledgement of what was expected".[10]

Within the literature a positive obligation is only discussed when civilians are under the 'control' of peacekeepers, such as the PoC sites in South Sudan.[11] Yet, the literature is undecided on the legal character of this obligation, or its implication to peacekeepers on the ground.[12]

While the protection of civilians is a central theme to the UN, there is minimal dialogue on what is the legal interpretation of the obligation to protect under the Security Council's mandate. As all Security Council decisions under Chapter VII of the UN Charter have a legal effect, so too must the protection of civilians mandate. Without a clear understanding of the obligation to protect it would be unreasonable to demand accountability of peacekeepers. Accordingly, before attempting to outline the interpretation of the protection mandate, first the legal obligation created by the mandate must be acknowledged.

In situations of unrest and armed conflict the international community relies on the obligations entrenched in international law as the benchmark associated with protection of civilians. As reiterated continually by the UN, compliance with international law is the primary answer to protection of

6 Ibid at 261.

7 Sheeran and Kent, above note 3 at 56.

8 Nasu, above note 4 at 81.

9 Hugh Breakey, 'The Protection of Civilians in Armed Conflict: Four Concepts' in Angus Francis, Vesselin Popovski and C. J. G. Sampford (eds), *Norms of Protection: Responsibility to Protect, Protection of Civilians and Their Interaction* (United Nations University Press, 2012) at 46.

10 Robert Schütte, *Civilian Protection in Armed Conflicts: Evolution, Challenges and Implementation* (Springer VS, 2013) at 162.

11 Hitoshi Nasu, 'Operationalizing the Responsibility to Protect in the Context of Civilian Protection by UN Peacekeepers' (2011) *18(4) International Peacekeeping* 364 at 368.

12 Ibid at 368.

civilians.[13] Therefore, any obligation surrounding the protection of civilians is synonymous with the obligations in IHL, IHRL, refugee law, and international criminal law.

This chapter will establish that the Security Council's mandate to protect civilians creates a legal obligation upon the UN, TCCs/PCCs and the host State. This conclusion will be reached by establishing that, as all decisions made under Chapter VII have a legally binding effect on Member States, so too must the protection of civilians mandate. Therefore, a legal obligation is formed on all Member States who willingly contribute to a UN peace mission. The legal obligation to protect will be a 'conditional obligation' binding on all Member States that enter into a UN peace mission and host States who consent to their deployment. Further as the UN is an international legal person, it will also be obliged by the mandate of the Security Council.

By scrutinising the Security Council's expression, it is apparent that there is no intention in creating a 'new' obligation, rather the Security Council is invoking existing obligations within the law. Thus, peacekeepers are obligated to protect civilians under the obligation in IHL and IHRL.

To reach this conclusion this chapter will frame the powers of the Security Council and the effect of the mandate on Member States and the UN as an organisation. As the obligation to protect is the protection under existing laws, this chapter will review 'protection' obligations in international law, in order to outline the meaning of the obligation to protect.

1 The Legal Obligation of the Protection of Civilians Mandate

Since the founding of the UN, the Security Council was granted specific powers that entrenched the Council as a distinct authority in international law. Primarily, under Article 24 of the UN Charter the Security Council was awarded the responsibility "for the maintenance of international peace and security."[14] As the expression of 'maintenance of international peace and security' is

13 United Nations Security Council, *Report of the Secretary-General on the Protection of Civilians in Armed Conflict,* UN Doc S/2016/447; United Nations Security Council, *Report of the Secretary-General on the Protection of Civilians in Armed Conflict,* UN Doc S/2017/414.

14 However, though the Security Council is given the responsibility over peace and security, according to the ICJ in the *Expenses* case, the ICJ has emphasised that the Security Council does not have exclusive authority over issues related to peace and security. The Court observed that Article 14 of the UN Charter also authorises the General Assembly to "recommend measures for the peaceful adjustment of any situation."[*Certain Expenses*

expansive, it appears to grant the Security Council with an extensive range of powers. As an example of the far-reaching use of this power, the creation of peacekeeping as a subsidiary organ of the UN was legally justified under Article 24(1).[15]

The power of the Security Council derives from States willingly consenting to be bound to the UN Charter. Therefore, alongside Article 24, Article 25 of the UN Charter binds all Member States "to accept and carry out the decisions of the Security Council". Thus, the combination of Articles 24 and 25 awards the Security Council a considerable volume of authority over Member States, as members to the UN Charter. Although Article 25 binds Member States to the decisions of the Security Council, the Security Council has only expressly referenced Article 25 in one resolution.[16] As set down in the *Namibia* case, the "obligation of states to comply with the decisions of the Council under Article 25 of the Charter extends to all decisions of the Council, not merely under Chapter VII", moreover, "to hold otherwise would be deprive this principal organ of its essential functions and powers under the Charter."[17]

The Security Council's authority is further extended with the insertion of Article 103 of the UN Charter, which specifies that if there is any conflict between UN obligations and any other international agreements, "their obligations under the present Charter shall prevail." However, it is emphasised by the International Court of Justice (*ICJ*) that Article 103 does not override

of the United Nations (Article 17, Paragraph 2, of the Charter), Advisory Opinion of 20 July 1962, ICJ Reports 1962, p.151] However, Article 14 is subject to Article 12 that specifies that the General Assembly is limited to making any recommendations if the Security Council is overseeing the same situation or matter. Thus, if the Security Council is discussing or investigating a specific situation, they are awarded exclusive decision-making powers over that matter.

15 Ibid.

16 *United Nations Security Council Resolution 2118* (2013); As Article 25 has been used infrequently, there has been contention to when Article 25 applies, and whether it has any limitations. As an illustration, in the foundational years of the UN it was asserted by the Security Council Permanent Members that Article 25 only comes into force with decisions made under Chapter VII. (Security Council Official Records, 1589th Meeting, 6 October 1971, S/PV 1589) However, in later years it was decided that nothing in the wording of Article 25 limits the power to Chapter VII, and as suggest by the ICJ that Article 25 applies to all decisions of the Security Council. (*Legal Consequences for States of the Continued Presence of South Africa in Namibia (South West Africa) Notwithstanding Security Council Resolution 276 (1970)*, Advisory Opinion of 21 June 1971, ICJ Reports 1971 p.16) (*Namibia case*).

17 *Namibia* case, ICJ at paragraph 116.

customary international law,[18] as Article 103 specifies "international agreements" and not "international obligations".[19] Nevertheless, not all Security Council resolutions are intended to bind Member States; as stated by the ICJ, Security Council resolutions "do indeed include certain recommendations but others have dispositive force and effect."[20] Thus, the language used within a resolution of the Security Council needs to be "analysed before a conclusion can be made as to its binding effect."[21]

It is commonly accepted as UN protocol that the Security Council would utilise 'calls upon' or 'urges' in order to indicate a recommendation that does not intend to have a binding effect.[22] On the other hand, when the Security Council employs 'decides' or 'demands' they intend a binding obligation imposed on the parties in question.[23] Nonetheless, when the Security Council utilises their power under Chapter VII, all decisions made within that section are considered to be binding on Member States. As Chapter VII is used by the Security Council as a form of assertive power, it is crucial to state that the protection of civilians mandate is continuously mandated under Chapter VII. Thus, the protection mandate is drafted as a legally binding provision under the Security Council's powers in Chapter VII.

Within the literature there is a suggestion that the protection of civilians mandate is not a legal obligation, but merely an authority to use force.[24] As stated earlier, when examining the legal effects of a resolution, the text must be examined to identify the intention of the Security Council. When the Security Council intends to authorise the use of force it is common practice for them to explicitly 'authorize'. For example, in 2001, the Security Council "Authorizes the Member States participating in the International Security Assistance Force

18 *Case Concerning Questions of Interpretation and Application of the 1971 Montreal Convention Arising From the Aeria Incident at Lockerbie (Libyan Arab Jamahiriya v United Kingdom)*, ICJ, Judgment of 27 February 1998.

19 Ibid.

20 *Certain Expenses of the United Nations (Article 17, Paragraph 2, of the Charter)*, Advisory Opinion of 20 July 1962, ICJ Reports 1962, p.151 at 163.

21 *Namibia* case, note16 at paragraph 53.

22 Security Council Reporter, *Security Council Action Under Chapter VII: Myths and Realities*, Speacil Research Report, 23 June 2008.

23 Hugh Breakey, 'Parsing Security Council Resolutions' in Vesselin Popovski and Trudy Fraser (eds), *The Security Council as Global Legislator* (Routledge, 2014) 51 at 53; Security Council Reporter, above note 22 at 23.

24 Carina Lamont and Emma Skeppström, *The United Nations at War in the DRC?: Legal aspects of the Intervention Brigade* (Defence Analysis, Totalförsvarets forskningsinstitut (FOI), 2013) at 12; Sheeran and Kent, above note 3 at 36.

to take all necessary measure to fulfil the mandate."[25] Further in *Resolution 1973* (2011) the Security Council 'authorised' the use of force under the protection of civilians doctrine.[26] In comparison, within UN peacekeeping resolutions, the Security Council 'decides' the mandate 'to protect civilians under the threat of physical violence' and 'authorises' them to use all necessary means. Therefore, the Security Council *authorises* peacekeepers to use all necessary means to realise the *decision* of the Security Council, which is the obligation for peacekeepers to protect civilians.

Though the Security Council is privileged with a substantial amount of power, it has been suggested that they are still bound and must adhere to the 'spirit and principles' of international law, in other words, they cannot mandate outside the existing legal structure.[27] As the UN is an institution created and rooted in international law, it cannot then be above that law,[28] for "[i]t is not logically possible to claim to represent the power and authority of the law, and at the same time, claim to be above the law."[29] Thus as suggested in the Dissenting Opinion of Judge Jennings in the *Lockerbie* case, Security Council resolutions and decisions cannot override a Member State's obligations under customary international law, especially IHL and IHRL.[30] Moreover, as the UN Charter creates and assigns these powers to the Security Council, as set down in the *Tadić*[31] case, the Security Council "has to remain, at the very least, within the limits of the purposes and principles of the Charter."[32] Specifically, as the UN Charter proposes to promote and protect international law norms, then the Security Council must also be bound by those norms.[33] Therefore, it is inferred that the Security Council in their decisions should only clarify or identify already existing obligations in the UN Charter or customary international

25 *United Nations Security Council Resolution 1386* (2001) at operational paragraph 3.

26 *United Nations Security Council Resolution 1973* (2011) at operational paragraph 4.

27 N. Jain, 'A Separate Law for Peacekeepers: The Clash between the Security Council and the International Criminal Court' (2005) *16(2) European Journal of International Law* 239 at 243.

28 Ibid at 243.

29 *Lockerbie* case, note 18 per Dissenting Opinion of Judge Jennings at 110.

30 James D Fry, 'The UN Security Council and the Law of Armed Conflict: Amity or Enmity?' (2006) *38(2) The George Washington International Law Review* 327 at 334; Erika de Wet, *The Chapter VII Powers of the United Nations Security Council* (Hart Publishing, 2004) at 203.

31 *Decision on the Defence Motion for Interlocutory Appeal on Jurisdiction*, International Criminal Tribunal for the former Yugoslavia, Appeals Chamber Decision, 2 October 1995.

32 Ibid at paragraph 29.

33 Mégret, Frédéric and Florian Hoffman, 'The UN as a Human Rights Violator? Some Reflections on the United Nations Changing Human Rights Responsibilities' (2003) *25 Human Rights Quarterly* 314 at 317.

law.[34] In other words, the Security Council was not intended to act as a legislative body creating 'new' law, but rather are to clarify the law in application to specific situations.[35]

As it is contended that the Security Council can only reiterate pre-existing legal obligations, theoretically, Security Council resolutions are not to be considered as legal documents per se. In other words, traditionally unlike other legal instruments, Security Council resolutions do not create further or newer legal obligations.[36] However, it is arguable that the Security Council can create practices that will ultimately affect international law norms. For although the Security Council was not empowered to create new legal obligations, they do make decisions that have a substantive legal effect on Member States.[37]

Recently, the Security Council has passed resolutions that would be considered 'legislative' in nature, as they form 'generic' overarching obligations that intend to cover the field and to supplement the gaps in the legal framework. As an example, the Security Council has mandated Member States on counter-terrorism measures;[38] women, peace and security;[39] children in armed conflict;[40] and on the non-proliferation of weapons of mass destruction.[41] Although there has been vast criticism that these resolutions impose a legislative "application on upon all Member States as a legally binding Charter obligation" that "goes beyond the powers of the Security Council",[42] nevertheless, these resolutions have been accepted as legally binding obligations under the UN Charter. This new wave of resolutions is now creating obligations on Member States similar in effect to that of a treaty,[43]

34 Sufyan Droubi, *Resisting United Nations Security Council Resolutions* (Routledge, 2014) at 2–3.

35 *Tadic* case note 31 at paragraph 43.

36 Carina Lamont and Emma Skeppström, *The United Nations at War in the DRC?: Legal aspects of the Intervention Brigade* (Defence Analysis, Totalförsvarets forskningsinstitut (FOI), 2013) at 12.

37 Marko Divac Öberg, 'The Legal Effects of Resolutions of the UN Security Council and General Assembly in the Jurisprudence of the ICJ' (2005) *16(5) European Journal of International Law* 879 at 881–882.

38 For example, *United Nations Security Council Resolution 2370* (2017).

39 For example, *United Nations Security Council Resolution 1325* (2000).

40 For example, *United Nations Security Council Resolution 1379* (2001).

41 For example, *United Nations Security Council Resolution 1540* (2004).

42 *Statement by Martin Scheinin,* Special Rapporteur on the Promotion and Protection of Human Rights and Fundamental Freedoms while Countering Terrorism, 65th Session of the General Assembly, Third Committee, 26 October 2010 at 3.

43 Droubi, above note 34 at 3.

allowing the Security Council to adopt an international legislative function.[44]

Distinct from other resolutions, peacekeeping resolutions can only bind those Member States that are involved within those missions, that being, host States and TCCs/PCCs. As TCCs/PCCs willingly enter into an agreement with the UN to provide these troops, it places itself under the obligation created by the Security Council's mandate. Thus, a State's contribution of troops should be considered as a representation of acceptance to be bound by the obligation created in the Security Council's mandate.[45] This acceptance is further cemented with the TCCs/PCCs entrance into a MOU with the UN. Thus, the protection mandate can be seen as a "conditional obligation",[46] that is, the obligation only manifests itself once a Member State willingly engages in the prescribed mission. Once a State willingly contributes troops to a UN peace mission, the TCC/PCC would be responsible for the 'failure' of the mandate if the 'failure' was within their control.

While commentators have suggested that "State and UN practice clearly does not treat PoC [protection of civilians] as a legal obligation",[47] recently there has been a shift towards the acknowledgment that a legal obligation does come into force from the protection mandate. As the UN Office of Internal Oversight Services (*OIOS*) report evaluating the protection mandate suggests, "resolutions have authorized missions to use force, including deadly force. Legally, this creates a requirement to do so within their capabilities when civilians are in imminent physical danger or actually being attacked in their areas of deployment."[48] Indeed, as stated by the former Secretary-General in his 2016 report on the protection of civilians, "the protection of civilians was an obligation of all United Nations peace operations."[49]

---

44 Sylvia Maus, 'Jus post bellum a la United Nations? Human rights, UN peace operations, and the creation of international law' (2014) *32(4) Wisconsin International Law Journal* 675 at 683.

45 *Vienna Convention on the Law of Treaties 1969*, Article 16 refers to exchanges.

46 Hugh Breakey, 'The responsibility to protect and the protection of civilians in armed conflict: Overlap and contrast' in Angus Francis, Vesselin Popovski and C. J. G. Sampford (eds), *Norms of Protection: Responsibility to Protect, Protection of Civilians and Their Interaction* (United Nations University Press, 2012) at 266.

47 Scott Sheeran and Stephanie Case, *The Intervention Brigade: Legal Issues for the UN in the Democractic Republic of the Congo* (International Peace Institute, 2014) at 46.

48 United Nations General Assembly, *Evaluation of the Implementation and Results of Protection of Civilians Mandates in United Nations Peacekeeping Operations*, UN Doc A/68/787 (*OIOS Report*) at paragraph 15.

49 United Nations Security Council, *Report of the Secretary-General on the Protection of Civilians in Armed Conflict*, UN Doc S/2016/447 at paragraph 55.

Since UNMISS' failures in the 2016 Juba attacks and 2017 attacks in CAR, the UN has slowly used more 'obligatory' language in evaluating the inaction of peacekeepers. For example, the UN report on the 2016 incident in South Sudan, asserted that the "[i]naction by peacekeepers when civilians are attacked within one kilometre of a peacekeeping base should be promptly investigated and peacekeepers, commanders and relevant troop contributing countries should be held accountable for failures to protect."[50] As seen in the Security Council open debates regarding peacekeeping, more Member States are demanding the accountability of TCCs/PCCs,[51] with some referencing the "cooperation with international legal mechanisms".[52] In the 2017 *Leuven Manual on the International Law Applicable to Peace Operations*,[53] it was asserted that when UN peace missions "witness violence against civilians [they] are required to do what they can to stop it in accordance with basic UN principles and consistently with the 'the perception and the expectation of protection of civilians created by a peace operation'. In certain situations, a proactive approach is required on the part of the Peace Operation."[54]

In 2018 the Security Council unanimously passed *Resolution 2436*, penned by the USA, on performance of UN peacekeepers. In *Resolution 2436*, the Security Council reaffirmed:

> its support for the development of a comprehensive and integrated performance policy framework that identifies clear standards of performance for evaluating all United Nations civilian and uniformed personnel working in and supporting peacekeeping operations … that specifies measures for performance accountability that include a range of responses proportionate to the identified performance failures, including, as appropriate, transparent public reporting, withholding

50 Executive Summary of the Independent Special Investigation into the Violence which Occured in Juba in 2016 and UNMISS Response at 6.

51 Statement of Ibrahim Balyan, on behalf of the Swedish Mission to the United Nations, Security Council Open Debate on Collective Action to Improve UN Peacekeeping Operations, 28 March 2018; Statement by Ambassador Jürgen Schulz, Permanent Mission of the Federal Republic of Germany to the United Nations, Security Council Open deabte on Reform of UN Peacekeeping: Implementation and Follow Up, 20 September 2017.

52 Statement of Karel JG van Oosterom, Permanent Representative of the Kingdom of the Netherlands to the United Nations, Security Council Open Debate: Implementation of the Note S/2017/507 – Working Methods, 6 February 2018.

53 Terry Gill,, Dieter Fleck, William H. Boothby, and Alfons Vanheusden, *Leuven Manual on the International Law Applicable to Peace Operations* (Cambridge University Press, 2017).

54 Ibid at 178.

> reimbursement, and repatriating or replacing units, including the possibility of replacement by units from another troop- or police-contributing country from the Peacekeeping Capabilities Readiness System (PCRS), as well as revocation of delegated authorities, performance improvement plans, training, change of duties, or dismissal or non-renewal of contracts for civilian personnel.[55]

Although *Resolution 2436* does not explicitly mention the existence of a legal obligation, the outlined consequences for a 'failure' of performance and demand for accountability could imply a breach of an existing obligation. Throughout the literature and the international community, it is accepted that Security Council decisions invoking Chapter VII of the UN Charter will have a binding effect on Member States.[56] However, this rationale is yet to be applied completely to UN peacekeeping mandates that invoke the same authority of Chapter VII. As Chapter VII identifies and places legal obligations, this must also apply to peacekeeping mandates.

In interviews with the UN Secretariat in 2018, members of the UN Secretariat had not considered that the protection of civilians mandate could create a legal obligation, nor did they want to consider its implication for fear that Member States would no longer provide peacekeepers.[57] However, in 2019 all interviewees in the UN Secretariat accepted that there is and must be some legal obligation created from the Security Council mandating under Chapter VII, though fascinatingly, there was no consensus on the meaning of the obligation.[58] In interviews conducted in 2023 all interviewees confirmed that the mandate must create a legal obligation, with one interviewee stating "I can't believe this is still opened for discussion",[59] nonetheless, there is still little consistency on its interpretation.[60]

---

55 *United Nations Security Council Resolution 2436* (2018) at operational paragraph 1.

56 Harry Aitken, 'The Security Council and International Law Enforcement: A Kelsenian Perspective on Civilian Protection Peacekeeping Mandates' (2017) 22(3) *Journal of Conflict and Security Law* 395; Carolyn M. Evans, 'Finding Obligation: Foundation for a More Accountable Security Council' (2016) 14 *New Zealand Journal of Public International Law* 129.

57 Interviews conducted in New York February 2018.

58 Interview conducted with HE Akuei Bona Malwal of South Sudan on 22 January 2019.

59 Interview with Member State in New York on 3 February 2023.

60 Interviews conducted with TCCs/PCCs in New York January 2023.

1.1 *The Positive Obligation to Protect on* TCCs *and UN*

Under the 'new' wave of Security Council resolutions[61] it could be assumed that Security Council intends to create a 'new' legal obligation to protect civilians. Nevertheless, within peacekeeping resolutions the Security Council has not expressed any intention to create a 'new' obligation, instead invokes the language of existing law, as will be discussed later in this Chapter. Therefore, as the Security Council has not indicated a 'new' norm, the protection mandate must be interpreted within pre-existing obligations in international law. As stated in the 2020 Handbook the protection mandate "is grounded in international law, including international humanitarian law, international human rights law and international refugee law, and reflects the desire of the Security Council to protect civilians from harm."[62]

In order for the obligations under IHL and IHRL to apply to UN peace missions, peacekeepers must either be parties to a conflict or in control over a territory or individual. However, even if the positive obligation in IHL and IHRL did not apply directly to UN peace missions, the Security Council's mandate places these existing legal obligations on the Mission. In other words, the existing legal obligation to take all practical measures to ensure the safety of civilians applies to all mandated missions, and so "this obligation applies to peacekeeping troops, even though they are not directly engaging in an armed conflict."[63]

As outlined in the *Draft Articles on Responsibility of States for Internationally Wrongful Acts* (*DAR*) and *Draft articles on the responsibility of international organizations* (*ARIO*), an omission of a State or an international organisation can be classified as a 'wrongful act' under the law.[64] Consequently the positive obligation to protect will not only cover peacekeepers' actions but must also include any omission. As will be discussed in Chapter 7, the UN and TCCs/PCCs have joint 'effective control' over UN peace missions, thus, an omission of peacekeepers to use force to protect civilians can be classified as a wrongful

61 For example, *United Nations Security Council Resolution 1325* (2000); *United Nations Security Council Resolution 1540* (2004).

62 United Nations Department of Peace Opertions, *The Protection of Civilians in United Nations Peacekeeping Handbook* at paragraph 2.3.1.

63 Hitoshi Nasu, 'The Protection of Civilians from Violence and the Effects of Attacks in International.

Humanitarian Law' in David W Lovell and Igor Primoratz (eds), *Protecting Civilians During Violent Conflict: Theoretical and Practical Issues for the 21st Century* (Ashgate Publishing Limited, 2012) 65 at 69.

64 Draft Articles on Reponsbility of States for Internationally Wrongful Acts, A/56/10 at Article 2; Draft Articles on Responsibility of International Organizations at Article 4.

act of the TCC/PCC and UN. As stipulated in Article 2 of DAR, a wrongful act of a State can consist of an "act or omission", and this omission would "constitute a breach of an international obligation" of that State. Thus, the TCC/PCC can be held accountable under the protection of civilians mandate for their troops failing to perform their duties under an international law obligation.[65]

Part of this positive obligation would be to ensure that proactive measures are taken to mitigate any harm created by military and police operations during a UN peace mission. As the UN and TCCs have joint responsibility, unmitigated harm caused by military operations will be a wrongful act of the UN and TCC. As such UN peace missions must ensure that all military operations take pre-emptive measures to ensure no harm fall upon civilians beyond what is necessary, this includes their already existing obligations under IHL.

Nonetheless, the creation of this positive obligation does not mean that the UN and TCCs/PCCs are now legally liable and damages can be sought by victims. In interviews with TCCs/PCCs and UN Secretariat, there was a concern that identifying the protection of civilians mandate as a legal obligation will create legal avenues in judicial institutions.[66] However, not all international law obligations create a legal avenue within domestic court systems. Similar to Common Article 1 of the Geneva Conventions UN peacekeepers are to ensure that they respect and adhere to the mandate to protect civilians. In regards to any positive obligations from Common Article 1, it is generally understood that all States have a "right to require respect for international humanitarian law by parties to any conflict".[67] For example, the Trial Chamber of the International Criminal Tribunal for the former Yugoslavia (*ICTY*) in its judgments in the *Furundžija* case,[68] when assessing the prohibition on torture, the Court set out that the IHL norm is owed *erga omnes*, and thus:

> the violation of such an obligation simultaneously constitutes a breach of the correlative right of all members of the international community and gives rise to a claim for compliance accruing to each and every member,

65 *Case Concerning Application of the Convention on the Prevention and Punishment of the Crime of Genocide (Bosnia and Herzegovina v Serbia and Montenegro)*, ICJ, 26 February 2007.

66 Interviews conducted in New York in February 2018 and January 2019.

67 International Committee of the Red Cross, Study on Customary Interantional Humanitarian Law (Customary IHL Database) at rule 144.

68 *Prosecutor v Anto Furundžija*, Trail Chamber Judgement, ICTY, it-95-17/1-T, 10 December 1998.

> which then has the right to insist on fulfilment of the obligation or in any case to call for the breach to be discontinued.[69]

Thus, similar to the obligation to ensure respect to IHL, the obligation for peacekeepers to protect civilians, 'gives rise to a claim for compliance' and 'the right to insist on fulfilment of the obligation'. As stated by ICRC in regards to breaches of Common Article 1, States can use "(i) diplomatic protest and (ii) collective measures through which States exert their influence, to the degree possible, to try and stop violations of international humanitarian law."[70] Thus, when the UN or TCC/PCC breach their obligation to protect, or place caveats that will undermine the protection of civilians mandate, the international community can insist on the fulfillment of the mandate. Issues arising over the accountability of peacekeepers will be discussed in Chapter 7.

1.2 *The Obligation on the UN*

Since the UN is considered a legal person under the law, it will also bear a positive obligation to protect civilians under the mandate. Specifically, the UN must take active steps to encourage and ensure respect for the obligation throughout the organisation. Under Article 14 of ARIO, if the UN 'aids or assists' in an internationally wrongful act, then the UN likewise will be responsible for that act. Therefore, the UN must not aid or assist any State to breach their obligation to protect under the mandate.

Consequently, the UN Secretariat and the Secretary-General would be in breach of their obligation by accommodating a caveat from a TCC that is in contravention of the protection of civilians mandate. For example, it would be a breach of the UN's obligation for the Secretary-General to accept a caveat that troop contingents would not use force, even if civilians are at risk. Accepting this caveat would be aiding the TCC/PCC to be in violation of their obligation, and therefore be a wrongful act under the law. Although caveats will be discussed in Chapter 3, the Secretary-General and the UN Secretariat must warrant the respect of the obligation to protect even when planning and implementing UN peace missions.

Moreover, the Secretary-General and DPO cannot accept a contingent if they have reasonable knowledge that the contingent will not comply with their obligation under the mandate. For example, if specific Member States consistently breach their obligation to protect, it would be negligent for the UN

---

69 Ibid at paragraph 151.

70 International Committee of the Red Cross, *Study on Customary Interantional Humanitarian Law* (*Customary IHL Database*) at rule 144.

to accept that contingent for future deployment. The UN under its obligation must ensure that each contingent is equipped and trained to adequately comply with the obligation to protect.

1.3 *The Obligation of the Host State*

As Security Council decisions are binding on all Member States, the host State will also have an obligation arising out of the protection mandate. Although host States have the primary responsibility to protect civilians, the protection of civilians mandate will also obligate them not to interfere or hinder a UN peace mission from fulfilling their mandate. If a host State limits the movement of peacekeepers, or hinders their ability to protect civilians, then the host State will be in breach of their obligation under the mandate. As the host State consents to the deployment of the Mission by signing the SOFA with the UN, they are voluntarily binding themselves to the obligation within the mandate. Similar to the UN, they are obliged to encourage and certify respect for the obligation to protect, and to ensure adequate mechanisms to aid UN peace missions.

2 The Content of the Obligation to Protect

Whether interpreting the protection mandate via traditional or contemporary literature, the protection mandate is still read through existing law. As the Security Council has not intended any 'new' obligation or a departure from existing laws, the mandate cannot be perceived as a new obligation. Thus, the content of the obligation mandated by the Security Council must be determined by examining existing legal structures, as the resolution has not indicated otherwise.

As will be discussed further in Chapters 3 and 6, within the current legal framework there are gaps that need clarification from the Security Council. While it can be argued that the Security Council can and should clarify these areas, the Security Council has yet to do so. So even for moderate commentators who envisage the Security Council as an international legislator, the Security Council has yet to declare any intention of clarifying these divergences in the law. Therefore, peacekeepers when interpreting the obligation to protect, must rely on existing laws to determine its content.

Even though the Security Council has explicitly mandated peacekeepers to protect civilians, there already exists differing legal obligations to protect under the prevailing international legal structure.[71] It is well accepted, since the *Reparations Advisory Opinion*[72] and the Bulletin, that the UN is a legal person and as such is subject to international law, therefore, are already obliged to protect civilians under existing laws. In order to establish the obligation under the Security Council's mandate, the obligation to protect under IHL and IHRL must first be examined.

2.1 *Obligation to Protect under IHL*

The obligations owed to civilians under IHL vary depending on the party and the circumstances being examined, however, broadly speaking these obligations can be either positive or mitigative in nature. On the one hand parties are obliged to ensure that their military actions are mitigated to ensure a limitation on the harm that occurs to civilians. And on the other hand, parties have a positive obligation to protect civilian and 'protected persons' within their control. Depending whether the conflict is an international armed conflict (*IAC*) or a non-international armed conflict (*NIAC*), will determine the obligation that falls on the parties. As will be discussed in Chapter 3, peacekeepers will find themselves in a NIAC, and therefore those obligations are contained in Common Article 3 to the Geneva Conventions, Additional Protocol II (where States are party to Additional Protocol II), and customary international law.

Under IHL parties to a conflict are obliged to distinguish between civilian and military targets; as provided in Article 13(2) of Additional Protocol II, civilians "shall not be the object of an attack." This is reiterated in international criminal law, as stipulated in the Rome Statute of the International Criminal Court (*Rome Statute*) where "intentionally direct attacks against the civilian population as such or against individual civilians not taking direct part in hostilities"[73] is considered a war crime in a NIAC. Moreover, this is reiterated as all Security Council resolutions on civilian protection and the adherence to IHL are targeted towards NIACs.[74] Therefore, the rule of distinction and the

---

71 *Geneva Convention (IV) Relative to the Protection of Civilian Persons in Time of War*, Geneva, 12 August 1949 at Article 27.

72 *Reparation for Injuries Suffered in the Service of the United Nations*, Advisory Opinion of April 11, 1949, ICJ.

73 *Protocol Additional to the Geneva Conventions of 12 August 1949 and realting to the Protection of Victims of Non-International Armed Conflicts (Protocol II)*, 8 June 1977 at Article 8(2)(e)(i).

74 *United Nations Security Council Resolution 1894* (2009); *United Nations Security Council Resolution 2286* (2016); *United Nations Security Council Resolution 2474* (2019).

non-targeting of civilians is considered a central part of customary international law.[75]

As an extension of the protection of civilian status, all military operations must ensure that all reasonable precautions are undertaken to avoid and mitigate any harm to civilians or civilian objects. Although this rule is not explicitly mentioned in the Geneva Conventions or Additional Protocols for NIACs, the ICRC in their *Study on Customary International Law* have suggested that this is part of customary international law and should apply to NIACs.[76] The ICRC's position was also used by the ICTY in *Kupreškić* case,[77] where it was noted that these provisions are part of customary international law, "not only because they specify and flesh out general pre-existing norms, but also because they do not appear to be contested by any State."[78] These obligations to mitigate harm and guarantee civilians are not deliberately targeted will apply to all parties to a conflict,[79] whether the party is a State or a non-State actor.

As will be discussed in Chapter 3, peacekeepers are obliged to protect civilians from military operations, therefore adhering to the principles of distinction, necessity and proportionality. Further, as will be discussed in Chapter 4, peacekeepers are to treat all detained individuals humanely under the provisions of Common Article 3.

2.2 *Obligation to Protect in IHRL*

Even in situations where UN peace missions are *not* involved in the armed conflict, they will nevertheless still be bound by the obligations to protect civilians entrenched in IHRL. Under IHRL, States are bound and obligated to ensure the protection of the human rights of civilians within their control. Under the *International Convention on Civil and Political Rights* (*ICCPR*) States are required to respect and fulfil the Covenant rights "to all persons who may be within

75 *United Nations Security Council Resolution 1001* (1995); *United Nations Security Council Resolution 1019* (1995); *United Nations Security Council Resolution 1041* (1996); *United Nations Security Council Resolution 1049* (1996); *United Nations Security Council Resolution 1173* (1998); *United Nations Security Council Resolution 1181* (1998).

76 International Committee of the Red Cross, *Study on Customary Interantional Humanitarian Law* (*Customary IHL Database*) at rule 15.

77 *Prosecutor v Kuprešbić et al*, International Criminal Tribunal of the former Yugoslavia, Judgment, 14 January 2000, Case No IT-95-16-T.

78 Ibid at paragraph 524.

79 There are other obligations, such as attacks that may cause civilian loss must be proportionate to the military advantage anticipated (International Committee of the Red Cross, *Study on Customary Interantional Humanitarian Law* (*Customary IHL Database*) *at rule 14*); obligation to verify targets as military objects (Ibid at rule 20).

their territory and to all persons subject to their jurisdiction."[80] Specifically, the Human Rights Committee references that this concept:

> also applies to those within the power or effective control of the forces of a State Party acting outside its territory, regardless of the circumstances in which such power or effective control was obtained, such as forces constituting a national contingent of a State Party assigned to international peace-keeping or peace-enforcement operation.[81]

The most notable rights under the ICCPR for the protection of civilians include the right to life, the prohibition against torture and ill- treatment, and the freedom from arbitrary detention.[82] States and international forces are bound by their positive obligation to respect, protect and fulfil these rights for individuals within their control.[83]

Where a State or authority is in 'effective control' of a territory outside their boundary,[84] or are in control of a foreign individual or individuals, their human rights obligations will apply to those within their control.[85] As noted by the UN Human Rights Committee in the *Lopez* case, "it would be unconscionable to so interpret the responsibility" under the ICCPR "as to permit a State party to perpetrate violations of the Covenant on the territory of another State, which violations it could not perpetrate on its own territory."[86] This extra-territorial nature also applies to other human rights treaties; as established by the European Court of Human Rights (*ECHR*), that the *European Convention on Human Rights* also applies extra-territorially when a Signatory State experiences effective control.[87] Unlike the obligations under IHL that insists on

80 United Nations Human Rights Committee, *General Comment No. 31 Nature of the General Legal Obligation Imposed on States Parties to the Covenant*, 26 May 2004, UN Doc: CCPR/C/21/Rev.1/Add.13 at paragraph 10.

81 Ibid.

82 *International Convenant on Civil and Political Rights*, adopted by General Assembly resolution 200a(XXI) of 16 December 1966, entry into force 23 March 1976 (*ICCPR*) at Articles 6(1), 7, and 9(1).

83 UN Human Rights Committee, *General Comment No 36 (2018) on Article 6 of the International Covenant on Civil and Political Rights, on the Right to Life*, CCPR/C/GC/36 at paragraph 69.

84 Effective control will be discussed further in Chapter 6.

85 *Lopez Burgos v Uruguay, Saldias de Lopez (on behalf of Lopez Burgos) v Uruguay, Merits*, Communication No 52/1979, UN Doc CCPR/C/13/D/52/1979, IHRL 2796 (UNHRC 1981), 29th July 1981.

86 Ibid at paragprah 12.3.

87 *Vlastimir and Borka Bankovic, Zivana Stojanovic, Mirjana Stoimenovski, Dragana Joksimovic and Dragan Sukovic v Belgium and Other States*, European Court of Human

protection within an armed conflict, IHRL requires mechanisms to be established to ensure protections from all parties and individuals, in all circumstances. In other words, an authority that has effective control is responsible to guarantee that there exist adequate mechanisms that ensure that individuals' rights are protected from all sources and in all contexts.

IHRL's obligation to protect an individual's human rights does not only apply to States but would also apply to UN peace missions. Whilst the UN as an organisation is founded in "promoting and encouraging respect for human rights",[88] so to must any subsidiary organ of the UN. Moreover, as UN peacekeepers remain within their national service, these peacekeepers will also be under any extra-territorial obligations owed by their TCC/PCC.

At this time, it is prudent to differentiate between a State's effective control over a territory and authority over an individual. As will be explored in Chapter 6, UN peace missions will not have effective control over territory, outside executively administered peace missions, yet in the majority of cases, peacekeepers will exercise authority over individuals, for example in situations of detention or IDP camps. The UN Human Rights Committee states in *General Comment 31* that the rights authorised in the ICCPR must be respected and ensured to anyone "within the power or effective control" of a party.[89] Although some commentators, such as Milanovic, have been critical of the UN Human Rights Committee's interpretation of the ICCPR, suggesting that their interpretation "is directly contrary to the test of the treaty" and therefore "to say that the concept of 'territory' includes control over persons is simply mind-boggling."[90] However, it has become well accepted that a party's obligation under IHRL will also apply to individuals within their control.[91]

Although IHRL demands that States take positive approaches to protecting human rights, such as legislative and judicial mechanisms, this cannot completely apply to UN peace missions. Therefore, IHRL obligations cannot apply

Rights, Application no. 52207/99, 12 December 2001 at paragraph 73; *Case of Al-Jedda v The United Kingdom (Application no 27021/08), European Court of Human Rights, Grand Chamber*, 7 July 2011; *The Queen on the application of Mazin Jumaa Gatteh Al-Skeini v Secretary of State for Defence* [2004] EWHC 2911.

88 *Charter of the United Nations* (1945) at Article 1.

89 UN HRC, General Comment No 31, note 80 at paragaph 10.

90 Marko Milanovic, *Extraterritorial Application of Human Rights Treaties: Law, Principles and Policy* (Oxford University Press, 2011) at 179.

91 Maus, above note 44 at 695; Noam Lubell, 'Challenges in applying human rights law to armed conflict' (2010) *87(860) International Review of the Red Cross* 737 at 739; Md Kamal Uddin, 'Human Rights Violations by un Peacekeepers' (2014) *25(1) Security and Human Rights* 130 at 134.

in their entirety to the UN and must be shaped to suit the relevant situation at hand. Although a fundamental principle of IHRL is that human rights are indivisible and interdependent, it would be unrealistic to expect UN peace missions to comply in full to IHRL. As stated by the ECHR in *Al-Skeini* a "State is under an obligation under Article 1 [of the European Convention] to secure to that individual the rights and freedoms under Section 1 of the Convention that are relevant to the situation of that individual."[92] Although the Court was applying this to the European Convention of Human Rights, it is analogous as UN peace missions will be obliged to protect the rights that are 'relevant to the situation of that individual'.

For IHRL obligations to apply to UN peace missions, there are two requirements that need to be fulfilled. Firstly, as discussed above, peacekeepers must have effective control over a territory or individual. This condition would apply to individuals detained by peacekeepers, or camps and areas protected and controlled by peacekeepers, such as UN bases or PoC sites in South Sudan. Secondly, to establish that a positive obligation has arisen it must be

> established that the authorities know or ought to have known at the time of the existence of a real and immediate risk to the life of an identified individual or individuals from the criminal acts of a third party and they failed to take measures within the scope of their powers which, judged reasonably, might have been expected to avoid that risk.[93]

This confirms that the positive obligation under IHRL "must be interpreted in a way which does not impose an impossible or disproportionate burden on the authorities."[94] Disregarding UN peace missions mandated to administratively control territories such as UN Peace Mission in Kosovo (*UNMIK*), it would be difficult to suggest that peacekeepers have 'effective control' over any territory and thus be bound by IHRL obligations to ensure that effective protection mechanisms have been established.

Nevertheless, with the creation of PoC sites in South Sudan, many commentators have suggested that UNMISS would have a positive obligation to protect under IHRL, specifically as the civilians within these camps would fall within

---

92 The Queen on the application of Mazin Jumaa Gatteh Al-Skeini v Secretary of State for Defence [2004] EWHC 2911 at paragraph 137.

93 *Kaya v Turkey*, Merits, App No 22535/93, ECHR 2000-III, [2000] ECHR 129, (1999) 28 EHRR 1.

94 Ibid at paragraph 86.

their control.[95] It is suggested that there "is little doubt that peacekeepers are under a legal obligation to protect civilians sheltering in their military camps."[96] Yet, it is unclear to the extent of this obligation, and whether a "full package"[97] of protection is warranted to satisfy the law. The obligation of UNMISS becomes ambiguous with the ever-growing nature of these camps. Further, the obligation UNMISS owes will change depending on the legal instrument that is being investigated. Under the ICCPR, UNMISS has a duty to protect an individual's rights "from all reasonably foreseeable threats, including from threats emanating from private persons and enemies."[98] The Convention on the Rights of the Child (*CRC*), which incorporates a range of international law instruments, will ensure not only that peacekeepers establish mechanisms to protect children from threats, but to also ensure a child's participation within their civil, cultural, economic and social rights.[99] Although, UN peace missions' obligations under IHRL will be determined on the factual scenario, a minimum core will still apply as will be discussed further in Chapter 6.

3 Protection of Civilians and Humanitarian Intervention

The evolution of the protection mandate is considered by the academic literature[100] to be the primary vehicle in widening of the Security Council's authority for the use of force in UN peace missions. Modern commentators correlate the use of force in UN peacekeeping directly with obligations under the protection mandate. However, within the academic discussions on the authorisation of the use of force, there is occasionally the blurring between

95 Nasu, above note 11 at 368; Ray Murphy, 'The United Nations Mission in South Sudan and the Protection of Civilians' (2017) *22(3) Journal of Conflict and Security Law* 367 at 378; Rachel Ibreck and Naomi Pendle, 'Community Security and Justice under United Nations Governance: Lessons from Chiefs' Court in South Sudan's Protection of Civilians Sites' (2017) *6(1) Stability: International Journal of Security and Development* at 3.

96 Nasu, above note 11 at 368.

97 Ibid at 368.

98 UNHRC, General Comment No 36, above note 83 at paragraph 18.

99 This is will be discussed further in Chapter 5.

100 Haidi Willmot and Ralph Mamiya, 'Mandated to Protect: Security Council Practice on the Protection of Civilians' in Marc Weller (ed), *The Oxford Handbook of the Use of Force in International Law* (Oxford University Press, 2015) at 376; Tardy, T. Tardy, 'The UN and the Use of Force: A Marriage Against Nature' (2007) 38(1) Security Dialogue 49 at 58; Haidi Willmot and Scott Sheeran, 'The Protection of Civilians mandate in UN peacekeeping Operations: Reconciling protection concepts and practices' (2013) *95(891/892) International Review of the Red Cross* 517 at 530.

the notions of humanitarian intervention and the protection mandate.[101] As the Responsibility to Protect (*R2P*) doctrine has recently been officially added to the General Assembly agenda,[102] it would be prudent to insist on the distinction between R2P and the protection of civilians mandate. Although both doctrines consider the use of force to protect, the legal and philosophical foundations of the protection of civilians mandate are distinct from R2P,[103] and this distinction is essential to appreciate when investigating the legal obligation of UN peace missions mandated to protect civilians.

While both doctrines remain distinct, an apprehension to use force in peacekeeping stems from the on-going tension between protection of civilians, the sovereignty of Member States and R2P. For even though the protection mandate has become its own thematic concept, there still exists tensions between the philosophy behind R2P and the protection of civilians mandate.[104] This tension is exacerbated when the Security Council distorts the distinction between the protection mandate and humanitarian intervention. As evidenced by the actions of UN peacekeepers in Côte d'Ivoire in 2010, their justification under the protection mandate "blurred the lines between human protection and regime change and raised questions about the role of the UN in overriding Côte d'Ivoire's Constitutional Court."[105] Although protection of civilians is separate from humanitarian intervention, it cannot be denied that the protection mandate has been utilised by the Security Council as a form of humanitarian intervention and regime change. The climax of this tension was reached in 2011 when the Security Council authorised "Member States that have notified the Secretary-General acting nationally or through regional

101 Hitoshi Nasu, 'Peacekeeping, Civilian Protection Mandates and the Responsibility to Protect' in Angus Francis, Vesselin Popovski and C. J. G. Sampford (eds), *Norms of Protection: Responsibility to Protect, Protection of Civilians and Their Interaction* (United Nations University Press, 2012) at 118; Sabine Hassler, 'R2P and the Protection Obligations of Peacekeepers' (2010) *1(1) Journal of International Humanitarian Legal Studies* 205 at 209–210; Frédéric Mégret, 'Between R2P and the ICC: "Robust Peacekeeping" and the Quest for Civilian Protection' (2015) *26 Criminal Law Forum* 101; Nasu, above note 11.

102 United Nations General Assembly, *Organization of the seventy-second regular session of the General Assembly, adoption of the agenda and allocation of items: First report of the General Committee*, UN Doc A/72/250.

103 For an example of R2Ps philosophical background see, Peter Hilpold, *Responsibility to Protect: A New Paradigm of International Law?* (Brill Nijhoff, 2014); Alex J Bellamy, *Responsiblity to Protect: A Defense* (Oxford University Press, 2014).

104 Lisa Hultman, 'UN Peace Operations and Protection of Civilians: Cheap Talk or Norm Implementation?' (2012) *50(1) Journal of Peace Research* 59 at 62.

105 Alex J Bellamy and Paul D Williams, 'The new politics of protection? Côte d'Ivoire, Libya and the responsibiity to protect' (2011) *87(4) International Affairs* 825 at 835.

organizations or arrangements ... to take all necessary measures ... to protect civilians".[106] Under *Resolution 1973*, and the protection of civilians doctrine, NATO intervened into Libya removing the Gadhafi administration.

One of the major reasons for the friction between the two doctrines, is that the literature and policy discussions of the UN on the protection mandate often revolve around the theoretical foundations of the R2P doctrine.[107] This confusion and amalgamation of the two concepts has also occurred within the academic literature, with some commentators suggesting that the difference between R2P and the protection mandate is mainly semantic.[108] Within the literature, commentators who observe the distinction as semantic cite two main distinctions; firstly it is contended that the protection mandate "is wider than R2P because it applies to protection of civilians from all violations of international humanitarian and human rights law in situations of armed conflict."[109] Secondly it is suggested that R2P "endeavours to protect *populations* facing the four main atrocity crimes, whereas PoC [protection of civilians] endeavours to protect *individuals* facing physical violence."[110] It is contended by these commentators that R2P attempts to protect 'populations' from mass atrocity crimes, while the protection mandate protects 'individuals' from crimes of war.[111] Thus, it is contended that the only difference between the two doctrines is a macro versus a micro approach to protection. While the literature on R2P is emerging,[112] there is increasing tension between the development of the R2P doctrine and its effects on the protection mandate.

This over-simplification of the two doctrines denies any further investigation and understanding of UN peacekeepers' failure and hesitation in

---

106 *United Nations Security Council Resolutuon 1973* (2011) at operational paragraph 4.

107 Sheeran and Kent, above note 3 at 29.

108 Breakey, above note 46; Nasu, above note 11; Hassler, above note 101.

109 Charles T. Hunt and Lisa Sharland, 'Implementing R2P Through United Nations Peacekeeping Operations: Opportunities and Challenges' in Cecilia Jacob and Martin Mennecke (eds), *Implementing the Responsibility to Protect: A Future Agenda* (Routledge, 2019) at 216; see also Breakey, above note 46.

110 Sheeran and Kent, above note 3 at 51.

111 Breakey, above note 46.

112 For example, see Andreas S. Kolb, *The UN Security Council Members' Responsibility to Protect A Legal Analysis*, Beiträge zum ausländischen öffentlichen Recht und Völkerrecht, Veröffentlichungen des Max-Planck-Instituts für ausländisches öffentliches Recht und Völkerrecht, 274 (Springer Berlin Heidelberg, 2018); Aidan Hehir, 'Sovereignty as Liability: The Security Council and R2P' in *Hollow Norms and the Responsibility to Protect* (Springer International Publishing, 2019) 117; Mark Busser, *Ethics, obligation, and the responsibility to protect: contesting the global power relations of accountability*, Global politics and the responsibility to protect (Routledge, 2019).

protecting civilians, and further denies the ability in creating a sufficient legal framework for the Security Council's mandate. While both doctrines are based on the premise of protection, the distinction between them is important to reiterate, as essentially both doctrines are based on opposing legal foundations. As Wills suggests the distinction between these two doctrines is not merely in their scope or their application, rather "the protection obligations of peacekeepers are distinct from the 'responsibility to protect' and they relate to different regimes of the law governing the use of force."[113] As was stated by the Secretary-General in his 2012 report, that "the work of peacekeepers may contribute to the achievement of RtoP [R2P] goals", however, "the two concepts of the responsibility to protect and the protection of civilians have separate and distinct prerequisites and objectives."[114] Even though both doctrines share the objective of 'protection', the two doctrines stem from differing legal issues and structures when assessing the use of force.[115] Primarily, the important distinction arises from R2P's notion that there exists a 'natural' obligation that falls on the international community to protect civilians from mass atrocity crimes; conversely, the protection of civilians doctrine is a mandate authorised by the Security Council, in specific situations with specific tasks.[116] Peacekeepers are obliged to act at the threat of 'mass atrocities' not from a 'natural obligation', but rather to protect the legal rights of civilians from the harms of armed conflict as authorised by the Security Council.

R2P attempts to expand the current legal structure, while conversely, the protection of civilians mandate functions within the existing boundaries, as it is based on Security Council authority. In other words, protection of civilians is not attempting to broaden or expand the current legal structure on the use of force.

Legally this becomes imperative as the protection mandate does not intend to override or shift the primary responsibility of the host States to protect their own civilians. For as stated earlier, the interpretation of the protection mandate is based on the protection of legal rights rather than a 'general' concept of protection. Therefore, the Security Council within their resolutions reiterate that "states bear the primary responsibility for protection of civilians throughout their whole territory."[117] This theoretical understanding of State responsibility

113 Wills, above note 2 at 2.

114 United Nations General Assembly and United Nations Security Council, *Responsibility to Protection: Timely and Decisive Response, Report of the Secretary-General*, UN Doc A/66/874-S/2012/578 at paragaph 16.

115 Wills, above note 2 at 2.

116 Nasu, above note 101 at 118.

117 *United Nations Security Council Resolution 2378* (2017) at the preamble.

to protect is further manifested within the Security Council's language, particularly when peacekeepers are mandated to engage in protection activities and use of force in order to "assist" local authorities.[118] As State responsibility is considered a philosophical foundation of the protection mandate, peacekeepers are not to be considered as "a substitute for political engagement to tackle sources of violence."[119]

As such, with the expansion of the protection mandate and threats being faced by civilians, the Security Council has endeavoured to balance the primary responsibility of States and peacekeepers obligation to act in order to protect civilians. In spite of this the doctrine of State responsibility to protect becomes problematic when host States are unable or unwilling to protect civilians. Moreover, in certain cases the threat to civilians is initiated from local authorities and forces, who are primary responsible to protect them. Due to the change in threats to civilians, the UN has affirmed that peacekeepers "should protect civilians irrespective of the origin of the threat."[120] For as reiterated by the HIPPO Report the primary responsibility of host States does not "dilute the obligation of United Nations missions to act within their capabilities when the host Government is not willing or unable to protect its citizens."[121] Although the Security Council has granted authority for peacekeepers to use force against any "origin" of threat, peacekeepers are reluctant to use force against government forces due to the theoretical foundations of State sovereignty. Moreover, many TCCs/PCCs believe that using force against a host State would constitute a breach of law and goes against the 'spirit of the UN'.[122]

The theoretical doctrine of primary responsibility of States evidences itself in the UN's requirement of consent from the host State before deploying peacekeepers.[123] Conversely, in the recent Mission to South Sudan, the South Sudanese Transitional Government had withdrawn its consent to the deployment of UNMISS in 2016; nonetheless, the Security Council extended UNMISS' mandate and peacekeepers had remained on the ground. Even though consent was ultimately granted, it was the first-time peacekeepers remained on the ground without the consent of the host State. The Security Council's departure

118 *United Nations Security Council Resolution 2313* (2016).

119 United Nations Security Council, *Report of the Secretary-General on the Protection of Civilians in Armed Conflict*, UN Doc S/2017/414 at paragraph 58.

120 United Nations General Assembly and Security Council, *Report of the High-level Independent Panel on Peace Operations on Uniting Our Strengths for Peace: Politics, Partnership and People*, UN Doc A/70/95-S/2015/446 at paragraph 126.

121 Ibid at paragraph 85.

122 Interviews conduct in New York in January 2019.

123 As will be discussed further in Chapter 2.

from the State's responsibility to protect is further seen in the Security Council's protection mandate for UNMISS, to "deter violence against civilians ... in particular when the GoSS [Government of South Sudan] is unable or failing to provide such security."[124]

The situation in South Sudan is seen as an exception to the agenda of the Security Council rather than development of a new regime. This was illustrated by the Security Council fervently negotiating an agreement with the South Sudanese government to allow peacekeepers to remain on the ground.[125] Although the Security Council did not legally need the consent of the South Sudanese government, as UNMISS as mandated under Chapter VII, it was believed a political imperative that the Security Council and South Sudan reach an agreement. As the UN is founded in State sovereignty, the protection mandate and its implementation are still grounded in State consent and authority. Thus, unlike R2P which sees an obligation for the international community to act that transcends political boundaries, the protection mandate is an authority granted by the Security Council that is firmly founded in State sovereignty and responsibility.

Although discussions in UN headquarters and the Security Council have demonstrated that there is an expectation that peacekeepers must protect civilians when States have failed in their responsibility, still the 'constitutional'[126] principles that stem from State responsibility to protect are theoretically adhered to by the Security Council. Thus, there is a contradiction amongst the UN and the Security Council discussions, as on the one hand, the international community's expectation that peacekeepers are to act when civilians are being threatened irrespective of origin of the threat or consent of local authorities, while on the other hand, the Security Council's constant reaffirmation in their resolutions of the sovereignty and primary responsibility of States. Particularly, the Security Council endorses the 'constitutional' principles of consent, impartiality, and the use of force in self-defence within the majority of resolutions. Due to the protection mandate's entrenchment in State sovereignty, there is confusion of when peacekeepers are actually authorised to use force, specifically without the consent of local authorities.

---

124 *United Nations Security Council Resolution 2459* (2019) at operational paragraph 7(a)(ii).

125 'South Sudan Rejects Unilateral Renewal of UNMISS Mandate', *Sudan Tribune* 6 September 2017 2017 <http://www.sudantribune.com/spip.php?article63427>.

126 The principles of consent, impartiality and the use of force in self-defence and defence of the mandate, are considered constitutional principles of peacekeeping, as will be discussed in Chapter 2.

For these reasons it is important to distinguish protection of civilians from R2P, for while R2P is based on international responsibility to protect, protection of civilians is founded in the authority of the Security Council. In order to determine the interpretation of what is intended by protection an investigation of the 'principles of peacekeeping' will be undertaken in Chapter 2. Further, as the protection of civilians is permitted by the authority of the Security Council, thus, the understanding of the obligation must come from the Security Council's expression. Unlike R2P, which insists on a 'natural' concept of protection, 'protection' in peacekeeping is directly correlated to the mandate of the Security Council.

4 Conclusion

As the Security Council mandates UN peacekeeping missions to protect civilians under their Chapter VII binding power, a legal obligation is formed on all Member States who willingly engage in that UN peace mission. Comparable to all Chapter VII decisions of the Security Council, UN peace mission mandates have the weight of Article 25 of the UN Charter, binding Member States to that decision. Distinct from general Security Council decisions, UN peace mission mandates are conditional to these Member States that engage within that mission. Thus, TCCs/PCCs, the host State and the UN have an obligation to ensure and encourage the respect of the obligation to protect. Further, the obligation to protect is not a 'new' obligation, but the invocation of existing legal obligations in the law.

As the protection of civilians mandate places an obligation on the TCC/PCC, UN and host State, the content of that obligation can only be examined by analysing the Security Council's language. In order to interpret the content of the obligation to protect, we must determine what the Security Council intends by 'protection', specifically in relation to UN peacekeeping. Although there are multiple reports and guidelines on protection of civilians, there is still minimal legal guidance on what is meant by 'protection' under the Security Council's mandate. Therefore, the next Chapter will determine the interpretation of the protection of civilians mandate's language, in order to construct an understanding of the content of 'protection' in UN peacekeeping.

CHAPTER 2

The Interpretation of Protection

As discussed in the previous chapter, the 'protection of civilians' is a central cross-cutting theme in the Security Council's composition of UN peace missions. Although there are numerous annual Secretary-General reports and Security Council open discussions on the protection of civilians, there remains a divergence between what is mandated by the Security Council and genuine protection received by civilians in the field. The variance between Security Council mandates and actual protection offered by peacekeepers is commonly attributed to the absence of any guidelines or operational instruction to assist peacekeepers in implementing the ever-growing mandate.[1] As 'protection' is used by multiple legal instruments, without guidance, each discipline will interpret 'protection' according to their body of law.

As UN peace missions will have differing impediments to civilian protection, a rigorous 'protection' definition becomes impossible. Additionally, a strict definition will hinder UN peace missions from being flexible and adaptive in responding to threats towards civilians. Therefore, a strict interpretation is not advocated here, however, there must be a minimum core to guide peacekeepers in their obligation under the mandate. As a legal obligation is created by the protection mandate, the obligation to protect needs to be clearly formulated. I do not propose to create a 'new' definition of the obligation to protect, but rather to interpret the Security Council's language when expressing pre-existing obligations in the law. Although 'protection' is an extremely broad term, from a reading of the Security Council's language, 'protection' is the protection of legal rights of civilians already existing in the law. Specifically, the Security Council implores the respect for obligations entrenched in IHL and IHRL.

This chapter will conclude that while the Security Council alters the language used in the protection mandate between each Mission, the mandate can however be divided into two broad categories – physical protection, and human rights protection. Although the protection of civilians mandate can be additionally divided into separate forms of protection, the primary focus of the Security Council's mandate still remains the protection from physical violence.

1 Nicholas Lamp and Dana Trif, 'United Nations Peacekeeping Forces and the Protection of Civilians in Armed Conflict' 47 (2009) *Hertie School of Governance – Working papers* at 3.

 | DOI:10.1163/9789004707313_004

As will be concluded, the obligation to 'protect' is entrenched in the obligation to respect the 'civilian' status as outlined in the law. Therefore, all protection activities engaged by peacekeepers must be embedded in legal protections and rights afforded to the status of 'civilians'.

Nevertheless, although the UN has been engrossed in the physical protection of civilians, the rights of civilians extend beyond physical threats. For this reason, peacekeepers are mandated to promote and protect human rights as well as humanitarian access. However, as the IHRL obligation relates to States, it is uncertain how the IHRL framework and human rights protections will apply to UN peace missions. Outside a UN peace mission's effective control over individuals, there is no indication of what UN peacekeepers can add to the current human rights landscape that is currently not being satisfied by humanitarian agencies.

This chapter will begin by examining the Security Council's meaning inferred from the language of what is intended under the protection mandate. Consequently, the chapter will examine the mandate in context of modern peacekeeping and difficulties that arise. Secondly, the language of the Security Council will be analysed to determine their intention; it will be concluded that the Security Council has divided the protection obligation into physical and human rights protection. This chapter will then be divided into two sections – protection against physical violence and human rights protection. Regarding the protection against physical violence, it will conclude that the minimum obligation to protect from physical violence is intertwined with the obligations in IHL, that is, to protect civilians from direct and indiscriminate attacks. This obligation will be owed to civilians within the vicinity of peacekeepers, UN headquarters, and areas of patrol. Regarding human rights protection, peacekeepers are obliged, at a minimum, to protect against human rights violations that can lead to physical violence, such as conflict-related sexual violence. Further it will be concluded that UN peace missions are obliged to respect, protect and fulfil the human rights of those individuals found within their control, however, that does not extend outside of those situations.

1 What Is Protection?

Since 1999, the Security Council has constantly inserted explicit 'protection' mandates in the majority of UN peace missions but have yet to define or clarify the functional and legal meaning of the 'protection of civilians'. Instead of offering plain guidance on the application of protection and the meaning of the obligation placed on peacekeepers, the UN Secretariat and Security Council have consistently proposed that the protection mandates can only be evaluated on a 'case-by-case basis'.[2] As suggested by the Secretary-General in his overarching 2001 report on the protection of civilians, 'protection' "is a complex and multi-layered process, involving a diversity of entities and approaches" and hence "depends on the circumstances and stages of a particular conflict."[3] Although each UN peace mission is deployed differing circumstances, nonetheless to ensure that peacekeepers fulfil their obligation under the mandate, a clear indication of what is 'protection' needs to be established. Without a plain explanation of peacekeepers' obligation to protect civilians, 'protection' will remain a political expression rather than an operational reality.

The lack of clarity in the protection of civilians mandate is a major component of the literature, as the "Security Council mandates are intrinsically political and consequently their language tends to be nuanced rather than clear."[4] Thus, there is "no universally accepted definition" of protection of civilians and "insufficient guidance on implementation,"[5] for the Security Council's protection mandate is an *authorisation* or *responsibility*, not an operational or legal instruction. Although the DPO and UN have drafted guidelines on the protection of civilians mandate, they omit any legal meaning of the obligation placed on peacekeepers.[6] Consequently, the absence of 'clarity' has led to "continuing and systemic failure" in protecting civilians.[7] The foremost deficiency in the narrative is the attention on the use of force as the lone method to execute the protection mandate, even though the mandate has expanded beyond the protection from physical attacks.[8]

---

2 United Nations Security Council, *Report of the Secretary-General to the Security Council on the Protection of Civilians in Armed Conflict* (2001) UN Doc S/2001/331 at paragraph 6.

3 Ibid at paragraph 6.

4 Siobhán Wills, *Protecting Civilians: The Obligations of Peacekeepers* (Oxford University Press, 2009) at 70.

5 Scott Sheeran and Catherine Kent, 'Protection of Civilians, Responsibility to Protect, and Humanitarian Intervention' in Haidi Willmot et al (eds), *Protection of civilians* (Oxford University Press, 2016) 29 at 42–43.

6 United Nations Department of Peacekeeping Operations and Department of Field Support, *Draft DPKO/DFS Operational Concept on the Protection of Civilians in United Nations Peacekeeping Operations*, 2009 at paragraph 2 (*Draft Operational Concept*).

7 United Nations General Assembly, Evaluation of the Implementation and Results of Protection of Civilians Mandates in United Nations Peacekeeping Operations, UN Doc A/68/787 (*OIOS Report*) at paragraph 80–81.

8 Haidi Willmot and Scott Sheeran, 'The Protection of Civilians mandate in UN peacekeeping Operations: Reconciling protection concepts and practices' (2013) 95(891/892) *International Review of the Red Cross* 517 at 518.

While protection from 'physical violence' is at the centre of peacekeeping literature, the Security Council is now utilising language associated with "human rights, humanitarian relief, and development activity".[9] Thus, many human right advocates have insisted that the Security Council's protection regime encompasses more than just protection against violence, "but should also include rights such as food, medicine and shelter."[10] With the expansion of tasks within the protection mandate, many commentators have dubbed the Security Council's protection regime as the "impossible mandate".[11]

As the literature mainly focuses on the military component of peacekeeping, there is no universal concept of 'protection' for the differing actors within a UN peace mission, nor how the mission's protection responsibilities relate to those of the host State. For while the concept of protection is "largely associated with the humanitarian realm, peacekeeping missions are perceived of in the realm of security and the military use of force."[12] This ambiguous nature of the protection regime is manifested in tensions between the varying UN bodies that have influence over the protection mandate. Even though the Office for the Coordination of Humanitarian Affairs (*OCHA*) claims 'ownership' over the protection regime, it is DPO that strategizes and manages the peace missions operationally, however, the two offices do not always agree on the practical implementation of the protection mandate.[13]

The confusion over of the meaning of 'protection' stems from the Security Council's use of borrowed language, that is, the terminology employed by the Security Council is derived from differing legal instruments.[14] Without sufficient explanation, each body and agency will interpret the mandate according to their expertise, resulting in differing readings of the same mandate. From

9 Sheeran and Kent, above note 5 at 43.

10 Conor Foley, 'What are the human rights obligations of unmiss to those sheltering on its protection sites?' (2016) 2 *Conflict Trends* 20 at 26.

11 Victoria K. Holt and Tobias C. Berkman, The Impossible Mandate? Military Preparedness, the Responsibility to Protect and Modern Peace Operations (The Stimson Center, 2006) at 86.

12 Benjamin de Carvalho and Jon Harald Sande Lie, 'Chronicle of a Frustration Foretold? The Implementation of a Broad Protection Agenda in the United Nations' (2011) *15(3–4) Journal of International Peacekeeping* 341 at 350.

13 Ibid at 352.

14 Within legal conventions implied and explicit protections can be found in, including but not limited to, the Geneva Conventions; International Covenant on Civil and Political Rights; International Covenant on Economic, Social and Cultural Rights; Convention on Rights of the Child; The 1951 Refugee Convention. Further, multiple international organisations such as UNCIEF, UNHCR, UNWOMEN, OCHA, and ICRC, have their own mandates and interpretation of protection.

IHRL to IHL, and even refugee law, all legal instruments and their related organisations have differing meanings of 'protection', and thus have differing interpretations.[15] This divergence was emphasised when various departments within the UN Secretariat were questioned on the definition of 'protection', with each individual outlining 'protection' according to their portfolio.[16]

The vagueness of the Security Council on the protection of civilians mandate is understandable as the Security Council is a diplomatic body and therefore their resolutions are inherently political in nature. The Security Council considers 'diplomatic' issues rather than legal or operational interests.[17] As the wording of the Security Council mandates are negotiated texts and intended to be political statements, they generally remain vague in nature.[18] Furthermore, endeavouring to examine the Security Council's intention behind their language becomes problematic as the Security Council is not a static body, but an ever-changing organism. From the rotation of the ten non-permanent members to the constant changing diplomats, determining the interpretation of the Security Council as one organisation is arduous.[19] Further complicating the issue of interpretation, the Security Council is constantly changing and expanding the protection of civilians mandate throughout the life of a single Mission. Since the initial insertion of the protection of civilians mandate, the Security Council has used various phrases and expressions to mandate peacekeepers to protect civilians. As expressed by peacekeepers in MONUSCO, "greater attention and clarity is needed from the Security Council on the issue of integration between *Resolution 2098* (2013) and the earlier mandates."[20] For as the Security Council develops the protection of civilians mandate, little attention is given to the application of the changing mandate in the field; in recent years "mandates have become lengthier and more specific, and at times less realistic or manageable."[21]

---

15 Willmot and Sheeran, above note 8 at 518.

16 Interviews conducted in New York in February 2018, January 2019, and January 2023.

17 Wills, above note 4 at 70.

18 Victoria K. Holt, Glyn Taylor and Max Kelly, *Protecting Civilians in the Context of UN Peacekeeping Operations: Success, Setbacks and Remaining Challenges*, Independent study jointly commissioned by the Department of Peacekeeping Operations and the Office for the Coordination of Humanitarian Affairs (2009) at 76.

19 Ibid.

20 OIOS Report, above note 7 at paragraph 39.

21 United Nations General Assembly and Security Council, *Report of the High-level Independent Panel on Peace Operations on Uniting Our Strengths for Peace: Politics, Partnership and People*, UN Doc A/70/95-S/2015/446 at paragraph 181.

With these tensions, and at times contradictions, there is contention on the actual obligations owed by peacekeepers under the protection of civilians mandate. Until the obligation of 'protection' is clarified, the expectation of the international community and civilians in conflict will not be sufficiently managed. This failure in community expectations was highlighted in the DRC protests in 2022, where protesters demanded the removal of MONUSCO for their failure to protect. For the Security Council "has a major responsibility to ensure that expectations are realistic",[22] as essentially the UN and the peacekeeping division "depends largely on their willingness and capability to act when civilians are threatened".[23]

2 Interpreting the Impossible Mandate

In order to determine the interpretation of the protection of civilians mandate, 'protection' in international law context must be first identified. As stated in the previous chapter, the Security Council has not indicated their intention to create a 'new' obligation, therefore, the protection of civilians mandate must be interpreted via the current international law framework.

The contemporary legal understanding of protection of civilians in armed conflict begins with its codification in the Geneva Conventions and birth of IHL, as it was the Geneva Conventions that gave rise to the legal conception of the category of 'civilian'. IHL and the Geneva Conventions are entrenched not in the concept of 'good' and 'evil', but rather in the principle of neutrality to the conflict.[24] That is to say, the classification of 'civilian' is not granted to the 'good' but rather to parties and individuals not involving themselves in hostilities. Therefore, IHL distinguishes between participants in conflict and non-participatory parties, that is, between those participating in hostilities and civilians. This classification of civilians also applies to former fighters that no longer participate in hostilities – *hors de combat* – either due to sickness, wounds or detention.[25] Therefore, depending on the legal category of the individuals involved, the rules founded in IHL offer differing protections and obligations. Hence, for 'civilians' to receive their specified legal protection they

22 Ibid at paragraph 103.

23 United Nations Security Council, *Report of the Secretary-General on the Protection of Civilians in Armed Conflict*, UN Doc S/2016/447 at paragraph 58.

24 Ralph Mamiya, 'A History and Conceptual Development of the Protection of Civilians' in Haidi Willmot et al (eds), *Protection of civilians* (Oxford University Press, 2016) at 67–68.

25 As established in Common Article 3 of the Geneva Conventions.

must not involve themselves directly in hostilities.[26] Due to 'civilians' neutral state, combatants are to ensure civilians specific protections, in order to mitigate and minimise the harm that occurs to them in armed conflict.[27]

Although IHL provides a clear and extensive legal structure for protection of civilians in armed conflict, this framework is constructed on the assumption that civilian casualties are an inevitable consequence of war.[28] Therefore, IHL's obligations of protection of civilians is rooted in an attempt to minimise and mitigate the harm created by parties to a conflict rather than maintaining peace and security. Even though IHL is a good foundation for the protections offered to civilians, it cannot cover the field regarding the Security Council's mandate on protection of civilians. Although IHL's obligations ensure 'positive' protections, such as to ensure the protection of human dignity of "protected persons" including Prisoners of War (*POWs*) and civilians, these 'protections' are intended to mitigate damage to protected persons from a party's engagement in conflict. In contrast to the protection offered in IHL, the protection mandate is not intended to 'mitigate' harm, but rather to positively protect civilians from physical violence by other actors. Dissimilar to the foundations of IHL, the protection of civilians mandate is not offered by parties to a conflict, but by an 'impartial' third party – UN peacekeepers. Further, the protection of civilians mandate is triggered with the deployment of peacekeepers rather than the existence of an armed conflict.

Therefore, to understand the content of 'protection' there must also be examination of IHRL and the protection of humanitarian assistance[29] in conflict. For although the concept of 'protection' was established in IHL, it was subsequently built upon and expanded in IHRL and refugee law.[30] Thus, the

---

26 Nils Melzer, *Interpretive Guidance on the Notion of Direct Participation in Hostilities Under International Humanitarian Law* (International Committee of the Red Cross, Reference Paper, 2009); Emily Crawford, *Identifying the enemy: civilian participation in armed conflict* (Oxford University Press, 2015).

27 Common Article 3 in the Geneva Conventions; Geneva Convention (I) Amelioration of the Condition of the Wounded and Sick in Armed Forces in the Field, Geneva, 12 August 1949 at Article 50; Geneva Convention (II) Amelioration of the Condition of Wounded, Sick and Shipwrecked Members of Armed Forces at Sea, Geneva, 12 August 1949 at Article 51; Geneva Convention (III) Treatment of Prisoners of War, Geneva, 12 August 1949 at Article 130; Fourth Geneva Convention at Article 147.

28 Jamie A Williamson, 'Protection of Civilians under International Humanitarian Law' in Haidi Willmot et al (eds), *Protection of Civilians* (Oxford University Press, 2016) at 165.

29 In this sense 'humanitarian assistance' is not to be confused with 'humanitarian intervention'. Here 'humanitarian assistance' denotes actions to maintain human dignity, for example, providing basic goods such as food, water and medical supplies.

30 Mamiya, above note 24 at 65.

understanding of protection "has expanded from a set of legal obligations in IHL to a conceptual and operational framework used by multiple 'protection actors' and practitioners – military and civilian, political and humanitarian."[31] Although IHRL protections are more expansive than protections offered against physical violence, the Security Council still emphasises that protection of civilians is physical protection.[32] In consultations with the UN Secretariat, the majority of interviewees emphasised the primacy of physical protection within the Security Council's mandate.[33] Although other human rights protections were identified as important, it was not seen as the priority of a UN peace mission's mandate.

Even though UN agencies and stakeholders focus on physical protection, the Security Council's language has extended beyond the boundaries of physical protection. Since the conception of IHL, protection of civilians has developed in the law from a military understanding to an imperative for humanitarian agencies and non-government agencies. Following the humanitarian landscape, in 2003 with the implementation of UNMIL, the Security Council's mandate on protection shifted from providing 'military' protection against 'imminent threat', to human rights protection.[34]

As governments are failing to ensure human rights protections, States in which peacekeepers are deployed are also seeing the deployment of humanitarian and UN agencies. As multiple humanitarian agencies have engaged in protection work, each humanitarian organisation interprets the protection of civilians differently. Specifically, this divergence of interpretation of protection will stem from each agency's legal mandate and portfolio. As identified by the ICRC, "[p]rotection means something different for each organization, depending on its mandate and its working methods, if any. Moreover, each organization uses a vocabulary of its own which is not necessarily consistent with that used by others and may therefore lead to misunderstanding."[35] For instance, the UN Office for the Coordination Of Humanitarian Affairs (*OCHA*) defines protection as encompassing "all activities aimed at ensuring full respect for the rights of the individual in accordance with human rights law, international

---

31 Phoebe Wynn-Pope, *Perceptions about Protection of Civilians: A Survey of Practitioners* (Australian Civil-Military Centre; Oxfam, 2014) at 5.

32 This is will be discussed further under 'Physical protection', as can be seen by the emphasis on the 'protection of civilians from imminent threat' and 'physical violence'.

33 Interviews conducted in New York in February 2018 and January 2019.

34 United Nations Security Council Resolution 1509 (2003).

35 International Committee of the Red Cross, *Strengthening Protection in War: A Search for Professional Standards*, Caverzasio, Sylvie Giossi (ed), Genenva, Switzerland, 1996–2000 at 38.

humanitarian law (which applies in situations of armed conflict) and refugee law."[36] In contrast, the UN International Children's Emergency Fund (*UNICEF*) defines protection "to prevention and response to violence, exploitation and abuse of children in all contexts. This includes reaching children who are especially vulnerable to these threats, such as those living without family care, on the streets or in situations of conflict or natural disasters."[37]

As each organisation has a different commission towards the protection of civilians, they naturally also have a different understanding and meaning of protection. This becomes crucial in UN peacekeeping as many of these humanitarian organisations are also involved in and work alongside UN peace missions, and therefore have a different level of expectation of the protection offered by the UN.

To reach some consensus among humanitarian agencies, the ICRC in 1999 held an open dialogue workshop to discuss an all-inclusive definition of 'protection' and the 'activities' associated with that protection.[38] At the conclusion of the workshop, protection was defined as "all activities, aimed at obtaining full respect for rights of the individual in accordance with the letter and spirit of the relevant bodies of law."[39] As this definition is intended to include all protection bodies and actors, it is drafted broadly and makes "it almost synonymous with human rights."[40] For this definition to be observed by all protection actors, 'protection' would not only cover "physical security but also civil, political, economic, social and cultural rights enshrined in international human rights law."[41]

In 2013, the ICRC produced the *Professional Standards for Protection Work*, which sets out standards and guidelines for all protection workers in the field. However, the ICRC did not expand or further clarify their 1999 definition, making "no attempt at further refining the definition of protection."[42] However, the

36 OCHA, *OCHA on Message: Protection*, https://www.unocha.org/publications/report/world/ocha-message-protection#:~:text=For%20humanitarian%20actors%20such%20as,rights%2C%20humanitarian%20and%20refugee%20law%20.

37 UNCIEF, *Child Protection Overview*, <https://data.unicef.org/topic/child-protection/overview/#:~:text=UNICEF%20uses%20the%20term%20'child,of%20children%20in%20all%20contexts.>.

38 Caverzasio, Sylvie Giossi (ed), *Strengthening Protection in War: A Search for Professional Standards*, International Committee of the Red Cross, Genenva, Switzerland, 1996–2000.

39 Ibid at 19.

40 Alex J Bellamy and Paul Williams, *Understanding Peacekeeping* (Polity Press, 2nd ed, 2010) at 345.

41 Ibid at 345.

42 International Committee of the Red Cross, *Professional Standards for Protection Work: Carried out by Humanitarian and Human Rights Actors in Armed Conflict and Other Siutations of Violence* (ICRC, Geneva, 2013) at 13.

ICRC definition does give privilege to 'legal' protection emphasising respect to 'rights' under international law.[43] For example, any relief assistance or 'preventive' advocacy can only be considered a protection activity if it is intended to promote or enforce a legal right under international law.[44] As reiterated in the 2020 Handbook the protection mandate is 'rooted' in international law, and should be perceived as the Security Council's intention for civilian protection founded in the law.[45] Therefore, although there are varying approaches to 'protection', there is a common understanding that protection must be that of a *legal* right.

Therefore, the 'protection of civilians' is the protection of 'legal rights' afforded to these who do not take direct part in hostilities. As the Security Council intends to compel peacekeepers under prevailing legal obligations, the protection of civilians mandate must be the protection of existing legal rights. Exclusively, the protection of civilians mandate invokes the legal status of 'civilian' and protections owed to them under the law. In other words, the Security Council's mandate to protect civilians must not be viewed as a generic concept, rather entrenched in international law and the rights that are owed to civilians.

Although 'civilian' status is connected to IHL, the insertion of human rights language was the Security Council's clear indication that the peacekeeping protection regime includes human rights protections. The Security Council regularly mandates that peacekeepers are to 'promote and protect' human rights. Unlike IHL that invokes the classification of 'civilian' and 'combatant', IHRL applies equally to all individuals regardless of their involvement in conflict.

With the insertion of human rights protections, the protection of civilians mandate becomes an all-encompassing protection of legal rights, making the mandate the 'impossible mandate'.[46] As the mandate expands, a clear minimum core of the obligation becomes paramount. Moreover, as modern peacekeeping now entails multiple actors within a single Mission, there is overall confusion on which component of a mission is to undertake which protection activity.

43 Mamiya, above note 24 at 74.

44 Ibid at 74.

45 United Nations Department of Peace Opertions, *The Protection of Civilians in United Nations Peacekeeping Handbook* at 2.3.1.

46 United Nations General Assembly and Security Council, *The Future of United Nations Peace Operations: Implementation of the Recommendations of the High-level Independent Panel on Peace Operations*, 17 June 2015, UN Doc A/70/357-S/2015/682 (*HIPPO Report*).

2.1 *Multi-dimensional Peacekeeping*

In modern UN peace missions peacekeepers are no longer merely monitoring peace agreements, nor are they solely military operations, rather, modern UN peace missions are made up of military, police and civilian components.[47] As protection of civilians is mandated across the entire Mission, it is considered a cross-cutting theme across all components. Nevertheless, with the increased role of peacekeepers and their activities, the UN Secretariat and Security Council have yet to identify the role that each component performs in the overall protection regime. Although the Security Council lists differing 'activities' within the peacekeeping mandates, it fails to attribute the tasks to the differing actors within the Mission.[48] Tasks mandated to peacekeepers not only include physical protection, but, inter alia reporting on hate speech,[49] protecting airports,[50] and removing landmines.[51]

As the Security Council gives no operational guidance, the strategic implementation of the mandate relies on the SRSG. While the SRSG oversees the overall Mission, there are reports that there is confusion on the ground regarding each component's role in the overall protection regime.[52] Consequently, the Secretary-General in his 2016 report on protection of civilians has recommended that the Security Council within its mandates, assign each protection task to a specific actor or group – whether military, police or civilian.[53] In order for each member to recognise their obligation under the mandate "a clear distinction must be drawn between political or military action and humanitarian action, the respective roles should be understood and opportunities for complementarity maximized."[54]

The need for clarification of roles originates from the observation that many protection actors misunderstand the roles of other actors within the

47 Sebastian von Einsiedel and Louise Bosetti, 'Realizing the UN's Protection Promise: A Central Challenge for the Next Secretary-General' (2016) *8(4) Global Responsibility to Protect* 366 at 367.

48 The Security Council has mandated specific tasks to Child and Women Protection Advisors, and the Force Intervention Brigade. But generally, in regard to the Protection mandates, the Security Council mandates for the entire mission at large, within the opening operational paragraphs of the mission mandates.

49 *United Nations Security Council Resolution 2327* (2016) at operational paragraph 7(b)(iii).

50 *United Nations Securityn Council Resolution 2304* (2016) at operational paragraph 10(b).

51 *United Nations Security Council Resolution 2227* (2015) at operational paragraph 14(d)(iv).

52 OIOS Report, above note 7 at paragraph 58.

53 United Nations Security Council, *Report of the Secretary-General on the Protection of Civilians in Armed Conflict*, UN Doc S/2016/447.

54 Ibid at paragraph 56.

same Mission.[55] Specifically, military and police personnel are reported to not understand the role of UN humanitarian agencies in the protection of civilians structure.[56] In MONUSCO, civilian personnel reported that "they are often informed of a Force operation only one or two days in advance, which does not give them enough time to prepare for or join the mission".[57] As many protection activities overlap and require different actors to effectively accomplish that protection activity, a clear understanding of the roles of each group is essential or the "level of overlap and the corresponding implications for implementation and coordination are likely to continue to be contested."[58]

This division of tasks is important as the 'culture of protection' no longer belongs to one entity, but rather involves different groups and actors, and at times within the same mission. A primary example of this difference in interpretation is the academic literatures' analysis of the protection of civilians mandate itself. While legal commentators focus on the use of force and physical protection offered to civilians,[59] human rights literature focuses on the protection of rights, and the importance of social, political and economic rights.[60] Yet the literature does not overlap, rather each discipline focuses on their own interests, creating a lack of holistic approach to protection.

In the Capstone Doctrine, the former DPKO and DFS sought to clarify the multiple interpretations of protection, by establishing a three tier set of activities – protection through political process; protection from physical violence; and the establishment of a protective environment.[61] However, nothing in the Capstone Doctrine gave a clear-cut definition of the meaning of protection and how that protection can be implemented in the field. More importantly, the Capstone Doctrine does not give a minimum core obligation of protection

---

55 Wynn-Pope, above note 31 at 38.

56 Ibid at 41–42.

57 Center for Civilians in Conflict, *Protection with Less Presence: How the Peacekeeping Operation in the Democractic Republic of Congo is Attempting to Deliver Protection with Fewer Resources*, 10 January 2018 at 19.

58 Wynn-Pope, above note 31 at 32.

59 For example, Dale Stephens, 'The lawful use of force by peacekeeping forces: the tactical imperative' (2005) *12*(2) *International Peacekeeping* 157; T. Tardy, 'The UN and the Use of Force: A Marriage Against Nature' (2007) 38(1) Security Dialogue 49; Siobhán Wills, 'Use of Deadly Force by Peacekeepers Operating Outside of Armed Conflict Situations: What Laws Apply?' (2018) *40*(*3*) *Human Rights Quarterly* 663.

60 *The Role of UN Peacekeeping Missions in the Protection of Civilians* (Oxfam Policy Compendium Note, July 2012) at 2.

61 United Nations Department of Peacekeeping Operations and Department of Field Support, *United Nations Peacekeeping Operations: Principles and Guidelines*, 2008 (*Capstone Doctrine*).

expected by the UN. Accordingly, after the Capstone Doctrine the UN Office of Internal Oversight Services (*OIOS*) that oversees the evaluation of accountability and improved performance, recommended to the General Assembly that the definition of protection of civilians should be 'narrowed' for a more focused and workable mandate.[62]

Additionally, the Security Council has not merely expanded the protection of civilians beyond physical protection, but has recognised differing groups in need of protection within UN peace mission resolutions, such as women and children,[63] and internally displaced persons.[64] Within the Secretary-General's and Security Council's reports several themes are acknowledged in order to improve culture of protection – physical attacks; internal displacement; effective location and protection of displaced camps; children in conflict; women in conflict; and human rights and humanitarian protection.[65] The above list is not intended to be exhaustive, rather an indication of the multiple and growing themes encompassing the UN concept of protection, and the 'culture' that they are mandating to be established.[66] Thus, the international community considers protection of civilians "to include many inter-connected activities including, for example, efforts to improve physical security, provide humanitarian assistance, support human rights, extend the rule of law and nurture transitional justice."[67]

As peacekeeping mandates are increasing in tasks and activities, they are generally referred to as 'Christmas tree' mandates,[68] that is, the Security Council adds language to the original mandate in similar fashion to a Christmas

---

62 OIOS Report, above note 7 at paragraph 54.

63 *United Nations Security Council Resolution 2363* (2017) at operational paragraph 15(i); *United Nations Security Council Resolution 2387* (2017) at operational paragraph 42(a)(ii).

64 *United Nations Security Council Resolution 2409* (2018) at operational paragraph 36(i)(a); *United Nations Security Council Resolution* 2327 (2016) at operational paragraph 7(a)(ii); or a variation of "securing IDP camps" in *United Nations Security Council Resolution 2296* (2016) at operational paragraph 4.

65 United Nations Security Council, *Report of the Secretary-General to the Security Council on the Protection of Civilians in Armed Conflict*, UN Doc S/2001/331.

66 United Nations Security Council, *Report of the Secretary-General on the Protection of Civilians in Armed Conflict*, UN Doc S/2017/414 at paragraph 73.

67 Mark Bowden, 'The Protection of Civilians' in Bertrand G Ramcharan (ed), *Human Rights Protection in the Field*, International Studies in Human Rights (Martinus Nujhoff Publishers, 2006) 59 at 67.

68 United Nations Security Council, 8218th meeeting, Wednesday, 28 March 2018, UN Doc S/PV.8218; United Nations Office for the Coordination of Humanitarian Affairs, *Building a Culture of Protection: 20 Years of Security Council Engagement on the Protection of Civilians*, OCHA Policy and Studies Series, May 2019 at 38.

tree ornament. So much so, that Secretary-General Guterres has declared that "Christmas is over" and urged "Security Council members to sharpen and streamline mandates and put an end to mandates that look like Christmas trees."[69] However, it has been suggested that the Security Council is "inclined to persist with the Christmas tree approach, not because they expect missions to implement the litany of tasks, but to give them the authority to do so if and when needed."[70] This fear of 'sharpening' the mandates or clarifying intent, is based on the belief that the protection of civilians mandate is merely an authority rather than a legally binding decision that entreats a legal obligation. Be that as it may, without a clear target identified by the Security Council, and a minimum standard of the protection, protection of civilian remains elusive.[71] As there is an increase in mandated tasks, each UN peace mission has been forced to prioritise some protection activities over other, as will be discussed further in Chapter 6.

In order to determine the minimum core obligation and legal problems in the protection mandate, this chapter will now examine the language of the protection of civilians mandate.

3 The Language of the Protection of Civilians Mandate

Even though each UN peace mission resolution expresses different language, protection mandates can be divided into two main categories – protection against physical violence and human rights protection. Particularly, the Security Council will entreat distinct obligations within the two categories, specifically the duties under IHL and IHRL.

3.1 *Protection from Physical Violence*

Before the Security Council entered into the protection landscape, humanitarian agencies were frequently involved in human rights and humanitarian protection. Humanitarian and human rights groups have for many years endeavoured to meet the humanitarian and material needs of civilians in armed conflict.[72] However, human rights and humanitarian agencies could not

69 UNSC, 8218th meeting at 3.

70 Alex J Bellamy and Charles T. Hunt, 'Benefits of Paring Down Peacekeeping Mandates Also Comes with Risks' (2019) *Global Observatory* <https://theglobalobservatory.org/2019/03/benefits-paring-down-peacekeeping-mandates-come-with-risks/>.

71 von Einsiedel and Bosetti, above note 47 at 379.

72 Elissa Goldberg and Don Hubert, 'Case Study: The Security Council and the Protection of Civilians' in Rob McRae and Don Hubert (eds), *Human Security and the New*

provide physical protection for these civilians from armed attacks, hence, the fundamental challenge, in the words of one commentator, was that too often civilians that received assistance ultimately became the "well-fed dead."[73]

As physical protection was the visibly missing element not provided for by local authorities or humanitarian agencies, the Security Council began mandating protection for civilians under "imminent threat of physical violence."[74] Though the Security Council has expanded the use and language associated with protection of civilians, as outlined in Chapter 1, the primary focus of the UN and the international community is still the physical protection of civilians from physical violence.

In current armed conflict, the civilian population are continually exposed to physical insecurity, making physical protection "central to the concept of the Protection of Civilians."[75] Even though peacekeeping protection activities have expanded beyond military protection, as stated by Secretary-General "[t]he credibility of United Nations peacekeepers depends largely on their willingness and capability to act when civilians are threatened."[76] While the protection of human rights and humanitarian needs advances the prevention of physical harm, and the development of preventive measures is essential for long-term peace and protection of civilians, "[s]uccess in prevention do[es] not, in the opinion of civilians, offset failures to intervene when they are under attack."[77] Although 'protection from physical violence' is only one of three forms of protection envisaged by the Capstone Doctrine, in practice, it has become the central theme within the mandate.

The physical protection of civilians from threat of physical violence is directly connected to armed conflict and the use of force and is considered to primarily fall within territory of military and police component. Due to this, it is still considered by the UN Secretariat that the mandate primarily applies to the military component of each Mission.[78]

When UN peace missions are mandated to protect civilians, it is exhorted that "uniformed personnel must play their part, including, where necessary,

Diplomacy: Protecting People, Promoting Peace (McGrill-Queen's University Press, 2001) 223.

73 Ibid at 225.

74 *United Nations Security Council Resolution 1270* (1999).

75 Wynn-Pope, above note 31 at 28.

76 United Nations Security Council, *Report of the Secretary-General on the Protection of Civilians in Armed Conflict*, UN Doc S/2016/447 at 58.

77 OIOS Report, above note 7 at paragraph 15.

78 Interviews conduct in New York in January 2019.

through the use of force."[79] This physical protection through the use of force has been defined to include "preventive, pre-emptive and tactical use of force to protect civilians under threat of physical violence."[80] As surmised in the third principle of the Kigali Principles on the Protection of Civilians, peacekeepers should:

> be prepared to use force to protect civilians, as necessary and consistent with the mandate. Such action encompasses making a show of force as a deterrent; inter-positioning our forces between armed actors and civilians; and taking direct military action against armed actors with clear hostile intent to harm civilians.[81]

The protection mandate expects peacekeepers to become the enforcers of the 'civilian' status, not only in response to a direct attack, but also in a preventive manner. Explicitly, UN peace missions are mandated to patrol and use their presence in 'high-risk' areas.[82] Unlike the obligations under IHL that are only applied once a conflict reaches the threshold of an 'armed conflict' under the Geneva Conventions,[83] the protection of civilians mandate is not dependant on the existence of a 'conflict' rather requires a pre-emptive and proactive response to threats of physical violence. Within the 2009 DPKO Concept Note, pre-emptive protection is not just the use of military presence, but also to "liaison with government and non-government armed actors, and potential parities to a conflict, enhanced human rights monitoring, reporting, and advocacy, as well as heightened political pressure."[84] Although UN guidelines mention the use of strategies outside the use of force, expressly human rights and the rule of law, independent reports such as HIPPO and Cruz reports focus mainly on the use of force in achieving protection.

The emphasis on military force in UN peacekeeping is apparent in the literature's fascination with the use of force and sole focus on the military

79 HIPPO Report, above note 46 at paragraph 18.

80 Ibid.

81 Report of the High-Level International Conference on the Protection of Civilians, *The Kigali Principles on the Protection of Civilians*, Kigali, Rwanda, 28–29 May 2015 Third principle.

82 *United Nations Security Council Resolution* 2327 (2016) at operational paragraph 7(a)(ii); *United Nations Security Council Resolution 2363* (2017) at operational paragraph 15(a)(ii).

83 *Decision on the Defence Motion for Interlocutory Appeal on Jurisdiction*, International Criminal Tribunal for the former Yugoslavia, Appeals Chamber Decision, 2 October 1995.

84 Draft Operational Concept, above note 6.

component of peacekeeping.[85] In the protection literature there is an expectation that peacekeepers will always position themselves between civilians and any threat of violence.[86] However, if the positioning of peacekeeping forces does not deter the threat, the literature is in consensus that force ought to be used in order to protect civilians.[87] Nevertheless, there still remains confusion on the operational or legal trigger for peacekeepers to use force. For even though protection from physical violence is central to the protection of civilians mandate, the UN has not clarified what would be considered a 'threat' of physical violence.[88] This becomes problematic as the protection mandate exists at all times of deployment, whether or not IHL has been activated, and therefore, the mandate lacks any legal trigger. As an example, should UN peacekeepers intervene with force if prisoners held by local authorities are being tortured? Or is lobbying local authorities sufficient to fulfil their obligation to protect?

As the Security Council has not intended a departure from the existing legal framework, a trigger for the use of force must be found within the law. Since the formation of the protection of civilians mandate is constantly correlated with armed conflict, for example, the Security Council's open debate on protection is titled 'the protection of civilians in armed conflict', and their overarching resolutions on protection of civilians constantly references "the protection of civilians in armed conflict."[89] Therefore, it is clearly the intention of the Security Council to interpret the protection of civilians in connection with armed conflict, and therefore the laws of IHL. In interviews conducted in

---

85 For example, Peter Nadin, *The Use of Force in UN Peacekeeping* (Routledge, 2018); Scott Sheeran, 'The Use of Force in United Nations Peacekeeping Operations' in Marc Weller (ed), *The Oxford Handbook of the Use of Force in International Law* (Oxford University Press, 2015); Tardy, above note 59; Thierry Tardy, 'The Reluctant Peacekeeper: France and the Use of Force in Peace Operations' (2014) *37(5) Journal of Strategic Studies* 770; Katarina Månsson, 'Use of Force and Civlian Protection: Peace Operations in the Congo' (2005) *12(4) International Peacekeeping* 503; Christopher K. Penny, "Drop That or I'll Shoot … Maybe': International Law and the Use of Deadly Force to Defend Property in UN Peace Operations' (2007) *14(3) International Peacekeeping* 353.

86 Bellamy and Williams, above note 40 at 349.

87 For example, Peter Nadin, *The use of force in UN peacekeeping* (2018); Mona Ali Khali, 'Legal Aspects of the Use of Force by Unitd Nations Peacekeepers for the Protection of Civilians' in Haidi Willmot et al (eds), *Protection of Civilians* (Oxford University Press, 2016); André Nolkaemper, 'Failures to Protect' in International Law' in Marc Weller (ed), *The Oxford Handbook of the Use of Force in International Law*, Oxford Handbooks in Law (Oxford University Press, 2015); Willmot and Sheeran, above note 8.

88 Robert Schütte, *Civilian Protection in Armed Conflicts: Evolution, Challenges and Implementation* (Springer VS, 2013) at 162.

89 *United Nations Security Council Resolution 1894* (2009) at operational paragraph 33.

2023, participants within DPO indicated that peacekeepers should only react in instances of armed conflict, and to leave all other matters to local police.[90]

Although IHL becomes the legal framework for physical protection, there needs to be a legal trigger to enforce the protection of civilians through the use of force. Specifically, as seen from the July 2016 'failure' of UNMISS, each contingent assessed the response to the threat differently, and hence, opposed the 'common' conception of the protection that was needed.[91] As identified by the Independent Special Investigation into the incident in Juba in 2016, the peacekeeping force "did not operate under a unified command, resulting in multiple and sometimes conflicting orders to the four troops contingents from China, Ethiopia, Nepal and India, and ultimately underusing the more than 1,800 infantry troops at UN House".[92] While Indian and Ethiopian troops kept their defensive positions protecting the civilians within the protection camps, the Chinese battalion abandoned their position leaving two protection camps opened to attack.[93]

As the fundamental protection offered by IHL is that no civilian will be directly targeted, this protection will become the minimum core of the obligation to protect from physical violence. Therefore, at a minimum UN peace missions are obliged to use military force to protect civilians from direct and indiscriminate attack in an armed conflict. Firstly, this obligation implies that the aggressors must be parties involved in armed conflict, in other words, IHL must be triggered. Secondly, the attack must be directed towards civilians, or in civilian-populated areas, that is to say the attack will be illegal. Thirdly, as this protection is against the threat of physical violence, peacekeepers do not have to wait for civilians to *actually* be attacked, rather that parties to a conflict are *going to* attack civilians. Furthermore, this obligation falls upon the military component to protect civilians from direct and indiscriminate attacks in armed conflict.

4 Qualifications to the Obligation to Protect

In order to clarify the scope of the protection mandate the Security Council has inserted caveats within the mandate, such as "within the capabilities" or

90 Interviews conducted with three participants in the DPO in New York in January 2023.

91 Executive Summary of the Independent Special Investigation into the Violence which Occured in Juba in 2016 and UNMISS Response.

92 Ibid at response 3.

93 Ibid at response 3.

in "areas of deployment". Nonetheless, similar to the mandate itself, the caveats are ambiguous and do not grant any operational or legal value. For example, it would be impossible to expect MONUSCO to protect the entire area of the DRC, since 'areas of deployment' can mean within the physical vicinity of peacekeepers and their mission headquarters, or within the entire 'area' of the mandated territory of the mission. Without a legal framework, peacekeepers will determine 'the area of their deployment' differently, leading to an inconsistent coverage. The 2020 Handbook gives little guidance on these caveats by interpreting these sections as:

> This limitation recognizes that peacekeeping operations have limited capacity and footprint and cannot protect everyone, everywhere, at all times. However, missions should consider the various threats to civilians when determining the mission footprint and deployment of resources and should be prepared to redeploy resources as necessary to respond to serious threats to civilians.[94]

For peacekeepers to effectively protect, and for civilians' expectations to be managed, a legal understanding is needed for 'area of their deployment'. As an example, in July 2016, in South Sudan, women were being sexually assaulted one kilometre from peacekeeping camps, yet peacekeepers refused to leave their encampments to assist.[95] For protection of civilians to become a more concrete principle, the UN and the Security Council need to determine the 'specific radius', or the territorial coverage of their obligation. However, until this radius of protection is defined by the Security Council, at a minimum, protection must be offered to all civilians within the immediate vicinity of peacekeepers or UN bases of operation.

Therefore, a reading of the Security Council's language shows that IHL will be the legal framework for the obligation to protect against physical violence. As such, military peacekeepers are legally obliged under the mandate, at a minimum, to protect civilians within their vicinity and the vicinity of UN bases of operations, against direct and indiscriminate attacks within an armed conflict.

4.1 *Preventive Protection*

When mandating the protection of civilians, the Security Council mirrors the obligations in Article 27 of the Fourth Geneva Convention, by mandating

94 The 2020 Handbook at 2.1.1.

95 Executive Summary of the Independent Special Investigation into the Violence which Occured in Juba in 2016 and UNMISS Response at 4.

not only against direct attacks, but "threats thereof". Thus, the protection of civilians mandate requires an element of proactive protection. Even though the Secretary-General and humanitarian agencies have identified differing activities to protect preventively, the Security Council has only explicitly mandated two preventative activities – patrolling and ensuring a creation of secure environments.[96]

The preventive protection measure that is dominantly mandated by the Security Council is the active patrolling of peacekeepers in vulnerable areas.[97] It is consistently reported that preventative deployment of peacekeepers in vulnerable areas is successful in ceasing mass violations of the law.[98] As the presence of UN peacekeepers deters attacks on civilians, patrolling has been successful in creating a secure environment. Due to the success of patrolling, the Security Council has consistently and explicitly mentioned patrolling as a protection activity that ought to be performed by peacekeepers.[99] In practice patrolling is undertaken by both the police and military component of a Mission, depending on the level of risk.[100]

Although the Security Council caveats the protection of civilians mandates within the "areas of their deployment", in regards to patrolling, the Security Council particularly mandates peacekeepers to "expand its presence, including through long-range patrols."[101] As it can be inferred from the wording of the mandates, these patrols are not only to occur within the proximity of

---

96 *United Nations Security Council Resolution 2164* (2014) at operational paragraph 13(a)(iv); *United Nations Secuirty Council Resolution 2149* (2014) at operational paragrpah 30(a)(i); *United Nations Security Council Resolution 2003* (2011) at operational paragraph 3; *United Nations Security Council Resolution 2063* (2012) at operational paragraph 3; *United Nations Security Council Resolution 2173* (2014) at operational paragraph 8(a); *United Nations Security Council Resolution 2155* (2014) at operational paragraph 4(a)(ii); *United Nations Security Council Resolution 2304* (2016) at operational paragraph 5; *United Nations Security Council Resolution 1856* (2008) at operational paragraph 3(e).

97 *United Nations Security Council Resolution 2499* (2019) at operational paragraph 32(ii); *United Nations Security Council Resolution 2480* (2019) at operational paragraph 28(c)(ii); *United Nations Security Council Resolution 2502* (2019) at operational paragraph 29(i)(b).

98 United Nations Security Council, *Report of the Secretary-General to the Security Council on the Protection of Civilians in Armed Conflict*, UN Doc S/1999/957 at paragraph 47 and recommendation 12; United Nations Security Council, *Report of the Secretary-General Pursuant to Security Council Resolution 1820*, UN Doc S/2009/362 at paragraph 41; also as the Center for Civilians in Conflict have identified the success of patrolling in South Sudan in Center for Civilians in Conflict, *Under Fire: The July 2016 Violene in Juba and UN Response* (Center for Civilians in Conflict, 2016) at 3.

99 Ibid.

100 The 2020 Handbook at 4.3.

101 *United Nations Security Council Resolution 2164* (2014) at operational paragraph 13(a)(iv).

peacekeeping camps, but rather to be performed "in areas of high risk conflict."[102] However, as with all protection mandates, patrolling is limited by the Security Council to the 'capabilities' of the mission. Therefore, if patrolling is within their capabilities, it is an obligation for UN peace missions to actively deploy peacekeepers in "areas of high risk" in order to ensure the safety of civilians.

As long-range patrolling is mandated as 'proactive deployment', in practice peacekeepers have dispensed patrolling once armed conflict erupts within these areas.[103] As an example in South Sudan, once conflict broke out around the peacekeeping compounds in 2016, UNMISS remained within the compounds and discontinued all patrols in that area, as patrolling was seen as a preventive and proactive measure, and not a 'combatant' approach to protection.[104]

Nonetheless, once conflict has broken out, even though peacekeepers can discontinue patrolling, they cannot dispense their obligation to protect civilians from 'physical' harm, as long as this territory falls within the 'area of their deployment'. Thus, to reiterate, it becomes essential to define what is intended by 'area of their deployment'; particularly, if peacekeepers are regularly patrolling a specific area, that territory could be deemed to be an 'area of deployment'. Even though these territories might be some distance from peacekeeping base of operation, the regular occurrence of peacekeepers patrolling would position that territory as an 'area within their deployment'. Thus, civilians residing in these regions should be able to expect a level of protection from UN peacekeepers from physical violence, adding areas of patrol to the substance of the obligation to protect.

The second preventive activity explicitly mandated by the Security Council is that peacekeepers are to "contribute to the creation of a more secure environment."[105] Particularly, UN peace missions are mandated to achieve these secure environments by assisting local authorities and forces. Even though the wording from mission to mission differs, all mandates imply that this 'coordination' is to be assumed as part of the military and police component of the Mission. Missions have been mandated to assist government and local forces

---

102 *United Nations Security Council Resolution 2003* (2011) at operational paragraph 3(a); *United Nations Security Council Resolution 2666* (2022) at operational paragraph 24(i)(d).

103 Executive Summary of the Independent Special Investigation into the Violence which Occured in Juba in 2016 and UNMISS Response.

104 Center for Civilians in Conflict, above note 98 at 3.

105 *United Nations Security Council Resolution 1778* (2007) at operational paragraph 2(b); *United Nations Security Council Resolution 1856* (2008) at operational paragraph 3(c).

to "stabilize the key population centers"[106] or to assist the local "military and police"[107] to create secure environments. However, it is unclear the role of the military and police components of peacekeeping operations within these areas. Specifically, whether the peacekeepers are to take an active approach to "stabilizing" certain areas, or to take a passive approach by training local authorities. Further, it is unclear whether UN peacekeepers are intended to take a lead role or are to follow the direction of the local forces. In practice, UN peace mission have deferred to 'training' local authorities and advocating and promoting the rule of law.[108] Without a clear indication from the Security Council, UN peace missions will take a 'supporting' role rather than a leading role in this area.

Additionally, there is no indication to peacekeepers of their course of action when local authorities are unable or unwilling to achieve or provide this protective environment. Moreover, tension arises when the local authorities and government forces are the ones creating an unsecure environment themselves. With the exception of UNMISS, as discussed later in this Chapter, the Security Council has remained silent on what peacekeepers are intended to do without the assistance or authority of local forces. Until the Security Council references otherwise, peacekeepers would not be legally obliged to take a leading role in creating a secure environment, but rather are to support local authorities.

4.2 *Proactive Protection and the Rise of Protection Forces*

Acting on the recommendations of Secretary-General Ban Ki-moon, in 2013, the Security Council embarked on a new regime to proactively protect civilians from physical threats by establishing the FIB in the DRC. With the continuing violence and human rights violations by armed groups, the Security Council created an 'offensive' peacekeeping force to eliminate the threat against civilians. Instead of a responsive approach, the FIB is "take the initiative and track down armed groups to prevent their expansion, disarm and ultimately neutralize them."[109] Thus, the FIB is "described as the first contingent of troops to conduct targeted offensive operations against armed groups."[110] However, the FIB is mandated to undertake the military operations in coordination with the

106 *United Nations Security Council Resolution 2227* (2015) at operational paragraph 14(a)(ii).
107 *United Nations Security Council Resolution 2175* (2014) at operational paragraph 8(iv).
108 Interview with UN Secretariat on 28 January 2019.
109 Lars Müller, 'The Force Intervention Brigade – United Nations Forces beyond the Fine Line Between Peacekeeping and Peace Enforcement' (2015) 20(3) *Journal of Conflict & Secuirty Law* 359 at 360.
110 Ibid at 360.

DRC state military. Further the Security Council has continually insisted that this proactive measure is a one-off and not a precedent for further missions; however, in 2016, the Security Council has mandated the Regional Protection Force (*RPF*) in South Sudan. In UNMISS' recent mandate, the RPF has been mandated to "[p]romptly and effectively engage any actor that is credibly found to be preparing attacks, or engages in attacks, against United Nations protection of civilians site."[111]

The introduction of the FIB expands the protection of civilians from ensuring that civilians are not directly targeted, to actively finding and eliminating armed groups that have breached their obligations to civilians under the law. Although the FIB was initially advocated in order to stop atrocities committed against civilians, the FIB has now entered the existing armed conflict, going beyond 'protection'.[112] This 'new wave' of proactive protection can be seen in the Security Council's recent wording when mandating MONUSCO and MINUSCA to take necessary means in "preventing, deterring and stopping all armed groups and local militias from inflicting violence on the populations."[113]

Therefore, adding these preventive and proactive measures to the minimum obligation, military peacekeepers are obliged to protect civilians who are in the vicinity of peacekeepers, UN bases of operations, and in areas of patrol, from direct and indiscriminate attacks. Part of this obligation is the patrolling of areas of 'high-risk', even when these areas are outside the direct proximity of bases of operation, if it is within their capability. Further, the application of this protection is not only responsive in nature but is to be preventative and pre-emptive to deter any threat of violence instigated from armed groups.

5 Protection and Promotion of Human Rights

Since its explicit inclusion in *Resolution 1509* (2003), the protection of human rights has become a norm and is constantly included in peacekeeping mandates. Ever since the inclusion of human rights protection, the Security Council has mandated peacekeepers to "protect and promote human rights"[114] and to carry out "human rights promotion, protection and monitoring activities."[115]

111 *United Nations Security Council Resolution 2459* (2019) at operational paragraph 10(iii).

112 The legal issues of the FIB will be discussed in Chapter 3.

113 *United Nations Security Council Resolution 2666* (2022) at operational paragraph 24(i)(a); *United Nations Security Council Resolution 2659* (2019) at operational paragraph 35(a)(iii).

114 *United Nations Security Council Resolution 1509* (2003) at opertaional paragraph 3(l); *United Nations Security Council Resolution 2659* (2022) at operationa paragraph 36(b)(iii).

115 Ibid at operational paragraph 3(m).

Since its inclusion human rights protection has become a prominent area of discussion and focus within the UN. As contended in the HIPPO report, human rights protection is "an integral component of every United Nations peace operation and a core consideration for United Nations development and humanitarian activities."[116] The protection of human rights is argued to be a fundamental objective, as "[w]idespread violations of human rights often trigger a United Nations peace operation, and progress in the protection of those rights is a basis for its exit."[117] Therefore, as the Security Council is continually mandating the protection and promotion of human rights, current UN peace missions are expected to be guardians to IHRL protections in the area of their deployment. This is further emphasised with the deployment of Human Rights Advisors, who are to assist and implement human rights related mandates across all mission operations.

It is considered by one member of the UN Secretariat that the protections of human rights should not be considered under the protection of civilians mandate.[118] In support of this argument this interviewee quoted *Resolution 2364* (2017), specifically that MINUSMA was explicitly mandated to protect human rights under a different sub-section to 'protection of civilians'.[119] This division of sections was used as evidence that the Security Council intends to separate human rights from the protection of civilians mandate. Nevertheless, within other mandates, human rights protections are placed under the division of 'protection of civilians'. For example, MONUSCO's is mandated to "ensure the protection of civilians from abuses and violations of human rights and violations of international humanitarian law",[120] whereas UNMISS is mandated under the umbrella of protection of civilians to establish "response mechanisms to threats and attacks against civilians that may involve violations and abuses of human rights".[121] Therefore, although some human rights protections are mandated under a distinct paragraph, other human rights protections will fall under the umbrella of protection of civilians. Nevertheless, even when the Security Council separates human rights protection from physical protection, DPO considers both elements as part of the larger protection regime.[122]

---

116 HIPPO Report, above note 46 at paragraph 16.
117 Ibid at paragraph 10.
118 Interview with UN Secretariat on 28 January 2019.
119 Ibid.
120 *United Nations Security Council Resolution 2277* (2016) at operational paragraph 35(i)(b).
121 *United Nations Security Council Resolution 2406* (2018) at operational paragprah 7(a)(iii).
122 The 2020 Handbook at 2.3.1.

5.1 *Human Rights Protection in UN Peacekeeping*

Before endeavouring to outline the minimum obligation of human rights protection, firstly, we must attempt to outline IHRL's jurisdiction over UN peace missions. IHRL is founded in the concept that the obligation to protect human rights is placed uniquely in the jurisdiction of States, that is, it is the responsibility of the State to guarantee protection.[123]

Differing human rights treaties impose differing obligations on States parties. Under the ICCPR, States must "respect and … ensure"[124] the rights within the Covenant, while the *International Convention on Economic, Social and Cultural Rights* (*ICESCR*) requires States to "take steps"[125] towards "the full realization of the rights recognized" within the Covenant. Henry Shue suggested in 1980 that IHRL imposes three obligations on States; the obligation to respect, protect and fulfil.[126] Shue's typology assisted in clearly identifying the obligations found within multiple human rights instruments, and is now commonly used by the UN Human Rights Committee and the Committee on Economic, Social and Cultural Rights (*CESCR*) when assessing human rights obligations.[127] Therefore, under this typology States not only have an obligation to respect and refrain from interfering with these rights, they must also protect against third parties by offering preventative and remedial aspects to these rights.

From the protection mandate, it can also be implied that the Security Council obliges peacekeepers to respect, protect and fulfil the human rights of civilians within their care. However, it would be unreasonable to expect the same obligation owed by States to be placed on UN peace missions. For example, States are obliged to protect human rights through positive steps such as enacting criminal and civil laws, which cannot be undertaken by peacekeepers. Nevertheless, using Shue's typology, at a minimum, peacekeepers must first

---

123 Johan D Van Der Vyver, 'Sovereignty ' in Dinah Shelton (ed), *The Oxford Handbook of International Human Rights Law* (Oxford University Press, 2013) at 379; Wiktor Osiatyński, 'The Historical Development of Human Rights' in Scott Sheeran and Nigel Rodley (eds), *Routledge Handbook of International Human Rights Law* (Taylor and Francis, 2014) at 9.

124 ICCPR at Article 2(1).

125 *International Convenant on Economic, Social and Cultural Rights*, adopted by General Assembly resolution 200A(XXI) oon 16 December 1966, entry into force 3 January 1976 (*ICESCR*) at Article 2(1).

126 Henry Shue, *Basic Rights* (Princeton University Press, 1980).

127 For example, United Nations Economic and Social Council, General Comment 24 on State Obligations under the International Covenant on Economic, Social and Cultural Rights in the Context of Business Activities, 10 August 2017, UN Doc E/C.12/GC/24; UN HRC, General Comment No 31.

respect the rights of civilians by not violating these rights themselves. As will be discussed in further chapters, when peacekeepers engage in human rights violations whether in military operations or in their private capacity (such as gender-based and sexual abuse), they are breaching their obligation to protect.

Further in Shue's typology and the Security Council's language, peacekeepers are not only to respect but to 'protect and promote' human rights. Within the current humanitarian landscape, the protection of human rights by international organisations is the "naming, blaming and shaming those bearing responsibility for human rights violations", as well as lobbying governments and groups for a change in policy and procedure, "and publishing informed reports on situations of concern."[128]

Interestingly, when mandating explicit protection of human rights, the Security Council will make reference to "promoting and protecting" separate to "monitoring and reporting". This separation of phrases implies that 'promoting and protecting' is distinct from 'monitoring and reporting'. Essentially, the Security Council is referencing the obligation to protect owed by States under IHRL. The obligation under IHRL requires States to protect individuals within their jurisdiction against any violations from third parties and the State's agents. To fulfil their obligation to protect, States must take positive measures to reduce the abuses of any individual's rights. If this is the intention of the Security Council, UN peace missions would be obliged to ensure that individuals within their area of deployment are protected from abuses from third parties and UN personnel.

When peacekeepers are obliged to protect, there needs to be an indication for peacekeepers of which rights place an obligation to protect, rather than just an obligation to respect. Particularly, as under IHRL human rights are indivisible,[129] as all human rights are equal and should not be considered in any hierarchical manner, this will include economic, social, political and civil rights.

However, when the Security Council mandates peacekeepers to 'promote and protect' human rights it is generally in reference to physical protection.[130]

---

128 Schütte, above note 88 at 146.

129 *The United Nations General Assembly Resolution 217(III) (A Universal Declaration of Human Rights)*, A/RES/217(III), as stated in the preamble, "the inherent dignity and of the equal and inalienable rights of all members of the human family".

130 *United Nations Security Council Resolution 1509* (2003) at operational paragraph 3(l); *United Nations Security Council Resolution 1528* (2004) at operational paragraph 6(n); *United Nations Security Council Resolution 1933* (2010) at operational paragraph 16(e); *United Nations Secuirty Council Resolution 2000* (2011) at operational paragraph 7(g); *United Nations Security Council Resolution 2162* (2014) at operational parapgraph 19(g); *United Nations Security Council Resolution 2164* (2014) at operational paragraph 13(c);

From the language used in Security Council resolutions, it is implied that protection is obliged if the human rights violation is also a threat against a civilian's physical security. For instance, within certain missions peacekeepers are asked to 'protect' human rights with "particular attention to sexual and gender-based violence."[131] As noted by one peacekeeping analyst, peacekeepers are only obliged to protect when that breach of human rights also leads to a breach of civilians' physical safety.[132] Moreover, it is implied from the mandate that the protection of human rights is correlated with armed conflict.[133]

In consultation with the UN, only one interviewee thought that protection of human rights should stand alone from armed conflict.[134] It has been suggested by this individual that peacekeepers should intervene in any human rights violation that would lead to physical violence, whether or not the abuse is related to armed conflict.[135] This includes the intervention in areas of domestic violence and female mutilation. However, when speaking to the host States, any forceful intervention by peacekeepers for human rights protection is seen as a violation of law and over-reaches the mandate.[136] As will be discussed in Chapter 5, sexual violence does not need to be inflicted by a party to a conflict to be associated with armed conflict. While the Security Council associates protection with armed conflict, violence needs to be 'conflict-related' rather than committed by a party to a conflict to trigger a peacekeeping response.

Outside human rights violations that lead to direct physical violence, it is unclear what other rights would demand an obligation to protect from peacekeepers. Although UN debates regarding human rights protections centre around sexual violence and child recruitment, human rights are interdependent and should not be divided. For example, starvation and a lack of shelter will also lead to physical insecurity. Conversely, when peacekeepers are in control over a territory or individuals, UN peace missions will be obliged to respect, protect and fulfil those individuals' rights.

United Nations Security Council Resolution 2227 (2015) at operational paragraph 14(e)(i); *United Nations Secuirty Council Resolution 2149* (2014) at operational paragraph 30(e)(iv); *United Nations Security Council Resolution 1778* (2007) at operational paragraph 2(e).

131 *United Nations Security Council Resolution 1778* (2007) at operational paragraph 2(e).

132 Interview with South Sudan on 22 January 2019; Interview conducted with protection of civilian researcher on 23 January 2019.

133 For example see *United Nations Security Council Resolution 2364* (2017) at operational paragraph 20(f)(i).

134 Interview with POC researcher on 23 January 2019.

135 Ibid.

136 Interview with South Sudan on 22 January 2019.

As will be discussed in Chapter 6, UN peace missions will not be considered in control over a territory but can and will be in control over individuals. Although all rights are interdependent, at a minimum, with the exception of individuals under their control, peacekeepers are obliged to protect against human rights violations that directly lead to conflict-related violence.

5.2 *Social, Political and Economic Rights*

One aspect of protection of human rights in armed conflict that has yet to be fully developed is the protection of social, political, economic and civil rights. As of 1992 the Security Council has already recognised that "nonmilitary source[s] of instability in economic, social, humanitarian, and ecological fields have become threats to peace and security."[137] Further, the UN's Inter-Agency Standing Committee has suggested that

> the focus on already existing rights helped clarify the extent and focus of protection, set minimum standards for the treatment of civilians in war and was comprehensive in scope, covering not just physical security but also civil, political, economic, social and cultural rights enshrined in international human rights law.[138]

The majority of the focus on social, political, economic and civil rights of civilians in conflict, specifically women and children, has come from Secretary-General reports rather than the Security Council. When discussing the social, political, economic and civil rights of civilians, the Secretary-General focuses on education, gender equality and empowerment, forced marriages of women and girls, and female participation in the electoral process.[139] Interestingly, the Security Council has not explicitly mandated the protection of these individual rights to specific UN peace missions, but has mentioned the protection of several of these rights in the cross-cutting protection of women and children resolutions. Specifically, the Security Council has consistently referred to the importance of education and "marginalization" of specific groups of civilians. In *Resolution 1889* (2009) on the protection of women, the Security Council

137 Goldberg and Hubert, above note 72 at 223.

138 Bellamy and Williams, above note 40 at 345.

139 United Nations Security Council, *Report of the Secretary-General to the Security Council on the Protection of Civilians in Armed Conflict*, UN Doc S/1999/957 at paragraph 12; United Nations Security Council, *Report of the Secretary-General on Women, Peace and Security*, UN Doc S/2002/1154 at paragraph 10; United Nations Security Council, *Women and Peace and Security: Report of the Security-General*, UN Doc S/2009/465 at paragraph 20.

expressed "its intention, when establishing and renewing the mandates of United Nations missions, to include provisions on the promotion of gender equality and the empowerment of women in post-conflict situations."[140] Even though not making specific reference to peace operations, the Security Council in 2000 reiterated "the importance of ensuring that children continue to have access to basic services during the conflict and post-conflict periods, including, inter alia, education and health care."[141]

Yet it is unclear whether any of the rights should be considered under the obligation to protect when mandating the protection of civilians, specifically as the Security Council is yet to explicitly mandate any UN peace missions with this form of protection. However, it can be argued that the overarching resolutions on protection apply to all UN peace missions, and thus places a duty on the peacekeepers to protect and fulfil these rights. In discussion with TCCs/PCCs and host States, both considered that interfering in these human rights, outside monitoring and reporting, or in support of local authorities, would fall outside the realm of the protection mandate.[142] However, human right advocates within the UN Secretariat have insisted that human rights protection is a vital element of the protection of civilians and should not be considered outside the realm of the obligation.[143]

Although not mandated by the Security Council, during times of armed conflict the protection of human rights is crucial.[144] Any neglect of economic, social and cultural rights will create more conflict, making it difficult in ensuring a secure environment.[145] Essentially, it becomes unimaginable to protect civilians without protecting their basic humanitarian needs, such as food, shelter and health care. Although the international community has focused on the use of force against direct attacks towards civilians, equally as important is the protection and fulfillment of the economic, social and cultural rights of civilians.

Although human rights are considered essential for sustaining peace and security, it has become a secondary priority to physical protection within UN peace missions. As such, until the Security Council identifies what UN peace

140 *United Nations Security Council Resolution 1889* (2009) at operational paragraph 7.

141 *United Nations Security Council Resolution 1314* (2000) at operational paragraph 14.

142 Interview with South Sudan on 22 January 2019; Interview with diplomate from the Perment Mission of Pakistan to the UN on 23 January 2019.

143 Interviews held in February 2018.

144 Harston Julian, *Protection of Civilians* (Peace Operations Training Institute, Williamsburg, 2016) at 16.

145 Goldberg and Hubert, above note 72 at 233.

missions will add to the current human rights landscape, human rights protection will be considered an activity of humanitarian workers.

5.3 *Humanitarian Protection*

As part of the human rights protection regime, the Security Council has also mandated the protection of civilians' access to humanitarian assistance, expressly the protection of humanitarian workers and organisations. Even though the protection of humanitarian assistance was mandated earlier than the protection of human rights,[146] the protection of humanitarian assistance has fallen under the umbrella of the protection of civilians mandate within Security Council resolutions.

Within the humanitarian community the notion of 'humanitarian protection' has been widely discussed and is "concerned with the safety, dignity and rights of people affected by disaster or armed conflict."[147] Within this description there are four basic 'protection principles' – "do not harm; ensure access to impartial assistance; protect from physical and psychological harm; and assist people to claim their rights, access remedies, and recover from abuse."[148] Therefore finding its foundation in IHL protection, humanitarian protection is concerned with mitigating the harm that occurs to civilians caught in an armed conflict.[149]

Yet peacekeepers under the protection of civilians mandate are not mandated to provide civilians with humanitarian assistance, but rather to ensure that civilians have access to that assistance.[150] Generally, this protection is manifested with peacekeepers being mandated to protect humanitarian actors in the field. In other words, peacekeepers are protecting humanitarian access by directly protecting aid and humanitarian workers, for "[a]ccess to humanitarian assistance and protection, or humanitarian access, is therefore an essential subsidiary or ancillary right that gives meaning and effect to the core rights of protection and assistance."[151] As access to humanitarian essentials become

146 *United Nations Security Council Resolution 733* (1992) at operational paragraph 2.

147 Wynn-Pope, above note 31 at 17.

148 Ibid at 17.

149 Bellamy and Williams, above note 40 at 345.

150 For example, in *Security Council Resolution 1881* (2009) at operational paragraph 2(b) UMISS was mandated to "ensuring safe, timely and unhindered humanitarian access, the safety and security of humanitarian personnel and the protection of humanitarian convoys."

151 United Nations Security Council, *Report of the Secretary-General on Protection for Humanitarian Assistance to Refugees and Others in Conflict Situations*, UN Doc S/1998/883 at paragraph 15.

paramount to long-term peace and security, the protection of humanitarian workers also becomes paramount. This protection and support of humanitarian actors was one of the primary reasons that the Security Council deployed missions in Somalia and the former Yugoslavia.[152] Although this is an important task of peacekeeping, with the increase in mandated tasks this form of protection is being neglected due to lack of capacity. However, interviewees from the UN Secretariat thought that this form of protection was part of the overall protection against physical violence, and humanitarian workers should be perceived as civilians, rather than this being a separate task.[153]

Conversely, many humanitarian organisations are concerned that this form of protection is manipulating their 'impartial' work into political manoeuvring.[154] This becomes a specific concern when UN peace missions are mandated with Chapter VII of the UN Charter, as "the use of the military for humanitarian activities, particularly in the context of Chapter VII operations, compromise their impartiality and neutrality, affect their ability to assist victims on all sides of the conflict and, at times, even lends to increased violence against United Nations and other humanitarian personnel."[155] Thus, to sufficiently protect civilians, humanitarian agencies have argued that it is better for a separation between humanitarian agents and UN peace missions. This is emphasised when peacekeepers are assisting local authorities, for example with the FIB in DRC,[156] as humanitarian actors can be tainted by association and might seem to lose their impartiality. Nonetheless, the Security Council mandates peacekeepers to protect humanitarian actors in order to ensure civilians access to their assistance. This form of protection will be discussed further in Chapter 6.

6 The Core 'Constitutional' Principles

Much of the literature is still focused on traditional peacekeeping, that is UN peace missions under Chapter VI of the UN Charter. Many authors within this

152 Mamiya, above note 24 at 73.

153 Interviews conduct in New York in January 2019.

154 Mamiya, above note 24 at 74.

155 United Nations Security Council, *Report of the Secretary-General on Protection for Humanitarian Assistance to Refugees and Others in Conflict Situations*, UN Doc S/1998/883 at paragraph 24.

156 Sijuade Sunday Kayode, "Intervention Brigade' for the Congo; A Precedent for UN Peace Enforcement?' (2014) *10(38)* *Uluslararasi Hukuk ve Politika* 99 at 113–114.

category still attempt to make a distinction between 'peacekeeping' missions under Chapter VI and 'peace-enforcement' missions made under Chapter VII of the UN Charter. Conversely, modern UN peace missions blur the distinction between Chapter VI or Chapter VII operations. Subsequently one peace operation will have the "characteristics of both types of operations".[157] Those making this distinction have insisted that the Security Council must maintain a distinction between Chapter VI and Chapter VII missions to confirm their legal basis.[158] Nevertheless with modern 'peacekeeping' and 'peace-enforcement' often having indistinguishable natures, a great deal of academic examination relies on unstable foundations.[159]

As discussed in Chapter 1, UN peacekeeping is based in the theoretical foundation of sovereignty of Member States; therefore, peacekeeping adheres to three primary principles – consent of parties to the conflict, impartiality, and non-use of force except in self-defence and in defence of the mandate.[160] These principles on their own have no legal authority, however, these principles are considered constitutional pillars of UN peacekeeping. As reasserted by the Special Court in Sierra Leone, these three principles are "widely understood as the necessary foundations for a peacekeeping operation[s]."[161] Thus, when mandating UN peace missions, the Security Council ensures that it is perceived to adhere to these 'constitutional' principles, by reaffirming "the basic principles of peacekeeping."[162]

Even though practically the three principles have been diluted,[163] the literature, and UN documentation, still considers them "the bedrock principles of

157 Ray Murphy, 'United Nations Military Operations and International Humanitarian Law: What Rules Apply to Peacekeepers?' (2003) *14(2) Criminal Law Forum* 153 at 167.

158 Joseph P Bialke, 'United Nations Peace Operations: Applicable Norms and the Application of the Law of Armed Conflict' (2001) *50(1) Air Force Law Review* 1 at 31.

159 Gary Anderson, 'Preparing for the Worst Military Requirements for Hazardous Missions' in Donald C.F. Daniel, Patricia Taft, and Sharon Wiharta (eds), *Peace Operations, Trends, Progress, and Prospects* (Georgetown University Press, 2008) 63 at 67.

160 Capstone Doctrine, above note 61.

161 *Prosecutor v Issa Hassan Sesay, Morris Kallon and Augustine Gbao*, Special Court for Sierra Leone, 2 March 2009, Case No SCSL-04-15-T at paragraph 225.

162 United Nations Security Council Resolution 2100 (2013); United Nations Secuirty Council Resolution 2149 (2014); United Nations Security Council Resolution 2155 (2014); United Nations Security Council Resolution 2659 (2022); United Nations Security Council Resolution 2666 (2022).

163 John Karlsrud, 'The UN at war: examining the consequences of peace-enforcement mandates for the UN peacekeeping operations in the CAR, the DRC and Mali' (2015) *36(1) Third World Quarterly* 40 at 42.

peacekeeping",[164] and contends that they are a 'constitutional framework'.[165] These principles technically only apply to 'traditional' peacekeeping missions mandated under Chapter VI of the UN Charter, and are not pertinent to tasks mandated under Chapter VII. Interestingly, UN documentation and non-academic institutions no longer make this distinction, thus, making it something solely encountered in the realm of academia. Currently six of the thirteen UN missions would be classified as 'traditional',[166] however, all these missions were formed prior to 1999.

With the expansion of peacekeeping activities under the protection mandate, it has been suggested that with over two decades of UN peacekeeping, the interpretation of the principles should be more "flexible and progressive."[167] For even though the UN and Security Council have continued to reiterate the importance of the three principles, with the introduction of the protection mandate "the principles of peacekeeping should never be used as an excuse for failure to protect civilians or defend the mission proactively."[168]

With the consistent encouragement for the UN to innovatively react to threats against civilians, the principles are organically being re-interpreted or disregarded completely under the protection regime.[169] As the principles are no longer connected to the reality of modern peacekeeping mandates, it has been suggested that the application of the principles should be "reviewed and adjusted to contemporary threats and to the context of violence that innocent civilians and peacekeeping personnel face in conflict areas."[170]

This disconnect between the three principles and the 'new' form of peacekeeping is exacerbated with the discussion of the use of force to protect civilians from the threats of physical violence. The gap between the theoretical and practical nature of the protection mandate further isolates peacekeepers from

---

164 United Nations, Report of the Panel on United Nations Peace Operations of 21 August 2000, UN Doc A/55/305 (*Brahimi Report*) at paragraph IX.

165 Nicholas Tsagourias, 'Consent, Neutrality/Impartiality and the Use of Foce in Peacekeeping: Their Constitutional Dimension' (2007) *11(3) Journal of Conflict and Security Law* 465 at 465–466.

166 These missions are MINURSO in Western Sahara; UNDOF in Golan; UNFICYP in Cyprus; UNIFIL in Lebanon; UNTSO in the Middle East; and UNMOGIP in India and Pakistan.

167 United Nations General Assembly and Security Council, Report of the High-level Independent Panel on Peace Operations on Uniting Our Strengths for Peace: Politics, Partnership and People, UN Doc A/70/95-S/2015/446.

168 Ibid at paragraph 125.

169 Karlsrud, above note 163 at 48.

170 United Nations Secuirty Council, *7275th Meeting, Thursday, 9 October 2014, 10am*, UN Doc S/PV.7275 at 2–3.

any legal or doctrinal framework of their obligation and expectation to protect civilians.

6.1 *Consent*

As the UN is founded on "the principle of the sovereign equality of all its Member States",[171] consent of the host State to deploy peacekeepers is thus a cornerstone of all UN peace missions. The principle of consent is rooted in Article 2(7) of the UN Charter that specifies that "[n]othing contained in the present Charter shall authorize the United Nations to intervene in matters which are essentially within the domestic jurisdiction of any state or shall require the Members to submit such matters to settlement under the present Charter." Thus, without the consent of the host State, deployed peacekeepers would be in breach of Article 2(7) of the UN Charter. Legally however, consent is only required for operations authorised under Chapter VI of the UN Charter, as Article 2(7) "shall not prejudice the application of enforcement measures under Chapter VII."[172]

Within the current peacekeeping landscape, the majority of UN peace missions are mandated under Chapter VII, rendering consent legally redundant. Particularly, all UN peace missions obligated to protect civilians are mandated under Chapter VII to 'use all necessary means' to protect civilians. Nonetheless, even though consent is not a legal requirement, the Security Council still attempts to attain consent from the host State.[173] As witnessed with UNMISS and the South Sudanese Transitional government, consent was considered a political necessity rather than a legal imperative. Even if consent is a legal requirement, some commentators have suggested that consent is a legal enigma, for it is most likely coerced by the UN rather than freely given.[174]

Even though the Security Council attempts to acquire consent, the principle of consent has been diluted as the majority of UN peace missions are deployed in politically unstable environments. As conflict areas are becoming more uncertain, the question of the ability or authority of 'governments' to grant consent comes into question.[175] As illustrated in the Ivorian crisis in 2010, the UN was faced with the dilemma of determining the legal ability to withdraw

171 UN Charter at Article 2(1).

172 Ibid at Article 2(7).

173 Eric David and Ola Engdahl, 'How does the involvement of a multinational peacekeeping force affect the classification of a situation?' (2013) 95(891–892) *International Review of the Red Cross* 659 at 668.

174 Sheeran and Kent, above note 5 at 53.

175 Nasu, above note 101 at 123.

consent, as the 'self-purported' president Gbagbo ordered peacekeepers to withdraw from Côte d'Ivoire. In the Côte d'Ivoire crisis, the UN deemed Gbagbo not to have any authority to withdraw consent, and UN peacekeepers remained on the ground. Moreover, the Security Council did not consider the denial of Gbagbo's authority as a breach or departure from the consent principle.[176]

Based upon the Montevideo Convention 1933,[177] modern practice defines a 'legitimate' government of a State as a government that is 'recognised' by the international community.[178] Recognition does not necessarily establish a legal classification it "simply constitutes a subjective (relative) statement on that status."[179] As recognition is determined by States,[180] the UN "does not possess any authority to recognize either a State or a Government."[181] However, despite this seeming absence of legal capacity or authority to recognise, the UN nonetheless engages in de facto recognition when determining a government's ability to grant consent.

Further, although a host State may 'consent', consent is an elusive term as demonstrated with the 2016 crisis in South Sudan. Although the Security Council had approved the deployment of the RPF into the troop construction of UNMISS, this was rejected by the South Sudanese Transitional Government.[182] However, within a few months of the removal of consent, President Salva Kiir was forced to consent to the RPF in order to avoid the threatened UN arms embargo.[183] Although consent was reluctantly granted, UNMISS has continually reported interference from the local authorities on the ground, ultimately hindering their ability to protect civilians.[184]

176 Bellamy and Williams, above note 40 at 837.

177 A State is defined as having four elements – a defined territory; a permanent population; an effective government; the capacity to enter into relations with other States.

178 James Crawford, *The Creation of States in International Law* (Oxford University Press, 2007) at 17.

179 Stefan Talmon, *Recognition of Governments in International Law* (Oxford University Press, 2001) at 29–30.

180 Hersch Lauterpacht, *Recognition in International Law* (Cambridge University Press, 1947).

181 https://www.un.org/en/about-us/about-un-membership#:~:text=The%20United%20Nations%20is%20neither,representatives%20of%20a%20new%20Government.

182 Sudan Tribune, above note 125.

183 Denis Dumo and Michelle Nichols, 'South Sudan Spells out Unresolved UN Protection Force Issues', *Reuters* 2016 <https://www.reuters.com/article/us-southsudan-security-un-idUSKCN11B22H>.

184 UNMISS, *UNMISS Urges Parties to Deescalate Tensions and Lift Movement Restrictions* <https://unmiss.unmissions.org/sites/default/files/160712_unmiss_urges_parties_to_deescalate_tensions_and_lift_movement_restrictions.pdf>; As reported, patrolling in South Sudan has been restricted as the mission first sought the permission of the local authorities to conduct armoured patrols.

The principle of consent technically extends beyond the consent of the host State, to consent of all parties involved within the conflict.[185] As historically UN peace missions were deployed to monitor peace agreements between States, consent of all parties was considered fundamental to align with the UN's State-centric framework.[186] However, this practice developed when peacekeeping was inter-State, rather than intra-State, as it is today. Thus, while, as the literature implies,[187] consent of all parties is desirable, Member States would consider this as interference into domestic affairs, as it would be a form of international recognition.[188] As the UN is ingrained in a State-centric realm, the Security Council only endeavours to attain the consent of the host State rather than consent of all parties.

The volatility of the consent principle has been observed with the protection of civilians becoming a cross-cutting theme across all UN peace missions. As peacekeepers are mandated to protect civilians, it is important for peacekeepers to recognise that in the field "the government itself contributes to the problem at hand."[189] To counter-balance concerns with consent and UN 'intervention', the Security Council mandates peacekeepers to protect civilians in 'assistance' to local authorities and forces.[190] This support function of UN peacekeeping leads to the one-sided execution of the protection mandate. Moreover, this 'caveat' to the protection mandate limits the situations in which peacekeepers may deem it necessary to respond to threats against civilians. In the 2012 OIOS report on the implementation of the protection mandate, it was reported that peacekeepers "determined not to act if local security forces were not present or had abandoned the scene."[191] As the majority of UN peace missions are mandated to assist and work with local authorities, it is construed on

185 Scott Sheeran and Stephanie Case, *The Intervention Brigade: Legal Issues for the UN in the Democractic Republic of the Congo* (International Peace Institute, 2014) at 5.

186 *Dispatches from the Field: Council Meetings in Juba and a Visit to Protection of Civilians Sites* Security Council Reporter <https://www.whatsinblue.org/2016/09/dispatches-from-the-field-council-meetings-in-juba-and-a-visit-to-protection-of-civilians-sites.php>.

187 Nicholas Tsagourias, 'Consent, Neutrality/Impartiality and the Use of Foce in Peacekeeping: Their Constitutional Dimension' (2007) *11(3) Journal of Conflict and Security Law* 465 at 475; United Nations Security Council, *Report of the Secretary-General to the Security Council on the Protection of Civilians in Armed Conflict*, (2001) UN Doc S/2001/331 at paragraph 19.

188 Tsagourias, above note 187 at 475.

189 Mats Berdal and David H. Ucko, 'The Use of Force in UN Peacekeeping Operations' (2015) *160(1) The RUSI Journal* 6 at 11.

190 *United Nations Security Council Resolution 2164* (2014) at operational paragraph 13(a); *United Nations Security Council Resolution 1778* (2007) at operational paragraph 2.

191 OIOS Report, above note 7 at paragraph 41.

the ground that the protection mandate is limited by the presence or consent of local forces. As an example, when the Security Council saw fit to make the protection mandate the core mission activity of UNMISS, it still insisted within the resolution that protection was the primary responsibility of the government.[192] As further illustrated by the Secretary-General in his 2011 report on Sudan, that while "the protection of civilians would be one of the core activities of the mission and the country team, the protection of civilians is first and foremost the sovereign responsibility of the Government", and the Mission must support "the Government in strengthening its capacity to fulfil its protection responsibilities under human rights and international humanitarian law."[193] However, in contradictory terms UNMISS is also mandated to protect civilians "irrespective of the source of such violence."[194]

In order to obligate peacekeepers to protect civilians regardless of the source of the threat, the Security Council must clearly outline the limitations and boundaries of the consent and 'authority' of the host State. While the Security Council mandates use politically nuanced language, peacekeepers are reluctant to implement their mandate without clear guidelines and departure from host State consent. While peacekeepers are expected to have an 'implied' authority to use force to protect civilians, however, due to the UN's political emphasis of State sovereignty, peacekeepers are reluctant to use force without consent of local authorities.[195]

Even though Secretary-General reports and the literature consider the protection of civilians mandate to exist outside the realm of host State consent,[196] this is not the reading of the text of the resolutions. Other than UNMISS, the Security Council has not explicitly authorised any other Mission to protect civilians against the host State. As UN peace missions rely on Security Council resolutions for their authority, unlike R2P, peacekeepers cannot rely on a general concept of 'protection'. As the Security Council qualifies the protection of civilians mandate with the consent principle, the authority of UN peace missions must be read with this limitation. Therefore, under the current text

192 *United Nations Security Council Resolution 2155* (2014); *United Nations Security Council Resolution 2406* (2018).

193 United Nations Security Council, *Special Report of the Secretary-General on the Sudan*, UN Doc S/2011/314 at paragraph 44.

194 *United Nations Security Council Resolution 2327* (2016) at operational paragraph 7(a)(i).

195 OIOS Report, above note 7 at paragraph 42.

196 For example, see Patryk I. Labuda, *With or Against the State? Reconciling the Protection of Civilians and Host-State Support in UN Peacekeeping* (International Peace Institute, May 2020).

(outside UNMISS), peacekeepers are not authorised to use force against the host State.

6.2 *Impartiality*

At the creation of UN peacekeepers, the principle of impartiality was imperative to ensure that the UN did not become nor be perceived as a 'party to the conflict'. As peacekeepers are mandated by the Security Council on behalf of the international community, peacekeepers "should not promote a particular national or other political agenda."[197] Peacekeepers needed to remain impartial to be considered as "international policemen"[198] rather than participating parties in the conflict.

It is important to note that impartiality should not be confused with the principle of neutrality.[199] As stated in the Capstone Doctrine, impartiality should be viewed as the equal treatment of all parties on the ground.[200] In other words, whether or not a party is considered 'legitimate' by the international community should not affect how peacekeepers apply their mandate, rather peacekeepers should only consider a party's commitment to the peace process, the Security Council's mandate, or the rule of law. As set out and defined in the Capstone Doctrine "peacekeepers should be impartial in their dealings with the parties to the conflict, but not neutral in the execution of their mandate. The need for even-handedness towards the parties should not become an excuse for inaction in the face of behaviour that clearly works against then peace process."[201] In other words, peacekeepers should be treating all parties and individuals equally, rather than supporting one party against another.

Conversely, with the implementation of the protection mandate, the Security Council has shifted from the principle of impartiality, in order to balance the tensions between R2P and protection of civilians. As stated previously, under the protection mandate peacekeepers have been mandated to "assist" and "work alongside" local authorities to fulfil State responsibility to protect. However, in conflicts where peacekeepers are deployed, local

---

197 Katrina Grenfell, 'Perspectives on the Applicability and Application of International Humanitarian Law: the UN Context' (2013) *95(891–892) International Review of the Red Cross* 645 at 647.

198 Ibid.

199 For a discussion of the difference between neutrality and impartiality in UN peacekeeping see Hitoshi Nasu, *International Law on Peacekeeping: A Study of Article 40 of the UN Charter* (Martinus Nijhoff Publishers, 2009) at 154–158.

200 Capstone Doctrine at 61.

201 Ibid.

authorities are not only parties to a conflict, but also at times violators of their obligations to civilians under the law. The support function of peacekeepers to local authorities in the protection mandate is a clear violation of the impartiality principle.[202]

Although UN peace missions are being taught not to hold prejudices towards participants in conflict, impartiality firstly "should also be a guiding principle for those writing mandates."[203] The Security Council's expanding protection regime has highlighted the unstable and unrealistic impartial ground on which UN peacekeeping is founded. As evidenced in 2010 under the protection mandate, peacekeepers assisting French forces attacked Gbagbo's forces disregarding any sense of impartiality.[204] Even though both Gbagbo's forces and the RFCI breached the ceasefire and attacked civilians, only Gbagbo's forces were targeted by peacekeepers, as the RFCI was considered by the UN to be the 'legitimate' government. This departure from the principle of impartiality reached its pinnacle when the Security Council mandated the FIB in the DRC to fight alongside local authorities against a common 'enemy'. In an unprecedented step, the FIB was mandated to 'neutralise' a pre-selected list of non-State armed and militia groups. With the implementation of the FIB, the Security Council has clearly dispensed with the principle of impartiality.[205] The FIB's deployment into the DRC creates "suspicion, showcasing bias and creating a wider divide between the armed groups and the Congolese government, and reducing to the minimal any chance for rapprochement, peace or cease-fire in the crisis."[206]

As impartiality is no longer drafted in the mandates, in many situations peacekeepers will not respond to threats against civilians unless they have received authority from local forces.[207] For example, in South Sudan UNMISS has started the procedure of seeking documentation from local authorities before conducting ground movements, although original considered a form of

---

202 International Committee of the Red Cross, *Professional Standards for Protection Work: Carried out by Humanitarian and Human Rights Actors in Armed Conflict and Other Siutations of Violence* (ICRC, Geneva, 2013) at 51.

203 Daniel H. Levine, *Peacekeeper Impartiality: Standards, Processes, and Operations* (Center for International and Security Studies in Maryland, April 2010) <https://drum.lib.umd.edu/items/49740ad1-d296-40db-a463-412ea6b38926> at 16.

204 Alex J Bellamy and Paul D Williams, 'The new politics of protection? Côte d'Ivoire, Libya and the responsibiity to protect' (2011) *87(4) International Affairs* 825 at 837.

205 Sheeran and Case, above note 185 at 5.

206 Kayode, above note 156 at 113–114.

207 OIOS Report, above note 7 at paragraph 41.

consultation it has now become a form of seeking approval from the government before beginning any ground movements.[208]

Consequently, when peacekeepers are faced with a situation where the host State is the aggressor, peacekeepers will choose "not to invoke their general mandate for protecting civilians although that was available to them."[209] Commentators have remarked that UN peace missions are reluctant to report violations committed by local bodies and forces under the protection mandate.[210] Peacekeepers inability to 'report' violations by host States is often observed to be mostly a political decision rather than a legal one.[211]

These tensions become more apparent when peacekeepers are mandated to assist government forces who are considered by civilians as aggressors. This was demonstrated in the DRC, where the DRC government-led force "were the beneficiaries of UN assistance", and "committed violations of human rights and international humanitarian law of the kind they were supposed to prevent with UN aid."[212] In the UN Organization Mission in the Democratic Republic of the Congo (*MONUC*), government forces with the assistance of MONUC committed serious violations of IHL and IHRL. Since the conclusion of MONUC the UN has established the Human Rights Due Diligence Policy (*HRDDP*) that insists that peacekeepers are to examine their 'partners' compliance with IHL, IHRL and refugee law before granting assistance. However, the HRDDP only tackles 'grave violations' rather than any violations of the law.[213] For example, even though the FARDC are reportedly violating IHRL, MONUSCO are still providing assistance to these forces in the name of 'protection of civilians', as the FARDC has not committed any 'grave violation'. As the protection regime stems beyond mass atrocities, so too must the UN's HRDDP. Specifically, as under the principle of impartiality, UN peacekeepers must only focus on a party's dedication to the rule of law rather than their legitimacy in the UN political structure.

208 Center for Civilians in Conflict, *Moving Towards Mobility: Providing Protection to Civilians Through Static Presence and Mobile Peacekeeping in South Sudan* (2019) at 11.

209 OIOS Report, above note 7 at paragraph 44.

210 von Einsiedel and Bosetti, above note 47 at 382; Sofia Sebastián and Aditi Gorur, *UN Peacekeeping & Host-State Consent: How Missions Navigate Relationships with Governments* (Stimson Center, 2017).

211 Månsson, above note 85 at 506–507.

212 H. P. Aust, 'The UN Human Rights Due Diligence Policy: An Effective Mechanism against Complicity of Peacekeeping Forces?' (2014) 20(1) *Journal of Conflict and Security Law* 1 at 3.

213 Ibid at 11.

6.3 *The Use of Force in Self-Defence*

As traditional peacekeeping was deployed on behalf of the international community, and originally authorised under Chapter VI of the UN Charter, peacekeepers were deemed under the final principle to be only authorised to use force in self-defence. As not to involve the UN in armed conflict, the principle of self-defence applied in order that peacekeepers "may never take the initiative in the use of armed force, but are entitled to respond with force to an attack with arms."[214] For example, peacekeepers' inaction in Rwanda was justified as peacekeepers were only allowed to use force in their self-defence.

Commentators discussing the principle of self-defence in peacekeeping mainly ground their discussion in Article 51 of the UN Charter and the "inherent right of individual or collective self-defence."[215] However, Article 51 was not intended as a provision for a right to personal self-defence, rather involving the self-defence of States. Within the international law framework there is no explicit provision for a personal right to self-defence.[216] Conversely the personal right of self-defence has been used by the UN and Member States in justifying the use of force by military personnel in UN peacekeeping. Although there is no explicit personal right to self-defence, it is suggested by commentators that it is an inherent right as it is included in most national rules of engagement,[217] and is implied in Article 31(1)(3) of the Rome Statute that excludes criminal responsibility on the grounds of self-defence.

In regard to peacekeeping, the principle of self-defence was initiated in order for peacekeepers not to be seen as 'soldiers'. In other words, the peacekeeping principle of self-defence was to correlate to a civilian's right to self-defence against an unlawful attack. As outlined by Hessbruegge, every jurisdiction in the world recognises that an individual has a right to defend themselves against an unlawful attack within their national laws.[218] Therefore, the peacekeeping

---

214 United Nations General Assembly, *Report of the Secretary-General: Summary Study of the Experience of Derived from the Establishment and Operation of the Force*, UN Doc A/3943 at paragraph 179.

215 UN Charter at Article 51; James Sloan, 'Peacekeepers under Fire: Prosecuting the RUF for Attacks against the UN Assistance Mission in Sierra Leone' (2010) 9(2) *The Law & Practice of International Courts and Tribunals* 243 at 282; Sheeran, above note 85 at 364.

216 Natalino Ronzitti, 'The Expanding Law of Self-Defence' (2006) 11(3) *Journal of Conventional Weapons Destruction* 343.

217 Erica Gaston, 'The View from the Ground – Emerging State Practice on Individual and Unit Self-Defense' (2019) *Soldier Self-Defense Symposium* <http://opiniojuris.org/2019/05/02/soldier-self-defense-symposium-the-view-from-the-ground-emerging-state-practice-on-individual-and-unit-self-defense/>.

218 Jan Arno Hessbruegge, *Human Rights and Personal Self-Defense in International Law* (Oxford University Press, 2017) at 239.

principle of self-defence is a reiteration of a right that already exists in a host-State or the TCC's/PCC's domestic criminal code. Further, as peacekeepers are authorised and mandated under Security Council resolutions, the authority to use force in self-defence finds its legal foundation in the Security Council's authority. As the Security Council authorises the use of force within their resolutions, the principle of self-defence was considered caveat of when that force can be used.

The principle of force in self-defence was expanded in 1964 with the deployment of UN peacekeeping force in Cyprus (*UNFICYP*) to include force used in 'defence of the mandate'.[219] This expansion of the principle of force in self-defence was confirmed in 1973 with the Security Council's approval of Secretary-General's proposal for the deployment of the Second UN Emergency Force (*UNEF II*) in the Egypt-Israel conflict.

With the expansion of duties mandated by the Security Council under the protection mandate, an increase in the situations in which peacekeepers would be authorised to use force has also arisen. Currently, under the principle of self-defence of the mandate, peacekeepers are authorised to use force "in order to assert their right to freedom of movement, and even more extensive enforcement rights, which were needed for example to secure the delivery of humanitarian assistance."[220] This broad authority to use force was highlighted in the UN operation in the Congo (*ONUC*), when in 1961 self-defence was the sole justification for peacekeepers to use force in order to neutralise and overturn the Katangan regime.[221]

Peace operations authorised under Chapter VII do not need to legally rely on the principle of self-defence as they have been authorised to use all necessary means to achieve their mandate. For example, all UN peace missions with a protection of civilians mandate are mandated under Chapter VII to use force to protect civilians. Even though all protection tasks are mandated under Chapter VII, commentators are still referencing the principle of self-defence to justify the use of force by peacekeepers.[222] Conversely, modern commentators have proposed that even without the express mandate to protect civilians, it is implied that peacekeepers are authorised to use force in order to protect civilians.[223] As it is contended that the protection mandate has become an

219 Sheeran, above note 85 at 352; Sheeran and Kent, above note 5 at 32.

220 Lamp and Trif, above note 1 at 4.

221 Nasu, above note 199 at 176–179.

222 Lamp and Trif, above note 1 at 4; Müller, above note 109 at 367; Sloan, above note 214 at 282.

223 Willmot and Sheeran, above note 8 at 524.

intrinsic norm of the UN, it is suggested that the protection mandate "is best understood as an implied power normatively connect to the UN Charter's purpose and principles."[224] Therefore, peacekeepers have an authority to use force in order to fulfil their mandate to protect civilians independent of their self-defence. As many legal ambiguities exist once peacekeepers begin to use force and engage in conflict, UN peace missions are reluctant to engage in force without clear authority to do so.[225]

Through a strict interpretation of the constitutional principle, peacekeepers are only to use force to protect civilians, against armed groups, or when assisting local authorities. In order for the Security Council to change this interpretation or to remove any ambiguities, they need to remove references to consent or clarify the parameters of the principles within the resolutions.

7 Conclusion

In interpreting the language of the Security Council, the obligation to protect is in relation to armed conflict and the status of 'civilian'. Thus, peacekeepers are obliged to protect the rights reserved under the law to civilians. However, the Security Council places qualifiers on this obligation, explicitly, that the obligation exists within areas of their deployment and within their capabilities. Further, the Security Council reiterates that the obligation to protect is to respect State sovereignty and not to be used against the host State.

Therefore, military and police peacekeepers are obliged to protect all civilians in the vicinity of bases of operation, their person, and areas of patrol, from direct and indiscriminate attacks. Moreover, this obligation to protect includes the protection from any violations of an individual's rights that would directly lead to conflict-related violence.

In order for the Security Council to expand the obligation to protect, expressions of State sovereignty and 'areas of deployment' need to be revised or explained. Particularly, for the obligation to encompass violations committed by the host State, the Security Council must refrain from mandating the obligation in 'assistance' of local authorities. Moreover, if the Security Council wishes for the mandate to reach beyond the vicinity of peacekeepers, there needs to be clarification of the defined area of deployment.

---

224 Ibid.

225 The legal consequence will be discussed further in Chapter 3.

Regarding human rights protections, without further clarifications from the Security Council, UN peacekeepers will mainly duplicate existing humanitarian agencies. Consequently, UN peacekeepers are solely obliged to 'monitor and report' any human rights violations to the UN, unless the individual is within their control.

In order to now determine the content of the obligation to protect, there must be an examination of the obligations that are triggered under international law. Thus, the obligation to protect will incorporate further obligations under IHL and IHRL. As the Security Council has not intended any departure from the law, peacekeepers under the obligation to protect are also obliged to respect IHL and IHRL. Particularly, when peacekeepers engage in the use of force, the substance of the obligation to protect will include further duties, such as ensuring their force is proportionate and distinguishes between civilian and military targets. Hence, to truly understand the obligation to protect under the mandate, an examination must occur of the obligations triggered once peacekeepers engage in force.

As such the substance of the obligation to protect can only be determined by examining the laws triggered when peacekeepers engage in protection activities. Therefore, the following chapter will examine the protection against the threat of physical violence and the expansion of the obligation once peacekeepers engage in force.

CHAPTER 3

Protection from Threats of Physical Violence and IHL

As stated in the previous chapter, the protection mandate has consistently included the "protection of civilians against threats of physical violence".[1] Consequently the central premise of the protection mandate is the ability to directly protect civilians via military and police presence or the use of force. Therefore, criticisms and failures of UN peace missions are themed around peacekeepers' inability or unwillingness to use force. As emphasised by the Cruz Report, "hostile forces do not understand a language other than force. To deter and repel attacks and to defeat attackers, the United Nations needs to be strong and not fear to use force when necessary."[2]

This emphasis on the use of force stems from accounts that peacekeepers remain passive when observing civilians under threat.[3] Under the protection mandate, peacekeepers are authorised to actively employ force in order to protect civilians, yet this authority is infrequently used. The 2014 OIOS report evaluating the protection mandate, reported that only "four missions indicated that they have ever fired a warning shot, and only three indicated that they have ever fired a shot with lethal intent."[4]

The passive behaviour of certain contingents is attributed to their fear of the consequences when force is used.[5] As the Security Council and UN have remained silent on the legal effects resulting from the protection mandate, peacekeeping contingents have defaulted towards a risk-averse approach to the use of force.[6] Fundamentally, peacekeepers can be punished for action but

1 In *United Nations Security Council Resolution 1270* (1999) the Security Council originally mandated UNAMSIL to "afford protection of civilians under imminent threat of physical violence."

2 Santos Cruz, *Improving Security of United Nations Peacekeepers: We Need to Change the Way We Are Doing Business* (United Nations, 2017) at 5.

3 United Nations General Assembly, Evaluation of the Implementation and Results of Protection of Civilians Mandates in United Nations Peacekeeping Operations, UN Doc A/68/787 (*OIOS Report*) at paragraph 25.

4 Ibid.

5 OIOS Report, above note 3 at paragraph 35.

6 Center for Civilians in Conflict, *Within and Beyond the Gates: The Protection of Civlians by the UN Mission in South Sudan*, May 2015 at 33.

 | DOI:10.1163/9789004707313_005

there is currently no consequence for any lack of action.[7] In particular, in discussion with the UN Secretariat and TCCs, the IHL ramifications of peacekeepers' use of force was not considered as a natural occurrence of the protection of civilians mandate.[8] While protection of civilians discussions have centred around the exhortation of the use of force, considerations of the effects of that force has been limited.

As concluded in Chapter 2, peacekeepers are obliged to protect civilians in their vicinity of UN bases and areas of patrol from direct and indiscriminate attacks. When using force to adhere to their mandate, peacekeepers will also trigger other international law obligations. As Security Council resolutions do not exist in a legal vacuum, prevailing international law obligations must also be considered by UN peace missions when engaged in protection activities. No legal duty will exist in isolation, rather international obligations function mutually, and must be examined thus. Essentially, when peacekeepers engage in force, the obligation under the mandate expands to include further obligations under IHL and IHRL.

As IHL is the legal framework within armed conflict, the Security Council's mandated obligation must also reflect the IHL obligations that are triggered once peacekeepers engage in the use of force. So as to obtain a holistic understanding of the obligation to protect, peacekeepers must also recognise their duties under the law once they engage in force. Thus, the content of the Security Council's obligation to protect must be incorporated with their obligations as a party to a conflict.

This chapter will conclude that, depending on the circumstance, UN peace missions will find themselves as parties to a conflict, and therefore, the obligation to protect will include IHL obligations. Consequently, when using force, as parties to the conflict, peacekeepers must ensure that all attacks follow the rules of proportionality and distinction. Therefore, the obligation to protect will incorporate an obligation that all force is proportionate to the advantage of protecting civilians, and force is not to be used if the attack cannot distinguish between civilian and military targets.

To reach this conclusion, firstly, this chapter will discuss how protection from physical violence has become and is considered the central platform of the protection mandate. Secondly, it will be concluded that UN peace missions that are parties to a conflict are bound by the rules and obligations of

7 United Nations General Assembly, *Evaluation of the Implementation and results of Protection of Civilians Mandates in United Nations Peacekeeping Operations: Report of the Office of Internal Oversight Services*, UN Doc A/68/787.

8 Interviews conduct in New York in January 2019.

IHL. Thirdly, UN peace missions will generally be engaged in NIACs, and thus the obligations under NIAC will apply to peacekeeping operations. Finally, as UN peace missions have limited resources, therefore, peacekeepers will need to assess the priority of protection activities to ensure they adhere to their mandate.

1 Central Theme of Physical Violence

While the protection of civilians mandate has been expanded to embrace multiple areas of legal protections, the lack of resources has forced UN peace missions to prioritise their protection activities. As such, UN peace missions and the international community focus on the protection against physical violence via the use of military and police presence. Although this physical protection will also correlate with the right to life and the freedom from inhumane treatment, the primary focus of the UN is the protection from direct attacks and the respect of IHL.

As suggested earlier, the literature predominately focuses on UN peace mission's failure to use force, as it is implied that peacekeepers chief vehicle in protection is the use of force.[9] Moreover, the literature contends that the protection mandate has become an intrinsic norm of the UN, and thus "is best understood as an implied power normatively connect to the UN Charter's purpose and principles".[10]

Frequent reports allege peacekeepers of not using force and failing their obligation to protect civilians.[11] Notwithstanding, the UN and the literature has diverged on how and when force is to be used. For even though the literature identifies the use of force as an integral element of the protection regime, scarcely any assistance is specified on "the condition nor the consequences of its application".[12]

9 Wi Haidi Willmot and Scott Sheeran, 'The Protection of Civilians mandate in UN peacekeeping Operations: Reconciling protection concepts and practices' (2013) *95(891/892) International Review of the Red Cross* 517 at 524.

10 Ibid.

11 Aditi Gorur and Lisa Sharland, *Prioritizing the Protection of Civilians in UN Peace Operations: Analyzing the Recommendations of the HIPPO Report*, Stimson Center, 2016 at 11.

12 T. Tardy, 'The UN and the Use of Force: A Marriage Against Nature' (2007) *38(1) Security Dialogue* 49 at 59.

This confusion over the use of force to protect civilians is rationalised by the literature as 'protection' is not a recognised scenario that soldiers perform.[13] Even though they are authorised to use force "up to, and including deadly force, to defend any civilian person who is in need of protection against a hostile act or hostile intent",[14] this is not reflected in any traditional military or peacekeeping situation. Subsequently, TCCs are directing their troops not to use force outside the traditional principle of self-defence, apprehending any legal consequence.[15]

Accordingly, due to the international community's stress on physical protection of civilians, the creditability and 'success' of a peacekeeping mission becomes largely dependent on a Mission's "willingness and capability to act when civilians are threatened."[16] The 2020 handbook highlights the UN's preoccupation with physical protection by only focusing on "sources of violence"[17] when advising on 'identifying and prioritising' protection activities. This magnitude placed on the need to physical protect is a consequential response to the UN's historically publicised 'failures' in Rwanda and Srebrenica.[18]

1.1 *The Focus on the Use of Force to Protect*

Due to this sensitivity around the UN's past failure to act, the expansion of the protection regime into areas of human rights has not shifted the core element of the protection mandate from the physical protection of civilians. Even though the language used by the Security Council in protection mandates has varied depending on the specific Mission, the core text that has remained consistent across all protection of civilians mandates is the protection of civilians

13 Scott Sheeran and Catherine Kent, 'Protection of Civilians, Responsibility to Protect, and Humanitarian Intervention' in Haidi Willmot et al (eds), *Protection of civilians* (Oxford University Press, 2016) 29 at 54–55.

14 As cited in Willmot and Sheeran, above note 9 at 530.

15 Nicholas Lamp and Dana Trif, 'United Nations Peacekeeping Forces and the Protection of Civilians in Armed Conflict' 47 (2009) *Hertie School of Governance – Working papers* at 3.

16 United Nations Security Council, Report of the Secretary-General on the Protection of Civilians in Armed Conflict, UN Doc S/2016/447 at paragraph 58.

17 United Nations Department of Peace Opertions, *The Protection of Civilians in United Nations Peacekeeping Handbook* (the *2020 Handbook*).

18 For example, Alexandra Thompson, 'After the Rwanda Genocide the UN Promised 'Never Again' – Now It's Time For Them To Take Action Against ISIS', *Forbes* 20 April 2017 <https://www.forbes.com/sites/realspin/2017/04/20/after-the-rwandan-genocide-the-un-promised-never-again-now-its-time-for-them-to-take-action-against-isis/#45226b641424>; Barbara Crossette, 'UN Details Its Failure to Stop '95 Bosnia Massacre', *New York Times* 16 November 1999 <https://www.nytimes.com/1999/11/16/world/un-details-its-failure-to-stop-95-bosnia-massacre.html>.

"under threat of physical violence". Although the Security Council originally mandated the protection of civilians 'under *imminent* threat of physical violence', since 2017 the Security Council has omitted the word 'imminent', broadening the circumstances of what is intended as a threat. As the Security Council has remained consistent in mandating physical protection across the board, it is implied that the Security Council clearly intends the physical protection of civilians to be the foundation of the UN's protection regime.[19]

Since 2016 the Security Council has branched out from its set language and has mandated UN peace missions with specific protection tasks, such as protecting airports[20] and schools,[21] and patrolling high risk areas.[22] Moreover, as discussed in the previous chapter, the Security Council is currently using 'proactive' language, mandating protection of civilian missions in preventing and proactive approach to protection.[23] Outside of the general protection of civilians mandate, the Security Council has also separated protections by explicitly identifying 'vulnerable civilians', explicitly women, children and IDPs.

When delving into the literature regarding the physical protection of civilians, commentators commonly envisage the use of force as the principal avenue for direct physical protection of civilians. Commentators have expressed their concern that peacekeepers are not willing to actively use force in response to threats and attacks against civilians.[24] However, in contrast the Secretary-General and Security Council have stressed that UN peace missions are ill-equipped and are incapable of creating sustainable peace through continuous use of force.[25] As the protection of civilians mandate has been rooted in the Security Council's responsibility for international peace and security, the use of force to physically protect is considered only an immediate and

---

19 Victoria K. Holt, Glyn Taylor and Max Kelly, *Protecting Civilians in the Context of UN Peacekeeping Operations: Success, Setbacks and Remaining Challenges*, Independent study jointly commissioned by the Department of Peacekeeping Operations and the Office for the Coordination of Humanitarian Affairs (2009) at 44.

20 *United Nations Security Council Resolution 2327* (2016) at operational paragraph 9 (ii).

21 *United Nations Security Council Resolution 2187* (2016) at operational paragraph 4(ii).

22 *United Nations Security Council Resolution 2364* (2017) at operational paragraph 20(c).

23 *United Nations Security Council Resolution 2502* (2019) at operational paragraph (i)(a); *United Nations Security Council Resolution 2499* (2019) at operational paragraph 32(a)(ii).

24 Haidi Willmot and Ralph Mamiya, 'Mandated to Protect: Security Council Practice on the Protection of Civilians' in Marc Weller (ed), *The Oxford Handbook of the Use of Force in International Law* (Oxford University Press, 2015) at 376 and 394; OIOS Report, above note 3 at paragraph 45.

25 United Nations General Assembly and Security Council, *The Future of United Nations Peace Operations: Implementation of the Recommendations of the High-level Independent Panel on Peace Operations*, 17 June 2015, UN Doc A/70/357-S/2015/682 (*HIPPO Report*) at 15.

necessary response to a threat of physical violence rather than a 'sustainable' answer to peace.[26] To reinforce this understanding, the use of force was considered a 'last resort' for UN peacekeepers, as physical protection should be first endeavoured through the non-use of force.[27] As the Security Council does not want to encourage the use of force, peacekeepers are mandated to create physical security through the non-use of force, such as patrolling and the use of their 'military' presence.[28] However, in recent reports and UN discussions it can be seen that peacekeepers should be utilising more proactive force as non-use of force methods are not enough to deter the threat against civilians and UN personnel. Expressly, the Cruz Report directed by the Secretary-General on improving peacekeeping security, insisted that "missions should identify threats to their security and take the initiative, using all the tactics, to neutralise or eliminate the threats. Missions should go where the threat is, in order to neutralise it."[29] Admittedly the Cruz Report has been highly criticised within the UN Secretariat for solely focusing on the use of force,[30] however, it does underscore the international community's attention on the use of force within UN peace missions.

As UN peace missions are currently engaged in unconventional warfare such as counter-terrorism operations in Mali, subsequently, attacks on UN personnel and civilians have amplified, aggregating the discussion on the use of force, not only to protect civilians but in self-defence.

1.2 *A Legal Indicator to the Use of Force*

Although the Security Council focuses on the protection from physical violence, throughout the resolutions there is no legal prompt to indicate when peacekeepers are compelled to use force in order to protect civilians. As stated in Chapter 2, peacekeepers are obliged to protect civilians from conflict-related violence, however, there lacks any legal trigger of when force ought to be used. Further the Security Council does not grant peacekeepers the insight into the priority of groups that need to be protected. As peacekeepers are now envisaged to protect civilians, women and children, humanitarian workers,

26 United Nations Security Council, *Report of the Secretary-General to the Security Council on the Protection of Civilians in Armed Conflict*, UN Doc S/1999/957 at paragraph 67.

27 Ibid.

28 *United Nations Security Council Resolution 2499* (2019) at operational paragraph 32(a)(ii); *United Nations Security Council Resolution 2480* (2019) at operational paragraph 28(c)(ii); *United Nations Security Council Resolution 2502* (2019) at operational paragraph 29(i)(b).

29 United Nations, *Improving Security of United Nations Peacekeepers: We Need to Change the Way We Are Doing Business*, 19 December 2017 at 4.

30 Interviews conduct in New York in January 2019.

UN workers and equipment, guidance is necessary to the precedence of each group. Throughout discussions with stakeholders, there was no agreement to the priority of protection or what peacekeepers are intended to do when priorities conflict.[31] While some participants consider protection of local civilians paramount,[32] others indicated that peacekeepers must protect UN workers and equipment first.[33] Peacekeepers continually confront opposing interests between protecting a vulnerable group versus defending themselves and UN assets. As demonstrated in October 2018 with rebel attacks on an IDP camp in Batangafo, CAR, peacekeepers within their capability were only permitted a small number of troops to defend the IDP camp.[34] It was contended by MINUSCA that the priority was the defence of UN assets, and therefore, was not within their capabilities to defend the IDP camp.[35]

As the protection mandate is the protection of legal rights, the physical protection mandate lacks any legal language or indication of when peacekeeping action is required, and which 'category' of civilian receives priority. As the mandate demands protection from 'threats' not just direct attacks, a threshold of 'threat' is needed, in order for peacekeepers to determine when a response is obliged.

Under IHRL, a State is obliged "to take adequate preventive measures in order to protect individuals against reasonable foreseen threats of being murdered or killed by criminals and organized crime or militia groups, including armed or terrorist groups."[36] However, States are equipped with legal avenues of protection, which UN peace missions would not have access too. As an example, Article 6 of the ICCPR specifies, the right to life "shall be protected by law." Without legal and administrative avenues for peacekeepers to preventively protect the right to life, peacekeepers are limited to use their military and police presence. As such, patrolling becomes the major instrument in attempting to prevent conflict-related violence. Unlike military operations, patrolling can be compared to domestic law enforcement, therefore, domestic police enforcement may give guidance to the obligations under patrolling.

31 Ibid.

32 Interview with UN Secretariat on 28 January 2019.

33 Interview with Pakistan on 23 January 2019.

34 'MSF says UN failed civilians in Central African Republic attack', *Al Jazeera* 19 February 2019 2019 <https://www.aljazeera.com/news/2019/02/msf-failed-civilians-central-african-republic-attack-190218075727242.html>.

35 Center for Civilians in Conflict, *The Primacy of Protection: Delivering on the MINUSCA Mandate in the Central African Republic*, 2017.

36 UNHRC, General Comment No 36 at paragraph 21.

In considering domestic police enforcement and their role in the protection from physical harm, there is disagreement on whether police, in principle, have an obligation to protect. As suggested by Hutchinson, unless imposed by domestic law, police officers have no duty to protect individuals from harm.[37] Specifically, it is suggested that a duty to protect only applies to civilians within their 'proximity' rather than to the populace at large. As police enforcement relies on domestic codes to outline their obligation to protect, and the domestic guidelines on the use of force, this cannot be relied upon in determining peacekeeping obligations.

In European human rights jurisprudence, the ECHR has established clear parameters for the positive obligation to the right to life under Article 2 of the European Convention. Specifically, the ECHR in *Osman v UK*[38] held the obligation to protect "extends beyond its primary duty to secure the right to life by putting in place effective criminal law provisions."[39] For the ECHR it was "sufficient for an applicant to show that the authorities did not do all that could be reasonably expected of them to avoid a real and immediate risk of life of which they have or ought to have knowledge."[40] For example in *Tagayeva v Russia,*[41] the Court concluded that Russia failed their positive obligation under Article 2 of the European Convention as they did not "prevent or minimise the known risk" of a terrorist attack.[42]

For IHRL and the positive obligation to apply to peacekeepers, UN peace missions must have jurisdiction over a territory or individuals. As will be discussed in Chapter 6, outside IDP camps and specific areas of patrol, it will be unlikely for peacekeepers to have jurisdiction that would trigger their obligation of IHRL. However, as will be discussed, patrolling activities could see peacekeepers in joint control over an area or territory, and therefore trigger their obligations under IHRL. If peacekeepers are found in control over a territory, then UNPOL would have a positive obligation to preventively protect

37 Adeel Hassan, 'Officers Had No Duty to Protect Students in Parkland Massacre, Judge Rules' (2018) <https://www.nytimes.com/2018/12/18/us/parkland-shooting-lawsuit-ruling-police.html>.

38 *Osman v The United Kingdom*, Judgment, merits and just satisfaction, App no 23452/94, Case No 87/1997/871/1083, ECHR 1998-VIII, [1998] ECHR 101.

39 Ibid at paragraph 115.

40 Ibid at paragraph 116.

41 *Case of Tagayeva and Others v Russia*, Application no 26562/07 and 6 other applications, European Court of Human Rights, 13 April 2017.

42 Ibid at paragraph 492.

civilians from deprivation of life.[43] However, this obligation becomes unclear with a conflict of priorities and differing groups in need of protection.

With varying threats materialising in the field, UN peacekeeping has grown organically, rather than being guided by a strategic framework. From the Protection Forces to the PoC sites in South Sudan, the protection mandate has grown and developed in reaction to the threats on the ground, forcing the Security Council to respond rather than dictate a clear architecture. With the organic development of the Security Council's protection regime and peacekeepers' obligation to use force, the Security Council and UN have yet to answer the many legal questions that arise under this 'new' peacekeeping regime. With the expectation that peacekeepers are to use force regularly and sporadically, there must be an established legal framework of the use of force, not only on the military and police component that are implementing the use of force, but on the entire UN peace mission. The classification of the legal implications of the use of force is imperative to outline the obligation that is invoked when the Security Council mandates peacekeepers to protect civilians.

2 The Application of IHL in UN Peace Missions

One of the major concerns with the use of force is a UN peace mission will be categorised as a 'party to the conflict'. With the perception that peacekeepers are the world's police, and deployed on behalf of the international community,[44] the UN has insisted that peacekeepers are not to be alleged as 'parties to a conflict'. Specifically, the UN has insisted that peacekeepers are granted 'special' status and cannot be legally targeted. In 1994 the UN attempted to codify the 'special' status of peacekeepers by endeavouring to ratify the *Convention on Safety of United Nations and Associated Personnel* (the *Safety Convention*). To further reiterate the 'special' protections offered to peacekeepers, the 'intentional and direct' attacks against peacekeepers was also included as a crime under the Rome Statue.[45]

43 UN Human Rights Committee, *General Comment No 36 (2018) on Article 6 of the International Covenant on Civil and Political Rights, on the Right to Life*, CCPR/C/GC/36 at paragraph 21.

44 Katrina Grenfell, 'Perspectives on the Applicability and Application of International Humanitarian Law: the UN Context' (2013) *95(891–892) International Review of the Red Cross* 645 at 647.

45 *Rome Statue of the International Criminal Court*, A/CONF.183.9 of 17 July 1998 at Article 8(2)(b)(iii).

However, with the introduction of the Safety Convention, and the inclusion of attacks against peacekeepers in the Rome Statue, many commentators have suggested that both instruments have not made any significant impact on the law.[46] Particularly, the majority of host States in which peacekeepers are deployed are not parties to the Safety Convention. Although Pacholska has suggested that a new category of war crime has been introduced,[47] currently to date, all individuals that have been charged with attacks against peacekeepers have not been charged under the new provisions of the Rome Statute, but rather under general provisions prohibiting attacks against civilians.[48] As confirmed by the Special Court for Sierra Leone, the "prohibition against attacks on peacekeeping personnel does not represent a new crime."[49]

Nonetheless, peacekeepers do not require the ratification of the Safety Convention to be granted 'special' protections. Firstly, host States are already bound by existing obligations to ensure the protection awarded to peacekeepers under the SOFA signed by them. Notwithstanding the SOFA, if peacekeepers are not parties to a conflict then they are granted the same protections awarded to civilians under the law. Hence, under the pre-existing conditions of IHL any deliberate attack on an individual, not participating in hostilities is illegal. This is reiterated within the Safety Convention, as Article 2(2) states that the Convention will not apply to Chapter VII operations, "in which any of the personnel are engaged as combatants against organized armed forces and to which the law of international armed conflict applies."

As the legal status of peacekeepers is connected to their participation in hostilities, force used in connection with a conflict could deem a UN peace mission as a party to that conflict under the law. Once peacekeepers are participating in hostilities, they lose their protected status and can be legally targeted by opposing parties.[50] This interpretation of the law is mirrored in the

46 Ola Engdahl, 'The Status of Peace Operation Personnel under International Humanitarian Law' (2010) *11 Yearbook of International Humanitarian Law* 109 at 135; Grenfell, above note 44 at 650; Dieter Fleck, 'The legal status of personnel involved in United Nations peace operations' (2013) *95(891–892) International Review of the Red Cross* 613 at 635.

47 M. Pacholska, '(Il)legality of Killing Peacekeepers: The Crime of Attacking Peacekeepers in the Jurisprudence of International Criminal Tribunals' (2015) *13(1) Journal of International Criminal Justice* 43 at 46.

48 *Prosecutor v. Issa Hassan Sesay, Morris Kallon and Augustine Gbao (the RUF accused)*, Special Court of Sierra Leone, Case No. SCSL-04-15-T.

49 Ibid at paragraph 215.

50 Additional Protocol I defines a combatant in an IAC under Article 43(2). In a NIAC there is no status of 'combatant', however, Article 4(1) does specify that "persons who do not take a direct part or who have ceased to take part in hostilities, whether or not their liberty

provisions of the Rome Statute, which specifies that an intentional attack on peacekeepers is considered a crime "as long as they are entitled to the protection given to civilians."[51]

3 Classification of Conflict Involving UN Peace Missions

In order for the legal status of peacekeepers to be affected, UN peacekeepers must be involved in an armed conflict under IHL. The mere existence of armed force does not mean that IHL has been activated, however, the armed force must fall under the definition an 'armed conflict' under the law. Whether the conflict is classified as an IAC or a NIAC will determine the assessment needed in order to classify the use of force as an 'armed conflict'.

According to the Geneva Conventions an IAC is an 'armed conflict' that involves military conflict between two States. Under the IAC classification low levels of intensity in the conflict is needed to initiate the governance of IHL.[52] Thus, if UN-led peacekeepers are considered a 'State' under the law and 'armed force' is used against local authorities or State forces, that force would constitute an 'armed conflict'. Advocates of the IAC classification for UN peace missions generally submit one of two arguments to justify applying the provisions of an IAC.[53] The first submission suggests that the involvement of UN-led peacekeepers intrinsically 'internationalizes' any conflict, compelling that the conflict to be classified as an IAC.[54] The second submission relies on the UN's role in the international community and insists that the UN should be considered a 'State' for international law purposes, and thus, any conflict

has been restricted, are entitled to respect for their person, honour and convictions and religious practices."

51 *Rome Statute of the International Criminal Court* (*Rome Statute*).

52 Common Article 2 of the Geneva Conventions; International Committee of the Red Cross, Commentary on the First Geneva Convention: Convention (I) for the Amelioration of the Condition of the Wounded and Sick in Armed Forces in the Field (Commentaries on the 1949 Geneva Conventions) (Cambridge University Press, 2016).

53 Whittle, Devon, 'Peacekeeing in conflict: The Intervention Brigade, MONUSCO, and the application of international humanitarian law to United Nations forces' (2015) *46(3) Georgetown Journal of International Law* 837 at 837; Ray Murphy, 'United Nations Military Operations and International Humanitarian Law: What Rules Apply to Peacekeepers?' (2003) *14(2) Criminal Law Forum 153* at 167; Daphna Shraga, 'The Secretary-General's Bulletin on the Observance by United Nations Forces of International Humanitarian Law–A Decade Later' (2009) *39 Israel Yearbook on Human Rights* 357.

54 Murphy, above note 53 at 180.

involving the UN should be considered a conflict between States.[55] The reasoning behind the arguments for an IAC classification is founded in a moral framework that insists that due to the UN's very nature and central place in the international community the 'highest standard' of IHL should always apply, and this standard is found in an IAC.[56]

Conversely, advocates of the NIAC classification base their arguments in a 'negative campaign', that is, a conflict involving peacekeepers cannot be an IAC under the law, and thus by default must be classified as a NIAC. Supporters of the NIAC classification contend that under IHL an IAC must involve two States, and as the UN cannot be considered a 'State', no conflict involving the UN can be considered an IAC.[57] Further, it is argued that the inherent 'internationalization' of a conflict has no legal basis and thus finds no support in the Geneva Conventions or customary international law.[58] This is further reaffirmed in the ICRC's 2016 Commentary on the Geneva Conventions, that any 'internationalized' arguments of armed conflict is not supported by law or State practice,[59] as two States must be in conflict for an IAC to exist. The UN itself cannot be considered a High Contacting Party of the Conventions; however, this does not mean that a State is not involved in UN peace missions. As will be discussed in Chapter 7, the TCCs retain an element of control over their contingents, therefore depending on the circumstances they can become a party to the conflict. If the TCCs have effective control, then the UN peace mission might be classified as a State (or multiple States) under the Geneva Conventions. Nevertheless, it is not enough for the UN peace mission to be classified as a State, rather all parties the conflict must be classified as States.

To add to the NIAC argument, modern conflict involving peacekeepers is generally engaged with non-State actors, and therefore are considered a NIAC. For even if it is conceded that the UN could be a 'State' under the law or the TCC is the State in the conflict, a conflict between a State and non-State actors would still be classified as a NIAC. The characterisation of an IAC or NIAC is dependent on the status of *all* parties to the conflict rather than the classification of the UN peace mission. Therefore, only when a UN peace mission is engaged against State forces could the conflict be potentially classified as an IAC. Due to the nature of peacekeeping mandates supporting local authorities,

55 Ibid.

56 Ibid at 180.

57 Fleck, above note 46 at 627; Whittle, above note 53 at 854.

58 Whittle, above note 53 at 854.

59 International Committee of the Red Cross, *Commentaries on the Geneva Conventions*, 2016 at paragraph 403.

majority of conflicts will be engaged with non-State actors, classifying the conflict as a NIAC. However, there are reported situations where UN peacekeepers are engaged against local authorities, which could classify that conflict as an IAC. Notwithstanding these situations, in majority of circumstances UN peacekeepers will be using force in a NIAC.

Unlike an IAC, a NIAC must reach a level of intensity to be classified as an 'armed conflict' to ensure it is not a mere 'internal disturbance'. When assessing the level of intensity to trigger IHL, commentators[60] rely on the judicial explanation set down by ICTY in the *Tadić* case. In the *Tadić* decision, the ICTY established that "an armed conflict exists whenever there is a resort to armed force between States or protracted armed violence between government authorities and organized armed groups or between such groups within a State."[61]

The literature assessing the use of force used by peacekeepers primarily focuses on the first condition of identifying 'protracted violence' rather than the second condition of an 'organised armed groups'. In determining whether the force used by peacekeepers can be 'protracted armed violence', commentators constantly assess the level of intensity of the force, and not the 'duration' of that intensity.[62] Currently the conventional literature only examines this criteria on a theoretical basis, and is yet to identify what level of 'intensity' is needed for force to be considered 'protracted armed violence'.[63] This lack of clarity regarding the level of intensity is further confused with the proposal that UN peacekeepers require a 'higher level of armed violence' in comparison to other parties.[64] Yet this approach finds no genuine support in the law, as requiring "a higher intensity of hostilities to reach the threshold of armed conflict involving multinational armed forces is neither supported by general practice nor confirmed by *opinio juris*."[65] Specifically, this approach disregards IHL's principle of equal application, as it does not consider the other parties in the conflict.

---

60 Engdahl, above note 46 at 112; Murphy, above note 53 at 187; Tristan Ferraro, 'The applicability and application of international humanitarian law to multinational forces' (2014) 95(891–892) *International Review of the Red Cross* 561 at 580.

61 *Decision on the Defence Motion for Interlocutory Appeal on Jurisdiction*, International Criminal Tribunal for the former Yugoslavia, Appeals Chamber Decision, 2 October 1995 at paragraph 70.

62 Engdahl, above note 46 at 112.

63 Ibid.

64 Whittle, above note 53 at 852; Engdahl, above note 46 at 117.

65 ICRC, 2016 Commentaries at paragraph 247.

Thus, if force used by peacekeepers reaches a level of 'intensity' against a non-state armed group, that conflict would be considered a NIAC under IHL. As UN peace missions MINUSMA, MINUSCA, and MONUSCO, are currently involved in high levels of violence and armed conflict, they would be considered parties to a NIAC. Indeed, the Rule of Law in Armed Conflict (RULAC) initiated by the Geneva Academy in 2007, classifies the UN's involvement in three conflicts – Mali, CAR and DRC – as NIACS.[66]

3.1 *Status of Peacekeepers in Armed Conflict*

When peacekeepers are 'directly participating' in a NIAC, they can no longer rely on their protected status. A concise definition of 'direct participation' does not exist under the Geneva Conventions,[67] and although, there is developing literature on 'direct participation',[68] the formulation within current legal discourse is not easily transferable to UN peace missions. In the Special Court of Sierra Leone, the Court was given an opportunity to investigate instances when peacekeepers could be directly participating in hostilities, and thus lose their protected status.[69] Article 4(b) of the Statute of the Special Court mirrors the peacekeeping provisions in the Rome Statute, granting the Court jurisdiction over crimes in attacking peacekeepers "as long as they are entitled to the protection given to civilians or civilian objects under international law of armed conflict". The Special Court, in assessing attacks directed towards peacekeepers, set down that peacekeepers retain their protected status if they are merely acting in self-defence. In this situation the accused RUF fighters were found guilty of directly targeting peacekeepers, for although UNAMSIL engaged in force to defend themselves,

> with all civilians, their protection would not cease if the personnel use armed force only in exercising their right to individual self-defence. Likewise, the Chambers opines that the use of force by peacekeepers in self-defence in the discharge of their mandate, provided that it is

66 http://www.rulac.org/browse/conflicts.

67 ICRC, 2016 Commentaries at paragraph 524.

68 For example, see Emily Crawford, *Identifying the Enemy: Civilian Participation in Armed Conflict* (Oxford University Press, 2015); Sandesh Sivakumaran, *The law of non-international armed conflict* (Oxford University Press, 2012); Yoram Dinstein, *The Conduct of Hostilities under the Law of International Armed Conflict* (*3rd ed*) (Cambridge University Press, 2016).

69 *Sesay* Case, above note 48.

> limited to such use, would not alter or diminish the protection afforded to peacekeepers.[70]

According to the interpretation of the Special Court of Sierra Leone, peacekeepers would remain as 'civilians' as long as they revert to using force only in self-defence or defence 'in the discharge of their mandate'. Hence, force used in order to protect civilians for the threat of physical violence may not classify peacekeepers as 'combatants', but rather civilians acting in self-defence.

Under IHL, 'attacks' are defined as "acts of violence against the adversary, whether in offence or in defence".[71] However, not all force is considered an 'attack'; for it would be irrational to suggest that civilians lose their protected status when using force to defend themselves, for "if individual self-defence against prohibited violence were to entail loss of protection against direct attack, this would have the absurd consequence of legitimizing a previously unlawful attack."[72] Thus, as concluded by the ICRC, "the use of necessary and proportionate force in such situations cannot be regarded as direct participation in hostilities."[73] The Special Court employed this line of reasoning to contend that peacekeepers are using 'necessary and proportionate' force to defend themselves or those in their protection, therefore should not lose their protected status.[74] Under this interpretation of 'direct participation' peacekeepers remain as 'civilians' when proportionate force is used on a 'reactional' basis against an attack. The Court further expanded this understanding of self-defence to cover attacks against civilians under a UN peace mission's protection.[75] Therefore, peacekeepers using force to protect civilians against a direct attack may still retain their specially protected status, providing that force is 'reactional' and proportionate to the threat at hand.

Conversely, when conflict occurs between a non-state group and UN peacekeepers, there must be a point in which the conflict ceases to be an action

---

70 Ibid at paragraph 233.

71 Protocol Additional to the Geneva Conventions of 12 August 1949 and realting to the Protection of Victims of International Armed Conflicts (Protocol I), 8 June 1977 at Article 49(1).

72 Nils Melzer, *Interpretive Guidance on the Notion of Direct Participation in Hostilities Under International Humanitarian Law, International Committee of the Red Cross*, (Reference Paper, 2009) at 61.

73 Ibid.

74 For example, as applying to medical personnel, they do not lose their protected status if they use force "in their own defence, or in that of the wounded and sick in their change." First Geneva Convention at Article 22(1).

75 *Sesay* Case, above note 48.

of self-defence and becomes an 'attack' or 'armed conflict' under IHL. For UN peacekeepers to solely rely on the self-defence approach confuses the jurisdiction of *jus ad bellum* and *jus in bello*. The justification or intention behind the use of force does not alter or affect the application of IHL.[76] Reliance on the justification of self-defence can suggest that there is a 'legitimacy' of force and confuse the two branches of law. Once peacekeepers are engaged in an 'armed conflict' against another party, irrespective of their intention behind the force, the laws of IHL must apply to that conflict unaltered. For if the conflict reaches a level of intensity, whether or not in self-defence, that conflict will be categorised as a NIAC. Moreover, if force is used in self-defence repeatedly, although not continuously, the combination of these military operations may also potentially lead to a level of intensity to trigger the application of IHL.[77] Thus, as UN peace missions have been deployed for extended periods of time, the prolonged or intensified levels of armed force encountered by peacekeepers will initiate the rules of IHL, and consequently, render UN peace missions party to a conflict. Indeed, at the deployment of the FIB, the office of Legal Affairs of the UN conceded that these troops would be classified as 'parties to the conflict', and thus can be legally targeted.[78]

Even when peacekeepers do not use direct force, their assistance to parties in an existing armed conflict may classify UN peace mission as participating in that conflict. The ICTY in their discussions in *Dragomir Miloševic*[79] and *Kordić and Čerkez*,[80] set down that an act will be a direct part in hostilities if there is some 'nexus' between the act and actual harm that is likely to be caused.[81] With this interpretation, the Court concluded that under IHL 'military support' would be considered as participation in hostilities. An illustration of this 'military support' was given by the ICTY in the *Strugar*[82] case, where the transportation of weapons was concluded to be a direct act in hostilities.[83] Nonetheless, even when peacekeepers are not engaged in force, the inclusion of the protection mandate has further complicated the legal status of

76 Grenfell, above note 44 at 645–646.

77 Ferraro, above note 60 at 579.

78 As cited in Murphy, above note 53.

79 *Prosecutor v Dragomir Milošević*, International Criminal Tribunal of the former Yugoslavia, Judgment, 12 December 2007, Case No IT-98-29/1-T.

80 *Prosecutor v Dario Kordić and Mario Čerkez*, International Criminal Tribunal of the former Yugoslavia, Judgment, 26 February 2001, Case No IT-95-14/2-T.

81 Dragomir Miloševic case; Kordić and Čerkez case.

82 *Prosecutor v Pavle Strugar*, International Criminal Tribunal of the former Yugoslavia, Appeals decision, 17 July 2008, Case No IT-01-42-A.

83 Ibid at paragraph 177.

peacekeepers. As peacekeepers have been mandated to support local authorities and government forces, a new method of analysis called the 'support base approach' has arisen within the literature.[84] Peacekeepers supporting government forces who are already involved in a NIAC, by association could be considered a party of that existing conflict. This support base approach has been specifically applied to mandated Protection Forces, particularly the FIB in the DRC.[85] Commentators primarily focusing on the FIB are in agreement that the 'support base approach' applies to MONUSCO, that is, the FIB is considered a party to the same conflict as the Congolese forces.[86] With the Security Council increasingly mandating peacekeepers to assist local authorities, many UN peace missions may be considered parties to conflicts by association of their support function.

Although it is currently accepted in the literature that the FIB is engaged in armed conflict,[87] it is contentious whether non-combatant peacekeepers are also engaged in an armed conflict. Even though civilian peacekeepers might not intend to cause actual harm, their support of UN components who are actively engaged in armed conflict could deem them parties to a conflict.[88]

Currently, MONUSCO is made up of civilians, police, non-combatant peacekeepers and the FIB. However, the FIB is using the same infrastructure, transportation and administration as the entire Mission. The administrative support of the FIB by the entire Mission "definitely raises some questions concerning the legal status of these different categories of personnel under IHL."[89] As the non-combatant peacekeepers in MONUSCO are actively collaborating with the FIB to achieve the overall protection mandate, the "non-combatant peacekeepers within MONUSCO mission may lose their protected status."[90]

However, not all involvement in hostilities will lead to the loss of the protection afforded to civilians, for individuals may be deemed to either be 'directly' or 'indirectly' participating in hostilities. As outlined in the Geneva Conventions, 'direct participation' will lead to a loss of protections under the law, implying that 'indirect' participation would not deprive an individual of their protected status. According to the ICRC, the distinction between direct and indirect

84 Ferraro, above note 60 at 583.

85 Scott Sheeran and Stephanie Case, *The Intervention Brigade: Legal Issues for the UN in the Democractic Republic of the Congo* (International Peace Institute, 2014).

86 Ibid.

87 Ibid at 6; Whittle, above note 53 at 855; Ferraro, above note 60 at 579.

88 Haidi Willmot, Scott Sheeran and Lisa Sharland, 'Safety and Security Challenges in UN Peace Operations' (2015) *International Peace Institute* at 20.

89 Ferraro, above note 60 at 600.

90 Whittle, above note 53 at 866.

participation "must be interpreted as corresponding to that between direct and indirect causation of harm."[91] Therefore, for peacekeepers to loss their protected status their conduct must directly cause harm. For example, the transportation of weapons will only be considered direct participation if it is "carried out as an integral part of a specific military operation designed to directly cause the required threshold of harm."[92] Therefore, if civilian peacekeepers are assisting in activities that are 'integral' to the military operation that will cause harm, they will be classified as taking direct part in hostilities.

To assist with the protection of those not participating in hostilities, parties to the conflict are obliged to distinguish themselves from civilians and non-combatants.[93] The principle that an armed fighter must distinguish themselves is applicable in an IAC, but not treaty law in NIAC.[94] However, on policy grounds combatant peacekeepers should distinguish themselves from non-combatant personnel within the same Mission to avoid any confusion of legal status. The FIB are still wearing the UN blue helmets, and using the same vehicles as non-combatant peacekeepers. In past practice, the Rapid Reaction Force in the UN Protection Force (*UNPROFOR*) operated "under the United Nations flag and insignia but without the blue helmets and without painting its vehicles white."[95] As the FIB is considered a party to the conflict and is using the administration and infrastructural support of the entire Mission, "MONUSCO as a whole not just the Intervention Brigade component is considered a part to the armed conflict."[96]

Besides the support of 'combatant' peacekeepers, UN peace missions are being mandated to logistically and administratively support UN-backed forces engaged in conflict. For example, MINUSMA in Mali has been mandated to support French Forces who are actively engaged in counter-terrorism measures and are considered to be involved in armed conflict. Even though police and civilian components of MINUSMA are themselves not engaged in armed conflict, their 'military' support would be considered a direct participation in

---

91 Melzer, above note 72.

92 Ibid.

93 Additional Protocol I at Article 48.

94 For IAC, ibid at Articles 48 and 51. The principle of distinction is considered customary in NIAC – https://ihl-databases.icrc.org/customary-ihl/eng/docs/v1_cha_chapter1_rule1. It also arguable that the prohibition on attacking civilians in APII means that the principle of distinction is treaty law in NIAC.

95 Lars Müller, 'The Force Intervention Brigade – United Nations Forces beyond the Fine Line Between Peacekeeping and Peace Enforcement' (2015) 20(3) *Journal of Conflict & Secuirty Law* 359 at 376.

96 Sheeran and Case, above note 85 at 1.

hostilities under the law, specifically, when MINUSMA is providing logistical and intelligent services to French armed operations that functions as a direct nexus to the harm created.

The confusion over the status of peacekeepers and legal consequences of the use force has been cited as to the reluctance of peacekeepers to use force to protect civilians.[97] As TCCs do not want their troops sacrificing their lives for 'foreign' civilians, they have placed caveats on when their troops are authorised to engage in any military action. For example, one interviewee stated that Japanese peacekeepers are prominent for not engaging in force, and are under strict orders not to use force no matter the order.[98] For as reported by the OIOS report on the protection mandate "the risk confronting peacekeepers has gradually increased and is now higher than troop-contributing countries are willing to accept."[99]

Thus, when peacekeepers use force that reaches a level of intensity, whether as a 'one-off' or multiple reactional operations, that force will initiate the application of IHL. As peacekeepers are now mandated and expected to use force to protect civilians, UN peace missions are liable to find themselves parties to a conflict. Even though some UN peace missions may not use force, their assistance to Protection Forces or local authorities who are engaged in conflict, can classify them as being direct participants in hostilities, and thus, engaged in armed conflict.

3.2 *Scope and Duration of IHL*

The literature and UN reports in discussing the application of IHL, limit their discussions to whether the law applies to peacekeeping, however, insufficient discussion has occurred on "when and for how long IHL applies."[100] Under international law, the application of IHL does not cease in a NIAC simply when hostilities between the two parties has halted. As established by the ICTY in *Tadić*, the scope of IHL applies in a NIAC "for the initiation of such armed conflicts and extends beyond the cessation of hostilities until a general conclusion of peace is reached."[101] However, as peacekeepers are deployed in continuous areas of conflict, it becomes difficult to assess when a 'general conclusion of peace is reached', specifically in regards to UN peace missions. Due to this difficulty, some commentators have suggested that IHL will cease to apply

97 OIOS Report, above note 3 at paragraph 50.
98 Interview with UN researcher and analysts on 28 January 2019.
99 OIOS Report, above note 3 at paragraph 30.
100 Grenfell, above note 44 at 649.
101 *Tadic* case, above note 286 at paragraph 70.

to peacekeeping operations when the 'combat mission' has concluded.[102] However, peacekeepers deployed under the protection mandate have no concise 'combat mission', rather force is to be utilised in order to protect civilians from on-going threats. Further, with the increased use of robust and multi-dimensional peacekeeping it becomes nearly impossible to determine the 'conclusion' of any 'mission'. Thus, when IHL applies to UN peace missions, there is little to no guidance to when the 'conflict' has concluded under IHL.

With a lack of clarity on the duration of IHL in UN peace missions the ability for peacekeepers to regain their protected status becomes questionable. Under the law, a civilian can reclaim their protected status after the conclusion of a 'specific hostile act'.[103] However, it is unclear if and when peacekeepers can return to their protected status after directly participating in hostilities and becoming a party to the conflict. In the ICRC guidance on *Direct Participation*, it is argued that members of an organised armed group do not benefit from the 'revolving door' protection offered to civilians in IHL.[104] Members of an organised armed group "cease to be civilians for as long as they remain members by virtue of their continuous combat function."[105] Consequently, an armed group whose continuous function is to take direct part in hostilities, will remain parties to a conflict even if they are not constantly using force.[106] Hence, peacekeepers engaged in conflict, or in a support-based role, may find themselves in a continuous combat function even after the use of force has been completed.

Thus, when peacekeepers engage in force to protect civilians or assist other active parties in the conflict, they will lose their protected status and trigger the application of IHL. Moreover, when peacekeepers consequently invoke the application of IHL, they may not easily regain their protected status. The deployment of peacekeepers under the protection mandate may deem the entire Mission as directly participating in hostilities by assisting the military component of that Mission. Even as new peacekeepers are deployed, their association and membership to the Mission as an 'armed group' would render them also direct participants in hostilities.

---

102 Ferraro, above note 60 at 604.

103 Siobhán Wills, 'Continuing Impunity of Peacekeepers: The Need For a Convention' (2013) 4(1) *Journal of International Humanitarian Legal Studies* 47 at 59.

104 Melzer, above note 72.

105 Ibid at 71.

106 Ibid.

4 The Obligation to Protect and IHL

Once peacekeepers engage in armed conflict they are obliged under the law to only target 'combatants' and military objects. However, in States where peacekeepers are deployed, combatants and civilians are generally indistinguishable. As armed groups are often entrenched in civilian populations, the ability for peacekeepers to distinguish military from non-military targets becomes challenging. Crucially, as many armed groups have abducted or have civilians held within their camps, civilian and military objects have become intertwined.

Under the protection mandate, peacekeepers have been mandated to engage and 'neutralize' armed groups that have entrenched themselves in civilian populations. For example since 2017, MONUSCO has been conducting regular 'reconnaissance' operations in North Kivu to monitor and engage with former M23 groups in the DRC who have entrenched themselves amongst the local population.[107] Although these rebel groups have many civilians within their camps, "there are still some civilian and military personnel within the mission who view these civilians in the armed groups' camps as legal targets."[108]

Even though IHL understands that civilian casualties are inevitable in armed conflict, the law also insists that armed forces must be able to distinguish between military and civilian objects, and to take reasonable care to mitigate civilian harm.[109] Distinctively, this must apply to peacekeepers who are mandated to protect civilians from the harms and threats of armed conflict. Even though a combatant camp is to be considered a military target, as peacekeepers are mandated to observe civilian harm mitigation, peacekeepers must ensure adequate mechanisms are in place to minimise civilian harm. This leads to tension between the strategy of removing armed groups in order to protect civilians, and creating immediate harm to civilians through military operations. Although peacekeepers are mandated to partake in military operations, they are also mandated to protect civilians, and bound by the rules of IHL, therefore their military campaigns must ensure that harm to civilians is mitigated. Particularly, all military operations implemented by UN peace

---

107 United Nations Security Council, *Report of the Secretary-General on the United Nations Organizations Stabilization Mission in the Democratic Republic of the Congo*, S/2017/206 at paragraph 14.

108 Center for Civilians in Conflict, *From Mandate to Mission: Mitigating Civilian Harm in UN Peacekeeping Operations in the DRC*, 2016 Report at 1.

109 Although precautions to attacks in NIAC are not outlines as they are in an IAC. Article 13 of Addtional Protocol II requires that "the civilian population and individual civilians shall enjoy general protection against the dangers arising from military operations".

missions must follow the rules of distinction and proportionality. As follows, before entering into a military camp, UN peacekeepers must guarantee that they have been able to distinguish between civilian and non-civilian targets. Although some civilian causalities are inevitable, UN peacekeepers must confirm that those casualties are proportionate to the military advantage that will be gained from that attack. The necessity to mitigate harm was codified in MINUSMA's and MONUSCO's recent mandate that "the risk to civilians are mitigated before, during and after any military or police operation."[110]

Under the IHL rule of proportionality, attacks would be classified as illegal "which may be expected to cause incidental loss of civilian life, injury to civilians, damage to civilian objects, or a combination thereof, which would be excessive in relation to the concrete and direct military advantage anticipated."[111] Although the rule is codified in Additional Protocol I, the rule of proportionality is accepted as customary international law and would be binding on UN peace missions.[112] Therefore, UN peace operations can only harm civilians, or civilian objects, if the attack is concretely proportionate to the 'military advantage' gained. Unlike standard military operations, the military advantage in peacekeeping is not of a military nature. Outside the FIB, UN peace missions engaged in conflict are not attempting to 'defeat' an opposing party but rather to protect civilians from physical violence. As the use of force is annexed to the protection of civilians, the mandate becomes the benchmark for the operation's military advantage. Therefore, any military operations of a UN peace missions must be proportionate to the advantage anticipated in protecting civilians, as authorised in the Security Council's mandate. The moment when peacekeepers' military operations are disproportionate to the advantage gained in protecting civilians, then that operation will be considered disproportionate, and peacekeepers would have failed their obligation under the law.

Therefore, the obligation to protect under the Security Council's mandate will also encompass a UN peace mission's obligation under IHL. When a UN peace mission becomes a party to a conflict, the obligation to protect will incorporate the obligation to distinguish between civilian and military targets,

110 *United Nations Security Council Resolution 2502* (2019) at operational paragraph 29(i)(a); *United Nations Security Council Resolution 2666* (2022) at operational paragraph 24(i)(a); *United Nations Security Council Resolution 2640* (2022) at operational paragraph 26(c)(i).

111 Additional Protocol I at Article 51(5)(b).

112 International Committee of the Red Cross, *Study on Customary Interantional Humanitarian Law (Customary IHL Database) at rule 14*; the rule of distinction and proportionality is also noted in The 2020 Handbook art 2.1.2.

as well as an obligation to ensure all operations are proportionate to the advantage of protecting civilians.

4.1 *Counter-terrorist Measures*

Within the conventional literature, discussions regarding peacekeepers' authority to use force generally focuses on self-defence or as a reactional response to threats against civilians.[113] However, under the protection mandate peacekeepers have been mandated to directly protect civilians, and in some cases to take a 'proactive' approach to protection. The proactive form of protection reached its height with the Security Council's formation of the FIB in the DRC and the counter-terrorism measures in Mali.

As to date, six States that have had UN peace missions deployed have had issues with terrorist organisations.[114] As of yet there is still no legal definition of 'terrorist', and this book will not go into this debate.[115] For the purpose of this book a 'terrorist organisation' is one that is identified by the Security Council in *Resolution 1566* (2004).

In the 2015 HIPPO report, the Panel firmly believed "the United Nations peacekeeping missions, owing to their composition and character, are not suited to engage in military counter-terrorism operations."[116] However, MINUSMA has been deployed in continuous conflict involving active terrorist organisations. To date MINUSMA is considered one of the "deadliest" missions in the history of the UN, due to the terrorist organisations involved in the conflict.[117]

Initially, the Security Council mandated MINUSMA assist French Forces actively engaged in military counter-terrorism. Yet in 2016, MINUSMA was mandated to "anticipate and deter threats and to take robust and active steps to counter asymmetric attacks against civilians or United Nations personnel."[118]

---

113 For example, Peter Nadin, *The use of force in UN peacekeeping* (2018); Mona Ali Khali, 'Legal Aspects of the Use of Force by Unitd Nations Peacekeepers for the Protection of Civilians' in Haidi Willmot et al (eds), *Protection of Civilians* (Oxford University Press, 2016); Thierry Tardy, 'A Critique of Robust Peacekeeping in Contemporary Peace Operations' (2011) *18*(2) *International Peacekeeping* 152.

114 Arthur Boutellis and Naureen Chowdhury Fink, *Waging Peace: UN Peace Operations Confronting Terrorism and Violent Extremism*, International Peace Institute, (2016) at 1.

115 For example of this debate Ben Saul, *Defining Terrorism in International Law* (Oxford University Press, 2006).

116 United Nations General Assembly and Security Council, *Report of the High-level Independent Panel on Peace Operations on Uniting Our Strengths for Peace: Politics, Partnership and People*, UN Doc A/70/95-S/2015/446 at paragraph 119.

117 John Karlsrud, 'Towards UN Counter-Terrorism Operations?' (2017) *38*(*6*) *Third World Quarterly* 1215 at 1215.

118 *United Nations Security Council Resolution 2295* (2016) at operational paragraph 19(d).

This contradiction between what was contended and what was mandated has "created a gap between the policy debate in NY and the realities confronting UN staff on the ground."[119]

Though initially MINUSMA would not be seen as taking 'direct' part in hostilities with their assistive function, since 2018, with numerous clashes, MINUSMA is now perceived as 'directly' participating in hostilities.[120] As the UN is based on a State-centric philosophy and ideology, this new challenge involves a party that does not associate itself with political boundaries. As MINUSMA is assisting French Forces in military counter-terrorist activities, peacekeepers (military and non-military) have become targets by these organisations. This creates a scenario where peacekeepers are putting at risk those who they are mandated to protect. As UN peacekeepers are in an armed conflict against a transnational organisation, it puts to question the status of other UN peace missions deployed in States that have elements of that same terrorist organisation. For example, in January 2013 the main extremist group in Mali, Ansar Dine, become associated with the larger Al-Qaeda group. As such Al-Qaeda has a growing presence within Central Africa, where MINUSCA is currently deployed. This connection between both Missions, increases the likelihood chance of MINUSCA becoming military targets by association with MIINUSMA. With an increase in extremist groups, the UN has conceded that they can no longer avoid counter-terrorism in peacekeeping and that they must "reflect on tools and means for UN peace operations to respond to terrorism and violent extremism."[121]

When peacekeepers are engaging with these terrorist organisations, peacekeepers are faced with a theoretical and philosophical difference from other non-State groups. Under the principles of peacekeeping, peacekeepers undertake activities that build international peace and security, and further engage all sides of the conflict to mitigate harm to civilians. As stated by one commentator "one can negotiate with insurgents, but not with terrorists."[122] Thus, counter-terrorism involves a different ethical understanding and a drastic change to the mindset of UN peacekeeping. Since counter-terrorism activities

---

119 Boutellis and Fink, above note 114 at 1.

120 From the attack in Aguelhok, in Northeast Mali in April and May 2018, in which two peacekeepers died and 13 were wounded. And in October 2018, were clashes between MINUSMA and armed groups in Timbuktu region, were two peacekeepers were killed.

121 Karlsrud, above note 117.

122 Charbonneau. Bruno, 'Intervention in Mali: Building Peace Between Peacekeeping and Counterterrorism' (2017) *35(4) Journal of Contemporary African Studies* 415 at 419.

depart from the moral application of the protection mandate, peacekeepers are found in undefined terrain.

5 Priority of Protection and Self-Defence

Under the Security Council's protection regime, peacekeepers are mandated not only protect civilians but to also protect humanitarian workers, UN personnel, and UN assets. When conflict arises, there is little guidance on what is the priority of physical protection and which actor or object takes precedence. With cuts in the peacekeeping budget, the majority of UN peace missions are under-resourced and military peacekeepers are unable to protect multiple areas or interests at the same time. Consequently, the position of most UN peace missions is to protect UN assets as first priority.[123] As peacekeepers withdraw back to UN bases in order to protect UN assets, so too do civilians flee to UN bases in order to seek refuge. This was evidenced in South Sudan, as civilians flocked to UN bases in order to be protected, spontaneously creating PoC sites.[124]

As conflict breaks out sporadically within a NIAC, peacekeepers are often faced with multiple trade-offs, between protecting civilians or protecting UN assets.[125] As evidenced in January 2016 UNMISS' internal memo, peacekeepers were instructed to protect UN staff and their humanitarian partners, if large scale attacks occurred in Juba.[126] As further evidenced in CAR, MINUSCA withdrew back to their base when movement of FPRC was reported, abandoning the Bria Hospital and leaving it undefended against attacks.[127] However, in discussions in New York it was suggested that the 'protection of UN assets and personnel' is at times used as an excuse not to engage in conflict to protect civilians.[128] Moreover, once peacekeepers have withdrawn within their bases, they tend to remain abandoning vulnerable civilians caught in the conflict in vicinity of their bases. This refusal to depart was demonstrated in South Sudan

123 Interview with POC researcher on 23 January 2019.

124 Mark Malan and Charles T. Hunt, *Between a Rock and a Hard Placel: The UN and the Protection of Civilians in South Sudan, Institute for Security Studies*, 2014.

125 Center for Civilians in Conflict, above note 108 at 21.

126 *Urgent South Sudan Consultations* Security Council Reporter <https://www.whatsinblue.org/2016/07/urgent-south-sudan-consultations.php>.

127 Center for Civilians in Conflict, *The Primacy of Protection: Delivering on the MINUSCA Mandate in the Central African Republic*, 2017 Report at 20.

128 Interviews conducted in New York in February 2018, January and March 2019.

when UNMISS peacekeepers refused to leave UN bases in order to answer the calls for help from humanitarian workers in 2016.

It is generally accepted that the protection mandate is to be interpreted broadly, as discussed in previous chapters, however, it is unclear whether peacekeepers are obligated to protect all civilians or to prioritise their protection activities over defence of UN assets. Moreover, with an increase in peacekeeping casualties, protection of civilians must also be put in context of risk to the individual peacekeepers. However, the protection of UN assets and civilians does not always have to be in conflict. Peacekeepers failing to protect civilians cannot always rely on the protection of UN assets, specifically if they have not assessed the threat sufficiently. Similar to a State's 'due diligence' to ensure their obligation to protect under IHRL,[129] UN peace missions must use all their available resources to protect civilians. Therefore, if a UN peace mission is under-resourced, they still should use all reasonable means in their capabilities to protect.

Under international law 'due diligence' is still not clearly identified,[130] however, an interpretation can be gleaned from the UN's HRDDP. Although the HRDDP is concerned with assisting of government forces, it can still be pertinent regarding due diligence assessments for protection priorities. Particularly, peacekeepers need to adequately assess the risk of omitting protection and be transparent with their assessment. In order to manage international expectations, all decisions need to be made transparent not only to the Security Council and DPO, but to civilians who have an expectation of protection.

6 Conclusion

As determined in Chapter 1 the mandate to protect civilians places a legally binding obligation on the UN, TCCs/PCCs and the host State. This obligation, as concluded in Chapter 2, is the protection of legal rights, that being, the civilian status. Moreover, as identified in Chapter 2, the primary focus of the protection mandate is the protection against physical violence. Therefore, as established in this chapter the content of the obligation to protect from physical violence will trigger the application and obligations under IHL.

---

129 Joanna Kuleza, *Due Diligence in International Law,* Queen Mary Studies in International Law (Brill Nijhoff, 2016) at 262–267.

130 Stephanie Farrior and Brice Clagett, 'State Responsibility for Human Rights Abuses by Non-State Actors' (Paper presented at the Proceeding of the Annual Meeting (American Society of International Law), 1998) at 305.

Although the Security Council has remained silent on the legal status of peacekeepers, the new protection regime of the UN has increased the prospects of UN peace missions being considered a party to a conflict. Therefore, the obligations under IHL will apply to all UN peace missions that are taking direct part in hostilities. The classification of a 'party to a conflict' will not apply only to military peacekeepers engaged in force, but to any component of the Mission assisting in an integral part of an operation that is designed to cause harm.

Once engaged in armed conflict peacekeepers are bound by their obligations under IHL when using force. Although IHL will guide UN peace missions in the manner of warfare, IHL does not give guidance on when peacekeepers are obliged to use force to protect civilians. With limited resources and multiple actors to protect, peacekeepers default to protecting UN assets and abandoning civilian areas. However, as a minimum obligation to protect, peacekeepers are obliged to protect civilians in the vicinity of UN bases of operations and areas of patrol from direct and indiscriminate attacks, as well as any conflict-related violence. Moreover, with the application of IHL, under the obligation to protect, all use of force must adhere to the rules of proportionality and distinction.

As the obligation to protect is triggered with the deployment of peacekeepers, peacekeepers will engage in protection activities outside the realm of armed conflict. Moreover, peacekeepers will be obliged to protect under IHRL even when engaged in armed conflict. Similar to the conclusion reached in this chapter, IHRL will expand the obligation to protect encompassing obligations under IHRL. Particularly IHRL will become the guiding framework for the law enforcement activities, such as detentions and arrests. Therefore, the following chapter will look at peacekeeping law enforcement activities, specifically the detention of individuals, active patrolling, and the obligations that are activated within those tasks.

CHAPTER 4

Law Enforcement under the Protection of Civilians Mandate

Throughout the life cycle of a mission, peacekeepers are mandated to protect civilians not only within the realm of an armed conflict, but at all times of deployment. Consequently, peacekeepers regularly engage in 'law enforcement' activities in order to protect civilians outside the application of IHL. As policing becomes a customary function of modern peacekeeping, UN police officers have become a stable component of all UN peace missions. Particularly as law enforcement protection activities are mandated and obliged regardless of the existence of an armed conflict.

UN police officers are currently deployed in all UN peace missions, however, there remains insufficient guidance on the role of UNPOL in the protection of civilians, and activities incurred from that mandate. Even within current literature, the primary focus of protection of civilians is the military component of each Mission.[1] However, with the ever-changing landscape of UN peacekeeping, UNPOL is participating in protection activities, blurring the line between them and their military counterparts.

As UNPOL will engage in force outside the realm of an armed conflict, they will be guided by 'police enforcement' principles rooted in IHRL.[2] As both counterparts, military and police, engage in the use of force under differing legal structures and purposes, there is confusion on each component's role in the protection regime. Significantly, UNPOL's obligation to protect remains unclear, as there is insufficient guidance to their role within the protection mandate.

From the Security Council's overarching resolutions on UNPOL,[3] the task explicitly assigned to UNPOL under the protection mandate is the prevention

1 For example Hitoshi Nasu, 'Operationalizing the Responsibility to Protect in the Context of Civilian Protection by UN Peacekeepers' (2011) *18(4) International Peacekeeping* 364; Conor Foley, *UN Peacekeeping Operations and the Protection of Civilians* (Cambridge University Press, 2017); Mona Ali Khali, 'Legal Aspects of the Use of Force by Unitd Nations Peacekeepers for the Protection of Civilians' in Haidi Willmot et al (eds), *Protection of Civilians* (Oxford University Press, 2016).

2 Siobhán Wills, 'Use of Deadly Force by Peacekeepers Operating Outside of Armed Conflict Situations: What Laws Apply?' (2018) *40(3) Human Rights Quarterly* 663 at 669.

3 *United Nations Security Council Resolution 2185* (2014); *United Nations Security Council Resolution 2382* (2017); and *United Nations Security Council Resolution 2447* (2018).

 | DOI:10.1163/9789004707313_006

and protection of sexual and gender-based violence to create a secure environment.[4] In particular the Security Council focuses on UNPOL's ability to mitigate sexual violence through active patrolling and to facilitate the protection of vulnerable displaced civilians.[5] As the role of UNPOL has grown organically in peacekeeping, UN police officers are increasingly involved in protection duties without a legal framework to adhere to.

As serious crimes are being committed in IDP camps and areas of patrol, UNPOL is forced to detain "individuals who constitute such threats, based on a mandate to maintain public safety and security within its sites for the protection of civilians, raising new legal and protection issues."[6] With the increase in protection activities, and the prevention of sexual and gender based violence, UNPOL has become more involved in local law enforcement. Particularly, as UNPOL is mandated to ensure 'secure environments' this has physically manifested in the form of detentions and investigations for security and criminal issues. Conversely, there is no consensus or guidance to the legal framework to govern these law enforcement activities in peacekeeping.[7]

It will be concluded in this chapter that IHRL is the legal body that outlines the obligations for law enforcement activities. As such, under the protection of civilians mandate, UNPOL will be legally permitted to detain individuals solely for security reasons, however, it is tenuous whether the mandate authorises detentions for criminal actions. Without legal authority to detain, UN peacekeepers will be partaking in the arbitrary detention of individuals and breaching their obligations under IHRL. However, although peacekeepers are in breach of IHRL for detaining individuals indefinitely, within the current landscape UNPOL will have no other operational alternative to detentions. Once peacekeepers have detained an individual, they exercise effective control and must guarantee the protection of that individual's rights under IHRL. Therefore, as part of the obligation to protect under the Security Council's mandate, peacekeepers must ensure that they respect, protect and fulfil the human rights of detained individuals.

---

4 United Nations Security Council, Report of the Secretary-General on United Nations Policing, 10 November 2016, UN Doc S/2016/952 (*Secretary-General Report on UNPOL*) at paragraph 8.

5 *United Nations Security Council Resolution 2409* (2018) at operational paragraph 36(a); *United Nations Security Council Resolution 2406* (2018) at operational paragraph 7(a)(ii); *United Nations Security Council Resolution 2363* (2017) at operational paragraph 15(a)(i).

6 United Nations Security Council, *Report of the Secretary-General on United Nations Policing, 10 November 2016*, UN Doc S/2016/952 (*Secretary-General Report on UNPOL*) at paragraph 34.

7 The Copenhagen Process will be discussed later in this chapter.

In order to reach this conclusion, this chapter will first give a brief introduction to UNPOL and their involvement in peacekeeping operations. Secondly, this chapter will focus on UNPOL's rising activity of the detention of individuals. Particularly, this chapter will analyse two legal aspects of detention, the authority to detain under the law, and the IHRL obligations to those individuals who are detained.

1 UNPOL in UN Peacekeeping

Since ONUC in 1960, UN police officers have been deployed to assist and support UN peace missions. With the introduction of executive mandates in UNMIK[8] and Timor-Leste (*UNMISET*),[9] UN police officers have become an integral part of the Security Council's peacekeeping landscape. The number of UN police officers deployed in UN peace missions has increased from 5,840 in 1995 to just under 8,000 as of October 2022.[10] In support of the increase in UNPOL's deployment, in 2006, the General Assembly authorised the creation of the UN Standing Police Capacity (*SPC*),[11] who is mandated to support UNPOL activities in UN peace missions. Although UNPOL is considered a standard component in UN peacekeeping, there has been slim guidance for their role in an overall Mission, specifically in the Security Council's protection regime. With the Security Council employing complicated mandates, there is confusion as to the division of tasks between the military and police components within a UN peace mission.

Due to the obscurity of the role of UNPOL, in 2011, OIOS was asked by the Secretary-General to review the overall role of UNPOL in UN peacekeeping and develop a strategic framework.[12] After years of consultation with Member States and PCCs, OIOS developed the Strategic Guidance Framework which was approved by the Secretary-General in 2014.[13] The Strategic Guidance Framework is a set of policies and guidelines that was proposed to assist UN police officers in identifying their duties within the overall peacekeeping structure. Similar to all

8 *United Nations Security Council Resolution 1244* (1999).

9 *United Nations Security Council Resolution 1410* (2002).

10 https://peacekeeping.un.org/en/data.

11 *United Nations General Assembly Resolution 60/268* (2006).

12 Office of Internal Oversight Services, *Review of the logical frameworks underlying selected aspects of United Nations peacekeeping operations*, 28 August 2015, Assignment No IED-15-007.

13 Ibid.

other peacekeeping doctrines and policies, the Strategic Guidance Framework lacks any legal or operational guidance, particularly to the division of tasks and an interpretation of the protection mandate. Nevertheless, in 2014 the Security Council handed down the first resolution regarding UNPOL, mandating "to include, as appropriate, policing as an integral part of the mandates of United Nations peacekeeping operations."[14]

Although the Secretary-General has repeatedly called for UN police officers to receive adequate training,[15] it has been reported that nearly 70% of individual police officers (*IPOs*) deployed do not receive any prescribed training from their PCC.[16] As UN police officers recruited for protection of civilians missions are mostly generalists, they do not receive any specific protection training.[17] While police officers are trained in general domestic protection activities this would differ to their expected function in peacekeeping. As outlined in Chapter 2, the interpretation of protection must come from the Security Council's mandate, therefore UN police officers cannot rely on their PCC's domestic codes for interpretation of protection tasks. Furthermore, police officers are not generally trained in protection during armed conflict, particularly the protection of IDPs and IDP camps.

In spite of calls to clarify the role of UNPOL, particularly the division of mandated tasks, the Security Council has yet to clarify UNPOL's role in the protection of civilians mandate. Without an indication of UNPOL's function in the protection regime, tension and miscoordination has been reported between the military and police components.[18] As the protection of civilians mandate is better served with the coordination of all components of a UN peace mission,[19] there is growing demand for an established framework to clarify the application of the protection mandate to UNPOL, specifically regarding the use of force.[20] In response to the growing confusion, the HIPPO report recommended

---

14 *United Nations Security Council Resolution 2185* (2014) at operational paragraph 1.

15 United Nations General Assembly and Security Council, *Sexual Violence in Conflict: Report of the Secretary-General*, UN Doc A/67/792-S/2013/149 at paragraph 4; Also see *United Nations Security Council Resolution 1820* (2008) at operational paragraph 12.

16 Sofia Sebastián, 'The Role of Police in UN Peace Operations' (2015) (3) *Civilians in Conflict Policy Brief* at 14.

17 External Review of the Functions, Structure and Capactiy of the UN Police Divison, 31 May 2016 at IV.

18 OIOS Report, above note 3 at paragraph 28.

19 *United Nations Security Council Resolution 2185* (2014) at operational paragraph 2.

20 United Nations General Assembly and Security Council, *The Future of United Nations Peace Operations: Implementation of the Recommendations of the High-level Independent Panel on Peace Operations*, 17 June 2015, UN Doc A/70/357-S/2015/682 (*HIPPO Report*).

that the "Secretariat should complete the strategic guidance framework on UN policing currently under preparation and propose commensurate resources for its implementation".[21] Although, DPO and SPC are both engaged in creating differing policies and doctrines, there still remains variance around UNPOL's function in the overall protection regime, and the legal framework governing those activities.

The role of local police in society centres around the police's function as an agent of the State and local authorities. Bittner, in his sociological works on the role of the police, suggests that definition of the police should be examined through their use of force, specifically the use of that force on behalf of the State.[22] Although the responsibilities of the police is not dependent on the use of force, as argued by Bittner, coercive force is always symbolically present and allows them to perform their duties.[23] Thus, an extension of this use of force is the police are only called upon when an individual is engaged in an activity that the State has prohibited or regulated.[24] Although the theory of policing has been discussed and debated by sociologists in a number of different ways,[25] Bittner's interpretation still remains prominent within the sociological community.[26]

As UN police officers are mandated by the Security Council and not the State, the role of UNPOL remains vague, especially with regards to their connection to local communities. For this reason, the Security Council initially mandated UNPOL to assist and work alongside with local police authorities, rather than undertaking police enforcement on their own.[27] As UNPOL was only to operate as a support function of local authorities, their authority would be granted to them by association with local communities.

Nevertheless, as UN peace missions have been mandated to protect civilians no matter the source of the threat,[28] the relationship between UNPOL and

21 United Nations General Assembly and Security Council, *Report of the High-level Independent Panel on Peace Operations on Uniting Our Strengths for Peace: Politics, Partnership and People*, UN Doc A/70/95-S/2015/446 at UNPOL recommendation 3.

22 Egon Bittner, *Aspects of Police Work* (Northeastern University Press, 1990).

23 Ibid at 131.

24 Ibid.

25 An example, of an opposing theory to Bittner, see Jean-Paul Brodeur, *The Policing Web* (Oxford University Press, 2010).

26 Trevor Jones and Trevor Newburn, *Private Security and Public Policing* (Clarendon Press-Oxford University Press, 1998) at 248–249.

27 *United Nations Security Council Resolution 143* (1960) at operational paragraph 2.

28 *United Nations Security Council Resolution 2156* (2014) at operationa paragraph 8; *United Nations Security Council Resolution 2304* (2016) at operational paragraph 5.

local police has become strained. As UNPOL is increasingly mandated to participate in the protection activities, guidance on the role on UNPOL is drastically needed. Moreover, as local authorities are not present in some high-risk areas, UNPOL can no longer rely on the State for legitimacy in the perception of the local community.

As discussed in Chapter 2, consent of a host State to a UN peace mission is not a clear assessment, as there are varying levels of consent that manifests in practice. Although the consent is granted before the deployment of a UN peace mission, this consent can be weakened through the actions of the host State or local authorities. For example, while the host State can agree with the deployment of UN peacekeepers, they may not agree with their mandated task, as was evidenced by South Sudan in 2016.

One major hindrance that occurs is when UN equipment and personnel are blocked by local authorities. For example, in March 2017, a total of 182 UN shipments were detained at customs in Sudan, with the government approval taking at times over a year, affecting UN efficiency on the ground.[29] Also in South Sudan, after the outbreak of civil conflict in 2013, the government restricted the movements of UNMISS, not allowing them to patrol high risk areas.[30]

Furthermore, although the host government might consent, this consent may not translate down to local soldiers and authorities. For example, although the South Sudanese government had reached an agreement with the UN on UNMISS' mandate, in July 2015, SPLA (South Sudanese local forces) launched "rocket-propelled grenades and heavy machine guns south of Malakal, rendering the [UN] engine and communication equipment of the barge temporarily inoperable."[31] This issue of consent becomes problematic for UNPOL, as UN police officers philosophically represent the 'rule of law' of the State. When the connection between the host State and the UN peace mission is severed, UN police officers are required to function in legal and theoretical isolation.

As UN peace missions are becoming more complicated in nature, UNPOL has been required to participate in protection activities beyond their initially mandated tasks of training and monitoring, as first envisaged in the 1960s. With the introduction of peace missions primarily mandated to protect civilians, UNPOL, as part of these missions, is also required to engage in protection

29 United Nations Security Council, *Report of the Secretary-Genereal on the African Union-United Nations Hybrid Operations in Darfur*, S/2017/250 at paragraph 34.

30 Sofia Sebastián and Aditi Gorur, *UN Peacekeeping & Host-State Consent: How Missions Navigate Relationships with Governments* (Stimson Center, 2017) at 23.

31 United Nations Security Council, *Report of the Secretary-General on South Sudan*, S/2015/655 at paragraph 65.

objectives. Without a coherent framework from the Security Council, "[m]andate implementation is at times hindered by inconsistent planning and unrealistic operational recommendations."[32] Though the Secretary-General in his 2016 report on UNPOL defined the functions of UN police officers as "a function of governance responsible for the prevention, detection and investigation of crime; the protection of persons and property; and the maintenance of public order and safety",[33] UN police officers are now mandated to engage in the prevention and response to sexual and gender-based violence, assisting in countering violent extremism, and building the rule of law.[34]

With the expanding nature of UNPOL mandates, it is important to distinguish between the 3 different categories of police officers – IPOs; Formed Police Units (*FPUs*); and Specialised Police Teams (*SPTs*). IPOs are considered the traditional UN police officer, and thus, are normally unarmed. IPOs are deployed for community-orientated policing, that being, investigations and information-gathering, and training and monitoring. IPOs were predominately deployed in traditional peacekeeping and seen as the traditional form of UNPOL. Conversely, FPUs are made up of 120 to 140 well-armed officers, deployed to provide "security support to United Nations operations by ensuring the safety and security of United Nations personnel and assets; contributing to the protection of civilians; and supporting police operations that require a formed response."[35] Members of FPUs are predominately paramilitary police using more robust means to control crowds and protect UN personnel and facilities. Between 2003, UN peace missions started to rely heavily on FPUs, specifically with the protection mandate.[36] The final category of SPTs have received little detail, other than they are a group of experts in special weapon and tactics, close protection units or forensics.[37] When examining the protection of civilians mandate, the majority of tasks are assigned to FPUs; however, with the growing nature of peacekeeping, demands for IPOs to also undertake protection activities is becoming more prominent.

32 Secretary-General Report on UNPOL, above note 6 at paragraph 32.

33 Ibid at paragraph 7.

34 Kari M Osland, 'UN Policing: The Security-Trust Challenge' in Cedric de Coning and Mateja Peter (eds), *United Nations Peace Operations in a Changing Global Order* (Palgrave Macmillian, 2018) at 191–192.

35 United Nations Department of Peacekeeping and Department of Field Support Policy (Revised) on *Formed Police United in United Nations Peacekeeping Operations* (1 March 2010) at paragraph 8.

36 William J Durch and Michelle Ker, 'Police in UN Peacekeeping: Improving Selection, Recruitment, and Deployment' (2013) *6 Providing For Peacekeeping* at 7.

37 https://police.un.org/en/specialized-police-teams.

2 Protection of Civilians Mandate for UNPOL

While UN police officers are expected to engage in protection activities, conversely, the current UNPOL structure does not anticipate this 'new' task of protection of civilians. Distinctively, the current UNPOL model does not differentiate between the two major UNPOL mandates – the protection of civilians mandate and the mandate to restructure and develop host State capabilities.[38] As evidenced in field reports, some UN police officers do not believe that the Security Council protection mandate applies to them;[39] further, it is perceived that all language under Chapter VII of the UN Charter is considered to only apply to the military component of the Mission.[40]

In order to highlight the centrality of protection of civilians in UNPOL functions, in *Resolution 2185* (2014) the Security Council affirmed "the central role of the protection of civilians, where mandated, in the work undertaken by United Nations Police Components."[41] The Security Council further confirmed UNPOL's role in the protection mandate "where mandated, in supporting the efforts of host authorities in the protection of civilians, particularly those under imminent threat of physical violence, including all forms of sexual and gender based violence."[42] Although protection of civilians is a central role in UNPOL, it was made clear within *Resolution 2185* that the protection mandate applies differently to UNPOL in comparison to their military counterparts. The Security Council in *Resolution 2185* qualifies the protection of civilians mandate for UNPOL with 2 caveats. Firstly, the Security Council reiterates that the protection of civilians is only to be undertaken by UNPOL "where mandated".[43] In contrast to the UN's Capstone Doctrine that identifies the 'protection of civilians' as one of the four cross-cutting themes that UN peace missions are expected to fulfil even when they are not explicitly mandated,[44] the Security

38 External Review of the Functions, Structure and Capactiy of the UN Police Divison, 31 May 2016 at VI.

39 Victoria K. Holt, Glyn Taylor and Max Kelly, *Protecting Civilians in the Context of UN Peacekeeping Operations: Success, Setbacks and Remaining Challenges*, Independent study jointly commissioned by the Department of Peacekeeping Operations and the Office for the Coordination of Humanitarian Affairs (2009) at 104.

40 Sebastián, above note 16 at 17.

41 *United Nations Security Council Resolution 2185* (2014) at operational paragraph 17.

42 Ibid at operational paragraph 18.

43 Ibid.

44 United Nations Department of Peacekeeping Operations and Department of Field Support, *United Nations Peacekeeping Operations: Principles and Guidelines*, 2008 (*Capstone Doctrine*).

Council has consistently emphasised that UNPOL must be explicitly mandated to protect civilians. Secondly, and more importantly, in *Resolution 2185*, UNPOL is to undertake the protection activities in supporting "the efforts of host authorities".[45] Conversely, in the Security Council *Resolution 2382* (2017) this 'supporting' language was disregarded; rather, the Security Council "recognizes the important role that United Nations Police Component can play, where and as mandated, in the protection of civilians, including in preventing and addressing sexual and gender based violence."[46] With *Resolution 2382*, the language of 'assisting' only remains in UNPOL's mandate in capacity-building of the host State.[47] Thus, with *Resolution 2382* the Security Council has severed the connection with local police enforcement, creating further uncertainty of the role UNPOL with the local communities, and their authority to use force outside the military scenario and the realm of armed conflict.

Although the Security Council has removed the second caveat from *Resolution 2382*, it is still considered by PCCs that UNPOL can only undertake protection activities, especially the use of force, in order to support or assist local authorities.[48] For example, UNMISS police officers have been reported to be uncertain "about whether and to what extend UN police may be allowed to take pre-emptive action to dissuade violence among IDPs seeking protection at UN bases."[49] As UN police officers have traditionally only engaged in protection activities with the support of local authorities, some host governments have assumed that UNPOL is deployed as an extension of their own police force. As illustrated with MINUSCA, the CAR government "at times seems to have interpreted the mandated urgent temporary measures as transforming United Nations police into the Government's operational arm for conducting sensitive arrests."[50]

In 2017, the former departments of DPKO with DFS published the Guidelines on *The Role of United Nations Police in Protection of Civilians*, and clarified that although,

> the host state has the primary responsibility for protecting civilians, in cases where the government is unable, unwilling or otherwise failing to do so, UN police in missions with POC mandates have both the authority

45 *United Nations Security Council Resolution 2185* (2014) at operational paragraph 18.

46 *United Nations Security Council Resolution 2382* (2017) at operational paragraph 6.

47 Ibid.

48 Interviews conduct in New York in January 2019.

49 Sebastián, above note 16 at 22.

50 Secretary-General Report on UNPOL, above note 6 at paragraph 38.

> and obligation to act independently to protect civilians under threat of physical violence, irrespective of the source of the threat, including through use of force.[51]

Although the Security Council has insisted that UNPOL use force regardless of the threat, as discussed in Chapter 2, because of the Security Council's use of 'supporting' language within peacekeeping mandates and the UN's emphasis on consent, UNPOL, like their military counterparts, still believe that the use of force can only be undertaken with the local authority's consent. More so, as police officers are intrinsically linked to the State, it becomes difficult for UN police officers to engage in law enforcement without State consent. As conceptualised by Bittner, the role of the police in society is to enforce the 'rules' of the State, therefore, force can only be used on behalf and with consent of the State.[52]

2.1 *Protection against Sexual and Gender-Based Violence*

As UNPOL is required to participate in protection of civilians, it is indistinct which tasks would fall in the realm of UNPOL, rather than their military counterparts. As both the military and police components are now mandated to protect civilians and to prevent violent threats, it becomes complicated "to maintain a clear understanding of the respective roles of the military and police."[53] However, when examining Security Council resolutions, UNPOL reports, and DPO's guidelines, UNPOL is consistently guided to focus their effort in the 'preventing and addressing sexual and gender based violence'.[54] Particularly, in the overarching resolutions on UNPOL, the Security Council has consistently emphasised the prevention and protection of sexual and gender based violence.[55]

As will be discussed in the next Chapter, when referencing sexual and gender-based violence in the protection mandate, this must be in context of armed conflict. This focus is a result of sexual violence becoming a culture within armed conflict, making women and children disproportionately

---

51 United Nations Department of Peacekeeping Operations and Department of Field Support, *Guidelines: The Role of United Nations Police in Protection of Civilians*, Ref 2017.12 at paragraph 13.

52 Bittner, above note 25 at 249.

53 Secretary-General Report on UNPOL, above note 6 at paragraph 40.

54 *United Nations Security Council Resolution 2382* (2017) at operational paragraph 6.

55 *United Nations Security Council Resolution 2185* (2014); *United Nations Security Council Resolution 2382* (2017).

targeted.[56] Under international law, sexual violence is not limited to rape, however includes a variety of violations related to conflict.[57] However, when examining Security Council resolutions, the prevention and protection of civilians against conflict-related violence encompasses two main mandated activities; patrolling and securing areas of risk, specifically IDP camps, and strengthening the rule of law through training and community engagement. While both the protection of conflict-related violence and IDP camps will be discussed in the next two Chapters, a primary task engaged by UNPOL to ensure protection in this area is detention of individuals. Although detention becomes a main task of UNPOL, it is unclear what authority they have under the law to detain individuals.

In order to assess the law that governs detentions made by peacekeepers, firstly it will have to be determined whether peacekeepers have the authority to even detain individuals. Then, secondly, it can be determined what legal framework applies to the conduct and treatment of the detainee.

3 Law Enforcement and Detention in UN Peace Missions

While the peacekeeping literature generally assess the use of force by peacekeepers under IHL, unless peacekeepers fall within the criteria of participating in an armed conflict, their engagement must be considered a form of law enforcement. As peacekeepers are engaging more in law enforcement, this raises the question of what legal authority do peacekeepers have to involve themselves in local law enforcement, and what body of law should regulate their activities?

As discussed previously, peacekeepers tend to only engage in these activities alongside local authorities or forces. Therefore, when arrests are made and weapons or contrabands are confiscated, peacekeepers tend to immediately return the individuals and contraband to local authorities so as not to overstep their authority.[58] However, local authorities are increasingly unable to assist due to their own administrative instability, forcing UN peace missions to deal with individuals without local support. For example, UNPOL in CAR have

56 United Nations Security Council, *Women and Peace and Security: Report of the Security-General*, UN Doc S/2009/465 at paragraph 13.

57 Ibid at paragraph 4; and as discussed in Chapter 4.

58 United Nations Security Council, *Report of the Secretary-General on the United Nations Organization Stabilization Mission in the Democratic Republic of the Congo*, S/2016/1130 at paragraph 32.

replaced the national police in most areas outside Bangui, and are mandated to take 'Urgent Temporary Measures' that include arrest and detention in the absence of local authorities.[59]

As the body of law that governs peacekeepers involvement in local law enforcement is indistinct, there is a lack of sufficient framework to guide their actions. While there are guidelines established by the DPO on the detention of individuals,[60] there is ambiguity over the UN's authority to involve themselves in law enforcement, and the consequences and obligations of those actions.

Although the UN has discussed the application of IHL within peacekeeping missions, specifically in the Secretary-General's Bulletin in 1999, the UN is yet to officially publish or specify the legal framework that applies to law enforcement within peacekeeping missions outside of IHL. The UN Office of Legal Affairs and DPO both consider that UN peacekeepers are only bound by their sanctioned mandate and are not bound by the IHRL principle of the right to life.[61] As Wills quotes in their interview with the UN Office of Legal Affairs:

> A person that would not be a military target under traditional IHL may become an authorized military target of a UN peacekeeping operation (and therefore killed) provided that: the peacekeepers' use of force is pursuant to an authorization in a Chapter VII mandate and is provided for in the mission's rule of engagement; that the use of force is proportionate to achieving the authorized objective; that minimum force is used; and that force is used only as a last resort. This framework applies across the board to all UN peacekeeping missions, regardless of whether the situation is one of armed conflict or not.[62]

Although the Security Council authorises peacekeepers to use force, this cannot extend to the use of force in domestic law enforcement, unless intended in the language of the resolution. Particularly, as domestic police are permitted

---

59 Charles T. Hunt, 'To Serve and Protect: The Role of UN Police in Protecting Civilians ' (2019) *Global Observatory* <https://theglobalobservatory.org/2019/09/to-serve-and-protect-the-role-of-un-police-protecting-civilians/>.

60 United Nations Department of Peacekeeping Operations and Department of Field Support, *Interim Standard Operating Procedures: Detention in United Nations Peace Operations*, 25 January 2010; the Detention SOP give practical guidance on how peacekeepers are to operate in detentions situations. For example, that individuals are to only be detained for 72 hours; the individual must be notified of reasons of their detention in their language; Detained individuals must have access to medical services and sanitary.

61 As quoted in interviews with UN departments, cited in Wills, above note 2 at 669–670.

62 As cited in ibid at 691.

to use force and detain individuals under the State's authority rather than under international law. The authority for UNPOL to participate in law enforcement is dubious as there is no indication from the Security Council or the UN Secretariat which legal framework will govern UNPOL.

As a minimum, when applying IHRL and law enforcement principles it is essential that UN police officers use the "minimum force required to counter the threat raised."[63] This would mean that UN police officers are to arrest and detain an individual instead of using lethal force. Further, any individual detained by UN peacekeepers must have all their rights respected and protected under the law. Interestingly, UN peace missions that are mandated to protect civilians are mandated to use "all necessary measures", however, as an international organisation, the UN cannot derogate from their obligations under IHRL unless in a State of emergency, as will be discussed in Chapter 6.

Although there exist uncertainties as to what body of law grants peacekeepers the authority to engage in local law enforcement, once an individual is detained peacekeepers must respect and adhere to their obligations under IHRL.

4 Detentions Made by Peacekeepers

Detention of individuals is the prominent law enforcement activity undertaken by UNPOL. As such a legal definition of 'detention' is essential in determining the status of a detained individual, and what obligations, if any, are owed to them. Although there is a clear definition and understanding of POW under international law, there is no equivalent for the status of 'detainees'.[64] In order for the existence of POW status to apply to a conflict, the conflict must be classified as an IAC. As stated in Chapter 3 when UN peacekeepers are engaged in armed conflict, that conflict would be classified as a NIAC. Consequently, the POW status and the associated obligations would not apply to individuals held by UN peacekeepers. Although there is literature on detentions in a NIAC,[65] not all detentions made by UN peace missions are associated with

63 Andrew Clapham, 'Protection of Civilians under International Human Rights Law' in Haidi Willmot et al (eds), *Protection of Civilians* (Oxford University Press, 2016) at 156.

64 Bruce Oswald, 'Detention by United Nations Peacekeepers: Searching for Definition and Categorisation' (2011) *15(1–2) Journal of International Peacekeeping* 118 at 132.

65 Ryan Goodman, 'The Detention of Civilians in Armed Conflict' (2009) *103(1) The American Journal of International Law* 48; Lawrence Hill-Cawthorne, *Detention in Non-International Armed Conflict* (Oxford University Press, 2016).

armed conflict, thus falling outside the realm of IHL. In order to fully assess the obligations owed to detainees and the law governing that detention, UN police officers need to look beyond IHL and create a holistic interpretation of 'detention' in UN peacekeeping.

Article 9(1) of ICCPR gives a starting point of detention, by stating that "no one shall be subjected to arbitrary arrest or detention. No one shall be deprived of his liberty except on such grounds and in accordance with such procedure as are established by law." Thus, according to the ICCPR detention is a deprivation of one's liberty in accordance with the law.

One of the few explicit definitions of 'detention' found in the law can be seen in the General Assembly's resolution *Body of Principles for the Protection of All Persons under Any Form of Detention or Imprisonment* (*Body of Principles*), which was adopted in 1988. Within the Body of Principles a 'detained person' is defined as "any person deprived of personal liberty except as a result of conviction for an offence."[66] The Working Group on Arbitrary Detention further clarified this definition in the Commission of Human Rights Resolution No. 1997/50, specifying that 'deprivation of liberty' is to be underpinned and governed by the obligations in IHRL.[67] As international laws do not always use the same terminology in reference to deprivation of liberty, it was concluded by the Commission on Human Rights that IHRL would be the interpreting and governing law for detentions[68] (unless IHL applies to that specific detention and thus takes precedence).

As the General Assembly's definition was targeted towards State detentions, it has been suggested by Oswald that when applying it to UN peace missions the element of 'consent' must be added to the classification. As many civilians willingly allow a limitation of their liberty to seek protection, these civilians should not be considered detainees. Thus, it can be surmised that within UN peace missions, the definition of 'detention' is "the deprivation of an individual's liberty by peacekeepers where the individual has not consented to that deprivation."[69] Consequentially, there is an element of 'belief' in the definition; a belief that the individual is not free to leave at any time. Therefore, if an individual is under the impression or believes that they do not have the right of

66 United Nations General Assembly, *Body of Principles for the Protection of All Persons under Any Form of Dentention of Imprisonment, Resolution 43/173*, 9 December 1988 at Use of Term (b).

67 Fact Sheet No. 26, The Working Group on Arbitrary Detention.

68 Ibid at Section IV subsection A.

69 Oswald, above note 64 at 135.

free movement, although in reality the peacekeepers would not hinder them, they would still fall under the definition of detainee.

It is important to note that the above definition assumes that an individual is automatically 'detained' the moment they are deprived of their liberty. In other words, the length of deprivation or its timing has no bearing on the classification of 'detention'. Thus, IHRL obligations are owed to an individual the instant they are deprived of their liberty. Finally, no individual can be deprived of liberty arbitrarily, thus UNPOL must have legal grounds and authority in detaining any individual, otherwise they would be in breach of their obligations under IHRL.

4.1 *Legal Grounds for Detention*

Outside the realm of IHL, only a territorial power is granted the authority to detain an individual under domestic laws.[70] Practically, although peacekeepers are not a territorial authority, they still detain individuals; however, there is no consensus on the legal authority peacekeepers have to detain individuals outside of an armed conflict.[71] As outlined in IHRL, individuals are not be deprived of their liberty "except on such grounds and in accordance with such procedure as are established by law."[72] Although it is a common practice, UNPOL cannot deprive an individual of their liberty without the legal grounds to do so, for without sufficient legal authority and justification, peacekeepers will be engaging in arbitrary detention and breaching their obligations under IHRL. Therefore, before outlining the body of laws that would govern the treatment of detainees, first it must be determined if peacekeepers *have* a legal authority to even detain.

If an individual is detained as a combatant in an armed conflict, then IHL must be considered as regulating the authority of that detention. As previously stated in an IAC, individuals are entitled to POW status per Article 4(A) of the Geneva Convention III and Article 43 of Additional Protocol I. Although the Geneva Conventions remain silent on detentions in a NIAC, as suggested by

70 Copenhagen Conference on 'The Handling of Detainees in International Military Operations', *Non-Paper on Legal Framework and Aspects of Detention*, of Foreign Affairs of Denmark, Legal Service, 4 October 2007, as annexed in 'The Copenhagen Processions – The Handling of Detainees in International Military Operations' (2007) *46 Mil L & L War Rev* 363 at 378.

71 Peter Vedel Kessing, 'Security Detention in UN Peace Operations' in Kjetil Mujezinović Larsen, Camila Guldahl Cooper and Gro Nystuen (eds), *Searching for a 'Principle of Humanity' in International Humanitarian Law* (Cambridge University Press, 2013) 272 at 273; Hill-Cawthorne, above note 65 at 193.

72 ICCPR at Article 9(1).

the ICRC, the Conventions do grant an implied right for States to detain individuals. It is maintained by the ICRC that as Common Article 3 of the Conventions makes explicit reference to detentions, consequently parties to a NIAC have an implied authority to detain.[73]

The recent 2014 UK High Court decision of *Serdar Mohammad v Ministry of Defence*[74] took an opposing view. The UK Court in their decision concluded that IHL does not confer any authority for a State to detain in a NIAC, and thus settled that any detention would go against the European Convention on Human Rights.[75] The Court reached this decision, as illustrated by the reasoning of Leggart J, that the Geneva Conventions do not explicitly mention the right of detention in a NIAC and States cannot rely on any implied right.[76]

However, the contention that the Geneva Conventions need to explicitly reference 'detention' goes against the established *Lotus* principle in international law.[77] As founded in the *S.S Lotus case*, unless a State is expressly prohibited from an action, they are legally allowed to do so.[78] However, it is unclear how the *Lotus* principle would apply to a NIAC and non-State actors or an international organisation. While the status of detainees in NIAC is contentious,[79] it is suggested that if peacekeepers award a status of detention to members of armed groups, expressly that detention is legal, belligerent groups will detain rather than fatally wound peacekeepers.[80]

Even if UNPOL cannot rely on IHL to detain, throughout the literature many academics have suggested that UN peace missions that are mandated to "use all necessary measures" have an implied authority to detain individuals in

73 International Committee of the Red Cross, *Internment in Armed Conflict: Basic Rules and Chanllenges*, Opinion Paper, November 2014.

74 Serdar Mohammed v Ministry of Defence [2014] EWHC 1369 (QB).

75 Ibid.

76 Ibid.

77 Hugh Handeyside, 'The Lotus Principle in ICJ Jurisprudence: Was the Ship Ever Afloat? (International Court of Justice)' (2007) 9(1) *Michigan Journal of International Law* 71.

78 *The Case of the S.S. Lotus (France v Turkey)*, PCIJ Judgment No.9, 7 September 1927 at paragraph 46; Also need literature on the Lotus principle.

79 Although some commentators have contended that customary international law now accepts the POW classification in both IAC and NIAC, however, this debate falls outside the scope of this thesis. For more on the debate please see, Hill-Cawthorne, above note 402; Gregory Rose and Bruce Oswald, *Detention of Non-State Actors Engaged in Hostilites: The Future Law*, International Humanitarian Law Series (Brill Nijhoff, 2016).

80 Andrew Clapham, 'Detention by Armed Groups under International Law' (2017) *93 International Law Studies* 1 at 3.

order to achieve and defend their mandate.[81] As the mandate 'to use all necessary measures' is generally interpreted to grant authority to use lethal force, it must also logically include all measures that are of a lesser means, such as operational detention.[82] However, the 'to use all necessary measures' language does not grant peacekeepers unchecked authority, rather is conditioned by their mandate. Therefore, the authority granted to peacekeepers must be read in context of the mandated language and is confined to the priorities and tasks assigned by the Security Council in each specific resolution. And as such the 'to use all necessary measures' wording is not intended to be an open authority for UNPOL.

Additionally, the authority to 'use all necessary measures' is legally too vague, and thus, does not give peacekeepers authority to deprive individuals of their liberty.[83] Unless the Security Council has explicitly mandated peacekeepers the authority to detain individuals, they have no legal authority to do so.[84] For example, MINUSCA has been mandated to 'use all necessary measures' to protect civilians, however in *Resolution 2387* (2017) MINUSCA has also been explicitly mandated "to arrest and detain in order to maintain basic law and order and fight impunity."[85] If MINUSCA has the authority to detain under the 'all necessary measures' mandate, then it would not be necessary for the Security Council to explicitly mandate the authority to also detain. Further, in comparison to UNMIK and UNMISET, the Security Council has mandated UNPOL "to give full effect" of "Public Security and Law Enforcement",[86] granting them authority to detain.

While UNPOL is not explicitly mandated to detain individuals, the DPO does instruct that UN police officers are authorised to detain individuals to protect civilians from threats of violence.[87] However, DPO guidelines are not legal documents and do not give legal authority for peacekeepers to detain. Nevertheless, detentions can be implied as an activity to protect civilians from

81 Kessing, above note 71 at 294; Bruce 'Ossie' Oswald, 'Some controversies of detention in multinational operations and the contributions of the Copenhagen Principles' (2014) 95(891–892) *International Review of the Red Cross* 707 at 717.

82 Kessing, above note 71 at 470.

83 Rose and Oswald, above note 79 at 717; Terry Gill,, Dieter Fleck, William H. Boothby, and Alfons Vanheusden, *Leuven Manual on the International Law Applicable to Peace Operations* (Cambridge University Press, 2017) at 160.

84 Rose and Oswald, above note 79 at 714.

85 *United Nations Security Council Resolution 2387* (2017) at operational paragraph 42(e)(iii).

86 *United Nations Security Council Resolution 1410* (2002) at operational paragraph 4(b).

87 DPKO/DFS, *The Role of United Nations Police in Protection of Civilians*, 2017 at paragraph 14.

individuals causing conflict-related violence, and hence, is authorised by the Security Council.

Within the majority of situations, individuals are detained by UNPOL for 2 main reasons – security or in relation to criminal offences being committed.[88] If an individual is a security threat, to either the UN peace mission or to civilians, that individual will be able to be held under the implied authority of the protection of civilians mandate, specifically, UNPOL's mandate to create a 'secure environment'. Some commentators have also contended that even without the protection mandate, peacekeepers will be able to hold security detainees under the principle of self-defence.[89] Nevertheless, neither the protection mandate or self-defence covers detentions of individuals who have committed a criminal act or detained outside security grounds.

In executive mandated UN peace missions, such as UNMIK, UNPOL are granted the authority of law enforcement, "including the areas of public safety, investigations and the conduct of special operations."[90] Recently, MINUSCA has been mandated under 'temporary measures' "to coordinate international assistance to the justice and correctional institutions to reinstate the criminal justice system, within the framework of the United Nations global focal point on rule of law".[91] However, excluding MINUSCA, non-executive UN peace missions are not explicitly granted the authority to detain outside their obligation to protect. Although FPUs are authorised to engage in direct protection activities, in non-executive mandated missions, they "do not have the power to arrest, and have no authority or limited capability to maintain law and order."[92] While the DPO Guiding Principles on detention seem to imply an authority to detain individuals that threaten civilians with imminent violence, the Guiding Principles are silent on arrests for non-violent criminal offences in non-executive mandates.

Under a strict interpretation of the law, unless peacekeepers are explicitly mandated the authority to detain, peacekeepers can only detain for security and violent conflict-related crimes under the protection of civilians mandate.

88 Oswald, above note 64 at 146; Frederik Naert, 'The Legal Framework and Main Categories of Detainees' (2006) *45 Military Law & Law War Review* 51 at 59–60; Jelena Pejic, 'Procedural principles and safeguards for internment/administrative detention in armed conflict and other situations of violence' (2010) *87(858) International Review of the Red Cross* at 381.

89 Oswald, above note 64 at 146.

90 United Nations Department of Peacekeeping Operations and the Department of Field Support, *United Nations Police in Peacekeeping Operations and Special Political Missions*, February 2014 at 49.

91 *United Nations Security Council Resolution 2301* (2016) at operational paragraph 34(d)(v).

92 Sebastián, above note 16 at 22.

Essentially, as 'all necessary measures' are conditioned by the mandate, the authority to detain can only be exercised to achieve that mandate. As outlined so far, the protection of civilians mandate is the protection against direct attacks or conflict-related violence, therefore, peacekeepers can only detain individuals that have committed these acts. Although UN peace missions are not granted the explicit authority to detain alleged criminals, in practice, they still do so. For example, MONUSCO has conducted patrols in the Bunia area, arresting and detaining individuals to prevent criminal offences such as theft.[93] Further, UNMISS being the only authority in the PoC sites, have had to administer police authority to arrest and detain individuals committing criminal acts within the sites. Although UNMISS has left the dealings of minor crimes to the Chiefs Courts, UNMISS has solely dealt with major crimes such as murder and battery.

As the Security Council has not mandated the authority to detain, many commentators have suggested that the host State has granted peacekeepers a deferred power to detain individuals.[94] Although, the model SOFA or the MOU do not explicitly grant a UN peace mission the authority to detain alleged criminals, some commentators have contended that an authority is implied with the host State's consent to allowing peacekeepers to be deployed within their territory.[95] However, the host State has only consented to activities undertaken for the Mission to discharge their mandate, in other words, like the implied authority of the Security Council it will be bound to the protection of civilians mandates and will not cover domestic criminal detentions.

As UN peacekeepers are still engaging in criminal detentions, it remains contentious as to the legal framework defining the offence that the individual has committed. Problematically, in order for UNPOL to determine whether a criminal offence has occurred, they must first have a legal framework that outlines that offence. In previous instances, it is unclear under which legal structure has UNPOL based their authority to arrest. As UNPOL would be unsure of the host State's domestic criminal code, most arrests and detentions have occurred under a concept of 'natural law'.[96] As UNPOL is continually engaging

---

93 Bruce Oswald, 'Detention in Military Operations: Some Military, Political and Legal Aspects' (2007) 46 *Military Law & Law War Review* 341 at 315.

94 Bruce Oswald, 'The law on military occupation: answering the challenges of detention during contemporary peace operations?' (2007) 8(2) *Melbourne Journal of International Law* 311 at 315; Katarina Grenfell, 'Detention in United Nations Peace Operations' in Greogry Rose & Bruce Oswald (eds), *Detention of Non-State Actors Engaged in Hostilities* (Brill, 2016) 345 at 347.

95 Grenfell, above note 94 at 347.

96 Interview with UN Secretariat on 14 March 2019.

in criminal detentions, it would be advisable that UN police are trained in local criminal laws. Nevertheless, as UNPOL functions as an agent of the State, the grounds and procedures codified in domestic laws should be adhered to by UN police officers. However, in situations where there is insufficient guidance or a lack of domestic laws, UNPOL should rely on IHRL principles.

4.2 *Treatment of Security Detainees*

Once UN peacekeepers have detained an individual there is limited guidance to the treatment and procedure of that detainee. In contemporary UN peace missions, host States do not have fully functioning legal mechanisms to sufficiently investigate and prosecute detained individuals.[97] For even if peacekeepers have the authority to detain, the Security Council's mandate does not give UNPOL any guidance to the treatment and procedures after detention.[98]

Some commentators have contended that "all international detention standards in IHL and IHRL are superseded by the UNSC mandate pursuant to Article 103 of the UN Charter, and that UN forces may detain individuals in peace operations for prolonged periods of time without any form of review, simply by referring to the authorisation from the Security Council to use 'all necessary measures'."[99] Even if it is accepted that Article 103 of the UN Charter overrides IHRL obligations, there is no indication that the Security Council has intended this to be the case. As decided in *Al Jedda* case,[100] the language used within a resolution needs to "unambiguously" indicate that the Security Council intends to place Member States "under an obligation to use measures of indefinite internment without charge and without judicial guarantees, in breach of their undertakings under international human rights instruments including the Convention."[101] Therefore, the Court concluded that in "the absence of clear provision to the contrary, the presumption must be that the Security Council intended States ... to contribute towards the maintenance of security in Iraq while complying with their obligations under international human rights law."[102]

Accordingly, even *if* a UN peace mission is granted the explicit authority to detain, this authority does not override the obligations owed to that individual

97 Naert, above note 88 at 62.

98 Oswald, above note 81 at 717.

99 Kessing, above note 71 at 294.

100 *Case of Al-Jedda v The United Kingdom (Application no 27021/08)*, European Court of Human Rights, Grand Chamber, 7 July 2011.

101 Ibid at paragraph 105.

102 Ibid.

under IHL or IHRL. This position was supported by the UN Commissioner of Human Rights when investigating States involved in Libya in 2011. The Commissioner concluded that although these States were mandated to 'use all necessary measures' to protect civilians, detentions are still bound by the requirements and conditions found in customary international law.[103] This is further emphasised by UN reports that stress UN peace missions are to "promote and encourage respect for international humanitarian, human rights and refugee law."[104] Thus, once an individual has been legally or illegally detained, UN peacekeepers must still adhere to the law in the treatment of that individual.

Within an armed conflict, as previously discussed, UN peace missions cannot look to the POW rules for clarification on the expected treatment of detainees, hence, they must look at Common Article 3. When examining Common Article 3, the only guidance given to peacekeepers for the treatment of detainees is the prescribed minimum protection of 'humane treatment', with explicit protections against outrages upon personal dignity, and against cruel treatment and torture.

Nonetheless, the Geneva Conventions do not define or outline the operational meaning of 'humane' in regard to detentions.[105] Article 75 of Additional Protocol I does provide some clarification, by prohibiting:

(a) violence to the life, health, or physical or mental well-being of persons, in particular:
  (i) murder;
  (ii) torture of all kinds, whether physical or mental;
  (iii) corporal punishment; and
  (iv) mutilation.[106]

Furthermore, Additional Protocol II gives additional guidance by articulating the obligation for the access to health care, food and water, protection against

103 United Nations Human Rights Concil, *Investigation by the Office of the United Nations High Commissioner for Human Rights on Libya: detailed findings*, A/HCR/31/CRP.3 at paragraph 128.

104 United Nations General Assembly and Security Council, *Human Rights Due Diligence Policy on United Nations Support to Non-United Nations Security Forces*, UN Doc A/67/775-S/2013/110 at paragraph 1.

105 Yateesh Begoore, 'Prisoner Dilemma: Ascertaining and Augmenting the Multinational NIAC Detention Regime' in *Max Planck Yearbook of United National Law Online* (United Nations, 2017) vol 20, 436 at 447.

106 Additional Protocol I at Article 75(2)(a); according to International Committee of the Red Cross, *Study on Customary Interantional Humanitarian Law* (*Customary IHL Database*) Article 75 is considered part of customary international law.

armed conflict and the dangers associated with that conflict.[107] Additional Protocol II also stresses the freedom and protection of religion,[108] and the separation of men and women in different quarters.[109] Unfortunately, Additional Protocol II is not universally ratified by States, and would not apply consistently over UN peace missions. Moreover, for Additional Protocol II to be applicable, the conflict must reach a specific threshold, that is, only where "organized armed groups exercise control over a part of the State's territory so as to enable them to carry out sustained and concerted military operations."[110] Accordingly, Additional Protocol II would not be able to be applied as a standard throughout UN peace missions,[111] as not all detentions would occur in an armed conflict.

Although there is literature on detention in armed conflict, the majority of the work is focused on the distinction between an IAC and NIAC.[112] It is contended that as the UN is seen as the promotors and protectors of international law, peacekeepers should treat all security detainees as POWs, regardless of the classification of the conflict.[113] As outlined by the Secretary-General in his 1999 Bulletin, peacekeepers should treat detainees "in accordance with the relevant provisions of the Third Geneva Convention of 1949."[114] The Secretary-General references the Geneva Conventions with no mention or distinction between whether the classification of the conflict should influence this. Further, the Secretary-General in the Bulletin states that this treatment of detainees should "[w]ithout prejudice to their legal status."[115]

Although IHL functions as *lex specialis* during times of conflict, some commentators have contended that IHRL will function as *lex specialis* in detentions.[116] Once an individual has been detained, they are no longer participating in hostilities, classifying them as a civilian under the law. Although

---

107 Addtional Protocol II at rule 118.

108 Ibid at rule 127.

109 Ibid at rule 119.

110 Ibid at Article 1.

111 For example, Sandesh Sivakumaran, *The law of non-international armed conflict* (Oxford University Press, 2012); Yoram Dinstein, *The Conduct of Hostilities under the Law of International Armed Conflict (3rd ed)* (Cambridge University Press, 2016).

112 For example, see Murphy, above note 53; Tristan Ferraro, 'The applicability and application of international humanitarian law to multinational forces' (2014) *95(891–892)* *International Review of the Red Cross* 561.

113 Kessing, above note 71 at 284.

114 United Nations, *Secretary-General's Bulletin: Observance by United Nations Forces of International Humanitarian Law*, UN Doc ST/SGB/1999/13 at Section 8.

115 Ibid at Section 8.

116 Kessing, above note 71 at 288.

IHRL becomes the governing law, there still needs to be a balance between the obligations under IHRL and the necessities under the protection mandate. While IHL identifies and balances operational necessity against protection of civilians, this is not clearly expressed in IHRL.[117] Although IHRL sets out obligations to individuals detained by authorities, it does not clearly envisage or intend to regulate detentions made by UN peacekeepers and multi-national forces. As the application of IHRL cannot be assessed in the same manner in peace as amidst conflict, the "application of human rights norms must be contextualised."[118] For example, IHRL does not give any indication on the place of detention holding areas, and their distance from areas of armed conflict.[119] Furthermore, Article 9(3) of ICCPR stipulates that individuals detained on a "criminal charge shall be brought promptly before a judge or other officer authorised by law to exercise judicial power." However, as peacekeepers are deployed in 'failing States' it might not be possible to adhere to Article 9(3).

As there is a lack of operational guidance for the treatment of detainees in UN peace missions, in 2010 the former departments of DPKO and DFS issued an interim Standard Operating Procedures (*SOP*) to all UN peace missions on *Detention in United Nations Peace Operations*. The SOP on detentions was not intended to clarify or grant authority for UN peace missions to detain individuals, rather was only to apply "to Missions for which such authority has been mandated by the Security Council of the General Assembly."[120] The purpose of the SOP on detention was "to ensure that persons detained by United Nations personnel in United Nations peace operations ... are handled humanely and in a manner that is consistent with applicable human rights, humanitarian and refugee law, norms and standards."[121]

The SOP on detention sets out three main general principles that UN peace missions must adhere to. Firstly, detainees are to be either handed over to local authorities or released as soon as possible.[122] In order for peacekeepers not to

117 Copenhagen Conference on 'The Handling of Detainees in International Military Operations', *Non-Paper on Legal Framework and Aspects of Detention,* of Foreign Affairs of Denmark, Legal Service, 4 October 2007, as annexed in 'The Copenhagen Processions – The Handling of Detainees in International Military Operations' (2007) *46 Mil L & L War Rev* 363 at 370.

118 Ömar Faruk Direk, *Security Detention in International Territorial Administrations: Kosovo, East Timor and Iraq* (Brill Nijhoff, 2015) at 90.

119 Tilman Rodenhäuser, 'Strengthening IHL protecting persons deprived of their liberty: Main aspects of the consultations and discussions since 2011' (2016) *98(903) International Review of the Red Cross* 941 at 944.

120 SOP, above note 60 at paragraph 2.

121 Ibid at paragraph 1.

122 Ibid at paragraph 7.

find themselves in a legal void, the SOP on detention envisaged that detainees should not be held by peacekeepers for longer than 72 hours.[123] The 72 hour rule can be breached if the host State has requested the Mission to do so, the Mission has been explicitly mandated to detain criminal offenders, or the Mission considers the extension of detention vital in carrying out their mandate. In other words, individuals can be held beyond 72 hours if the UN peace mission has legal grounds to do so. Secondly, the SOP stresses that detainees are entitled to their rights under international law.[124] However, the SOP does not give guidance on which rights are to apply and which can be derogated or limited during the times of conflict. Finally, the SOP reiterates that the 1999 Bulletin and its principles are to apply to detentions.[125]

While the former DPKO attempted to clarify detentions with the introduction of the SOP, there still remains confusion over a UN peace mission's obligation to detainees under the law. In response to this confusion, Denmark has attempted to create a soft-law approach to help establish some guidelines for UN peace missions. During Denmark's presidency of the Security Council in 2007, they set on the agenda the need for the Security Council to clarify a UN peace mission's expectation in regards to detention.[126] As nothing was finalised during their presidency, the Danish government began working with other Member States to establish a set of guidelines.[127] In October 2012, the *Copenhagen Process Principles and Guidelines* (*Copenhagen Process*), was drafted to apply in non-armed conflict detentions. Specifically, the Copenhagen Process was to apply to all UN peace missions that are mandated "to restore or maintain order."[128]

Although there remains contention on what obligations are owed to detainees, there are some accepted principles found in IHRL that are reiterated in the Copenhagen Process that would apply to UN peacekeeping. Firstly, under Article 7 of the ICCPR detainees are to be treated humanely, including a prohibition on torture and other cruel and degrading treatment.[129]

Secondly, under Article 9 of the ICCPR the individual has the right to be informed of their detention and reasons for their detention.[130] Expanding the

123 Ibid at paragraph 73.
124 Ibid at paragraph 8.
125 Ibid at paragraph 9.
126 Oswald, above note 81 at 15.
127 Ibid.
128 The Copenhagen Process Principles and Guidelines at Commentary paragraph 1.2.
129 ICCPR at Article 7.
130 Ibid at Article 9; The Copenhagen Process at Principle 7.

right under Article 9, the Copenhagen Process includes a right to explain what this detention means (delivered in their own language), in order to enable the detainee to participate or raise grounds for the review of their detention.[131] However, it remains unclear the mechanism in appealing that detention with UN peacekeeping.

Thirdly, under Principle 7 of the Copenhagen Process all detentions must be recorded and registered by the UN peace mission.[132] This is to ensure that UN peacekeepers can be held accountable for the treatment of the detainees. The UN currently does not appear to have a formal procedure in reporting to the public or the ICRC of the number of individuals detained at any given time.[133] The Copenhagen Process obliges peacekeepers, even in a NIAC, to inform the ICRC of all detentions and to provide them access to the detainees.[134]

Fourthly, under Article 11 of ICESCR detainees need adequate access to food and water, and health care. The Copenhagen Process takes this right one step further and contends that a detainee has a right for "access to open air" and "protection against the rigours of the climate and the dangers of military activities."[135]

Fifthly, taken from the conditions of POWs in IHL, it is suggested that detainees have a right to access their families.[136] Conversely, the Copenhagen Process places a caveat that this right is "subject to reasonable conditions relating to maintaining security and good order in the detention facility and other security considerations."[137]

Finally, detainees have a right of internal review of their detention, if they are detained for security reasons,[138] or have proceedings initiated against them, if they are accused of committing a criminal offence.[139]

While the majority of rights in the Copenhagen Process are merely reflections of Articles 9 and 10 of the ICCPR, there are some expansions to those articles. Specifically, the Copenhagen Process mimics certain safeguards entrenched in IHL, such as registration with the ICRC and access to family. These extensions to the ICCPR imply that drafting States have assumed that UN peacekeepers will be functioning in the realms of IHL and armed conflict.

131 The Copenhagen Process at Commentary 7.1.
132 Ibid at Principle 8.
133 Oswald, above note 64 at 124.
134 The Copenhagen Process at Principle 11.
135 Ibid at Principle 9.
136 Pejic, above note 88 at 389.
137 The Copenhagen Process at Principle 10.
138 Ibid at Principle 12.
139 Ibid at Principle 13.

However, local police enforcement, not being participants in hostilities, will not be functioning within the IHL framework, consequently, there would exist two different legal structures – local police and UNPOL. That being said, the Copenhagen Process is based on the assumption that detainees will not be held indefinitely but transferred to local authorities promptly.

5 Transferring and Releasing Detainees

The obligations outlined by the Copenhagen Process do not seem onerous to Member States, as UN policies on detentions envisage that individuals will be transferred to local authorities as quickly as possible.[140] However, the transfer of detainees is based on the assumption that local authorities have the legal structure in place to deal with these individuals. As the majority of host States are experiencing civil conflict, the governments of these States may not have effective control over certain territories. Moreover, under international law, UNPOL cannot transfer an individual if they have a belief that they would not be treated humanely.[141] Although the UN reiterated the principle of non-refoulement, it does not give guidance on what UN peace missions are to do with individuals that cannot be transferred to local authorities.

5.1 *The Principle of Non-refoulement*

As the first reference of 'non-refoulement' appears in Article 33 of the Refugee Convention, the concept is generally considered tied to refugee law, however, non-refoulement is also entrenched in IHL and IHRL. Under the principle of non-refoulement, peacekeepers cannot transfer detainees to local authorities if they have the belief that those individuals would be treated inhumanely or that they are at risk of torture.[142]

Since the Refugee Convention the principle of non-refoulement is explicitly mentioned in numerous human rights instruments.[143] The principle of non-refoulement was further reiterated by the UN Human Rights Committee

140 SOP, above note 60.

141 Although non-refoulement is not stated expressly in a NIAC, the ICRC have suggested that the transfer of a detain with the belief that they would not be treated humanely would be a violation of Common Article 3, see International Committee of the Red Cross, *Study on Customary Interantional Humanitarian Law* (*Customary IHL Database*).

142 Scott Sheeran and Stephanie Case, *The Intervention Brigade: Legal Issues for the UN in the Democractic Republic of the Congo* (International Peace Institute, 2014) at 3.

143 Convention against Torture and Other Cruel, Inhuman or Degrading Treatment or Punishment, adopted by General Assembly resolution 39/46 of 10 December 1984 at

that expressed that States parties of the ICCPR have a duty not to deport or expel an individual in their control "where there is a real risk of irreparable harm, such as the contemplated by articles 6 and 7 of the Covenant."[144] Notwithstanding IHRL, during times of armed conflict Common Article 3 of the Geneva Conventions obliges that civilians "shall in all circumstances be treated humanely", and so it is contended that a State would be in breach of their IHL obligations in transferring an individual that they believe would be treated contrary to Common Article 3.[145]

In order for UN peace missions to ensure their obligations under the principle of non-refoulement, UN peace missions will attempt to sign a memorandum of understanding (*MOUs*) with the host State to give reassurances that transferees will be treated humanely. While the MOUs help to identify a host State's obligations and understanding under the law, the MOUs do not relieve a UN peace mission's obligation under the law. Although a host State has signed a MOU, peacekeepers will still need to make an individual assessment with each transfer.[146] Once the assessment has been made, an individual is then able to be transferred to the local authorities, it is to be noted that there is no obligation under the principle of non-refoulement to keep monitoring a detainee post-transfer.[147] However, peacekeepers will be obliged under the protection of civilians mandate to monitor and report the treatment of detainees under local authorities. Still, it is unclear what UNPOL or military peacekeepers can do if they have belief that a transferee is now being tortured by local authorities, other than monitoring and reporting the incident to UN headquarters.

In situations where a UN peace mission cannot transfer an individual to local authorities, detained individuals are found in a legal void. When a host State cannot give reassurances that individuals will be treated humanely, detainees are held by peacekeepers indefinitely. This problem is illustrated by the situation in South Sudan, where UNMISS has no legal authority to prosecute criminal offences, yet the South Sudanese government had refused to agree and sign

Article 3; International Convention for the Protection of All Persons from Enforced Disappearance, adopted by the General Assmebly by resolution A/RES/61/177 at Article 16.

144 United Nations Human Rights Committee, *General Comment No. 31 Nature of the General Legal Obligation Imposed on States Parties to the Covenant*, 26 May 2004, UN Doc: CCPR/C/21/Rev.1/Add.13 at paragraph 12.

145 Cordula Droege, 'Transfers of Detainees: Legal Framework, Non-Refoulement and Contemporary Challenges' (2008) *90(871) International Review of the Red Cross* 669 at 674–675.

146 Ibid at 694.

147 Oswald, above note 81 at 719.

a MOU on treatment of detainees.[148] As the government has still refused to guarantee that detainees would not face the death penalty, detainees are held by UNMISS indefinitely.[149] Consequently, UNMISS is forced to create ad hoc holding cells within the PoC sites, where some individuals were held for more than a year.[150] Although UNMISS has clearly breached their obligation under Article 9 of ICCPR, they are denied any other operational option but to hold these individuals indefinitely.

With on-going conflict, UN peace missions are holding more individuals where host State's cannot guarantee human rights standards. Consequently, when host States are known to torture and execute prisoners, insurgents refuse to surrender to local forces, but rather surrender to peacekeepers who have better human rights standards. As reported in the DRC, armed rebels try "to surrender to the UN forces, rather than government authorities, including due to fears of being tortured or harmed by the FARDC."[151] In these situations, peacekeepers cannot transfer individuals under the principle of non-refoulement, meaning that they will be holding the individuals for longer than the anticipated 72 hours, even though they do not have the legal authority to do so.

More importantly, part of the Security Council's obligation to 'promote and protect' human rights is to ensure that UN peace missions respect the rights of all individuals, specifically those within their control. Consequently, by holding individuals indefinitely not only are they breaching their obligations under Article 9 of the ICCPR, but under the protection of civilians mandate.

6 Conclusion

As established thus far the mandate to protect civilians places a legally binding obligation on the UN, TCCs and the host State, to protect legal rights of civilians. While the primary focus of the protection mandate is the protection against physical violence, which may trigger the application of IHL and its obligations, UN peacekeepers must also undertake activities outside the realm

148 Eli Stamnes, *Policy Brief: The United Nations Mission in the Republic of South Sudan (UNMISS): Protecting Civilians in a Volatile Environment* (Norwegian Institute of Internatioanl Affairs, 2015) at 3.

149 Ray Murphy, 'The United Nations Mission in South Sudan and the Protection of Civilians' (2017) 22(3) *Journal of Conflict and Security Law* 367.

150 Sebastián, above note 16 at 23.

151 Sheeran and Case, above note 142 at 12.

of armed conflict. Specifically, in order to protect against physical violence, UNPOL will continually engage in law enforcement activities.

As the UN has failed to discuss the legal framework guiding and interpreting UN law enforcement, UNPOL is operating in a legal vacuum when detaining individuals. Although detaining individuals indefinitely is a breach of Article 9 of the ICCPR, peacekeepers are limited in other operational avenues as the transfer detainees would be a breach of the principle of non-refoulement. On the other hand, if they release the individual, they would be in breach of their obligation to protect civilians.

The Security Council and UN need to establish operational and legal guidelines when detainees cannot be transferred to local authorities within the prescribed 72 hours. Without clear legal guidelines peacekeepers will continue to function without a legal structure, and in breach of their obligations under IHRL.

However, whether individuals are detained legally or illegally, peacekeepers are still obliged to respect, protect and fulfil the rights of individuals under their control, which will be discussed further in Chapter 6. For though detentions are occurring outside a legal structure, they have become the main avenue in the protection of women and children from conflict-related violence.

In order to complete a holistic picture of the content of the obligation to protect, the next two chapters will look at the two differing groups identified by the Security Council for needing special attention. Essentially, an examination of the content of the obligation discussed thus far needs to be evaluated via these specific groups.

CHAPTER 5

The Protection of Women and Children

With the increase of the scope of the protection of civilians mandate, as discussed in Chapter 2, the Security Council has begun to identify specific groups of civilians that are regarded as 'vulnerable' and require explicit protection. In the Secretary-General's first report on the protection of civilians in armed conflict, he identified three general groups that require the Security Council's 'special' consideration, particularly, women, children, and IDPs.[1] Since the Secretary-General's recommendation that "special protection and assistance requirements of children and women are fully addressed in all peacekeeping and peace-building operations",[2] the Security Council has identified women and children explicitly when mandating UN peace missions.

Since 2003 the Security Council has mandated that peacekeepers give particular attention to women and children when planning and implementing protection activities. The Security Council has explicitly mandated for the protection against sexual and gender-based violence, and child recruitment. Other than focusing the attention of peacekeepers on these issues relating to women and children, it is unclear whether this is an extension of the standard protection mandate, or rather a clarification.

It is concluded in this chapter that the Security Council mandates the protection of women and children under their authority to maintain international peace and security, therefore, implying that this form of protection is in connection to the harms associated with armed conflict. Therefore, peacekeepers are obliged to protect women and children from conflict-related violence, including sexual and gender-based violence, and the recruitment of children. While peacekeepers are to use their physical presence and the use of force to protect woman from sexual and gender-based violence, they are to take a 'support role' in the Disarmament, Demobilisation and Reintegration (*DDR*) of child soldiers.

As discussed in the previous Chapter, individuals under the control of peacekeepers will be owed obligations under IHRL. Thus, children that are captured by peacekeepers are owed the respect, protection, and fulfilment of their rights under the *Conventions on the Rights of the Child* (*CRC*). When peacekeepers

1 United Nations Security Council, *Report of the Secretary-General to the Security Council on the Protection of Civilians in Armed Conflict*, UN Doc S/1999/957.

2 Ibid at recommendation 20.

 | DOI:10.1163/9789004707313_007

engage in infiltrating armed camps, they need to guarantee their obligations under IHL to women and children within these camps, particularly, to only target those civilians directly participating in hostilities. Further, their obligation to protect will encompass warranting that mechanisms are in place for any child soldier forcibly removed from these camps, to ensure the protection of their rights under the law.

In order to reach this conclusion, this chapter will firstly look at women and children as a vulnerable group and examine how they are perceived by the Security Council within the mandate. Secondly, an examination of women as a vulnerable group will be undertaken and the Security Council's focus on sexual and gender-based violence. Finally, the protection of children will be assessed with a focus on child soldiers and the protection afforded to them.

1 Women and Children as 'Vulnerable' Civilians

As women and children are "disproportionately targeted in contemporary armed conflicts and constitute the majority of all victims",[3] UN peace missions are to ensure that they prioritise them in mission strategies. Even though the Geneva Conventions afford women and children 'special' protections,[4] in current armed conflict women and children have become susceptible to unconventional forms of attacks not considered in the Conventions, "in particular sexual violence and exploitation."[5] In armed conflict women and children are not merely causalities of war, but are being targeted as a form of tactical warfare.

Currently in modern conflict, violence and exploitation are used as "a tactic of war in order to deliberately target civilians or as a part of a widespread or systematic attack against civilian populations" and "can significantly exacerbate situations of armed conflict and impede the restoration of international peace and security."[6] Therefore, the targeting of civilians has become

3 United Nations Security Council, *Report of the Secretary-General on Women, Peace and Security*, UN Doc S/2002/1154 at paragraph 6.

4 For example, Article 27 of the Fourth Geneva Convention, protecting women from attacks; Article 24 of the Fourth Geneva Convention, offering protection to children under the age of 15 not to be left alone; or Article 89 of the Fourth Geneva Convention to requires children under the age of 15 to be given additional food.

5 United Nations Security Council, *Report of the Secretary-General on Women, Peace and Security*, UN Doc S/2002/1154 at paragraph 7.

6 United Nations Security Council, *Women and Peace and Security: Report of the Security-General*, UN Doc S/2009/465 at paragraph 5.

a "weapon of war",[7] and hence has increased the violence against civilians to "unprecedented levels"[8] which has led "to dramatic increase of grave violations."[9] Thus, as emphasised by the Security Council and the reports of the Secretary-General, the attacks on women and children are being used by armed groups on a systematic basis.[10]

Shadowing the Secretary-General's report on protection of civilians,[11] the Security Council adopted *Resolution 1261* (1999) exclusively focusing on the effects of armed conflict on children. Within *Resolution 1261* the Security Council 'emphasised' that regarding issues of security in armed conflict the Council will "give special attention to the protection, welfare and rights of children."[12] In the following year, the Security Council adopted *Resolution 1325* (2000) giving consideration to the protection of women and girls against sexual violence in armed conflict, and that "where appropriate, field operations include a gender component."[13] *Resolution 1325* (unlike *Resolution 1261*) did not specifically mention the Security Council's intention to include 'protection' of women in UN peace missions, but rather that the Security Council is to "incorporate gender perspective into peacekeeping operations."[14] Further it was mandated in *Resolution 1325* that UN peace missions should "take into account gender considerations and rights of women."[15]

Not surprisingly, the Security Council did not identify how these protections or 'gender perspectives' would manifest operationally, yet have continued to include references to these resolutions in UN peace missions' mandates.[16] Notwithstanding this lack of clarification, *Resolution 1261* and *1325* did instigate dialogue on protection activities for women and children. In the following year in 2001, the Security Council passed *Resolution 1379* (2001), where it expressed

7 Ibid at paragaph 9.

8 United Nations General Assembly and Security Council, *Children and Armed Conflict: Report of the Secretary-General*, A/69/926-S/2015/409 at paragraph 11.

9 Ibid at paragraph 11.

10 United Nations Security Council, *Women and Peace and Security: Report of the Security-General*, UN Doc S/2009/465 at paragraph 5.

11 United Nations Security Council, *Report of the Secretary-General to the Security Council on the Protection of Civilians in Armed Conflict*, UN Doc S/1999/957.

12 *United Nations Security Council Resolution 1261* (1999) at operational paragraph 16.

13 *United Nations Security Council Resolution 1325* (2000) at operational paragraph 5.

14 Ibid at operational paragraph 5.

15 Ibid at operational paragraph 15.

16 For example *United Nations Security Council Resolution 2363* (2017) at operational paragraph 15; *United Nations Security Council Resolution 2387* (2017) at operational paragraph 42(a); *United Nations Security Council Resolution 2364* (2017) at operational paragraph 20(f).

"its readiness explicitly to include provisions for the protection of children, when considering the mandates of peacekeeping operations."[17] However, it was not until 2003 that the protection of women and children was explicitly mandated by the Security Council in a UN peace mission. In 2003, UNMIL was mandated to "contribute towards international efforts to protect and promote human rights in Liberia, with particular attention ... [to] women, children, and demobilized child soldiers."[18] Since 2003, the Security Council has frequently mandated the protection of human rights of women and children, commonly mandating peacekeepers to "monitor, help investigate and report to the Council" human rights violations associated with women and children.[19] The Security Council in 2011 expanded the protection of women and children by mandating the protection of women and children against physical threats and abuses.[20] Since 2011, the Security Council has regularly referenced 'women and children' when mandating UN peace missions "to take all necessary means" to protect civilians against physical threats.[21]

When mandating the protection of women and children, the Security Council mainly focuses on the protection from sexual and gender-based violence and the recruitment of child soldiers. Although women and children demand varying forms of protection, the Security Council generally ties the two groups together, by instructing UN peacekeepers "to provide specific protection for women and children affected by armed conflict."[22] This category of 'vulnerable civilians', that is, women and children, is also mirrored in the Security Council's mandates on the 'promotion and protection' of human rights.[23]

Even with multiple Secretary-General reports and Security Council resolutions on the protection of women and children, there is still no understanding

---

17 *United Nations Security Council Resolution 1379* (2001) at operational paragraph 2.

18 *United Nations Security Council Resolution 1509* (2003) at operational paragraph 3(l).

19 For example, *United Nations Security Council Resolution 2164* (2014) at operational paragraph 13(c), and *United Nations Secuirty Council Resolution 2149* (2014) at operational paragraph 30(e)(ii).

20 *United Nations Secuirty Council Resolution 2000* (2011) at operational paragraph 7(a).

21 See note 16.

22 *United Nations Security Council Resolution 2100* (2013) at operational paragraph 16(c)(ii); *United Nations Security Council Resolution 2164* (2014) at operational paragraph 13(a)(iii); *United Nations Security Council Resolution 2227* (2015) at operational paragraph 14(d)(iii).

23 Multiple resolutions for UNOCI reference this, the latest resolution being UNOCI at operational paragraph 19(g); other missions with similar references include *United Nations Security Council Resolution 2100* (2013) at operational paragraph 16(d); *United Nations Security Council Resolution 2164* (2014) at operational paragraph 13(c); *United Nations Secuirty Council Resolution 2149* (2014) at operational paragraph 30(e)(ii).

of the specific protections that peacekeepers are intended to provide outside of the general protection mandate. In *Resolution 1674* (2006) on the protection of children, the Security Council identified precise atrocities and attacks that women and children need protection from, including "(i) torture and other prohibited treatment, (ii) gender-based and sexual violence, (iii) violence against children, (iv) the recruitment and use of child soldiers (v) trafficking in humans, (vi) forced displacement, and (vii) the intentional denial of humanitarian assistance."[24] Even though the Security Council has identified distinct abuses that require peacekeeping attention, with multi-components of UN peace missions on the ground, there is an absence of how this is deciphered with each component.

More importantly, the Security Council is yet to identify which activities are intended for peacekeepers and which for the humanitarian community. As each UN peace mission is deployed in distinct conflicts, and working with differing humanitarian organisations, it is unclear the role peacekeepers play in the current humanitarian landscape. Indeed, this uncertainty and division was demonstrated in interviews, with the suggestion that peacekeepers should only engage in protection activities that protect against physical violence, such as sexual violence,[25] while other protection activities should be delegated to humanitarian actors. This is maintained by commentators even though, the "facilitation of humanitarian assistance"[26] is one of the mandated tasks of peacekeepers.

On a theoretical level, in regards to protection there is no agreement whether protection should be offered and implemented to women and children as a group or to individual civilians in need.[27] As there is no agreement or understanding on this concept, this "leads to inevitable fragmentation of responsibility that forces failure of protection."[28] Practically, this impacts whether UN peace missions are to merely react when it comes to women and children, such as police enforcement activities, or whether they are to take a strategic and pre-emptive stance in order to ensure protections for the overall 'group'.

24 *United Nations Security Council Resolution 1674* (2006) at operational paragraph 5.

25 Interview with POC researcher on 23 January 2019.

26 *United Nations Security Council Resolution 2363* (2017) at operational paragraph 15.

27 Carolyn Hamilton, 'Child Protection in Complex Emergencies' in Charles W Greenbaum, Philip Veerman and Naomi Bacon-Shnoor (eds), *Protection of Children During Armed Political Conflict: A Multidisciplinary Perspective* (Intersentia, 2006) at 291.

28 Ibid at 291.

2 Protection under the Maintenance of International Peace and Security

As the UN Charter does not explicitly authorise the Security Council to create peace missions, the Security Council's authority and power stems from their obligation founded in Article 24 of the UN Charter, which specifies that the Security Council has the primary responsibility to maintain international peace and security. As outlined in *Advisory Opinion on Certain Expenses*,[29] the ICJ (in deciding whether the expense of peacekeeping should be paid by the General Assembly), had to assess whether peacekeeping is a legitimate 'activity' of the organisation, in order to fall under Article 14 (II) of the UN Charter. The ICJ stated that the creation of a peacekeeping force must adhere to the 'purpose' of the UN under Article 1 of the UN Charter. The ICJ summed up the purpose of the UN into three main categories, noting that the:

> first two purposes as stated in paragraph 1 and 2, may be summarily described as pointing to the goal of international peace and security and friendly relations. The third purpose is the achievement of economic, social, cultural and humanitarian goals and respect of human rights. The fourth and last purpose is: "To be a center for harmonizing the actions of nations in the attainment of these common ends".[30]

Consequently, in mandating peacekeepers to protect civilians the Security Council has continually relied on the first purpose, that is, the maintenance of international peace and security.

Since the commencement of the protection regime, both the Security Council and the Secretary-General have repeatedly insisted that the protection of children and women is done primarily to ensure international peace and security. Thus, in *Resolution 1261*, the Security Council emphasised that it will consider the protection of children "when taking action at promoting peace and security"[31] and that "widespread impact of armed conflict on children and the long-term consequences this has for durable peace, security and development."[32] In a similar fashion, when adopting *Resolution 1325*, the Security Council identified that the prevention and action against sexual violence

29 *Certain Expenses of the United Nations (Article 17, Paragraph 2, of the Charter)*, Advisory Opinion of 20 July 1962, ICJ Reports 1962, p.151.

30 Ibid at 167–168.

31 *United Nations Security Council Resolution 1261* (1999) at operational paragraph 16.

32 Ibid at operational paragraph 1.

"significantly contributes to the maintenance of international peace and security."[33] Therefore, the targeting of women and children in conflict should no longer be considered a mere side-effect of that conflict, but rather "a front-line consideration."[34] Following *Resolutions 1261* and *1325*, the Security Council adopted numerous resolutions focusing on the specific themes of women and children within the Security Council's protection regime.[35]

The protection of women and children is therefore directly correlated to international peace and security; it can be thus inferred that this protection is connected to the circumstances of armed conflict and the threat to peace and security. However, while as stated in Chapter 2, the protection mandated is associated with armed conflict, some members of the UN Secretariat believe that the protection of women and children is to stand alone outside the realms of conflict.[36] It is maintained that as the Security Council mandates against 'sexual and gender-based violence', this is to be interpreted as all 'sexual violence', whether or not it is associated with armed conflict. However, from the Security Council's language there is a clear connection between protection of women and children, and armed conflict. For example, the Security Council mandated MINUSMA to "provide specific protection for women and children affected by armed conflict."[37]

Furthermore, in the overarching mandates on women and children, the Security Council consistently references protection in relation to armed conflict. For example, in *Resolution 1325* (2000) the Security Council recognised the importance "for specialized training for all peacekeeping personnel on the protection, special needs and human rights of women and children in conflict situations."[38] Although the Security Council is not always explicit in their language, their authority to mandate peace missions stems from their responsibility to maintain international peace and security, thus making 'international peace and security' the underlying foundation. Moreover, this connection to

33 *United Nations Security Council Resolution 1820* (2008) at operational paragraph 1.

34 United Nations Security Council, *Women and Peace and Security: Report of the Security-General*, UN Doc S/2009/465 at paragraph 8.

35 *United Nations Security Council Resolution 2100* (2013) at operational paragraph 16(c)(ii); *United Nations Security Council Resolution 2164* (2014) at operational paragraph 13(a)(iii); *United Nations Security Council Resolution 2227* (2015) at operational paragraph 14(d)(iii); *United Nations Security Coucil Resolution 2173* at operational paragraph 8(a); *United Nations Security Council Resolution 2155* (2014) at operational paragraph 4(a)(i).

36 Interview with UN Secretariat on 28 January 2019.

37 *United Nations Security Council Resolution 2364* (2017) at operatioal paragraph 20(c)(iii).

38 *United Nations Security Council Resolution 1325* (2000) at the preamble.

conflict was confirmed in DPO's CRSV Handbook, which is solely focused on 'conflict-related' violence.

However, this does not mean the violence or threat of violence has to occur by one of the parties to a conflict for peacekeepers to intervene. Rather peacekeepers are to protect against 'conflict-related' sexual and gender-based violence. Perpetrators of conflict-related violence do not have to be part of, or participating in, the conflict, rather "may include members of government armed force, paramilitary groups, non-State armed groups, peacekeeping personnel and civilians."[39]

Although conflict-related sexual and gender-based violence has a wide scope, practically, members of the UN Secretariat did not think that peacekeepers would have the resources to protect in any situations outside parties to a conflict and IDP camps.[40] Moreover, host States and TCCs that were interviewed believed that any interference in local criminal conduct, without local consent, would be a breach of the sovereignty of the host State.[41] As peacekeepers are mandated under the implied power of Article 24 of the UN Charter, protection must be tied to international peace and security, rather than domestic laws. Therefore, peacekeepers are only authorised to intervene in *conflict-related* sexual and gender-based violence.

3 The Protection from Conflict-Related Sexual Violence

Although the Secretary-General and the Security Council have identified multiple issues affecting women and girls in conflict, the major focus within the UN protection mandate is the prevention and response to sexual violence. Sexual violence is constantly mentioned as the primary protection activity, as "[s]exual violence as a tool of war can become a way of life: once entrenched in the fabric of civilian society, it lingers long after the guns have fallen silent."[42]

To that end, in 2009 the Secretary-General recommended that the Security Council "impose enforcement measures under Chapter VII of the Charter of the United Nations, contain provisions, as appropriate, on the prevention of,

39 Committee on the Elimination of Discrimination Against Women, *General Recommendation No. 30 on Women in Conflict Prevention, Conflict and Post-Conflict Situations*, 1 November 2013, UN Doc. CEDAW/C/GC/30.

40 Interviews conduct in New York in January 2019.

41 Interview with Pakistan on 23 January 2019; Interview with South Sudan on 22 January 2019.

42 United Nations Security Council, *Women and Peace and Security: Report of the Security-General*, UN Doc S/2009/465 at paragraph 14.

and response to, sexual violence, with corresponding reporting requirements to the Council."[43] In the same year the Security Council in *Resolution 1888* (2009) duplicated the language of the Secretary-General and mandated "its intention to ensure that resolutions to establish or renew peacekeeping mandates contain provisions, as appropriate, on the prevention of, and response to, sexual violence, with corresponding reporting requirements to the Council."[44]

While the Security Council has specifically mandated peacekeepers to protect women from all forms of sexual violence in multiple missions, it has yet to define what is considered 'sexual violence' and 'gender-based violence'. Under Article 27 of the Fourth Geneva Convention, and reiterated in Article 4 of Additional Protocol II, 'protected persons', specifically women are to be protected, "against any attack on their honour, in particular against rape, enforced prostitution, or any form of indecent assault." In the report of the Secretary-General on sexual violence in conflict, the Secretary-General defined sexual violence, duplicating Article 7(g) of the Rome Statute, as "rape, sexual slavery, forced prostitution, forced pregnancy, enforced sterilization and any other form of sexual violence of comparable gravity perpetrated against women, men or children with a direct or indirect (temporal, geographical or casual) link to a conflict."[45]

In international tribunal jurisprudence the definition of 'rape' was outlined in the *Akayesu* case, where the ICTR defined sexual violence as "any act of a sexual nature which is committed on a person under circumstances which are coercive."[46] In the later ICTY case of *Kunarac*,[47] the Tribunal considered rape as an act "which would render an act of sexual penetration non-consensual or non-voluntary on the part of the victim."[48] In the CRSV Handbook DPO reference the Secretary-General's definition of conflict-related sexual violence:

> The term "conflict-related sexual violence" refers to rape, sexual slavery, forced prostitution, forced pregnancy, forced abortion, enforced sterilization, forced marriage and any other form of sexual violence of

43 United Nations Security Council, *Report of the Secretary-General Pursuant to Security Council Resolution 1820*, UN Doc S/2009/362 at paragraph 56(c).

44 *United Nations Security Council Resolution 1888* (2009) at operational paragrah 11.

45 United Nations General Assembly and Security Council, *Sexual Violence in Conflict: Report of the Secretary-General*, UN Doc A/67/792-S/2013/149 at paragraph 5.

46 *The Prosecutor v Jean-Paul Akayesu*, International Court Tribunal for Rwanda, ICTR-96-4-T, 2 September 1998 at paragraph 598.

47 *Prosecutor v Dragoljub Kunarac, Radomir Kovac and Zoran Vukovic*, ICTY, IT-96-23-T & IT-96-23/1-T, 22 February 2001.

48 Ibid at paragraph 438.

> comparable gravity perpetrated against women, men, girls or boys that is directly or indirectly linked to a conflict. That link may be evident in the profile of the perpetrator, who is often affiliated with a State or non-State armed group, which includes terrorist entities; the profile of the victim, who is frequently an actual or perceived member of a political, ethnic or religious minority group or targeted on the basis of actual or perceived sexual orientation or gender identity; the climate of impunity, which is generally associated with State collapse, cross-border consequences such as displacement or trafficking, and/or violations of a ceasefire agreement. The term also encompasses trafficking in persons for the purpose of sexual violence or exploitation, when committed in situations of conflict.[49]

The law defines and establishes a framework to the 'crime' of sexual violence yet does not give guidance to the preventive and protective response needed regarding that crime. This is significant as peacekeepers need a legal prompt of when to respond to sexual violence, and more explicitly a 'threat' of sexual violence. Further, the Security Council not only mandates protection from sexual violence, but also gender-based violence. As stated in CEDAW General Recommendation No 30, conflict-related gender-based violence ranges from "arbitrary killings, torture and mutilation, sexual violence, forced marriage, forced prostitution and forced impregnation to forced termination of pregnancy and sterilization."[50]

In 2014, the Security Council first mandated that peacekeepers are to "report on sexual and gender-based violence",[51] but it was not until 2016 that the Security Council first mandated that peacekeepers "deter and prevent sexual and *gender-based violence* within its capacity and areas of deployment."[52] In the UNMISS mandate, peacekeepers are mandated to "deter, prevent and respond to sexual and gender-based violence, including by actively intervening to protect civilians threatened by, and survivors of, sexual violence, irrespective of its source"[53] Therefore, with the inclusion of 'gender-based violence', it is implied that peacekeepers obligations have expanded capturing a wider range of 'threats', outside the IHL definition of sexual violence.

49 United Nations Security Council, *Conflict-Related Sexual Violence: Report of the Secretary-General*, 29 March 2019, UN Doc. S/2019/280 at paragraph 4.

50 CEDAW, General Recommendation No 30.

51 United Nations Security Council Resolution 2173 (2014) at operational paragraph 24.

52 *United Nations Security Council Resolution 2327* (2016) at operational paragraph 7(v) – emphasis added.

53 *United Nations Security Council Resolution 2677* (2023) at operational paragraph 3(a)(ii).

In consideration of the prevention of gender-based violence, it is relevant to note Article 2(f) of the CEDAW, which obliges States "to take all appropriate measures, including legislation, to modify or abolish existing laws, regulations, customs and practices, which constitute discrimination against women." The Committee on the CEDAW defines discrimination to include "gender-based violence, that is, violence that is directed against a woman because she is a woman or that affects women disproportionately."[54] The recommendation of CEDAW regarding the prevention of sexual and gender-based violence generally references States, thus using the State's legal and administrative mechanisms to protect and prevent. For example, the CEDAW suggest that preventive measures include "public information and education programmes to change attitudes concerning the roles and status of men and women."[55]

Although peacekeepers do not have access to administrative and legal avenues, they are obligated under the mandate to protect women from sexual and gender-based violence. Of course, this obligation to protect will also obligate them to respect the rights of women, including prohibiting the promotion of or participation in sexually violent acts, or facilitating those acts by their administration of IDP camps.[56]

UN peacekeeping contingents are drawn from different cultural and legal backgrounds, with each contingent having diverse cultural and legal norms of what would be considered a 'threat' of sexual violence. In order for there to be consistent protection, the UN must have an accepted understanding of what is a threat to the sexual protection of women. Nonetheless, as outlined in the previous Chapter, from the over-arching resolutions on UNPOL, the Security Council expects that this form of protection will be undertaken by the police component. UN police officers through their presence are intended to position themselves between civilians and the threat of sexual or gender-based violence, and if their presence is not a deterrent, then to use force in order to

54 General Recommendations Adopted by the Committee on the Elimination of Discrimination Against Women, *General Recommendation No 19: Violecne Against Women*, Eleventh Session, 1992 at paragraph 6.

55 Ibid at paragraph 24(t)(ii).

56 For articles on the debate of sexual exploitation and abuse by peacekeepers, see Anthony J Miller, 'Legal Aspects of Stopping Sexual Exploitation and Abuse in UN Peacekeeping Operations' (2006) 39 *Cornell International Law Journal* 71; Marie Deschamps, Hassan B Jallow and Yasmin Sooka, 'Taking Action on Sexual Exploitation and Abuse by Peacekeepers: Report of an Independent Review on Sexual Exploitation and Abuse by International Peacekeeping Forces in the Central African Republic' (United Nations, 17 December 2015 2015); Gabrielle Simm, 'Regulating Sex in Peace Operations' in Peter Drahos (ed), *Regulatory Theory: Foundations and Applications* (ANU Press, 2017).

protect women and children. Therefore, if a report of sexual violence has been obtained, and the incident is within the Mission's area of deployment, peacekeepers are obliged to respond in order to protect.

Outside the immediate stopping of a violent act, it is not clear what legal authority UNPOL has in detaining or separating perpetrators of sexual violence. In domestic law enforcement, a major part of protection against sexual and gender-based violence is the response and legal ramifications once violence has been reported. However, in peacekeeping there are few methods that can be used by UN police officers once violence has been reported. Consequently, as discussed in the previous Chapter, UN police officers will detain individuals indefinitely, although this would be a breach of their obligations under IHRL.

4 Child Protection

Within more recent UN peace missions, the Security Council has separated the protection of children from women, by mandating "that child protection concerns are integrated into all operations and strategic aspects."[57] Moreover, the Security Council has begun mandating specific protection activities primarily related to child protection, explicitly in "ensuring that the protection of children's rights is taken into account, inter alia, in the DDR and DDRR process."[58] Although the language and emphasis differ in each mission, the majority of child protection mandates are connected to the protection of civilians 'under threat of physical violence'.

With the exception of the mandate to assist in the DDR process, the Security Council omits any interpretation of protection of children and the activities that are encompassed by it. As the Security Council mandates a general protection of civilians against "threat of physical violence", when specifically referencing the protection afforded to 'children', the Security Council intends an expansion to the general protection of civilians mandate. In other words, the protection of children mandate implies a different obligation to the general protection of civilians mandate.

An indication of the content of the protection of children can be found in the Security Council's cross-cutting resolutions on children in armed conflict.

---

57 *United Nations Security Council Resolution 2098* (2013) at operational paragraph 12(a)(iii).

58 *United Nations Secuirty Council Resolution 2149* (2014) at operational paragraph 34; also mandated to demobilise children in *United Nations Security Council Resolution 1509* (2003) at operational paragraph 3(l).

For example, the Security Council in *Resolution 1539* (2004), outlines multiple abuses that require protection against, such as:

> the recruitment and use of child soldiers by parties to armed conflict in violation of international obligations applicable to them, killing and maiming of children, rape and other sexual violence mostly committed against girls, abduction and forced displacement, denial of humanitarian access to children, attacks against schools and hospitals as well as trafficking, forced labour and all forms of slavery and other violations and abuses committed against children affected by armed conflict.[59]

From the list of violations and abuses highlighted by the Security Council it can be gleaned that the Security Council intends protection of children to be centred around violence against children and the recruitment of children in armed conflict. As reiterated in *Resolution 1674* (2006), which outlines violations and protections needed by all civilians, the Security Council specifically reference two issues related to children, that is 'violence against children' and 'recruitment and use of child soldiers'.[60]

4.1 *The Protections Afforded to Children in Armed Conflict*

Within a NIAC, children will be covered by the protections offered to persons not taking direct part in the hostilities found in Common Article 3.[61] Further, children will be granted special protections found in the Fourth Geneva Convention, however, "the principles on which the rules relating to children is based is not stated explicitly anywhere in that Convention."[62] The Additional Protocols to the Conventions attempted to codify child protections in Article 4 'fundamental guarantees', specifically, that children "shall be provided with the care and aid they require."[63] Additional Protocol II sets out further specific protections:

59 *United Nations Security Council Resolution 1539* (2004) at operational paragraph 1.

60 *United Nations Security Council Resolution 1674* (2006) at operational paragraph 5.

61 Common Article 3, Fourth Geneva Convention; Addtional Protocol II at Article 4.

62 Denise Plattner, "Protection of Children in International Humanitarian Law" (1984) 24 *International Review of the Red Cross* 140 at 142.

63 Addtional Protocol II at Article 4.

in particular:

(a) they shall receive an education, including religious and moral education, in keeping with the wishes of their parents, or in the absence of parents, of those responsible for their care;

(b) all appropriate steps shall be taken to facilitate the reunion of families temporarily separated;

(c) children who have not attained the age of fifteen years shall neither be recruited in the armed forces or groups nor allowed to take part in hostilities.[64]

Article 77 of Additional Protocol I sets out protections against using children in hostilities and offering protections in order to stop child recruitment. Although Additional Protocol I applies to IAC, the CRC, which has been almost universally ratified,[65] extends the field of application of Article 77 of Additional Protocol I to NIAC by reiterating it within Article 38 of the CRC.[66] The CRC sets out a full range of protections for children that encompass rights of civil freedoms, family, basic health and welfare, and education. Although the Optional Protocol to CRC goes further than the CRC, the Optional Protocol has not been universally ratified.

One of the primary protections owed to children in armed conflict is that they will not be recruited or used in hostilities. Children under the age of 15 cannot be recruited or used by armed groups, whether or not they are directly participating in hostilities.[67] However, States are asked to "refrain"[68] from the general recruitment of children under the age of 15; as they only forbidden from using children under age of 15 for active participation in hostilities, but can recruit them for non-combatant functions.

4.2 *Defining the 'Child' under the Law*

The explicit protections afforded to children within the framework of international law is documented in an array of treaties and conventions. Within the current legal framework there is no collective approach to the determination or definition of what constitutes a 'child'. As there is no universal definition across the bodies of international law, the legal categorisation of a 'child' will depend solely on the legal instrument being examined and utilised. This varying definition of a 'child' is recognised in the CRC, which defines a 'child' as

64 Ibid at Article 4(3).

65 https://www.unicef.org/why/why_rights.html.

66 *United Nations Convention on the Rights of the Child*, A/RES/44/25 (*CRC*) at Article 38.

67 Addtional Protocol II at Article 4(3)(c).

68 CRC, above note 66 at Article 38.

any person under the age of 18, "unless under the law applicable to the child, majority is attained earlier."[69]

As international law is drafted to oblige or regulate State actions, the differing legal definitions of a 'child' is not considered problematic, as States will define a 'child' under the legal instrument which obliges or regulates a specific action that is being undertaken. For example, each State will have differences between the age of recruitment, criminal responsibility, and sexual consent. Although a concise definition will be needed for human rights and humanitarian protections, this lack of a universally accepted definition is emphasised when peacekeepers engage, detain, or demobilize child soldiers.

As the Security Council focuses on protection of children in armed conflict, it is essential to first examine IHL and definitions found within its differing legal instruments to formulate a legal classification of 'children' under the Security Council's protection mandate. Although the Geneva Conventions do not explicitly define a 'child' for the purpose of the Conventions, it is generally accepted that unless specified to the contrary, that a 'child' is any person under the age of 18 years.[70]

When examining the current structure of IHL, there are two differing categories of 'children', that is, persons under the age of 18 years, and those under the age of 15 years. Under the Geneva Conventions, children under the age of 15 years are granted 'extra' care and protection, similar to expectant mothers or the sick and wounded.[71] When awarding these 'special' protections, the Fourth Geneva Convention does not intend to define children as persons under the age of 15 years, rather it creates a secondary category of 'children'. From the text in the Conventions that states "*children* under the age of 15", it can be inferred that there exists two categories of 'children': over the age of 15 years (but under the age of 18) and under the age of 15 years. This terminology of '*children* under the age of 15' is reused in the Additional Protocols, confirming the intention to create a subcategory of children who are awarded special protections.[72]

---

69 Ibid, Article 1.

70 This omission of any definition was reiterated and discussed during negotiations of the Additional Protocols to the Geneva Conventions, where during the negotiations, discussions arose of inserting a concise definition of 'children' into the Protocols. However, at the conclusion of negotiations, any definition of 'children' was omitted. See the ICRC Customary Law database.

71 Fourth Geneva Convention, specifically refer to Articles 14, 24, 38(5), 50 and 89 More citations needed.

72 Consequently, some legal commentators have contended that for all intents and purposes, under IHL children should only be defined as any person under the age of 15 years. It is contended that as the majority of 'special' obligations specify 'children under the age of 15', this classification could be considered as the only real definition of a 'child'. For

Rather than interpreting these special provisions as re-defining what constitutes a child, these provisions should be seen as establishing a 'special class' of children. This distinction in class of children should be perceived as similar to the distinction between combatants and wounded combatants, that is, one category does not nullify the other. Within the Fourth Geneva Convention, Articles 23, 24, 38, 50 and 89 grant special protections for children under the age of 15, mainly around access to food and family life, granting a special class of children within armed conflict.

The classification of a 'child' becomes paramount when implementing the process of DDR for combatants and the legality of children recruited into armed groups and combat activities. Under the legal obligations founded in IHL, it is customarily accepted that the recruitment of any person under the age of 15 years is strictly forbidden.[73] The prohibition of recruiting children under the age of 15 years and their participation in hostilities is reiterated in the CRC[74] and the Rome Statute.[75] In contrast, Article 3(a) of the *Convention on the Worst Forms of Child Labour* states that "forced or compulsory recruitment of children [under 18 years] for use in armed conflict"[76] is to be considered one of the worst forms of child labour. International Labour Organization (*ILO*) Recommendation 190 calls on all State parties to make such recruitment practices a criminal offence.[77] However, the Convention on Child Labour fails to mention and reference 'voluntary' recruitment, or whether voluntary recruitment can exist for persons under the age of 18. Notwithstanding any disparity in the law, this distinct category of the age of recruitment is confirmed in the ICRC's *Study of Customary International Humanitarian Law*, which echoes that the illegality of recruitment of children under the age of 15 years is a norm of customary international law.[78]

The Optional Protocol to the CRC raises the minimum age of recruitment from 15 years to 18 years.[79] The Optional Protocol has been signed by all African

example, see, Claire Breen, 'When is a Child Not a Child? Child Soldiers in International Law' (2007) *8*(2) *Human Rights Review* 71.

73 Addtional Protocol II, Article 4(3)(c).

74 CRC, above note 66 at Article 38.

75 Rome Statute at Article 8(2)(b).

76 *Worst Forms of Child Labour Convention*, 1999 (No. 182) at Article 3(a).

77 International Labour Organization, *Worst Forms of Child Labour Recommendation 190*, 1999 (No.190).

78 International Committee of the Red Cross, *Study on Customary Interantional Humanitarian Law* (*Customary IHL Database*), Rule 136.

79 *Optional Protocol to the Convention on the Rights of the Child on the Involvement of Children in Armed Conflict*, A/RES/54/263 of 25 May 2000 at Article 2.

host States where UN peace missions are deployed. Furthermore as the protection of civilians Missions are deployed in Africa, the *African Charter on the Rights and Welfare of the Child* (the *African Charter*) defines the term of the 'child' as "every human being below the age of 18 years."[80] Additionally, the African Charter defining a 'child' as a person under 18 years of age, obliges all State parties to "take all necessary measures to ensure that no child shall take a direct part in hostilities and refrain in particular, from recruiting any child."[81] Thus, although customary international law will defines the lawful age of recruitment as 15, as the African host States signed and ratified the Optional Protocol to the CRC and the African Charter, the age of recruitment will be 18. Thus, child protection activities including DDR, are obliged to all individuals under the age of 18.

4.3 *Protection Provided to Child Soldiers*

The prime protection required by children in armed conflict, as identified by the UN, is the protection from recruitment and involvement in armed groups.[82] In recent UN reports, it has been reported that the use of children in armed conflict has been on the increase.[83] The recruitment of children includes not only children directly participating in hostilities, but involving them in the military 'life' of an armed group. Child soldiers are not commonly utilised in the 'front line', but rather the bulk of child soldiers have been identified in performing "supporting roles, such as cooks, porters and bodyguards, for senior commanders."[84] Thus, even though the greater part of child soldiers are not directly involved in hostilities, they are not removed from the risk of harm associated with armed conflict. The demands of military life and its incidental effects can be a severe burden on the physical wellbeing of children, as child soldiers "frequently collapse under heavy loads and suffer from malnutrition, respiratory and skin infections, and other ailments."[85] Critically, girls are being recruited by armed groups for the purposes of sexual exploitation or forced

80 *African Charter on the Rights and Welfare of the Child*, 1 July 1990, Article 2.

81 Ibid, Article 22(2).

82 United Nations General Asssembly, *Promotion and Protection of the Rights of Children: Impact of Armed Conflict on Children*, UN Doc A/51/306; United Nations General Assembly and Security Council, *Children and Armed Conflict: Report of the Secretary-General*, UN Doc A/63/785-S/2009/158.

83 United Nations Security Council, *Report of the Secretary-General on the Protection of Civilians in Armed Conflict*, UN Doc S/2017/414 at paragraph 13.

84 United Nations Security Council, *Report of the Secretary-General on Children and Armed Conflict in South Sudan*, S/2014/884 at paragraph 20.

85 Breen, above note 72 at 73.

marriage, leading to vulnerability to sexual transmitted diseases and unwanted pregnancies.[86] Furthermore, children that are recruited into armed groups are occasionally forced to perform violent acts on their own family members, or against members of their community, as an isolation tactic to force the children to become solely dependent on the armed group.[87] With long-term consequences and psychological damage, protecting children from recruitment becomes a primary objective in all child protection activities.

The explicit legal provisions on the recruitment of children can be found in the Additional Protocols to the Geneva Conventions under the title of "victims of armed conflict".[88] Accordingly, it is implied in IHL that children become victims by the mere fact of being 'combatants', that is, that "there is a class of combatants who are victims *in virtue of being combatants in the first place*."[89] This notion of the victimisation of child soldiers is echoed in international criminal law jurisprudence, as children under the age of 18 years, or under the age of 15 in the case of the Special Court of Sierra Leone, are not prosecuted for any war crimes committed while they are recruited. Thus, it can be inferred that under international law and the protection mandate, child soldiers cannot be considered or treated similarly to other civilians participating directly in hostilities.

In the Secretary-General reports, references are made to the correlation between easy access to small arms and the recruitment of children into armed forces.[90] The Secretary-General considers the removal of the access and circulation of small arms as a vital element to protect children from illegal recruitment.[91] In comparison to other weaponry, small arms are light weapons that can be easily used and carried, allowing children to be able to bear weapons and participate in hostilities. Even though UN reports and academic literature considers the access of light and small weapons as a major contributor to the continuation of violence and the victimisation of women and children, the Security Council is yet to explicitly mandate UN peace operations to forcefully

86 Sonja Grover, "Child Soldiers' as 'Non-Combatants': The Inapplicability of the Refugee Convention Exclusion Clause' (2008) *12(1) The International Journal of Human Rights* 53 at 54.

87 Franklyn Bai Kargbo, 'International Peacekeeping and Child Soldiers: Problems of Security and Rebuilding' (2004) *3(3) Cornell International Law Journal* 485 at 488.

88 Additional Protocol I.

89 G. Alex Sinha, 'Child soldiers as super-privileged combatants' (2013) *17(4) The International Journal of Human Rights* 584 at 587.

90 United Nations General Assembly and Security Council, *Children and Armed Conflict: Report of the Secretary-General*, UN Doc A/55/163-S/2000/712 at paragraph 21.

91 Ibid at paragraph 21.

deal with their removal.[92] However, both the DPO and UNDP have recognised and advised peace operations to consider small arms as a key factor in all DDR agreements and processes.[93]

As can be gleaned from Security Council resolutions and UN reports, child protection must be centred around the DDR process, with the Secretary-General stating that "one of the most urgent priorities is to remove everyone under 18 years of age from armed forces."[94] However, when the Security Council explicitly mandates the protection of children, they have utilised vague language making no reference to the Secretary-General's recommendations. The Security Council has mandated peacekeepers to protect civilians and to "provide specific protection for women and children affected by armed conflict,"[95] and, regarding children, to consider 'children' issues in planning and implementation of the mandate.

In order for the protection of children from recruitment and exploitation in armed conflict to be achieved, the Secretary-General indicates multiple avenues that need to be explored – the prevention and response to child abductions; the disarmament of small arms; and the reintegration of child soldiers into society. Even though the abduction of children "has primarily been a precursor to other violations, such as killing and maiming, recruitment and use, or sexual violence",[96] little has been explicitly mandated to prevent or respond to child abductions outside of the reports of the Secretary-General. Rather, the Security Council has underscored

92 The Security Council mainly mandates that peacekeepers assist local authorities with the process. For example, *United Nations Security Council Resolution 2399* (2018) at operational paragraph 3; *United Nations Security Council Resolution 2364* (2017) at operational paragraph 46; or *United Nations Security Council Resolution 2313* (2016) at operational paragraph 34.

93 Th United Nations Department of Peace Opertions, *The Protection of Civilians in United Nations Peacekeeping Handbook* at 12.3; Mark Malan, 'Disarming and Demobilising Child Soldiers: The Underlying Challenges' (2000) *9(5/6) African Security Review* at 2.

94 United Nations General Asssembly, *Promotion and Protection of the Rights of Children: Impact of Armed Conflict on Children*, UN Doc A/51/306 at paragraph 49.

95 *UnitedNationsSecurityCouncilResolution2100*(2013)atoperationalparagraph16(c)(l);*United Nations Security Council Resolution 2164* (2014) at operational paragraph 13(a)(iii); *United Nations Security Council Resolution 2227* (2015) at operational paragraph 14(d)(iii); *United Nations Security Council Resolution 2098* (2013) at operational paragraph 12(a)(iii); *United Nations Security Council Resolution 2155* (2014) at operational paragraph 4(a)(i).

96 United Nations General Assembly and Security Council, *Children and Armed Conflict: Report of the Secretary-General*, A/69/926-S/2015/409 at paragraph 6.

> the importance of disarmament, demobilization and reintegration of ex-combatants (DDR) in the protection of civilians affected by armed conflict, and, in this regard, emphasizes (i) its support of the inclusion in mandates of United Nations peacekeeping and other relevant missions, where appropriate and on a case-by-case basis, of specific and effective measures for DDR.[97]

Even though UNICEF, humanitarian agencies, and the Secretary-General have focused on multiple issues regarding child welfare, the Security Council has only expressly mandated peacekeepers to focus on child soldiers, outside the general protection against violence. The Security Council's focus on child soldiers and recruitment has manifested in their mandates that instruct peacekeepers to assist in the DDR and Sector Security Reform (*SSR*) processes,[98] and the embargo on small arms.[99] Although the mandate to assist with DDR and SSR falls in a separate section to the protection of civilians mandate, the Security Council will mandate missions "to take fully into account child protection as cross-cutting issue throughout its mandate" and to assist the local authorities to insure "that the protection of children's rights is taken into account, inter alia, in DDR and DDR/R processes and in SSR in order to end and prevent violations and abuses against children."[100]

In contrast to the DDR mandate, in the DRC, MONUSCO was mandated "to ensure that children protection concerns are integrated into all operations and strategic aspects of MONUSCO's work."[101] Specifically as the preamble of operational paragraph 12 opens "Authorizes MONUSCO, through its military component, in pursuit of the objectives described in paragraph 11 above, to take all necessary measures to perform the following tasks".[102] When the Security Council mandates a UN peace mission 'to take all necessary means',

97 *United Nations Security Council Resolution 1674* (2006) at operational paragrpah 18.

98 *United Nations Security Council Resolution 2327* (2016) at operational paragraph 7(c)(iv); *United Nations Security Council Resolution 2295* (2016) at operational paragraph 19(a)(v); *United Nations Security Council Resolution 2399* (2018) at operational paragraph 3.

99 *United Nations Security Council Resolution 2399* (2018) at operational paragraph 3; *United Nations Security Council Resolution 2364* (2017) at operational paragraph 46.

100 *United Nations Security Council Resolution 2387* (2017) at operational parapgraph 50; *United Nations Security Council Resolution 2399* (2018) at operational parapgrah 3; *United Nations Security Council Resolution 2364* (2017) at operational paragraph 27; *United Nations Security Council Resolution 2277* (2016) at operational paragraph 37.

101 *United Nations Security Council Resolution 2098* (2013) at operational paragraph 12(iii).

102 Ibid at operational parapgraph 12.

it is generally implied to be a responsibility of the military and police, specifically allowing the use of force.

4.4 DDR *Process and Child Soldiers*

The DDR process does not merely separate a child from an armed group, it also

> aims to deal with the post-conflict security problem that arises when combatants are left without livelihoods and support networks during the vital period stretching from conflict to peace, recovery and development. DDR also helps build national capacity to assist in the reintegration of ex-combatants and to support communities receiving ex-combatants and working for their peaceful and sustainable reintegration.[103]

The UN's DDR general process is based on the existence of a peace agreement, which sets out a DDR procedure.[104] However, as child recruitment is a violation of international law, the DDR process regarding children does not depend on any peace settlement, and can occur during on-going conflict.[105] As codified in Article 1 of the CRC, a child's right to life, survival and development is paramount, and so children need to be demobilised and reintegrated even without the existence of peace. Due to the very nature of child recruitment, their reintegration process becomes more complicated due to the psychological and medical harm that is associated with children involved in armed conflict.

Since 1989, with the deployment of the UN Transition Assistance Group (*UNTAG*) in Namibia, DDR mandates have been explicitly inserted into UN peace missions. UNTAG was mandated to assist in the independence of Namibia, including overseeing of the elections and the DDR of ex-combatants.[106] Even though DDR mandates have preceded the protection of civilians regime, currently, DDR has become a core consideration in the Security Council's regime for the protection of children and peacebuilding efforts. The Security Council has "[u]nderscored the importance of disarmament, demobilization and reintegration of ex-combatants (DDR) in the protection of civilians",[107] and DDR specifically has become a cornerstone of child protection: as reported by the Secretary-General, "particular attention should be given to demobilization

---

103 United Nations, *Operation Guide to the Integrated Disarmament, Demoblilization and Reintegration Standards* (IDDRS), 2014.

104 Ibid.

105 Ibid at 225.

106 *United Nations Security Council Resolution 435* (1978).

107 *United Nations Security Council Resolution 1674* (2006) at operational paragraph 18.

and reintegration of child soldiers."[108] However, the DDR process is a complicated and intricate procedure that demands the efforts of multiple agents and actors, ranging from the UN, States, and to non-state actors. It is not sufficient to simply disarm and separate child soldiers from armed groups; child soldiers must also be reintegrated within their communities and previous support networks. Thus, with logistical considerations, the reintegration of soldiers "has always required significant and long-term resources."[109] Moreover, children being distinct from other members of armed groups, require more support and resources in order to be integrated successfully into their communities and social networks.

During armed conflict, the scale of separation of children from their families and communities is extensive, complicating the reintegration component of former child soldiers.[110] As peacekeepers are increasingly being deployed into territories with ongoing conflicts and insecure environments, the communities and support networks of children are either vastly diminished or virtually non-existent.[111] With insecure environments, the DDR process for child soldiers becomes complicated, as children cannot be reintegrated into civilian life unless a support framework can be first established. Unlike their adult counterparts, children are 'dependant' individuals who are unable to support or provide for themselves, and hence, in need of a guardian. Moreover, with displacement of individuals within conflict, this further complicates the reintegration of children, as their families might be displaced in unknown areas.

Ex-combatants cannot be successfully reintegrated in civilian life with ongoing conflict, poor political structures, and a struggling economy.[112] Thus, unless an effective and sustainable reintegration process can be established after disarming and demobilising, "ex-combatants may be at a high risk of rejoining armed groups and criminal gangs and continuing to pose a threat

108 United Nations Security Council, *Report of the Secretary-General to the Security Council on the Protection of Civilians in Armed Conflict*, UN Doc S/1999/957 at recommendation 3.

109 United Nations General Assembly and Security Council, *Children and Armed Conflict: Report of the Secretary-General*, A/69/926-S/2015/409 at paragraph 15.

110 K. Williamson, P. Gupta, L.A Gillespie, H. Shannon, and D. Landis, *The Impact of Protection Interventions on Unaccompanies and Separated Children in Humanitarian Crises*, Humanitarian Evidence Programme, Oxford, 2017 at 3.

111 United Nations General Asssembly, *Promotion and Protection of the Rights of Children: Impact of Armed Conflict on Children*, UN Doc A/51/306 at paragraph 25.

112 United Nations Department of Peacekeeping Operations, *Second Generation Disarmament, Demobilization and Reintegration (DDR) Practices in Peace Operations: A Contribution to the New Horizon Discussion on Challenges and Opportunities for UN Peacekeeping*, 2010.

to security and the overall peace process."[113] Consequently, in regards to child soldiers, it is a common occurrence that children are re-recruited into armed groups after they have been demobilised by UN peacekeepers.[114]

Although the majority of DDR processes focus on the social and psychological problems encountered by child soldiers, rarely do UN peace missions dedicate their resources to the economic and humanitarian requirements needed for these children to adequately return to civilian life.[115] As claimed by the Secretary-General's reports, that "emphasis should be placed on schooling, potentially combined with some economic support to the family."[116] Without economic support, and an increase in their access to health and educational resources, ex-child soldiers are more likely to return to the armed groups than remain in an unstable community.

With the limitations in traditional DDR, the former DPKO has attempted to shift the DDR activities away from traditional DDR processes, as "the UN is mandated to conduct DDR programmes where the preconditions are not fulfilled".[117] As modern NIACs no longer subscribe to traditional structures enabling traditional DDR, DPKO altered its procedure to what has been named "second generation DDR."[118] For where traditional DDR programs focus on combatants in military organisations, "the focus of Second Generation programmes shift away from military structures towards the larger communities that are affected by armed violence."[119] That is, the UN intends to expand the DDR process beyond the mere traditional 'combatant' to a more flexible approach targeting non-traditional combatants and armed groups. However, even though DDR activities are being increased, there is currently a disconnect between activities expected and resources allocated.

Since 2017, the Office of Rule of Law and Security Institutions (*ORLSI*) has provided advisory support to UN peace missions with the DDR mandate.[120]

---

113 United Nations General Assembly, *Disarmament, Demobilization and Reintegration: Report of the Secretary-General*, UN Doc. A/65/741 at paragraph 17.

114 United Nations Security Council, *Report of the Secretary-General on Children and Armed Conflict in the Central African Republic*, UN Doc S/2016/133 at paragraph 19.

115 Malan, above note 93.

116 United Nations General Assembly, *Disarmament, Demobilization and Reintegration: Report of the Secretary-General*, UN Doc. A/65/741 at paragraph 33.

117 United Nations *Department of Peacekeeping Operations, Second Generation Disarmament, Demobilization and Reintegration (DDR) Practices in Peace Operations: A Contribution to the New Horizon Discussion on Challenges and Opportunities for UN Peacekeeping*, 2010 at 8.

118 Ibid.

119 Ibid at 3.

120 United Nations General Assembly, *Restrucuting of the United Nations Peace and Security Pillar: Report of the Secretary-General*, UN Doc A/72/525, 13 October 2017 at paragraph 32.

Regarding child DDR, UN peacekeepers are not leading the process but rather are assisting the host State infrastructure and UN organisations, such as UNICEF and UNDP. As specified in the UN Operation Guide on DDR, "[t]he primary responsibility for DDR programmes rest with national actors; the UN's role is to support the process as a neutral actor."[121] UN peace missions are to assist in identifying and registering the children to be released from these groups. Subsequently, one of the greatest contributions to the DDR process is educating non-State actors on their obligations under the law, in order for them to identify children within their groups.

Historically, UN peace missions have been strongly against any direct or forceful implementation of disarming and demobilising combatants. As US-led forces learnt in their peace operations in Somalia, that "[f]orcible disarmament is the 'bright line' of peace operations: when you cross it, you have entered a de facto state of war."[122] For in a modern NIAC, to attempt to forcibly disarm an armed group is to actively attempt to disarm and demobilise an entire community. Thus, any forcible disarmament should be considered as direct participation in armed conflict, and "there should be no mistaking the fact that the troops given this mission have been committed to combat."[123] Appropriately, from lessons learnt in Somalia, the UN as an organisation, is unfit and ill-equipped to engage in any non-voluntary disarmament of combatants.[124] Specifically, as stated earlier, DDR is more than merely removing arms from those participating in hostilities, but is to socially and economically reintegrate those individuals back into their communities.

Therefore, under the protection of civilians mandate, peacekeepers are not obliged to take an active role in DDR, rather they are obliged to assist and support the DDR process. For example in the CAR, MINUSCA has worked alongside UNICEF to hold training seminars for armed groups on the protection of children and their personal obligations under the law.[125] Specifically, MINUSCA has been mandated by the Security Council to "support, within its capabilities, efforts aimed at strengthening the capacity of the Governments of Chad and the Central African Republic and civil society through training in international

121 United Nations, *Operational Guide to the Integrated Disarmament, Demobilization and Reintegration Standards*, 2004 at 29.

122 Allard, Kenneth, *Somalia Operations: Lessons Learned*, CCRP Publication Series, 1995/2005 at 56.

123 Ibid at 80.

124 Malan, above note 93 at 7.

125 United Nations Security Council, *Report of the Secretary-General on Children and Armed Conflict in the Central African Republic*, UN Doc S/2016/133 at paragraph 57.

human rights standards, and efforts to put an end to recruitment and use of children by armed groups."[126] Moreover, linked to this educational approach, Child Protection Advisors generally pursue those who attended these seminars to sign and implement agreements to desist in actively recruiting children into their armed groups. Even though these agreements are not the definitive approach to abolishing child recruitment, they do assist local authorities and international organisations to continue an open dialogue with these armed groups on the agreed action plan.[127] Similarly in the DRC, Child Protection Advisors in MONUSCO have successfully negotiated agreements with numerous armed groups to stop the recruitment of children and to demobilise enlisted children.[128]

Due to the success of Child Protection Advisors in UN peace missions, DDR activities are generally considered in the realm of civilian peacekeepers. Accordingly, DDR activities in UN peace missions commonly encompass peacekeepers monitoring, investigating, and reporting on the situation to other bodies. As such, DDR activities fall within the jurisdiction of Child Protection Advisors to advocate for armed groups to respect and adhere to their obligations under international law, and to register child soldiers to begin the DDR process. However, as experienced in DRC and South Sudan, due to security issues, reporting and monitoring cannot be observed by Child Protection Advisors alone, but rather needs coordination with the military or police component of the Mission.[129]

Although peacekeepers should solely pursue the DDR mandate in a separate function, some commentators have suggested that the Security Council intends otherwise, specifically citing the mandate of the UN peace operation in Sierra Leone (*UNAMSIL*). In 2000, the Security Council mandated UNAMSIL to "provide security in and at all sites of the disarmament, demobilization and reintegration programme ... [and] authorizes UNAMSIL to take the necessary action to fulfil the additional tasks set out above"[130] The UNAMSIL mandate has been interpreted by some commentators as the Security Council's authority

126 *United Nations Security Council Resolution 1778* (2007) at operational paragraph 2(f).

127 United Nations Security Council, *Report of the Secretary-General on Children and Armed Conflict in the Central African Republic*, UN Doc S/2016/133 at paragraph 66.

128 United Nations General Assembly and Security Council, *Children and Armed Conflict: Report of the Secretary-General*, UN Doc A/59/695-S/2005/72 at paragraph 19.

129 United Nations Security Council, *Report of the Secretary-General on the United Nations Organization Stabilization Mission in the Democratic Republic of the Congo*, S/2016/1130 at paragraph 46; United Nations Department of Peacekeeping, *Child Protection in United Nations Peacekeeping: 2014 Review* at 13.

130 *United Nations Security Council Resolution 1289* (2000) at Operational Paragraph 10(c).

for UNAMSIL to use force to achieve DDR, as it is contended that the text "provides a legal framework for coercive action by UNAMSIL in pursuit of its disarmament mandate."[131] However, the mandate does not give authority for force to be used for the DDR process, rather that peacekeepers are mandated to "take necessary action" to protect DDR sites. In other words, UNAMSIL is to ensure the security and protection of the DDR sites, rather than directly engage with armed groups to forcibly disarm and demobilise combatants.

4.5 *Incidental Removal of Children from Armed Groups*

As stated previously, UN peace missions are not obliged to take a 'leading role' in DDR, however, with UN peace missions engaging in conflict with non-State actors, peacekeepers are required to deal directly with child soldiers. When peacekeepers actively disarm children, the legal responsibility of the welfare and the rights of the ex-child soldier must be prioritised. Once a child soldier is disarmed and demobilised, until they are reunited with a guardian, the UN has a legal duty to ensure their welfare and the protection of their rights. As the scale of separation of children from their families and community is "greater in conflicts than in natural disasters",[132] peacekeepers must consider the possibility that child soldiers might not be able to be easily reunited with family. Hence, before UN peacekeepers engage in actively disarming armed groups containing child soldiers, they must ascertain the resources to protect and ensure the rights of those children.

At times when a child's family or support network cannot be identified, consideration must be taken in who bears the duty of care and protection of the child once removed from the armed group. Within the humanitarian organisation landscape, humanitarian workers rely on a 'no harm' principle in all their protection activities.[133] A similar principle of 'no harm' must be adopted by UN peacekeepers as the foundation of all protection and peacekeeping activities involving children. Essentially when engaging with child soldiers, "the best interests of the child shall be a primary consideration."[134] When the FIB or RPF is engaged in neutralising the threat of these armed groups, a framework must be implemented to ensure the welfare and rights of child soldiers within these groups. Consequently, UN peacekeepers that disarm and demobilise children

131 Malan, above note 93 at 5.

132 Williamson et al, above note 110 at 3.

133 International Committee of the Red Cross, 'ICRC Protection policy' (2009) 90(871) *International Review of the Red Cross* 751.

134 CRC, above note 66 at Article 3(1).

are encumbered with the legal responsibility to ensure the protection of those children under the law.

Therefore, UN peacekeepers must identify a child's support network, or a sufficient alternative, before disarming and demobilising children. If a child is removed from an armed group without a suitable guardian, UN peace missions must take legal responsibility for the protection of the rights of the child, as required by law.[135] When State forces and local authorities assisting a UN operation are unable or unwilling to take responsibility for the child, then the UN peace mission under their legal obligations and the obligations under the protection mandate, must take responsibility for the protection of the child. Currently, UN peace missions do not have a mechanism in ensuring the protection of the welfare of ex-child soldiers, but rather are dependent on other actors. However, as part of their due diligence of their minimum obligation, a mechanism must be in place when children are forcibly removed from an armed group. As discussed in Chapter 3, force used by UN peace mission must be proportionate to the advantage of protecting civilians, therefore, part of their obligation to mitigate harm is to establish a mechanism to ensure the protections owed to ex-child soldiers.

4.6 *Use of Force against Child Soldiers*

With the commencement of the FIB and the Security Council's continuation of the use of Protection Forces, UN peace missions are increasingly interacting with child soldiers as 'enemy fighters'. Peacekeepers are thus confronted with two opposing issues: the legality of military engagement and the use of force against those child soldiers, and simultaneously their obligation to protect those children and other civilians under the protection mandate. Even though all UN peacekeepers encounter similar predicaments, these issues are more heightened for peacekeepers participating in offensive operations that are deployed to directly pursue protection activities and engage with armed groups. When using force against child soldiers, peacekeepers must balance their obligations to protect these child soldiers under the protection mandate, and simultaneously adhere to their obligation to protect other civilians and UN personnel. Thus, guidance is required regarding how "peacekeepers should respond to the presence of children and women on the battlefield – whether armed, being used as shields, or serving in support functions – is needed."[136]

---

135 Ibid at Article 3.

136 Center for Civilians in Conflict, *From Mandate to Mission: Mitigating Civilian Harm in UN Peacekeeping Operations in the DRC, 2016 Report* at 11.

While child soldiers should be considered victims, a child bearing a weapon, in the majority of situations, should be considered more dangerous than their adult counterpart.[137] Essentially, children will assess risk differently to their adult counterparts, making them less predictable on a battlefield. Consequently, peacekeepers are faced with balancing their mandate to neutralise these armed groups, with their overall obligation to protect these children and ensure the DDR process.

Notwithstanding the moral dilemma encountered by peacekeepers, nor the circumstances behind a child's involvement in the armed conflict; under international law a child will lose their protected status once they have directly participated in hostilities. Subsequently, when a child is directly participating in hostilities, they become a military target. Even though IHL specifies clear rules for the age of recruitment, it does not exclude children from the classification as a legal military target. The legality of the involvement of an individual in armed conflict does not nullify their status as a 'target' under the law. NIAC does not have a category of 'combatant', rather pursuant to Article 13(3) civilians are not protected from targeting if they are taking direct part in hostilities. Hence, in a NIAC the legal factor that must be considered is whether or not the child is directly participating in hostilities, rather than their actual age and the legality of their recruitment.

This is further evidenced in Article 77(3) of Additional Protocol I, in which a captured child soldier who has directly participated in hostilities is to be awarded prisoner of war (*PoW*) status; as suggested by the literature, PoW status can only be awarded "if they have previously attained the primary status of combatants by being unlawfully recruited into the armed forces of one of the parties to the conflicts."[138]

Although child soldiers can become military targets, international criminal law jurisprudence adds an additional complication to this situation, namely, children that are members of an armed group, and not directly participating in hostilities, will preserve their civilian status.[139] As handed down by the ICC in the decision of *Ntaganda*,[140] a child recruited in an armed group and being a member of that armed group is not in itself enough for that child to lose his or her civilian status under the law.[141] It was stated by the Court that "to hold

137 Grover, above note 86 at 54.

138 Knut Ipsen, 'Combatants and Non-Combatants' in Michael Bothe (ed), *The Handbook of International Humanitarian Law, 3rd Edition* (Oxford University Press, 2013) 301 at 306.

139 *Prosecutor v Bosco Ntaganda*, International Criminal Court, Pre-Trail Chamber II, NO: ICC-01/04-02/06, 9 June 2014.

140 Ibid.

141 Ibid.

that children under the age of 15 years lose the protection afforded to them by IHL merely by joining an armed group, whether as a result of coercion or other circumstances, would contradict the very rationale underlying the protection afforded to such children against recruitment and use in hostilities."[142]

However, the *Ntaganda* decision has been criticised for broadening the civilian classification under IHL, as this construction is not consistent with the law in regards to ordinary members of an armed group.[143] As discussed in Chapter 3, civilians who are members of an 'organised' armed group lose their civilian status and are seen to be continuing their direct participating in hostilities for the purposes of the law.[144] For the 'revolving door' protection of civilian status and "the restriction of loss of protection to the duration of specific hostile acts was designed to respond to spontaneous, sporadic or unorganized hostile acts by civilians and cannot be applied to organized armed groups."[145]

To allow members of organised armed groups to regain their civilian status, while still remaining members, would give an unfair advantage to these armed groups over State forces. Thus, it is commonly accepted that the "revolving door" of civilian status no longer applies to any member of an organised armed group.[146] However, as handed down by the ICC, children are considered the exception to the continuous combat function, that is, that their membership does not indicate a loss of their civilian status. According to the decision of *Ntaganda*, children must only be seen as military targets when they are directly participating in hostilities, and accordingly, they automatically return to their protected status once they are no longer 'directly' participating in hostilities,[147] although they remain members of the armed group.

Further to the distinction between child and adult soldiers, the ICC in their decision of *Lubanga*,[148] made a further distinction between 'active' and 'direct' participation in hostilities when it comes to children. As according to Article 8(2)(b)(xxvi) and (e)(vii) of the Rome Statute, using children to "participate

142 Ibid at paragraph 31.

143 Joanna Nicholson, 'Is Targeting Naked Child Soldiers a War Crime?' (2016) *16(1) International Criminal Law Review* 134 at 134.

144 Nils Melzer, *Interpretive Guidance on the Notion of Direct Participation in Hostilities Under International Humanitarian Law, International Committee of the Red Cross* (Reference Paper, 2009) at 71.

145 Ibid at 71–72.

146 Ibid at 72.

147 *Ntaganda* Case, above note 139.

148 Michael E Kurth, 'The *Lubanga* Case of the international Criminal Court: A Critical Analysis of the Trial Chamger's Findings on Issues of Active Use, Age, and Gravity' (2013) *5 Goettingen Journal of International Law* 431.

actively in hostilities" is a war crime in both an IAC and NIAC. As set down by the ICC, the use of the word 'active' participation is intended to give a wider interpretation when it comes to child recruitment, to allow a wider range of activities outside fighting in the front line.[149] In the *Lubanga* decision, the Court insisted that the "use of the expression 'to participate actively in hostilities', as opposed to the expression 'direct participation' (as found in Additional Protocol I to the Geneva Conventions) was clearly intended to import a wide interpretation to the activities and roles that are covered by the offence of using children under the age of 15 actively to participate in hostilities."[150] Although intended for criminal liability of the recruitment of children, it does reflect the difference in children and adult fighters.

The use of the terminology of "using children to participate actively in hostilities" enclosed in the Rome Statue, has been interpreted by the Court to:

> cover both direct participation in combat and also active participation in military activities linked to combat such as scouting, spying, sabotage and the use of children as decoys, couriers or at military checkpoints. It would not cover activities clearly unrelated to the hostilities such as food deliveries to an airbase or the use of domestic staff in an officer's married accommodation. However, use of children in a direct support function such as acting as bearers to take supplies to the front line, or activities at the front line itself, would be included within the terminology.[151]

The ICRC adopted the distinction of the *Lubanga* decision, however, "the committee made a distinction between 'combat' and 'military activities linked to combat', not between 'active' and 'direct' participation."[152] The ICRC employed different language to the ICC; as previously suggested by the ICRC "the treaty terms of "direct" and "active" indicate the same quality and degree of individual participation in hostilities."[153] However, irrespective of the wording, both the ICC and ICRC have the same practical implication in construing differing levels of 'participation' when taking children into account. Therefore, when

149 *Situation in the Democractic Republic of the Congo, in the case of the Prosecutor v Thomas Lubanga Dyilo*, International Criminal Court, Trail Chamber I, Judgment pursuant to Article 74 of the Statute, ICC-01/04-01/06, 14 March 2012 at paragraph 627.

150 Ibid at paragraph 627.

151 United Nations, *Report of the Preparatory Committee on the Establishment of an International Criminal Court, Addendum, Part One*, UN Doc. A/CONF.183/2/Add.1, 14 April 1998 at 21.

152 Melzer, above note 144 at footnote 84.

153 Ibid at 45.

determining the legal status of children, both the ICC and the ICRC have taken a broad interpretation to the "revolving door" of civilian status insisting that children must not be merely 'actively' participating but rather be 'directly' participating in hostilities. That is, children will regain their civilian protection as long as they are not 'directly' participating in hostilities, even though they are active members of an armed group.

As previously discussed in Chapter 3, there is no well-defined interpretation of 'direct participation', however, in the ICRC's Interpretative Guidance 'direct participation' is defined as "a direct causal link between the act and the harm likely to result either from that act, or from a coordinated military operation of which that act constitutes an integral part (direct causation)."[154] However, the 'nexus' interpretation of 'direct participation' seems not to apply to children, as there is a distinction made between 'active' and 'direct', or 'combat' and 'military activities linked to combat'. Consequently, there seems to be two conflicting interpretations of 'direct participation' under the law, one for adults and another for children. The implication of this interpretation of 'direct participation of hostilities', is that peacekeepers engaging in armed conflict must take reasonable measures not to target children unless they are 'directly' involved in hostilities. Moreover, once child soldiers have ceased their 'direct' participation in hostilities, they regain their protected civilian status, even if they remain an active member of an armed group.

Although the law would allow peacekeepers to target child soldiers who are directly participating in hostilities, some academic commentators have contended that children should never be considered as 'combatants', but rather should always be respected as 'victims'.[155] Notwithstanding the victimisation of child soldiers, however, to demand that peacekeepers not engage with child soldiers who are directly participating in hostilities, is to instruct peacekeepers to relinquish their basic right to defend their person and others in their surroundings.[156]

---

154 Ibid at 46.

155 Shannon Bosch, 'Targeting and prosecuting 'under-aged' child soldiers in international armed conflicts, in light of the international humanitarian law prohibition against civilian direct participation in hostilities' (2012) *45(3) The Comparative and International Law Journal of Southern Africa* 324 at 330; Jacques Kabano, 'The Criminal Responsibility of Child Soldier Under International Criminal Law, Case Study: Northern Uganda and Democratic Republic of Congo (DRC)' (2016) *2(2) E-Journal of Law* 15; Nicholson, above note 143.

156 Emily Kalah Gade, 'The Child Soldier: The Question of Self-Defense' (2011) *10(4) Journal of Military Ethics* 323 at 323–324.

Once children are directly participating in hostilities, they lose the protections offered to 'civilians', placing them outside the protection of the law and the protection mandate. Although some commentators have made moral arguments against the targeting of child soldiers,[157] legally, UN peacekeepers can target child soldiers when they are directly participating in hostilities.

While child soldiers can be targeted, peacekeepers still need to maintain the rule of distinction entrenched in Article 13(2) of Additional Protocol II. When UN peace missions infiltrate armed groups, they must distinguish between permissible and impermissible targets. Particularly, as the presence of children and women within these camps does not make them lawful targets. Reports from the FIB in the DRC, have indicated that UN peacekeepers consider anyone within an armed group's camp as a lawful target.[158] Subsequently, as peacekeepers are not distinguishing between military and civilian targets, they are in breach of their obligations under the law. When peacekeepers infiltrate camps with child soldiers they first must identify whether or not the children are 'directly participating in hostilities' before engaging in lethal force. Without sufficient assessment, peacekeepers will be in breach of their obligations under IHL and the protection of civilians mandate.

4.7 *Protection against Child Soldiers*

Although peacekeepers should consider child soldiers as 'victims' in need of protection, conversely, occasionally these child soldiers have themselves been responsible for multiple IHL and human rights violations against other civilians. Therefore, children can adopt the dual role of victim and abuser simultaneously. This contradiction is also found within the academic literature that portrays child soldiers paradoxically "as exploited victims of adult abuse of power and, two, as enraged, virtually uncontrollable killers."[159] There are multiple examples of children being commanders over groups of child soldiers who have been reported as committing serious atrocities, including murder and sexual violence, "who were clearly willing and acted without coercion, and who may have forced other children to commit such acts".[160] In UN peace missions in the DRC and Sierra Leone, peacekeepers were confronted with the

157 Guy Goodwin-Gill and Ilene Cohn, *Child Soldiers: The Role of Children in Armed Conflict* (Clarendon Press, 1994).

158 Center for Civilians in Conflict, above note 136 at 1.

159 David Rosen, *Armies of the Young: Child Soldiers in War and Terrorism* (Rutgers University Press, 2005).

160 Amnesty International, *Child Soldiers: Criminals or Victims?*, London, Amnesty International, 2000 at 6.

dual obligation of protecting civilians from atrocities committed by the same child soldiers that they are also obliged to protect.[161]

When peacekeepers are faced with a divergence in their obligations, the priority of protection under the mandate must be the physical protection and dignity of civilians, as discussed previously. The obligation to protect includes the protection from direct targeting "irrespective of the source of such violence."[162] When children participate in violations of international law and threaten the physical protection and dignity of civilians, they become a 'threat' that prompts a peacekeeping response.

When peacekeepers are combatting children outside the IHL framework, they are bound by principles under IHRL, that is, they should use minimal force to subdue or detain those individuals and diminish the threat. Lethal force can only be used as a last resort outside the realms of an armed conflict.

Once the child soldier has been disarmed and detained, and thus the threat ended, the 'soldier' returns to be a 'child' in need of protection under the law and the Security Council mandate. Children are generally not considered ex-combatants, but rather return entirely to their civilian status even if detained or captured by peacekeepers. As stated previously, international tribunals and courts do not exert jurisdiction over persons under the age of 18 years. This restriction in jurisdiction of international tribunals and courts implies that international criminal law deems individuals under the age of 18 years as 'victims' of conflict and thus cannot be held legally responsible for actions committed while being victims themselves.[163] Particularly, international law prohibits and punishes the recruitment of child soldiers, but not the act of child soldiering itself.

Under customary international law children over the age of 15 can be legally recruited into an armed group, which would indicate that they should no longer be considered victims under the law. Although IHL considers a dual category of children, in contradictory fashion international criminal law generally sees a sole category of any person under the age of 18 years. The exception under international criminal law was the establishment of the Special Court of Sierra Leone, which gave the Court jurisdiction over persons over the age of 15.[164] Even though the Court of Sierra Leone had jurisdiction over children over the age of 15, they did not prosecute anyone in that age group. Thus, with the exception of the Court of Sierra Leone, it is implied that although

161 Ibid.

162 *United Nations Security Council Resolution 2155* (2014) at operational paragraph 4(a)(i).

163 Breen, above note 72 at 80.

164 *Statute of the Special Court for Sierra Leone* (2000) at Article 7.

children over 15 years of age can be legally recruited into armed forces, under international criminal law they are not to be considered legally responsible nor accountable for their obligations under IHL. However, this only applies to international courts and tribunals, as domestic courts will require differing ages of legal responsibility. Domestically, the age of legal responsibility will depend on the host State's criminal codes. For example, while CAR places the age of legal responsibility at 14,[165] Sudan places the age at 7 (if the child has reached puberty).[166] This raises questions on whether peacekeepers are compelled to transfer detained child soldiers accused of crimes, to local authorities or to reintegrate them back into their community. In other words, there is a conflict between duties owed under domestic law, and duties owed under the protection mandate.

5 Protection Advisors and Training

The manifestation of the Security Council's 'intention' to ensure that UN peace mission mandates have provisions regarding the protection of women and children, is the creation of women and children protection advisers. Women and children protection advisers are inserted during preparations and the tactical planning of UN peace missions. As recommended by the Secretary-General, in regards to women's protection, peace missions should "[i]ncorporate gender perspectives explicitly into mandates of all peacekeeping missions, including provisions to systematically address this issue in all reports to the Security Council."[167] These gender perspectives are intended to be dealt by the women protection advisers and their inclusion in UN peace missions. Other than having these advisers participate in the planning of UN peace missions, they are also deployed in the field in order to continue assisting UN peace missions to understand and tackle women and children protection issues.[168]

The role of the protection advisers is used by the UN to guide mission leadership to ensure that women and children are constantly considered in peacekeeping strategy.[169] Even though not explicitly mandated, the protection

165 Loi No. 10.001 portant code penal Centrafricain at Article 9.

166 *Criminal Act 1991*, Sudan at Sections 3 and 9.

167 United Nations Security Council, *Report of the Secretary-General on Women, Peace and Security*, UN Doc S/2002/1154 at Action 10.

168 *United Nations Security Council Resolution 1539* (2004) at operational paragraph 7.

169 United Nations Security Council, *Report of the Secretary-General on Children and Armed Conflict*, UN Doc S/2002/1299 at paragraph 9.

advisers work on the preventive protection of women and children, by lobbying and working with local authorities to establish political and social change.[170] However, their role remains vague in respect to the military or police component of UN peace missions, particularly, as the Security Council is yet to identify the specific duties intended to protect women and children. In discussions with a peacekeeping analyst it has been identified that many of the military and police components do not fully understand what these civilian advisors bring to the overall mission strategy.[171] Moreover, the civilian components do not understand the working of the military and thus cannot effectively give guidance.[172] It was commented that civilian peacekeepers do not grasp military preparations, becoming frustrated when military components cannot react quickly or adapt as women and children advisers envisage.[173]

Moreover, due to human resourcing issues it becomes difficult to relocate or temporarily deploy civilian peacekeepers, therefore, deployment of troops generally occurs without civilian peacekeepers.[174] Consequently, women and children advisors cannot advise or assist in operations outside of UN bases of operations.

To succeed in the prevention of sexual violence and child recruitment, lobbying and the strengthening of the rule of law is needed, which is considered the role of the civilian component.[175] As adopted by the Security Council, it is necessary "when establishing and renewing the mandates of United Nations missions, to include provisions on the promotion of gender equality and the empowerment of women in conflict and post-conflict situations, including through the appointment of gender advisers as appropriate."[176] In order to prevent the increase in sexual violence and the recruitment of children, there needs to be a change in "social attitudes in tandem with legal and policy reforms to reduce stigmatization."[177] However, this political change can only

170 United Nations Security Council, *Women and Peace and Security: Report of the Security-General*, UN Doc S/2009/465 at paragraph 34.

171 Interview with Protection of Civilains researcher on 23 January 2019.

172 Ibid.

173 Ibid.

174 Center for Civilians in Conflict, *Moving Towards Mobility: Providing Protection to Civilians Through Static Presence and Mobile Peacekeeping in South Sudan* (2019) at 23.

175 United Nations Security Council, *Women and Peace and Security: Report of the Security-General*, UN Doc S/2009/465 at paragraph 34.

176 *United Nations Security Council Resolution 2122* (2013) at operational paragraph 4.

177 United Nations Security Council, *Women and Peace and Security: Report of the Security-General*, UN Doc S/2009/465 at paragraph 21.

be achieved with a clear mandate of the priorities under the protection of civilians mandate.

Within UN peace missions there are growing tensions between protection in the long-term versus immediate protection of individuals. There is no clear indication of priorities between establishing a post-conflict secure and protective environment and immediate protection using force. Peacekeepers using force in order to protect civilians may be more disruptive to the overall peace process, causing a delay in peace. When planning UN peace missions there needs to be more interaction between the military, police and civilian components of a mission, to ensure that all levels of protection are being considered. Part of the emphasis on physical protection as discussed in Chapter 2 and 3, protection advisors are the most vulnerable with the current budget cuts resulting in protection advisors no longer being deployed in missions.[178]

Outside the deployment of protection advisors, the Security Council attempts to ensure the protection of women and children, by mandating and encouraging the training of peacekeepers in issues particular to women and children. As early as 1999, the Security Council has been requiring all peacekeepers to be trained in issues of women and child protection.[179] In regards to sexual violence, as mandated by the Security Council in 2008, peacekeepers need to be granted adequate training "to help them better prevent, recognise and respond to sexual violence and other forms of violence against civilians."[180] However, instead of establishing mandatory training, or specific content and training scenarios, the Security Council has left the training with the TCCs, for the Security Council:

> [e]ncourages troop and police contributing countries, in consultation with the Secretary-General, to consider steps they could take to heighten awareness and the responsiveness of their personnel participating in UN peacekeeping operations to protect civilians, including women and children, and prevent sexual violence against women and girls in conflict and post-conflict situations, including wherever possible the deployment of a higher percentage of women peacekeepers or police.[181]

178 Aïssata Athie and Sarah Taylor, *UN Peacekeeping: Where is the Gender Expertise?* <https://theglobalobservatory.org/2017/10/un-peacekeeping-where-is-the-gender-expertise/>.

179 *United Nations Security Council Resolution 1261* (1999) at operational paragraph 19.

180 *United Nations Security Council Resolution 1820* (2008) at operational paragraph 6.

181 Ibid at operational paragraph 8.

As stated in Chapter 1, TCCs are obliged to ensure respect of the legal obligations under the protection mandate, thus, part of that obligation is to warrant adequate training to all military and police officers deployed in protection missions. By failing to adequately train their troops and police, they are breaching their obligation under the protection mandate. In recent interviews with TCCs, many States have indicated that DPO's policies and manuals are only offered in English rather than translating them in any of other language, making them useless to troops on the ground.[182]

The prominent training model for peacekeeping is the scenario-based model, however, what is required is to train the 'mindset' of peacekeepers.[183] Training needs to focus on the correct mindset regarding protection of women and children. Mindset training is paramount as it becomes impossible to predict all situations that will be faced by peacekeepers. Although examples become useful in illustrating the mindset that is needed, they must only be used as a means to an end. Specifically, as peacekeeping has grown organically, so too must the protection offered on the ground. However, in order to train peacekeepers in a specific rationale, the legal interpretation of protection must be first articulated.

6 Conclusion

The protection of civilians mandate creates a legally binding obligation to protect the legal rights of civilians. The Security Council has primarily focused on the protection against physical violence, which may trigger the application of IHL and its obligations. Specifically, peacekeepers are to protect civilians within the vicinity of UN bases, their person, and areas of patrol. Moreover, peacekeepers are obliged to ensure that all force is used in proportion to the overall protection of civilians. As concluded in this chapter, peacekeepers are obliged to ensure that children and women are not being targeted under the principle of distinction. Furthermore, as IHRL applies whether or not there is an armed conflict, IHRL principles become the governing principles for law enforcement activities undertaken by UNPOL. Therefore, peacekeepers must ensure that they adhere to IHRL when engaging in any law enforcement activity. Specifically, as concluded in this chapter peacekeepers must ensure the IHRL protections to children forcefully removed from armed groups.

---

182 Interviews conducted in New York in January 2023.

183 Paolo Tripodi, 'Peacekeepers, Moral Autonomy and the Use of Force' (2006) 5(3) *Journal of Military Ethics* 214 at 221.

The Security Council, in explicitly mandating the protection of women and children proposes to appoint further obligations on peacekeepers outside the scope of the standard protection mandate. This expanded obligation under the protection of women and children is concerned with 'protections' in connection with armed conflict and violations of IHL. Hence, the main obligation under the protection of women and children, is the protection against sexual and gender-based violence, and the recruitment of children. Moreover, TCCs are obliged under the mandate to ensure that military and police contingents are adequately trained in women and children protection before deployment.

Regarding the protection of children, civilian peacekeepers are obliged to monitor, investigate and report on children recruited in armed groups to begin the DDR process. While military peacekeepers are not to forcibly remove children from armed groups, when engaging in military operations that involve child soldiers, peacekeepers will be obliged to ensure that children are only targeted if they are taking direct part in hostilities. If children are removed from these armed groups, a mechanism must be established to ensure that all protections are being offered to them. Without adequate safeguards to protect ex-child soldiers, peacekeepers will be in breach of their obligation to protect.

Further, UN police officers are obligated to protect against conflict-related sexual and gender-based violence. However, outside of using direct force to halt the violence, it is unclear what avenues can be used to prevent and protect from 'threats' of that violence. Other than detaining aggressors, which was discussed in Chapter 4 as being problematic under the law, UN police officers are hindered from preventing or protecting women from conflict-related violence.

When the Security Council mandates peacekeepers to protect women and children from conflict-related violence, a correlation is made between these protections and protections to IDPs. As a large number of civilians are internally displaced in areas of conflict, women and children become more vulnerable to conflict-related violence. Therefore, to achieve the obligation to protect women and children, the Security Council also mandates the protection of IDPs, which will be explored in the next chapter.

CHAPTER 6

The Protection of IDPs

According to the Internal Displacement Monitoring Centre, by the end of 2021, nearly 59.1 million people were internally displaced.[1] As civilian areas have become conflict battle grounds, civilians are systematically forced to abandon their homes to seek safety from armed violence. In modern NIACs armed groups intentionally "intimidate, attack and displace local populations to further their pursuit of economic control over natural resources."[2] Therefore, armed groups become reliant on the profitability gained from the displacement of civilians.

As such, the foremost threat to civilian protection, specifically connected to the protection against sexual violence, is internal displacement;[3] as reported by the Secretary-General there are "cause-and-effect linkages between displacement and conflict-related sexual violence."[4] As UN peace missions deployed to protect civilians in conflicts with substantial numbers of displaced civilians, peacekeepers must consider IDPs and their specific protections in order to fulfil their obligation to protect. Problematically, as IDPs are considered legally distinct from refugees, the infrastructure and guidance for protecting IDPs is not well established in dealing with their particular protection needs.[5] Specifically, IDPs, unlike refugees, remain close to conflict areas frequently becoming trapped in areas of armed conflict.[6]

As will be concluded in this chapter, in order to protect IDPs UN peacekeepers will find themselves in control over individuals, triggering their IHRL obligations. Therefore, as part of obligation to protect, peacekeepers may also be obligated to respect, protect and fulfil IDPs rights under IHRL, including the

1 http://www.internal-displacement.org/database/displacement-data.

2 United Nations Security Council, *Report of the Secretary-General to the Security Council on the Protection of Civilians in Armed Conflict*, UN Doc S/1999/957 at paragraph 13.

3 Catherine Phuong, *The International Protection of Internally Displaced Persons* (Cambridge University Press, 2004) at 117; Kamel Morjane, 'The Protection of Refugees and Displaced Persons' in Bertrand G Ramcharan (ed), *Human Rights Protection in the Field*, International Studies in Human Rights (Martinus Nijhoff Publishers, 2006) 79 at 84.

4 United Nations Security Council, *Women and Peace and Security: Report of the Security-General*, UN Doc S/2009/465 at paragraph 9.

5 United Nations General Asssembly, *Promotion and Protection of the Rights of Children: Impact of Armed Conflict on Children*, UN Doc A/51/306 at paragraph 82.

6 Morjane, above note 3 at 84.

 | DOI:10.1163/9789004707313_008

right to food, water, education and healthcare. This conclusion will be reached by first discussing the Security Council's mandate on the protection and security of IDPs as vulnerable civilians. Secondly, that the chief component of the Security Council's agenda for the protection of IDPs is the security and protection of IDP camps. Thirdly, with organic nature of IDP camps, unneeded risks to civilians have consequentially been created, and diverted the majority of UN resources. Finally, due to the nature of IDP camps UN peacekeepers have become the only authority and in effective control of IDPs within these camps triggering their IHRL obligations.

1 Protection of IDPs

The protection of civilians in the control and authority of a State that is not their own, can be found both in IHL and refugee law.[7] However, while IHL is concerned with, inter alia, the protection of enemy combatants and civilians in the control of an opposing party, refugee law is concerned with individuals who have "sought refuge from persecution on the territory of a third country."[8] Therefore, under refugee law 'protection' is the protection sought within another-State's territory by victims or potential victims of persecution.[9]

As refugee law is concerned with individuals fleeing persecution, and taking refuge in another State's territory, consequently, international protection under refugee law is "to make up for the failure of the State to protect the concerned person against the persecution feared."[10] With the establishment of UN Refugee Agency (*UNHCR*), the international community was granted an agency to oversee this form of protection. UNHCR was given a clear mandate: that "a person fearing persecution who flees across an international border deserves international protection because he or she cannot avail himself or herself of the protection of his/her Government."[11] As detailed by Weiss, the first legal adviser to UNHCR, the purpose of international protection is "to remedy the situation created by the fact that they lack the protection which is usually afforded to nationals abroad by the State of nationality."[12] Therefore,

7 Mélanie Jacques, *Armed Conflict and Displacement: The Protection of Refugees and Displaced Person under International Humanitarian Law* (Cambridge University Press, 2012) at 156.

8 Ibid at 156.

9 Antonio Fortin, 'The Meaning of 'Protection' in the Refugee Definition' (2000) *12 International Journal of Refugee Law* 548 at 550–551.

10 Ibid at 551.

11 Morjane, above note 3 at 79.

12 As qutoed in Fortin, above note 9 at 569.

the mandate of UNHCR is not to replace the primary responsibility of the State, rather UNHCR is to promote the protection of refugees, and assist in coordinating and providing emergency operations when needed.

For refugee law to apply, and thus the protections found within, individuals must be classified as 'refugees' under the law, specifically under the 1951 *Convention Relating to the Status of Refugees*. That is, individuals must be persecuted or potentially persecuted, as defined under the Convention, and flee across territorial borders seeking refuge within another State's territory. Thus, as noted by UNHCR, "[p]ersons compelled to leave their country of origin as a result of international or national armed conflict are not normally considered refugees under the 1951 Convention or 1967 protocol."[13] Additionally, with mass influxes of individuals fleeing a territory, it becomes impractical in determining refugee status of that group of individuals. In such situations, a group-based recognition of refugee status is generally applied.[14] In practice, protection and recognition of refugee status is offered to any mass influx of individuals seeking refuge from armed conflict, "whether or not they are deemed to fall within the terms of the Convention".[15]

With the majority of conflict being classified as NIAC,[16] the majority of fleeing civilians in those conflicts do not seek refuge across international borders but are internally displaced within their home State's territory. Unlike 'refugees', IDPs do not have an explicit international law instrument outlining specific protections, rather have to rely on protections offered in existing legal structures. IDPs, as a group, are in greatest need of protection, for although their "needs may be as acute as those of refugees, but their plight is more precarious because of the lack of smoothly functioning and predictable arrangements to deal with them."[17]

IDPs have become the foremost humanitarian problem, demanding protection from daily threats, with at least half IDPs being children.[18] However, the

---

13 UN High Commissioner for Refugees (UNHCR), UNHCR Note on the Principle of Non-Refoulement, November 1997, available at: http://www.refworld.org/docid/438c6d972.html.

14 UN High Commissioner for Refugees, *UNHCR Guidelines on the Application in Mass Influx Situations of the Exclusion Clauses of Article 1F of the 1951 Convention relating to the Status of Refugees*, 2006 at paragraph 9.

15 UN High Commissione for Refugees, *The Scope of International Protection in Mass Influx*, EC/1995/SCP/CRP.3, 1995 at paragraph 8.

16 www.reliefweb.int/.

17 Morjane, above note 3 at 84.

18 United Nations General Asssembly, *Promotion and Protection of the Rights of Children: Impact of Armed Conflict on Children*, UN Doc A/51/306 at paragraph 66.

question of the precise protection needed by displaced people "has not always received appropriate attention, in spite of the view, that the main problem is not assistance but rather protection for internally displaced persons."[19] When considering the protection required by IDPs, two elements are mainly focused on – physical protection and the protection of their human rights.[20]

As concluded in Chapter 1 the protection mandate is interpreted as the protection of legal rights, hence, the protections offered to IDPs must be protections that are guaranteed to them under the law. Unlike refugees, IDPs have traditionally been considered a domestic issue, meaning that their protection remained the prime responsibility of the host State.[21] As the UN and international law are both rooted in the principle of State sovereignty, there still remains contention on the international legal protections afforded to IDPs. However, as internal displacement is becoming increasingly complicated, in 1993, at the request of the Commission on Human Rights, the Secretary-General's Representative on IDPs prepared a report on the legal framework to protect IDPs. The Report (*Deng's Report*)[22] identified that although protections of IDPs can be covered under the existing laws, there still remain essential protections not considered within the current framework. In response to Deng's Report, a set of non-binding *Guiding Principles on Internal Displacement*[23] was drafted and presented to the UN in 2001.

In order to mitigate unneeded opposition by Member States it was considered a political necessity to create a set of guidelines rather than a hard law instrument.[24] Therefore, the drafting of the Guiding Principles was not intended to establish 'new' norms but rather "reflect and are consistent with international human rights law and international humanitarian law."[25]

The Guiding Principles seek to emphasise the protection needed under each phase of forced displacement, in other words, dealing "with protection

---

19 Phuong, above note 3 at 117.

20 Ibid at 120.

21 Ibid at 185.

22 United Nations Economic and Social Council, *Internally Displaced Persons: Report of the Representative of the Secretary-General, Mr. Francis M.Deng, submitted pursuant to Commission on Human Rights resolution 1995/57 – Compliation and analysis of legal norms*, E/CN.4/1996/52/Add.2.

23 United Nations Office for the Coordination of Humanitarian Affairs, *Guiding Principles on Internal Displacement*, 1998.

24 A. M. Abebe, 'Legal and Institutional Dimensions of Protecting and Assisting Internally Displaced Persons in Africa' (2009) 22(2) *Journal of Refugee Studies* 155 at 157.

25 United Nations Office for the Coordination of Humanitarian Affairs, *Guiding Principles on Internal Displacement*, 1998 at paragraph 3.

against, during and after displacement."[26] The Guiding Principles not only place emphasis on physical protection, but also identifies the importance of social, political and economic protection. As protection of IDPs cannot be summarised in any legal instrument, such as refugee law, consequently, "it can only be rooted within the broader human rights framework."[27] As reiterated by the Inter-Agency Standing Committee (*IASC*), the Guiding Principles, "do not seek to create a privileged category of person or to establish a separate legal status for the internally displaced. Rather, they are based on the assumption that internally displaced persons have the same rights and obligations as other persons living in their own state."[28]

When defining 'protection' afforded to IDPs, the IASC in their 1999 Policy Paper have adopted the definition formulated in the ICRC 1999 Workshop, that is, "all activities, aimed at obtaining full respect for the rights of the individual in accordance with the letter and spirit of the relevant bodies of law."[29] Human Rights Watch and other human rights agencies have taken on the IASC's approach to protection of IDPs, but have added another aspect, contending that "protection encompasses both security of persons and property, as well as guarantees of legal protection and redress for rights abuses."[30] Human Rights Watch's insertion of 'property' is highlighted with the deliberate targeting of civilians in order to forcefully displace local populations for their pursuit of economic control over property and natural resources.[31]

In response to the Guiding Principles, the African Union's (*AU*) Executive Council requested the AU secretariat draft a legal instrument to outline IDP protections in Africa. In October 2009, the *AU Convention for the Protection and Assistance of Internally Displaced Persons in Africa* (*Kampala Convention*)

26 Phuong, above note 3 at 119.

27 Ibid at 119.

28 United Nations Inter-Agency Standing Committee, *Protection of Internally Displaced Persons*, Policy Paper, New York, December 1999 at 5.

29 International Committee of the Red Cross, *Strengthening Protection in War: A Search for Professional Standards*, Caverzasio, Sylvie Giossi (ed), Genenva, Switzerland, 1996–2000 at 19.

30 Human Rights Watch, *Summary Report Kenya*, 1997, https://www.hrw.org/reports/1997/kenya2/3.htm.

31 United Nations Security Council, *Report of the Secretary-General to the Security Council on the Protection of Civilians in Armed Conflict*, UN Doc S/1999/957 at paragraph 13; With numerous conflicts centred around natural resources, the protection of property has become a serious consideration especially in the context of ensuring the safe return of IDPs. However, the Security Council has yet to mandate the protection of civilians' property in any UN peace mission, however, it is implied within the mandate to ensure secure environments and 'areas of return'.

was adopted. As of April 2022, the Kampala Convention has been signed by 40 Member States and ratified by 33. In contrast to the Guiding Principles, the Kampala Convention intends to "[e]stablish a legal framework for preventing internal displacement, and protecting and assisting internally displaced persons in Africa."[32] However, while the AU has attempted to create a legal framework for the prevention and protection of IDPs, this has not decreased the number of IDPs nor created sufficient protections. Though the Kampala Convention retains the protection of IDPs with African States, as the majority of UN peace missions deployed in Africa are made up of AU troops, the Security Council still look to UN peace missions to protect IDPs.

While the existing legal structures offer protections to IDPs, at times IDPs need protections that do not exist in international legal instruments. For example, internally displaced women lack protection in determination of their legal status, as the current procedures "may not take gender-based persecution into consideration."[33] Additionally, many IDPs are women and children, who are either lost or do not have access to identification and 'official' State documents, and hence are at risk of being exploited. As expressed by the Security Council in the preamble of *Resolution 2122* (2013), there is concern "at women's exacerbated vulnerability in armed conflict and post-conflict situations particularly in relation to forced displacement, as a result of unequal citizenship rights, gender-biased application of asylum laws, and obstacles to registering and accessing identity documents which occur in many situations."[34]

Although IDPs require a myriad of protections, as outlined in the Guiding Principles, when mandating peacekeepers to protect IDPs, the Security Council generally focuses on only two aspects – the securing and protection offered to individuals in IDP camps, and the safe return of displaced individuals to their place of origin. As established in Chapter 3, although multiple violations are identified by the Security Council, mandates still revolve around physical protection.

Problematically, IDP camps are at times "poorly designed and security inside and outside camps is inadequate."[35] Moreover within the camps, control over resources such as food, water, and firewood, becomes a source of power, and

32 *African Union Convention for the Protection and Assistance of Internally Displaced Persons in Africa (Kampala Convention)* at Article 2(b).

33 United Nations Security Council, *Report of the Secretary-General on Women, Peace and Security*, UN Doc S/2002/1154 at paragraph 11.

34 *United Nations Security Council Resolution 2122* (2013) at preamble.

35 United Nations Security Council, *Report of the Secretary-General on Women, Peace and Security*, UN Doc S/2002/1154 at paragraph 50.

as men are normally responsible for their distribution, they "often abuse their power by demanding bribes or sexual favours."[36] For this reason the Security Council has generically mandated peacekeepers to prioritise "securing IDP camps and adjacent areas"[37] or to protect civilians from "physical violence, including civilians gathered in displaced and refugee camps."[38] As peacekeepers take direct part in the security of these camps, they begun to exert 'control' over IDPs, triggering peacekeepers' human rights obligations to those under their control. However, the UN and Security Council are yet to acknowledge the concerns that the UN is a controlling power and hence, that IHL and IHRL obligations must be considered.

Regarding the mandate on safe return, the Security Council has been inconsistent with their use of language. As an example, in UNMISS, the Security Council mandated UNMISS to create a "secure environment for eventual safe and voluntary return"[39] of IDPs, while the UN Peace Mission in Darfur (*UNAMID*) has been mandated to assist in "supporting the development and training of community policing for IDP camps and areas of return."[40] However, most commonly the Security Council has mandated that peacekeepers "work closely with humanitarian agencies, particularly in relation to areas of tension and of the return of displaced persons."[41] However, with such vague language there is no indication of the duty and obligation expected of peacekeepers in regards to the return of IDPs. Moreover, with the limited resources given to UN peace missions, peacekeepers are forced to prioritise activities, thus, as can be evidenced by UNMISS, peacekeepers focus their resources on defending and securing the PoC sites, rather than ensuring secure environments for IDPs safe return.

---

36 United Nations General Asssembly, *Promotion and Protection of the Rights of Children: Impact of Armed Conflict on Children*, UN Doc A/51/306 at paragraph 78.

37 *United Nations Security Council Resolution 2003* (2011) at operational paragraph 3(a); *United Nations Security Council Resolution 2063* (2012) at operational paragraph 3(a); *United Nations Security Council Resolution 2173* (2014) at operational paragraph 3(a).

38 *United Nations Security Council Resolution 2098* (2013) at operational paragraph 12(a)(i); *United Nations Security Council Resolution 1861* (2009) at operational paragraph 7(a)(i).

39 *United Nations Security Council Resolution 2155* (2014) at operational paragraph 4(a)(vi).

40 *United Nations Security Council Resolution 2113* (2014) at operational paragraph 4(a).

41 *United Nations Security Council Resolution 1933* (2010) at operational paragraph 16(b); *United Nations Secuirty Council Resolution 2000* (2011) at operational paragraph 7(b); *United Nations Security Council Resolution 2162* (2014) at operational paragraph 19(a).

2 Protection of IDP Camps

When mandating protection activities in regard to IDPs, the Security Council focuses on 3 main tasks – protection of IDP camps,[42] active patrolling,[43] and the creation of 'secure environments'.[44] In mandating the protection of IDPs, the Security Council mandates peacekeepers to pay "particular attention to civilians gathered in displaced persons and refugee camps."[45] Within UN peacekeeping the primary protection activity in regard to IDPs is the protection and supervision of IDP camps.

As civilians are becoming internally displaced at alarming rates, UN peace missions are required to divert their resources to the security of IDP camps. With the outbreak of sporadic armed conflict, civilians are forced to seek refuge in ad hoc areas, creating unplanned camps and sites. As evidenced in South Sudan, civilians have sought refuge at peacekeeping bases, transforming the adjacent areas into unplanned IDP camps. Since 2017 there has been more than 1.85 million people internally displaced in South Sudan, "including 223,994 sheltered in United Nations sites for the protection of civilians".[46]

In order to sufficiently monitor and coordinate IDP concerns, UNHCR uses a 'cluster approach', coordinating a group of agencies to work together to set up, manage and assist; including IDP camp set up and management. However, with the unpredictable nature of internal conflict, many IDP camps are not being planned or created by the Global Protection Cluster; rather areas become camps simply by the gathering of displaced civilians. As camps are not being designed under international standards, they are putting civilians housed within these camps at risk.

The issue of ad hoc camps is perfectly illustrated by the PoC sites in South Sudan. Since 2014, South Sudanese displaced persons have been taking refuge

---

42 *United Nations Security Council Resolution 2296* (2016) at operational paragraph 4; *United Nations Security Council Resolution 2301* (2016) at operational paragraph 3.

43 *United Nations Security Council Resolution 2327* (2016) at operational paragraph 15; *United Nations Security Council Resolution 2364* (2017) at operational paragraph 20.

44 *United Nations Security Council Resolution 2387* (2017) at operational paragraph 42(f); *United Nations Security Council Resolution 2295* (2016) at operational paragraph 19(g); *United Nations Security Council Resolution 2301* (2016) at operational paragraph 33(c).

45 *United Nations Security Council Resolution 2409* (2018) at operational paragraph 36(i)(a); *United Nations Security Council Resolution 2327* (2016) at operational paragraph 7(a)(ii); or a variation of "securing IDP camps" in *United Nations Security Council Resolution 2296* (2016) at operational paragraph 4.

46 United Nations Security Council, *Report of the Secretary-General on the Protection of Civilians in Armed Conflict*, UN Doc S/2017/414 at paragraph 64.

in and around UN bases from the outbreak of armed violence. Although UNMISS was not originally mandated to create these camps, nor create a safe haven for these civilians, the PoC sites were created organically as a response to the outbreak of violence. As such, IDPs within these sites are facing increased risks of exploitation and violence due to their poor design. As reported by the Secretary-General, "[w]omen and girls face the risk of violence when camps are poorly designed and security inside and outside of camps is inadequate."[47]

2.1 *UN Effective Control over Individuals and IDP Camps*

As UN peace missions are deployed in failed States, IDP camps lack government authority, thus UN peacekeepers might become the only authority within these camps. At first instance, the PoC sites were run in conjunction with local authorities, specifically the local police force, however, with the development of these camps, the only remaining authority has become UNMISS.[48] The current PoC sites are isolated from any government control, leaving UNMISS as the only effective authority or administration within these camps. As noted in reports, the "core reality is that, due to lack of government capacity, both UNMISS and humanitarian actors have been mandated to assume the responsibilities inherent in the protection of civilians."[49] Although UNMISS has been mandated to undertake only security and protection activities, when the security situation within the PoC sites has become too dangerous for the humanitarian actors to operate, "UNMISS has had to take on humanitarian responsibilities, such as food and water provisions, site management and the building of latrines."[50]

With the conflict in South Sudan, UNMISS has been forced to adopt a quasi-authoritative role within the sites.[51] Notwithstanding UNMISS's function in the sites, the UN has contended that as UNMISS has not received an executive mandate granting them authority for full administrative control, they cannot be in control of these camps.[52] It is contended that UNMISS cannot have

47 United Nations Security Council, *Report of the Secretary-General on Women, Peace and Security*, UN Doc S/2002/1154 at paragraph 50.

48 International Organization for Migration, *We Leave We Are Killed: Lessons Learned from South Sudan Protection of Civilians Sites 2013–2016*, 2016 at 39.

49 Ibid at 40.

50 Eli Stamnes, *Policy Brief: The United Nations Mission in the Republic of South Sudan (UNMISS): Protecting Civilians in a Volatile Environment* (Norwegian Institute of Internatioanl Affairs, 2015) at 2.

51 Ray Murphy, 'The United Nations Mission in South Sudan and the Protection of Civilians' (2017) 22(3) *Journal of Conflict and Security Law* 367 at 378.

52 Jenna Stern, *Establishing Safety and Security at Protection of Civilians Sites* (Stimson Center, September 2015) at 10.

effective control as UNMISS is limited by its mandate and the SOFA signed with the South Sudanese government.[53] This limitation of control is illustrated with UNMISS police officers' inability to deal with civilian disputes and to prosecute any criminal behaviour though legal mechanisms.

As determined by the ICJ the question of an authority's control over a territory is a question of fact.[54] Thus, whether or not UNMISS has been given an executive mandate does not affect the determination of 'effective control'. Due to the South Sudanese government's insufficient presence, UNMISS has been required to create quasi-structures in order to maintain order within the PoC sites. For example, the UNPOL component of UNMISS has been forced to develop procedures and internal site structures to ensure a level of order.[55] UNMISS has delegated the running of the camps to 'leaders' and 'chiefs' of differing groups within the camps, however, as these chiefs are empowered by UNMISS, chiefs have referred back to UNMISS in politically charged situations.[56]

As outlined under Article 5 of DAR,[57] the "conduct of a person or entity which is not an organ of the State under [this] article but which is empowered by the law of that State to exercise elements of the governmental authority shall be considered an act of the State under international law." Interestingly, these provisions are not explicitly mentioned in ARIO, however, ARIO defines an "agent" as a "person or entity, other than an organ, who is charged by the organization with carrying out, or helping to carry out, one of its functions, and thus through whom the organization acts."[58] UNMISS have 'empowered' these chiefs with the day-to-day administration of these camps, therefore, suggesting that these chiefs are 'agents' of UNMISS under ARIO. As agents of UNMISS, UNMISS will be responsible for their actions and omissions under the law.

To deal with civilian disputes Chiefs Courts have been established in the PoC sites to deal with internal civilian disputes and minor law prosecutions. While UNMISS does not 'officially' recognise the authority of these courts, they have allowed them to exist and have referred civilians to them.[59] Moreover,

53 Rachel Ibreck and Naomi Pendle, 'Customary Protection? Chiefs' Courts as Public Authority in UN Protection of Civilian Sites in South Sudan' (The Justice and Security Research Programme, September 2016 2016) at 3.

54 *Armed Activities on the Territory of the Congo (Democractic Republic of the Congo v Uganda)*, Judgment, ICJ Reports 2005, p.168 at paragraph 173.

55 Ibreck and Pendle, above note 53 at 7.

56 Ibreck and Pendle, above note 53.

57 DAR at Article 5.

58 ARIO at Article 2(d).

59 Ibreck and Pendle, above note 53.

UNPOL has set regulations on these courts by removing the court's jurisdiction over murder cases and more serious criminal offences. Civilians accused of serious criminal offences are dealt directly by UNPOL.[60] Although UNMISS cannot prosecute criminals, they have created temporary measures as a form of punishment, one example being removing individuals from the sites.[61] Further, UNPOL has had to constructed "holding facilities and assessments to determine when a suspect or offender could be excluded from the camp."[62]

Effective control does not have to be held by one entity, rather it can be attributed jointly to multiple bodies or authorities.[63] So although peacekeepers might have some limitation on their control, particularly that of legal and enforcement mechanisms, they can still share the responsibility jointly with other legal bodies. As specified in Article 48(1) of ARIO when there is joint responsibility for the same act, "the responsibility of each State or organization may be invoked in relation to that act." Thus, even when UNMISS possess control with local authorities, depending on the situation, the responsibility can be shared jointly.

The UN peace mission's control can be over a territory, or over individuals. Although the UN can contend that they do not have territorial control, it would be difficult to suggest that they do not have control over individuals within these camps. UNMISS' control is evidenced by their authority over civilians' entrances and decision to who remains within these camps. Moreover, UNMISS grants authority to individuals within these camps for administrative purposes. Although the PoC sites contains multiple agencies, it has been reported that these agencies regard UNMISS as the 'final' authority within these camps.[64] As it is perceived by civilians that UNMISS has become the substitute legal authority, it would indicate that they have 'effective control' over these camps,[65] and are thus bound by IHRL obligations.

While UNMISS' control cannot be correlated with territorial control, this level of control is vaster than individual control, such as detentions. As the current legal structure does not have a 'middle' between territorial and individual

---

60 Ibid; Also, Chapter 4 on detentions to see what procedures are used by UNPOL with detained individuals.

61 Ibreck and Pendle, above note 53.

62 Ibid.

63 Paolo Palchetti, 'The allocation of responsibility for internationally wrongful acts committed in the course of multinational operations' (2013) 95(891–892) *International Review of the Red Cross* 727 at 739.

64 IOM report on South Sudan Migration.

65 Conor Foley, 'What are the human rights obligations of unmiss to those sheltering on its protection sites?' (2016) 2 *Conflict Trends* 20.

control, at the very least, UNMISS must adhere to their obligations under the jurisdiction over individuals within the camp.

While UNMISS exerts effective control, the laws of occupation will not apply, as a "territory is considered occupied when it is actually placed under the authority of the hostile army."[66] As UN peace missions receive consent from the host State, they cannot be classified as a 'hostile army'. While consent is an elusive concept, as discussed in Chapter 2, nevertheless, in these instances, generally UN peacekeepers are deployed on the proviso of State consent, placing them outside the realm of the laws of occupation. While the laws of occupation may not apply, this does not exempt them from their obligations under IHRL owed to civilians within these camps. If UNMISS exercises effective control over individuals, then they are bound by their obligations under IHRL to ensure that these individuals' rights are respected, protected and fulfilled.

When the first PoC site was established, the Security Council refused to support its construction demanding that UNMISS remove IDPS to a UNHCR-run IDP facility. However, as more civilians began seeking refuge at UN bases, the Security Council has accepted their continuation and has mandated UNMISS to protect and secure these sites. In 2016, the Security Council mandated UNMISS to "deter violence against civilians ... with particular attention to IDPS, including, but not limited to, those in protection sites and refugee camps",[67] specifically, to "maintain public safety and security of and within UNMISS protection of civilians sites."[68] Therefore, even if UNMISS does not have a legal obligation under their 'effective control', they must still ensure the safety and security of those civilians under the Security Council's mandate.

2.2 *Security Risks Due to Lack of Planning of IDP Camps*

Within the international community the coordination of IDP camps and humanitarian assistance should be coordinated by UNHCR.[69] According to UNHCR Emergency Handbook, sites for refugee and IDP camps should be located away from "conflict zones and other potentially sensitive areas (such as military installations)."[70] Unlike IDP camps that are planned and organised by humanitarian agencies, in South Sudan fleeing civilians congregate around UN

66 Regulations Concerning the Laws and Customs of War on the Land (Hague Regulations) 1907 at Article 42.

67 *United Nations Security Council Resolution 2327* (2016) at operational paragraph 7(a)(ii).

68 Ibid at operational paragraph 7(a)(iv).

69 http://www.globalprotectioncluster.org/about-us/who-we-are/.

70 United Nations High Commissioner for Refugees Emergency Handbook, "Camp Planning Standards" at section 2.3.

bases to seek protection by peacekeepers. As UN bases are generally located in strategic and high-risk areas,[71] civilians attempting to find shelter around UN bases in actuality place themselves in greater danger. For example, one of the largest PoC sites in South Sudan was formed around the UNMISS base in Juba that was strategically placed in a high-tension area. The risk of congregating in UN Juba headquarters came to fruition in the incident in 2016, where violence overflowed from the city into the Juba PoC site.

As a consequence of the location of these sites, UN police officers have been required to 'actively patrol' the areas surrounding the PoC sites to ensure their security. As these camps are vast and complicated in their structure, the protection of these sites has transformed the entire Mission in South Sudan; in particular, UNMISS has diverted their resources to the PoC sites to ensure the camps' security. Although the PoC sites provided temporary protection for civilians, "they did not necessarily present the best way UNMISS might protect the great majority of those at risk."[72] Notwithstanding the creation of PoC sites, UN peace missions are generally under resourced, for although UN peace missions are authorised for a maximum number of troops, rarely is that number of troops deployed. For example, UNMISS has had 12% fewer troops deployed than they have been authorised by the Security Council.[73] As resources become scarce, UNMISS has had to forgo protection activities in order to secure IDP camps and UN bases. For example, UNMISS is calculated to spending $12 million per year on the Bor PoC site, which hosts fewer than 2,000 civilians.[74]

The PoC sites have given the illusion that UNMISS is fulfilling its protection mandate, however, with the concentration on the PoC sites inadequate protection is offered to vulnerable civilians outside these sites.[75] Unfortunately, as identified by the ICRC, IDPs not within camps are not receiving the protection that they require.[76] Therefore, UN peace missions protecting IDP camps confront a protection dilemma; to protect vulnerable civilians outside the camps, they must leave the camps defenceless; to protect the camps, they must forgoing protection to those outside the camps.

---

71 Murphy, above note 51 at 381.

72 Ibid at 377.

73 https://peacekeeping.un.org/en/mission/unmiss.

74 Center for Civilians in Conflict, *Moving Towards Mobility: Providing Protection to Civilians Through Static Presence and Mobile Peacekeeping in South Sudan* (2019) at 17.

75 International Committee of the Red Cross, *Internal Displacement in Armed Conflict: Facing up to the Challenges*, November 2009.

76 Ibid at 13.

This protection dilemma has resulted in UN peace missions predominately remaining within the camps that they are mandated to protect, abandoning other protection activities. Although the PoC sites initially saved many civilians from armed violence, they have forced UNMISS to fall "into a pattern in which the protection of civilians mandate has become about maintaining and protecting the POC sites, despite the fact that the vast majority of people in need of both physical protection and humanitarian services remain outside of the camps."[77]

Additionally, with the structure of the PoC sites, UNMISS is restricted to protecting the areas within PoC sites. Due to UNMISS' limited resources, UNPOL does not have sufficient resources to actively patrol areas in close proximity to the sites.[78] This resource limitation has left vulnerable civilians defenceless to physical violence outside the camps, not only those in greater distances, but also those in close proximity to the camps. As highlighted by the Human Rights Commissioner's report, the majority of incidences of sexual violence, "took place at checkpoints close to the PoC sites" and this would occur "when IDP women and girls from the PoC sites (mostly from the Nuer community) were returning from collecting firewood or from the market."[79] For example, in November 2018, in the Unity region, armed groups committed a series of attacks on women and girls traveling to collect food aid.[80] The attacks occurred approximately 15 kilometres from a UN base and PoC site, in the span of two weeks, 125 women had reported experiencing sexual violence.

By the PoC sites' very nature, they lack basic necessities, and thus, IDPS must often exit the camps in order to acquire basic goods; such as food, fuel, or firewood. As women and girls are generally those exiting the sites in order to acquire food and other necessities, the routine of exiting has made women and girls targets of sexual violence. As specific travel routes to and from the camps become widely known, "UNMISS HRD/Women's Protection Advisors (WPAS) have documented many incidents of sexual violence occurring within the perimeter of UNMISS PoC sites."[81] Through the threat and fear of sexual

77 Center for Civilians in Conflict, *Within and Beyond the Gates: The Protection of Civlians by the UN Mission in South Sudan*, May 2015 at 29.

78 Human Rights Watch, *"They Burned It All": Destruction of Villages, Killings, and Sexual Violence in Unity State, South Sudan*, 2015.

79 Office of the High Commissioner for Human Rights, *A Report on Violations and Abuses of International Humanitarian Law in the Context of the Fighting in Juba*, South Sudan, in July 2016, January 2017 at paragraphs 49–50.

80 Center for Civilians in Conflict, above note 74 at 3–4.

81 United Nations Mission in South Sudan, *The State of Human Rights in the Protracted Conflict in South Sudan*, 4 December 2015 at paragraph 53.

violence, civilians within these sites are being denied their basic right to an adequate standard of living,[82] specifically their "fundamental right to freedom from hunger and malnutrition."[83] In order to protect the IDPs' rights to adequate living standards, and the protection against inhumane treatment,[84] UNMISS has attempted to increase their protective measures outside the camps, such as patrolling the perimeters and escorting women to and from the sites, however, sexual and gender-based violence has not diminished.[85] Precisely as with limited resources, UNPOL has been unable to conduct this level of protection consistently.

As peacekeepers are mandated to patrol high-risk areas, in States such as Mali and CAR, peacekeepers are patrolling areas that are either lack local authorities or is under non-state control. For example, in CAR, UNPOL have become the substitute for the national police just outside Bangui and are engaging in arrests and detention in the absence of State authority.[86] In comparison to the PoC sites, UNPOL have become the only authority within these areas, consequently, compelling them to take on an element of control. Particularly, when civilians begin to rely and perceive UN police officers as the authority within the area.[87] As such, peacekeepers patrolling could trigger the UN peace mission's obligations under IHRL.

2.3 *Security Risk from Poor Design of IDP Camps*

Even when UN peacekeepers concentrate their resources within these camps, the spontaneous creation and design of these camps have manifested further security problems. Under UNHCR recommendations, the IDP camp size should equate to 45 square-meters per person, with each person having a living space of 3.5 square-meters.[88] However, the PoC sites have become dense living environments, as more civilians are arriving to seek refuge.[89] The dense nature

82 ICESCR at Article 11(1).

83 Ibid at Article 11(2).

84 ICCPR at Article 7.

85 Office of the High Commissioner for Human Rights, *A Report on Violations and Abuses of International Humanitarian Law in the Context of the Fighting in Juba, South Sudan*, in July 2016, January 2017 at paragraph 49–50.

86 Charles T. Hunt, 'To Serve and Protect: The Role of UN Police in Protecting Civilians ' (2019) *Global Observatory* <https://theglobalobservatory.org/2019/09/to-serve-and-protect-the-role-of-un-police-protecting-civilians/>.

87 Charles T. Hunt, *Protection through Policing: The Protective Role of UN Police in Peace Operations* (International Peace Institute, February 2020) at 6.

88 UNHCR Emergency Handbook, Camp Planning Standards at section 2.2.

89 Ray Murphy, 'The United Nations Mission in South Sudan and the Protection of Civilians' (2017) 22(3) *Journal of Conflict and Security Law* 367 at 378 at 377.

of these camps has seriously affected the security of civilians, and UNPOL's ability to maintain order and protection. As an example, the Malakal PoC site in 2016 had over 40,000 IDPs residing, from 3 separate tribes – the Dinka, Nuer and Shiluk tribes.[90] Due to the division of the living spaces for the 3 tribes, ethnic violence broke out throughout the site in February 2016; armed men from the Dinka tribe entered the Malakal PoC site during the outbreak, and it took over 12 hours for UNMISS police officers to react or intervene.[91] An internal UN inquiry found that the "external and internal physical protection infrastructure of the POC site was not sufficient, nor its repair when breaches were reported."[92] As spontaneous camps are crowded and dense, the use of force by UN police officers within these camps becomes problematic. Peacekeepers are faced with conflicting interests of using force to stop outbreaks of violence within the camps, with harming or injuring innocent civilians who might get caught in the crossfire.

As a consequence of growing armed conflict, not only are IDPs seeking refugee within the camps, rather, members of armed groups are also concealed within the PoC sites. The presence of members of armed groups have naturally caused instability within the PoC sites, creating growing tensions between the differing ethnic groups. As identified by the Secretary-General, those guarding the entrances to the PoC sites "have failed to deny access to the armed actors, many of whom have entered camps freely, in uniform and carrying weapons."[93] In the PoC sites' initial stages, the entrances to the sites were being patrolled by the national police, however, they were unable to stop the inflow of members from armed groups.[94] Since then, UNMISS has taken it upon themselves to patrol the entrance to the PoC sites, yet due to their lack of knowledge of the local populace, they have been unable to prevent the entrance of armed groups within the camps.[95]

A consequence of UNMISS' inability to regulate entrances is their inability to control the flow of arms and drugs. Although UNMISS has been actively

---

90 Ibid at 379.

91 Ibid at 380.

92 United Nations Headquarters Board of Inquiry, *Board of Inquiry Report on Malakal – Executive Summary*, 5 August 2016 at paragraph 23.

93 United Nations Security Council, *Report of the Secretary-General on Children and Armed Conflict in South Sudan*, S/2014/884 at paragraph 29.

94 Ibid at paragraph 29.

95 As identified by UNHCR, if combatants cannot be identified, other agencies such as the UN country team or other UN agencies are to be used to assist with the identification of combatants – https://emergency.unhcr.org/coordination-and-communication/cluster-system/camp-coordination-and-camp-management-cccm-cluster-iasc

searching all those entering the camps for contraband, there still remains an increased presence of arms and contraband within the sites. Due to the accumulation of small arms, drugs and other contrabands, there is the growing presence of organised gangs and violent crimes.[96] Humanitarian agencies have reported multiple criminal activities occurring within the camps, such as "alcohol-related assault, sexual violence, murder, possession and smuggling of illegal drugs, gang violence, [and] violence in the course of disputes between individuals, families or communities."[97]

When establishing IDP and refugee camps, planning of the camp's infrastructure becomes essential to ensure humanitarian standards and the protection of vulnerable civilians. However, the PoC sites have fallen well below the basic human rights standards expected from IDP camps, with problems ranging from poor sanitation to lack of basic access to humanitarian assistance.[98] Due to the unplanned nature of these IDP camps, their very design works against the protection mandate, creating further risks to civilians.

The flaws in the infrastructure of the PoC sites have amplified the risks of sexual and gender-based violence. As an example, many of the PoC sites lack sufficient lighting, subsequently making women "feel at risk of using the latrines at night, where there is no lighting."[99] Further, as UNMISS has left a lot of the day-to-day running of the camps to 'male' chiefs, it has been reported that women are being forced to trade sex for access to camp facilities.[100] Further, many of the sites lack sufficient humanitarian assistance to women and girls that have faced this type of violence, not providing them with basic medical assistance.[101] Consequently UNPOL is mandated to prevent and protect against sexual violence, by "the construction of shelter, water and sanitation facilities in camps which must be carefully designed to avoid creating opportunities for gender-based aggression against displaced women and children."[102]

When UN peace missions engage in administration of IDP camps, they must ensure that they adhere to the humanitarian standards established by UNHCR. As these camps are established out of necessity, UNPOL must safeguard that no further risks occur to vulnerable civilians. Unfortunately, due to the density

---

96 Center for Civilians in Conflict, above note 77 at 24.

97 Stern, above note 52 at 10.

98 Ibid.

99 Human Rights Watch, above note 78 at 26.

100 Stern, above note 52.

101 Human Rights Watch, above note 78 at 26.

102 United Nations General Asssembly, *Promotion and Protection of the Rights of Children: Impact of Armed Conflict on Children*, UN Doc A/51/306 at paragraph 108.

of the living areas and the limited UNPOL presence within the camps, many civilians remain at risk of being exploited or under attack.

3 Protection of Human Rights in IDP Camps

IHRL as a body of law is concerned with the protection of individuals from violations by the State.[103] Therefore, IHRL obligations lie with government authorities to protect and defend these rights through their legislative and judicial systems.[104] Even though it is accepted that the UN and UN peace missions can influence and 'promote' human rights, the violations and safeguarding of these rights is conventionally the principal responsibility of States.[105]

Although the UN cannot technically 'violate' IHRL, this does not mean that UN peace missions do not have obligations under IHRL. Within the literature and UN reports, 'violations' by peacekeepers is commonly a reference to a UN Peace Mission's lack or inability to 'respect' or 'ensure' human rights throughout a peace operation.[106] Interestingly the literature is indecisive to the ramifications of peacekeepers themselves 'violating' fundamental human rights.[107]

Human rights commentators suggest that UN peace missions should be intimately integrated with fundamental principles of IHRL.[108] This stance is supported by three submissions – the 'purpose' of the UN; the obligations of member states; and IHRL as customary international law.

It is first submitted that the opening Article of the UN Charter specifies that the purpose of the UN is the "promoting and encouraging respect for human rights."[109] It is further proposed that this Article constitutes a "constitutional requirement" on the UN as an organisation, forcing human rights as an integral

103 Wills, above note 3 at 112.

104 Ibid.

105 Mégret, Frédéric and Florian Hoffman, 'The UN as a Human Rights Violator? Some Reflections on the United Nations Changing Human Rights Responsibilities' (2003) 25 *Human Rights Quarterly* 314 at 322.

106 Ibid at 320.

107 Andrew Clapham, 'Detention by Armed Groups under International Law' (2017) 93 *International Law Studies* 1 at 144; Howland, Todd, 'Peacekeeping and Conformity with Human Rights Law: How MINUSTAH Falls Short in Haiti' (2006) 13(4) *International Peacekeeping* 462 at 462; Katarina Månsson, 'Integration of Human Rights in Peace Operations: Is There an Ideal Model?' (2006) 13(4) *International Peacekeeping* 547; Sylvia Maus, 'Jus post bellum a la United Nations? Human rights, UN peace operations, and the creation of international law' (2014) 32(4) *Wisconsin International Law Journal* 675.

108 Ibid.

109 Månsson, above note 107 at 549.

part of all UN operations.[110] The second submission is that the UN is bound by the responsibility that is deemed to be fulfilled by its Member States.[111] So it is proposed that the obligations of Member States incidentally rests with the UN. Finally, it is submitted that the majority of rights under IHRL are customary international law and so is binding on all international organisations.[112] Furthermore, it is contended that human rights have become customary within peace operations that "mirrors an 'established practice of the organization', and has thus become a rule of the organization."[113] Therefore, even though the UN is not a State, they must still adhere to the human rights framework established in IHRL. As set down in the ICJ *Advisory Opinion on Nuclear Weapons*, IHRL applies even in armed conflict, unless a party "lawfully derogated from it."[114] However, the majority of UN peace missions are deployed in States that do not have an effective human rights infrastructure, so it is still doubtful the framework "concerning remedies, procedures for making individual complaints, and reparations mechanisms."[115]

When UN peace missions are in control over an individual, they must ensure and are obliged to 'promote and protect' their human rights. These rights extend beyond the right to life and food, to their economic, social, cultural, political and civil rights. For example, in regards to children, according to the Office of the Special Representative of the Secretary-General for Children and Armed Conflict, in their paper *The Six Grave Violations Against Children During Armed Conflict*, the "full range of children's rights, economic, social and cultural as well as political and civil, must be respected, protected and fulfilled."[116]

Within the literature, there is deliberation on whether the UN, and by default UN peace missions, can derogate from their obligations under IHRL.[117] Under IHRL, States are permitted to 'derogate' or temporarily suspend certain

---

110 Ibid at 549.

111 Ibid at 549.

112 Clapham, above note 107 at 144.

113 Maus, above note 107 at 686.

114 Ray Murphy, 'United Nations Military Operations and International Humanitarian Law: What Rules Apply to Peacekeepers?' (2003) *14*(2) *Criminal Law Forum* 153 at 158.

115 Maus, above note 107 at 679.

116 Office of the Special Representative of the Secretary-General for Children and Armed Conflict, *Working Paper No 1: The Six Grave Vioaltions Against Children During Armed Conflict: The Legal Foundation*, October 2009 (Updated November 2013) at 9.

117 See Clapham, above note 107 at 143–144; in comparison Scott Sheeran and Catherine Bevilacqua, 'The UN Security Council and International Human Rights Obligations: Towards a Theory of Contrainst and Derogation' in Scott Sheeran and Nigel Rodley (eds), *Routledge Handbook of International Human Rights Law* (Taylor and Francis, 2014) 371.

rights due to extraordinary situations, such as armed conflict. For example, Article 4 of ICCPR permits in "time of public emergency which threatens the life of a nation" States "may take measures under the present Covenant to the extent strictly required by the exigencies of the situation" Thus, in order for a State to derogate from the obligations under the ICCPR there must be a State emergency and the derogation is required by the 'exigencies of the situation'. The literature examining whether the UN can derogate or limit their human right obligations mainly focusses on whether a Security Council resolution can violate individuals' human rights, for example, economic sanctions.[118] However, there is limited discussion on whether UN peacekeepers are allowed to derogate or limit their responsibilities under IHRL when exercising control over individuals.[119]

To be able to determine whether a UN peace mission can derogate or limit obligations, it must first be determined whether an international organisation, which is not a signatory State, can rely on the rules of derogation.[120] The rule of derogation is a cornerstone of IHRL, as it allows a balance between the protection of individual human rights, with the protection of the collective.[121] Without the rule of derogation unreasonable demands will be placed on the controlling entity and sacrifices will be made to collective security. Therefore, the rule of derogation becomes an essential and foundational element of IHRL.[122] Consequently, although the UN is not a signatory to the covenants, they must also have access to the rule of derogation not to place unreasonable demands that would sacrifice the protection of the collective. Therefore, UN peace missions cannot be denied from derogating from their human right obligations, as long as they fulfil the criteria set out in IHRL. Under the ICCPR, derogation may be made if it threatens the life of a nation, that is, when a threat is made to the collective. Following the same rationale, peacekeepers are permitted to derogate from their obligations under the ICCPR if there is a threat to the life of the collective. In other words, if there is a threat to the life of the camp or the 'collective individuals' under their control they can be permitted to derogate from their obligations.

118 Sheeran and Bevilacqua, above note 118.

119 Clapham, above note 107.

120 Ibid.

121 Jaime Oraá, *Human rights in states of emergency in international law*, Oxford monographs in international law (Clarendon Press, 1992) at 1.

122 Sheeran and Bevilacqua, above note 118 at 397.

However, the presence of an armed conflict alone is not enough to establish a state of public emergency.[123] Rather, even in an armed conflict, derogations "are allowed only if and to the extent that the situation constitutes a threat to the life of the nation [or the collective]."[124] Moreover, the measures taken by peacekeepers are "limited to the extent strictly require by the exigencies to the situation."[125] This means that UN peacekeepers cannot ignore or forgo a specific protection simply because of the situation of surrounding conflict; rather they must show that the derogation was 'strictly required'.

Conversely, rights under the ICESCR cannot be derogated from, but rather can be limited. According to Article 4 of the ICESCR, rights can only be limited "in so far as this may be compatible with the nature of these rights and solely for the purpose of promoting the general welfare in a democratic society." Thus, unlike the ICCPR, UN peace missions cannot depend on security to derogate from their obligations, however, they can limit their obligation solely for 'promoting the general welfare' of the collective.

Although protection of civilians missions may find themselves amidst armed conflict, this does not mean that they can limit their IHRL obligations. As set out by the ICJ in the *Advisory Opinion on Nuclear Weapons*,[126] and throughout the literature,[127] IHRL will continue to apply in times of conflict unless a party has legally derogated from or limited their obligations. However, parties involved in a conflict would be unable to commit to a fall range of obligations, therefore, they must at least adhere to a minimum core of obligations.

A minimum core of obligations was first introduced by the CESCR "to ensure the satisfaction of, at the very least, minimum essential levels of each of the rights is incumbent upon every State party."[128] Although the CESCR has been criticised for being inconsistent in defining what this 'minimum core' would entail,[129] it would be problematic in attempting to set a rigid structure.

---

123 United Nations Commissioner on Human Rights, *General Comment No 29: States of Emergency (Article 4)*, UN Doc CCPR/C/21/Rev.1/Add.11, 31 August 2001 at paragraph 3.

124 Ibid.

125 Ibid.

126 *Legality of the Threat or Use of Nuclear Weapons*, Advisory Opinion, ICJ Reports 1996, p.226.

127 Murphy, above note 114; Peter Rowe, *The Imact of Human Rights Law on Armed Forces* (Cambridge University Press 2006); Daragh (ed) Murray, *Practitioners' guide to human rights law in armed conflict* (Oxford University Press, 2017).

128 Office of the High Commissioner for Human Rights, *CESCR General Comment No 3: The Nature of States Parties Obligations (Art 2, Para 1, of the Covenant)*, Adopted at the Fifth Session of the Committee on Economic, Social and Cultural Rights, on 14 December 1990, UN Doc. E/1991/23.

129 Katharine G. Young, 'The Minimum Core of Economic and Social Rights: A Concept in Search of Content' (2008) *117 Yale International Law Journal* 113.

Rather than considering the 'minimum core' as 'core content', it should be considered as 'core obligations'. In other words, the minimum core is concerned with the duties required rather than the outcome. For example, it would be wrong to expect the same minimum content from developed and developing nations. As the CESCR outlines that the minimum core obligation "must also take account of resource constraints applying within the country concerned."[130] Therefore, even with limited resources, a party must show that they have used all resources in their disposition to attempt to satisfy their minimum obligation.

While there is an array of rights specified in IHRL, the UN mainly focuses on two rights – education and access to healthcare. Even though these two rights are focused on by the UN, in the literature there is also a focus on the right to food and water.

3.1 *The Right to Food and Water*

When the literature addresses the minimum core, there is a general focus on food, water, health and education.[131] Although the Security Council focuses on health and education, IHRL will still oblige UNMISS to fulfil their minimum obligation to give substance to IDPS rights to food and water.[132] As IDPS are under the control of UNMISS, UNMISS must "ensure the satisfaction of, at the very least, the minimum essential level required to be free from hunger."[133] Therefore, not providing sufficient security for women to safely exit and re-enter the camps to acquire food is a violation of their right to adequate food. As part of peacekeepers' obligations, they must protect individual's access to food, and take positive steps to certify the realisation of this right under their obligation to fulfil. For example, in central Mali, UNPOL organises patrols on market days to protect women and children traveling to and from marketplaces in order to safely access basic supplies.[134]

This will equally apply to IDPS right to access to water. Although not explicitly mentioned in the ICESCR, the CESCR has suggested that the right to water is implied in the reading of Article 11 and 12 of the ICESCR. The CESCR states

130 CESCR General Comment No 3 at paragraph 10.

131 Murray, above note 128.

132 ICESCR at Articles 11 and 12.

133 Office of the High Commissioner for Human Rights, *CESCR General Comment No. 12: The Right to Adequate Food (Art. 11)*, Adopted at the Twentieth Session of the Committee on Economic, Social and Cultural Rights, on 12 May 1999, UN Doc. E/C.12/1999/5 at paragraph 17.

134 Hunt, above note 87 at 6.

that the "right to water clearly falls within the category of guarantees essential for securing an adequate standard of living, particularly since it is one of the most fundamental conditions for survival."[135] Part of the minimum core obligation in relation to the right to water is to ensure "the right of access to water and water facilities and services on a non-discriminatory basis, especially for disadvantaged or marginalized groups."[136]

When UNMISS empowers men from specific tribes with the running of the camps, access to food and water becomes a political tool to discriminate against minorities within the camps. Moreover, as discussed earlier, many women and children are forced to trade sexual acts to have access to water sources. By not providing adequate security to access of water sources, UNMISS is in breach of ensuring "personal security is not threatened when having to physically access to water."[137]

Therefore, in order for the UN to fulfil their minimum core obligation they need to provide adequate safety and security for IDPs to access food and water. The minimum core does not require them to provide food and water themselves, but to allow safe and adequate access. Although UN peace missions are under-resourced, in order not to fail in their obligation, they must demonstrate that they used all their available resources in an attempt to satisfy this obligation.

3.2 *The Right to Education*

When mandating the protection of human rights, particularly regarding children, the Security Council focuses on the right of education. This importance of education is reiterated in the CRC, which "reinforces this by setting out detailed obligations on states, compliance with which is essential for the right to education to be adequately realized."[138] During armed conflict it is imperative to ensure "that children continue to have access to basic services during conflict and post-conflict periods, including, inter alia, education and health care."[139] Even though there are varying rights associated with children, the right to education and access to health care is seen by the UN as paramount.

135 Office of the High Commissioner for Human Rights, *General Comment No 15: The Right to Water (Arts 11 and 12 of the Convenant)*, Adopted at the Twenty-ninth Session of the Committee on Economic, Social and Culture Rights, on 20 January 2003, (UN Doc. E/C.12/2002/11) at paragraph 3.

136 Ibid at paragraph 37(a).

137 Ibid.

138 Global Coalition to Protect Education from Attack, Commentary on the "Guidelines for Protecting Schools and Universities from Military Use during Armed Conflict" at 4.

139 *United Nations Security Council Resolution 1314* (2000) at preamble paragraph 44.

While under IHRL there exists no 'hierarchy' of rights, an examination of UN reports and Security Council resolutions indicates that a child's right to education and health care is seen by the UN as the primary focus of the protection regime and the mandate to protect children's rights.

The removal of children from a learning and educational environment isolates the child, often forcing them into the cycle of conflict. Therefore, continuing the access to education for children assists dramatically in preventing the recruitment of children into armed groups, as education diminishes the child's separation from their community. As stated in *Resolution 1539* (2004), education of children plays a fundamental role in "conflict areas in halting and preventing recruitment and re-recruitment of children contrary to the obligations of parties to conflict."[140] Consequently, the UN considers the access to education as a cornerstone to the human rights protection of children and the strategic implementation of maintenance of peace and security. As codified in Article 13 of ICESCR, "education shall enable all persons to participate effectively in a free society, promote understanding, tolerance and friendship among all nations and all racial, ethnic or religion groups, and further the activities of the United Nations for the maintenance of peace."

This importance of continuing education during conflict is emphasised in the Geneva Conventions that obliges occupying powers to address the right of a child to education, that is, to cooperate with "national and local authorities, facilitate the proper working of all institutions devoted to the care and education of children ... Should the local institutions be inadequate for the purpose, the Occupying Power shall make arrangements for the maintenance and education."[141] Although, the UN could not be seen as an occupying power, Article 50 is a good reference for the expectation that exists for UN peacekeepers once they have taken control of an IDP camp. Additional Protocol II also specifies that in NIAC "[c]hildren shall be provided with the care and aid they require, and in particular: (a) they shall receive an education, including religious and moral education, in keeping with the wishes of their parents, or in the absence of parents, of those responsible for their care."[142]

The majority of PoC sites controlled and supervised by UNMISS have established basic levels of education.[143] It is important to note that UNMISS does not have to educate the children themselves as part of their minimum obligation

---

140 *United Nations Security Council Resolution 1539* (2004) at operational paragraph 9.

141 Forth Geneva Convention Article 50.

142 Addtional Protocol II at Article 4(3)(a).

143 https://peacekeeping.un.org/en/unmiss-peacekeepers-support-local-nursery-and-primary-school-juba.

but to allow access to education. Although UNMISS do not have the capability to enforce compulsory education, as outlined in Article 13 of ICESCR, they work with UNICEF in providing educational materials and promoting the importance of education within the PoC sites.[144]

However, many of the schools established within the PoC sites do not cater for any persons with an intellectual disability. As children with intellectual disabilities are being separated, this isolation is causing risks to their mental and physical wellbeing. As outlined in Article 24(a) on the Convention on the Rights of Person with Disabilities (*CRPD*), an individual must "receive the support required ... to facilitate their effective education." When UN peace missions exercise effective control over individuals or IDP camps, they must ensure that they are not disregarding the rights of people with disabilities. People with disabilities must have equal access to facilities and protections offered by UN peacekeepers. This access to facilities includes support and access to education and humanitarian assistance.

3.2.1 Military Use of Schools

In modern NIAC schools and educational buildings are often used for military purposes by State and non-State actors.[145] Even though schools are generally used temporarily as a form of barracks or accommodation,[146] nonetheless the temporary use of schools is enough to affect the rights of children's access to education.[147] In South Sudan, for example, it has been reported that the military use of schools "has affected the access of more than 50,000 children to education and safe spaces during times of conflict."[148]

Moreover, the military use of schools is also clearly correlated with recruitment of children into armed groups, as there are reports and "verified cases of the use of schools for recruitment of children."[149] Critically, the use of schools as military bases, "can render them vulnerable to lawful attack under the law of armed conflict, in some circumstances even if students and teachers remain

144 Ibid.

145 Global Coalition to Protect Education from Attack, Commentary on the "Guidelines for Protecting Schools and Universities from Military Use during Armed Conflict".

146 United Nations Security Council, *Report of the Secretary-General on Children and Armed Conflict in South Sudan*, S/2014/884 at paragraph 13.

147 Ibid at paragraph 49.

148 Ibid at paragraph 17.

149 Ibid at paragraph 49.

on site."[150] Under the provisions of IHL there is no explicit obligation forbidding the use of educational buildings for military purposes.

In infrequent cases, educational buildings can be classified as being of great cultural importance, and thus protected under Additional Protocol II.[151] Although it is suggested by the ICRC that the majority of schools and universities can be captured by the protection of cultural property,[152] many States have yet to agree with this interpretation.[153] To counterbalance the militarisation of schools the Global Coalition to Protect Education from Attack, has constructed the *Safe Schools Declaration* which is intended to be a political commitment for States to support the protection of education. Even though, the *Safe Schools Declaration* has been endorsed by many States, it has no legal authority, as the Coalition's *Guidelines for Protecting Schools* specifies that "it is acknowledged that certain uses [of schools] would not be contrary to the law of armed conflict."[154]

Of greater concern than armed forces using educational buildings, is peacekeepers themselves utilising schools as a base of operations. For example, MINUSCA in 2014 reportedly used five schools as a base for UN activities.[155] In 2015, MINUSCA peacekeepers received standing orders to remove themselves from all schools and no longer use educational buildings as a base of operations. Even with the standing order there are still reports that some peacekeeping contingents are still using schools as operational bases.[156] While UN peacekeepers are not expected to use force to protect schools from military use, they themselves cannot use educational buildings for any operational purposes, as this would be a violation of their obligation to respect the right to education.

---

150 Global Coalition to Protect Education from Attack, Commentary on the "Guidelines for Protecting Schools and Universities from Military Use during Armed Conflict" at 4.

151 Addtional Protocol II at Article 16.

152 International Committee of the Red Cross, Study on Customary Interantional Humanitarian Law (Customary IHL Database).

153 Global Coalition to Protect Education from Attack, Commentary on the "Guidelines for Protecting Schools and Universities from Military Use during Armed Conflict".

154 Ibid.

155 United Nations Security Council, *Report of the Secretary-General on Children and Armed Conflict in the Central African Republic*, UN Doc S/2016/133 at paragraph 54.

156 United Nations Multidimensional Integrated Stabilization Missions in Central African Republic, *Inter-Office Memorandum: Directive on the Protection of Schools and Universities Against Military Use*, 24 December 2015, MINUSCA/OSRSG/046/2015.

3.3 *Protection of Access to Health Care*

In current armed conflict, humanitarian aid and deliveries of "life-saving assistance" is denied or impeded "through bureaucratic impediments and attacks on humanitarian personnel and assets."[157] These restrictions and impediments to humanitarian access is carried out by non-state as well as State actors. For example, in South Sudan UNMISS has recorded the killing of 24 aid workers in 2016.[158] According to the Aid Worker Security Database, in 2021 there was 268 incidences of attacks on aid works with 141 workers being killed, and another 203 injured.[159]

Under Common Article 3 of the Geneva Conventions, the wounded and sick "shall be collected and cared for."[160] While in IHL the obligation is to provide health care to injured and sick civilians, under IHRL the obligation is to respect, protect and fulfil their right to healthcare. Under Article 12(d) of ICESCR, State parties must take steps to facilitate the "creation of conditions which would assume to all medical service and medical attention in the event of sickness". Therefore, under IHRL UN peace missions are not obliged to provide health care, rather to ensure access to humanitarian and medical aid. Within the Security Council mandates, this protection is implied with the protection of humanitarian workers and aid supplies. Thus, by protecting humanitarian workers and their security, they implicitly protect civilians' right to health. As stated in DPO's Principles and Guidelines, in regard to the access of humanitarian assistance, the responsibility:

> rests primarily with the relevant civilian United Nations specialized agencies, funds and programmes, as well as the range of independent, international and local NGOs which are usually active alongside a United Nations peacekeeping operation. The primary role of United Nations peacekeeping operations with regard to the provision of humanitarian assistance is to provide a secure and stable environment within which humanitarian actors may carry out their activities.[161]

---

157 United Nations Security Council, *Report of the Secretary-General on the Protection of Civilians in Armed Conflict*, UN Doc S/2017/414 at paragraph 49.

158 Ibid at paragraph 54.

159 https://aidworkersecurity.org/incidents.

160 This obligation to care for the sick and wounded is further expanded in Articles 7 and 8 of Additional Protocol II.

161 United Nations Department of Peacekeeping Operations and Department of Field Support, *United Nations Peacekeeping Operations: Principles and Guidelines*, 2008 (*Capstone Doctrine*) at 30.

Although peacekeepers are not mandated to provide humanitarian aid themselves, with IDP camps they have occasionally provided a range of health services to local communities, including "emergency care, ongoing medical care, health system development and delivery, and health care training and education".[162] Due to security risks, aid workers have been unable to provide healthcare to IDP camps, placing an obligation on UNMISS in providing these services, within their limited resources.

The DPO has acknowledged that UN peacekeepers must periodically take a lead role in providing access to humanitarian aid, specifically when humanitarian workers are unable to – that is, during times of conflict and emergencies. As UN peace missions have effective control over these camps, they must ensure and establish conditions of medical services, when humanitarian workers cannot get access to these camps. However, the DPO has emphasised that the provision of humanitarian assistance is an exception, and that the primary duty is rather to protect humanitarian workers.[163] For example, in April 2020 with the outbreak of COVID-19, in Africa, UN peace missions were forced to take an active role in providing health assistance to IDPs. This included providing facemasks,[164] hand washing facilities,[165] and locking down camps to ensure social distancing.[166]

The DPO articulates that during these moments when peacekeepers must provide direct support of humanitarian provisions, "it is important to keep longer-term objectives in mind and begin planning for the more comprehensive humanitarian programs that will be possible in a more stable environment."[167] However, the UN and DPO are quick to stipulate that providing medical assistance and health is not and should not be a core activity of UN peacekeepers, but is only a temporary measure.[168] Nevertheless, as evidence

162 Sara E, Davies and Simon Rushton, *Healing or Harming? United Nations Peacekeeping and Health*, International Peace Institute, March 2015 at 17.

163 United Nations Department of Peacekeeping Operations, *Handbook on United Nations Multidimensional Peacekeeping Operations*, December 2003.

164 https://peacekeeping.un.org/en/unmiss-hands-over-locally-produced-masks-to-protection-of-civilians-site-wau.

165 https://peacekeeping.un.org/en/unmiss-installs-handwashing-facilities-rumbek-town-to-prevent-spread-of-covid-19.

166 https://peacekeeping.un.org/en/unmiss-protection-site-displaced-people-bans-visits-to-prevent-spread-of-covid-19.

167 United Nations Department of Peacekeeping Operations, *Handbook on United Nations Multidimensional Peacekeeping Operations*, December 2003 at 175.

168 Capstone Doctrine, above note 162 at 23.

with the current humanitarian crisis, it is no longer uncommon that peacekeepers are providing health services directly to local communities.

4 Conclusion

As the Security Council has identified IDPs as a special category of protection, the protection and security of IDP camps has become a cornerstone of UN peacekeeping. As women and children are most vulnerable during displacement, the protection of IDP camps is considered the strategic avenue in providing physical protection to IDPs.

While the protection of IDP camps appears valid to fulfil the obligations under the protection of civilians mandate, supporting ad hoc camps has generated further risks to IDPs. Poor design and infrastructure have created dependency on UNPOL's presence, limiting peacekeeping resources, which resulted in the abandonment of tasks that would protect civilians outside these camps. Due to the organic nature of these camps, UNPOL has also been unable to adequately protect those civilians *within* these camps, and the poor design of these camps has created unneeded risks to already vulnerable civilians.

Therefore, although they are mandated to protect these camps, there is a clear conflict with their obligation to protect civilians. As resources are being poured into the IDP camps, peacekeepers are forced to forgo other protection activities. This conflict between activities cannot be easily resolved, unless a clear indication of priorities is stated by the UN.

As UN peace missions exert effective control over the individuals within these camps, under the law they must ensure the promotion and protection of the IDPs' rights. Thus, if peacekeepers are in control over IDP camps, their obligation to respect, protect and fulfil individuals' rights to food, water, education and healthcare.

In summary, peacekeepers are obliged to protect civilians from physical violence. The military component is obliged to protect civilians within the vicinity of UN bases and areas of patrol, from direct and indiscriminate attacks. Further, UN police officers are obliged to protect civilians within the same area from conflict-related violence, specifically sexual and gender-based violence.

When using force to protect, military peacekeepers must guarantee that the force is proportionate to the advantage of protecting civilians, and distinguishes between military and civilian targets. Moreover, when engaging with non-State actors, mechanisms need to be in place to protect child soldiers removed from these groups.

Finally, the obligation to protect will also encompass the obligation to respect, protect and fulfil individuals' human rights who are under peacekeepers' control. Practically, this will include detainees and IDPs in UN-controlled IDP camps.

As the minimum core obligation to protect has been established, the international community and civilians can seek accountability for UN peace missions for a failure to protect. This accountability can be sought from the TCC/PCC, host State or the UN.

CHAPTER 7

Accountability for Failure to Protect

This chapter is derived in part from an article published in *International Peacekeeping*, 15 March 2022, Taylor & Francis, available online: http://www.tandfonline.com/ <https://doi.org/10.1080/13533312.2021.1989304>.

As the literature has yet to acknowledge a legal obligation to protect, the accountability of peacekeepers is composed in separate forums that are yet to intersect. The divergence between the two main channels of peacekeepers' misconduct and failure to perform has created a fragmented approach to accountability. Moreover, even within each forum, arguments are divided between the accountability of the UN, Members States and individual peacekeepers. Yet as discussions omit a legal obligation as a foundation to accountability, the failure to perform is perceived to reside in the realm of 'best practice', while misconduct is considered in the realm of policy and domestic codes.

The ambiguity over the accountability of peacekeepers is that there is no consensus over the responsibility of peacekeepers to protect. For although peacekeepers are criticised for their failure to protect civilians, these discussions are mainly regarding military strategy rather than an obligation under the law.[1] Once a legal obligation is recognised the accountability of peacekeeping conduct or misconduct has a legal footing. In comparison to IHL and IHRL, a legal framework aids in managing and evaluating a minimum expectation of the UN and the international community.

It is concluded in this chapter that the responsibility of peacekeepers breaching their obligation to protect will be jointly apportioned to the UN and the TCC/PCC. As both the TCC/PCC and the UN hold joint effective control, they will also bear joint responsibility. However, legal responsibility does not always lead to legal remedy. Analogous with the obligation to respect IHL, found in Common Article 1, the obligation to protect will allow the international community to demand and pressure performance from the UN and the TCC/PCC.

1 Scott Sheeran and Catherine Kent, 'Protection of Civilians, Responsibility to Protect, and Humanitarian Intervention' in Haidi Willmot et al (eds), Protection of civilians (Oxford University Press, 2016) 29 at 46.

 | DOI:10.1163/9789004707313_009

1 Accountability of Peacekeepers' Actions

Within the last decade UN peace missions have been overwhelmed with accusations of criminal misconduct and a failure to protect civilians.[2] Significantly, peacekeepers have been reported as violating their obligations under international law by committing serious crimes against those civilians which they are mandated to protect. Although UN peacekeepers have been accused of sexual abuse,[3] gender-based abuse,[4] and child pornography,[5] little has been undertaken in order to seek a legal accountability.[6]

As reports of UN peacekeepers violating their obligations under international law have dramatically increased, there is a rising concern within the international community as to the lack of accountability of peacekeepers' actions.[7] Particularly, best practice in dealing with accusations against peacekeepers remains unresolved. Until it is decided which body or organisation is responsible for peacekeepers' actions, peacekeeper impunity will continue.[8]

1.1 *UN Operational Control and TCC/PCC Disciplinary Responsibility*

At the outset of peacekeeping the UN has insisted that the TCCs are solely responsible for disciplinary action of their troops and thus retain jurisdiction over their contingent.[9] Although the UN maintains that they have 'operational control' over UN peace missions, it is asserted by the UN that the accountability of a peacekeeper's misconduct rests with the TCC.[10] As the UN has no mechanism or legal infrastructure to deal with misconduct of peacekeepers, they maintain that they cannot claim responsibility for that misconduct.[11]

The UN assumes their only avenue for accountability is to demand TCCs to investigate and prosecute accused peacekeepers. Subsequently, the

---

2 M. Odello, 'Tackling Criminal Acts in Peacekeeping Operations: The Accountability of Peacekeepers' (2010) *15*(2) *Journal of Conflict and Security Law* 347 at 357.

3 Anna Shotton, 'A Strategy to Address Sexual Exploitation and Abuse by United Nations Peacekeeping Personnel' (2006) *39 Cornell International Law Journal* 97 at 97–98.

4 Ibid.

5 Ibid.

6 Odello, above note 2 at 350.

7 Siobhán Wills, 'Continuing Impunity of Peacekeepers: The Need For a Convention' (2013) 4(1) *Journal of International Humanitarian Legal Studies* 47 at 53.

8 Md Kamal Uddin, 'Human Rights Violations by un Peacekeepers' (2014) *25*(*1*) *Security and Human Rights* 130 at 132.

9 United Nations Security Council, Report of the Secretary-General to the Security Council on the Protection of Civilians in Armed Conflict, UN Doc S/1999/957 at recommendation 32.

10 Ibid.

11 Odello, above note 2 at 366.

Secretary-General constantly demands within his reports that TCCs/PCCs must "prosecute members of their armed forces who have violated international humanitarian and human rights law while in service of the United Nations."[12] As the UN has absolved itself from any responsibility of peacekeepers' misconduct, its only authority is to pressure the TCC/PCC to hold an accused peacekeeper legally accountable. Consequently, in response to issues of sexual misconduct and grave violations, the UN has requested all TCCs submit their 'legal structures' governing their contingents. The UN sustains that these submitted structures will improve "transparency and accountability in the handling of cases of misconduct".[13] Unfortunately, these submissions merely outline the legal structures of each TCC, rather than their willingness to investigate and take action.

While the TCCs/PCCs retain disciplinary authority, the UN has continually insisted that UN-led peacekeepers are "under the sole authority of the organization and not their respective states."[14] As the UN claims responsibility for a UN peace mission as a whole, the misconduct of individual peacekeepers taints the UN as an organisation. As contended by the Permanent Representative of South Sudan to the UN, the UN is solely responsible for peacekeepers' actions, for "they wear the blue hat, with the UN flag. Can I blame their [peacekeeper's] home country? No."[15] Although the UN constantly references the accountability of the TCCs, international perception is still that the UN is to manage the misconduct and end violations within UN peace missions.

As both the UN and the TCC/PCC share differing responsibilities, the command and control structures of UN peace missions are built on conflicting accountabilities. The obscured command and control structure complicates the responsibility of the UN and the TCC/PCC over peacekeeping misconduct and failures. This confusion allows the accountability of UN peace missions to fall within a political and jurisdictional gap.

12 United Nations Security Council, Report of the Secretary-General to the Security Council on the Protection of Civilians in Armed Conflict, UN Doc S/1999/957 at recommendation 32.

13 https://peacekeeping.un.org/en/standards-of-conduct.

14 Devon Whittle, 'Peacekeeing in conflict: The Intervention Brigade, MONUSCO, and the application of international humanitarian law to United Nations forces' (2015) *46(3) Georgetown Journal of International Law* 837 at 857.

15 Interview with South Sudan on 22 January 2019.

2 Law of State and Organisational Responsibility

As set out in the ICJ *Reparations Case*,[16] under international law the UN as an organisation is considered a legal person,[17] and hence is able to bear responsibility for actions committed by UN peace missions.[18] Under ARIO, the conduct of an organ or agent of an organisation will be considered the actions of that organisation under international law.[19] Whether peacekeepers are defined as 'agents' or 'organs' of the UN will determine which section of ARIO is applied; Article 2(c) of ARIO defines an 'organ' as "any person or entity which has the status in accordance with the rules of the organization", while Article 2(d) differentiates 'agent' from 'organ', by defining an 'agent' as any person "who is charged by the organization with carrying out, or helping to carry out, one of its functions, and thus through who the organization acts."

Though UN peace missions are at times considered subsidiary organs of the UN, individual peacekeepers are considered 'agents' of the UN, as they are still in service of their home States.[20] In the *Behrami* decision, the ECHR saw that UNMIK was a "subsidiary organ of the UN created under Chapter VII of the Charter" and thus, the alleged "inaction was, in principle, 'attributed' to the UN in the same sense."[21] However, UNMIK differs in nature to other UN peace missions, as UNMIK was "endowed with all-inclusive legislative and administrative powers in Kosovo",[22] and therefore was strictly overseen by the UN. Though UNMIK is considered a subsidiary organ of the UN, conversely within non-administrative peace missions, military peacekeepers remain within their national contingent and thus remain organs of the TCC.[23] While an overall UN peace mission can be described as an 'organ' of the UN, this cannot be considered the same for individual peacekeepers, and hence their actions. Thus, to

16 *Reparation for Injuries Suffered in the Service of the United Nations*, Advisory Opinion of April 11, 1949, ICJ.

17 Ibid at 9.

18 Terry D. Gill, 'Legal Aspects of the Transfer of Authority in UN Peace Operations' (2011) *42 Netherlands Yearbook of International Law* 37 at 52.

19 *Draft Articles on Responsibility of International Organizations* at Article 6.

20 Paolo Palchetti, 'The allocation of responsibility for internationally wrongful acts committed in the course of multinational operations' (2013) *95(891–892) International Review of the Red Cross* 727 at 729.

21 *Behrami and Behrami v France* and *Saramati v France, Germany and Norway*, Application no 71412/01 and 78166/01, 2 May 2007 at paragraph 143.

22 Ibid at paragraph 118.

23 *Attorney General v Nissan (Right of UK National to Compensation for Porperty Seized by UK Forces in Cyprus; Relationship of UK Forces to Cyprus Goverment and to United Nations)* [1969] UKHL 3.

determine the authority that is legally responsible for peacekeepers' actions, it must be assessed which authority has 'effective control' over these actions.

When assessing the legal responsibility of the UN, there has been contention over which article of ARIO would be more suited – Article 6 or 7. As Article 6 assumes that peacekeepers are organs of the UN,[24] Article 7 considers peacekeepers agents of the UN loaned by the home State. Commentators such as Perova have suggested that Article 7 is the more appropriate article when examining UN peacekeeping as peacekeepers still remain under the jurisdiction of the TCCs.[25] Essentially, the contention is whether peacekeepers are organs of the UN (under Article 6), or organs of the State placed at the disposal of the UN (under Article 7). In *The Netherlands v Nuhanović*[26] the Dutch Court settled the matter in affirming that in consideration of a UN peace mission, Article 7 is the correct provision to oversee UN responsibility.[27] In the *Nuhanović* case, the family of one of the victims of Srebrenica massacre sought action against the Dutch State for their failure to prevent the massacre from occurring. The Court in applying Article 7 concluded that peacekeepers remained organs of The Netherlands, and therefore, the Dutch State could be held liable.

2.1 *Effective Control Test*

In employing Article 7, the UN as an organisation, is legally responsible for peacekeepers' actions if it exercises 'effective control'. As outlined in Article 7 of ARIO:

> The conduct of an organ of a State or an organ or agent of an international organization that is placed at the disposal of another international organization shall be considered under international law an act of the latter organization if the organization exercises effective control over that conduct.

Parallel to Article 7 of ARIO, Article 8 of DAR outlines that conduct will be considered the acts of the State if individuals are "acting on the instructions of, or under the direction or control of, that State". Thus, under the principles of

24 Palchetti, above note 20 at 731.

25 Natalia Perova, 'Disentangling 'Effective Control' Test for the Purpose of Attribution of the Conduct of UN Peacekeepers to the States and the United Nations' (2017) *86(1) Nordic Journal of International Law* 30 at 38–39.

26 *The Netherlands v Hasan Nuhanović*, Supreme Court of the Netherlands, First Chamber 12/03324, 6 September 2013.

27 Ibid.

international law, the organisation or State that exhibits effective control will be considered legally responsible for those actions. Contrarily, differing characterisations of 'effective control' do exist within the international framework.

Within the ICJ's two leading cases – the *Nicaragua* case[28] and the *Bosnian Genocide* case[29] – the Court has applied a strict narrow criterion of 'effective control'. In the *Genocide* case the Court elaborated on the 'effective control' test founded in *Nicaragua*, in that,

> It is not necessary to show that the persons who performed the acts alleged to have violated international law were in general in a relationship of 'complete dependence' on the respondent State; it has to be proved that they acted in accordance with the State's instructions or under its 'effective control'. It must however be shown that this 'effective control' was exercised, or that the State's instructions were given, in respect of each operation in which the alleged violations occurred, not generally in respect of the overall actions taken by the persons or groups of persons having committed the violations.[30]

Conversely, the ICTY in the *Tadić* decision attempted to widen the test to 'overall control' for State responsibility, however, this was ultimately rejected by the ICJ.[31] As such the UN cannot reply on their notion of 'operational control', yet each alleged action needs to be investigated to determine who had effective control.[32]

Though there are numerous discussions on UN responsibility and peacekeeper accountability, there is still no consensus to whether the UN has

---

28 *Case Concerning Military and Parmilitary Activities In and Against Nicaragua (Nicaragua v United States of America)*, ICJ, Judgment of 27 June 1986.

29 *Case Concerning Application of the Convention on the Prevention and Punishment of the Crime of Genocide (Bosnia and Herzegovina v Serbia and Montenegro)*, ICJ, 26 February 2007.

30 Ibid at paragraph 400.

31 Ibid at paragraph 406; The ICTY varied the test used by the ICJ, considering whether a State has 'overall control' rather than 'effective control' over the action in question. The ICJ in the *Genocide* case, discussed the ICTY's 'overall control' test and rejected the 'overall control' test as a broadening of the existing principles under the law, and thus a departure from customary international law.

32 Christopher Leck, 'International Responsibility in United Nations Peacekeeping Operations: Command and Control Arrangements and the Attribution of Conduct' (2009) *10 Melbourne Journal of International Law* 346 at 348; Haidi Willmot, Scott Sheeran and Lisa Sharland, 'Safety and Security Challenges in UN Peace Operations' (2015) *International Peace Institute* at 14; Perova, above note 25 at 37.

'effective control' over peacekeepers. Ferraro, in agreement with the UN, has suggested that the UN's operational control "means that it has 'effective control' (and a fortiori 'overall control') over military operations conducted by the troops lent by the TCCs."[33] Presently, however, there is no legal definition to 'operational control' or 'operational command', nor can it be equated to the legal definition of 'effective control'. Particularly the concept of 'operational control', as was discussed, can be correlated to the 'overall control' test in *Tadić*, which was rejected by the ICJ as being a departure from customary international law.

Even if 'operational control' is accepted as 'effective control', the practice of the UN's command structure differs greatly from its theoretical foundations.[34] In other words, although the UN contends that they have 'operational control', this 'control' is not always executed in the field. With the continuation of TCC/PCC intervention and national caveats, the command of the UN is more accurately 'aspirational' than actuality.[35]

Before contributing troops, Member States are permitted to place caveats over intended operations and mandated tasks to be performed by their contingent. Interestingly many of these caveats remain 'hidden' and are not reported to the Security Council or the UN Force Commander.[36] Due to political considerations, Member States do not want their caveats publicised to the international community, thus, the majority of caveats remain 'hidden' from those designing and implementing UN command. Distinctively, some TCCs place a caveat forbidding their troops from engaging in the use of force unless for their personal protection.[37] Consequently, in situations where the UN Force Commanders order troops to use force to protect civilians, certain contingencies will disobey UN command to adhere to their State's orders.[38] Thus, in the Declaration of Shared Commitments on UN Peacekeeping Operations, paragraph 15 states:

33 F Tristan Ferraro, 'The applicability and application of international humanitarian law to multinational forces' (2014) *95(891–892) International Review of the Red Cross* 561 at 589.

34 Leck, Christopher, 'International Responsibility in United Nations Peacekeeping Operations: Command and Control Arrangements and the Attribution of Conduct' (2009) *10 Melbourne Journal of International Law* 346 at 352.

35 Willmot, Haidi, Scott Sheeran and Lisa Sharland, *Safety and Security Challenges in UN Peace Operations* (International Peace Institute, 2015) at 16.

36 United Nations General Assembly and Security Council, Report of the High-level Independent Panel on Peace Operations on Uniting Our Strengths for Peace: Politics, Partnership and People, UN Doc A/70/95-S/2015/446 at paragraph 222.

37 Interview with diplomate from Western Member State on 30 January 2019.

38 Interview with UN researcher on 28 January 2019.

> We stress the importance of avoiding all caveats which have a detrimental impact on mandate implementation and performance. We as Member States commit to redouble all efforts to identify and clearly communicate any caveats or change in status of caveats, and to work with the Secretariat to develop a clear, comprehensive and transparent procedure on caveats.[39]

Furthermore, many contingents will function under their own national rules of engagement, which will mirror their State's restraints on the use of force, rather than following the UN's issued rules of engagement.[40] As stated by the Under-Secretary-General for peacekeeping "[f]ailures by units to respect the chain of command and to adequately implement the ROE [rules of engagement] have, on some occasions, led to critical failures of missions to protect civilians and on others have placed mission personnel in considerable danger. This is unacceptable."[41]

This tension between UN and host State command originates in the TCCs/PCCs rejection that their troops would be under any foreign jurisdiction.[42] The status of military and police peacekeepers remaining as representatives of their States is reiterated in the Model MOU.[43] The Model MOU stipulates that the TCC retains the exclusive jurisdiction over their troops and further they are accountable for investigations and any corrective action.[44] However, as the UN wishes to still appear to have 'operational control', the Model MOU further stipulates that States are to ensure that legal action is taken against troops for alleged misconduct, and must inform the Secretary-General of the outcome of the investigation.[45]

While disciplinary authority solely resides in the jurisdiction of the Contingent Commander, the UN Force Commander is deprived the most effective avenue to enforce their orders. As the UN Force Commander cannot enforce any of their command, UN peacekeepers have "explained that there

39 *Declaration of Shared Commitments on UN Peacekeeping Operations*, Action for Peacekeeping, Secretary-General António Guterres, 16 August 2018 at paragraph 15.

40 Dale Stephens, 'The lawful use of force by peacekeeping forces: the tactical imperative' (2005) *12*(2) *International Peacekeeping* 157 at 164.

41 As cited in Willmot, Sheeran and Sharland, above note 35 at 16.

42 Odello, above note 2 at 366; United Nations General Assembly, *Model Status of Force Agreement* (*SOFA*), 9 October 1990, UN Doc. A/45/594 at paragraph 47.

43 Model Memorandum of Understanding between the United Nations and Participating State, Chapter 9 of UN Doc A/C.5/63/18.

44 Ibid.

45 Ibid.

was little deterrent to refusing to act or to follow command."[46] As the UN lacks any military structures to impose orders, peacekeepers rely on the confirmation from their home States before following UN orders.[47]

As contingents are perceived to remain within their respective jurisdictions, Contingent Commanders constantly refer back to their home State before complying with orders given by the UN Force Commander.[48] As an example, the failure of peacekeepers in Juba in South Sudan in 2016 was attributed to the breakdown of command, as each contingent followed the instructions of their Contingent Commander rather than UN command.[49] With multiple contingents existing within a single UN peace mission, it remains indistinct as to who realistically has effective control at any given time.[50]

The problems in determining effective control become further exacerbated with the expansion of multinational peacekeeping missions.[51] This issue was illustrated in Mali, as MINUSMA was mandated to assist French troops with French controlled operations, and work alongside French forces. In this situation it would become hard to determine who had 'effective control' over a number of MINUSMA's operations. With the increase in multinational peacekeeping missions, there arises a possibility to expose third party States to the responsibility of the actions of those peacekeepers, and hence, accountable for any violations of the law. As an example, on 23 February 2018 the UN, EU and the G5 Sahel signed an agreement that MINUSMA is to provide "specific operational and logistical support"[52] to French forces in Mali. Through their operational support, France might share an element of responsibility for the actions of MINUSMA within these operations, precisely when those operations violate international law. Moreover, even if third parties are not in effective control, this still brings issues of assisting and aiding other States, as discussed in Chapter 3.

---

46 Center for Civilians in Conflict, *Within and Beyond the Gates: The Protection of Civlians by the UN Mission in South Sudan*, May 2015 at 33.

47 Róisín Burke, 'Status of Forces Deployed on UN Peacekeeping Operations: Jurisdictional Immunity' (2011) *16(1) Journal of Conflict & Secuirty Law* 63 at 71.

48 United Nations General Assembly, Evaluation of the Implementation and results of Protection of Civilians Mandates in United Nations Peacekeeping Operations: Report of the Office of Internal Oversight Services, UN Doc A/68/787.

49 Ray Murphy, 'The United Nations Mission in South Sudan and the Protection of Civilians' (2017) *22(3) Journal of Conflict and Security Law* 367 at 381.

50 Scott Sheeran and Stephanie Case, *The Intervention Brigade: Legal Issues for the UN in the Democractic Republic of the Congo*, International Peace Institute, 2014 at 14.

51 Marten Zwanenburg, 'International humanitarian law interoperability in multinational operations' (2013) *95(891–892) International Review of the Red Cross* 681 at 696.

52 www.un.org/press/en/2018/sc13353.doc.htm.

In practice, whereas the SRSG and the UN Force Commander hold the 'operational control' over the Mission, the Contingent Commander is vested with authority to discipline and direct their contingents.[53] Consequently, while the UN Force Commander retains strategic control, the Contingent Commander practically has effective control over their contingent. Therefore, the assessment of effective control over peacekeeping conduct will depend on whose instructions the Contingent Commander is following.

The reporting procedure of UN operations creates difficulties in determining who had effective control over the operation. UN Force Commanders presently receive reports from Contingent Commanders on the amount of activities engaged and completed, however, there is no reporting on effectiveness, outcomes, duration or response.[54] As such, only the Contingent Commander would be truly aware of whether or not their contingent is adhering to UN orders.[55] As an example, Contingent Commanders only need to report on 'number of patrols' the contingent have engaged in; they do not report on duration, area of patrol, or time of day this was undertaken. In other words, there are no records of where, when, or how long the contingent undertook these activities.

Although members of the UN Secretariat emphasised that the UN has overall command over the UN peace missions, when asked directly who has actual control on the ground, it could not be certified by any participant that it was the UN. As one participant stated that "this is the million-dollar question."[56]

2.2 *Joint Responsibility of UN Peace Operations*

To reconcile this divergence between State and UN control, legal commentators have suggested that both the UN and the TCCs share the control, and hence the responsibility.[57] As suggested by Palchetti the "acts committed by a national contingent in the context of an authorised operation are to be attributed to the sending states does not exclude the possibility that the same acts could also give rise to the responsibility of the organisation."[58] This issue of joint responsibility was discussed in the Dutch case of *Nuhanović*, where the

53 Model Memorandum of Understanding at paragraph 7.5.

54 Interview with UN researcher in New York on 28 January 2019.

55 Ibid; Interview with UN Secretariat on 28 January 2019.

56 Interview with UN researcher in New York on 28 January 2019.

57 Keiichiro Okimoto, 'Violations of international humanitarian law by United Nations forces and their legal consequences' (2003) 6 *Yearbook of International Humanitarian Law* 199 at 225; Leck, above note 34 at 360.

58 Palchetti, above note 20 at 737.

Supreme Court of The Netherlands concluded that if the UN is determined in having effective control, this does not mean that the UN had "exclusive responsibility."[59]

The question of responsibility becomes essential, not only for legal responsibility but for a State's obligations under IHL. As UN peace missions are directly participating in hostilities, the authority or organisation that is legally responsible for the military operation will consequently become a party to that conflict.[60] Significantly, when the UN is considered to be in control of peacekeepers who are directly participating in hostilities, the UN as an organisation would be deemed as a party to the conflict. As the UN continually insists that it retains responsibility of peacekeeping operations, that control could determine that UN, as an organisation, is a party to multiple conflicts. Equally, the TCC/PCC may also be classified as a party to the conflict when they retain control over their contingents, as was discussed in Chapter 3.

2.3 *Civilian Peacekeepers*

Remarkably in relation to peacekeeping responsibility, discussions have centred around the military and police components of peacekeeping. Recently however, non-military members of UN peace missions have also been reported to violate international law or accused of underperformance. Civilian personnel, unlike their military counterparts, are not 'provided' by Member States and are not considered under national service. Rather civilian personnel are selected on an individual basis and should be considered sole organs of the UN.[61] Although the responsibility under Article 6 of ARIO would apply to non-military peacekeepers, some commentators have suggested that these personnel would be "subject to host state jurisdiction"[62] and thus under the responsibility of the host State rather than the UN. However, under the principles of organisational responsibility, civilian personnel would be under the legal responsibility of the UN as outlined in Article 6. Although, reports of civilian

59 *The Netherlands v Hasan Nuhanović*, Supreme Court of the Netherlands, First Chamber 12/03324, 6 September 2013 at paragraph 3.11.2.

60 Eric David and Ola Engdahl, 'How does the involvement of a multinational peacekeeping force affect the classification of a situation?' (2013) *95(891–892) International Review of the Red Cross* 659 at 671.

61 Perova, Natalia, 'Disentangling 'Effective Control' Test for the Purpose of Attribution of the Conduct of UN Peacekeepers to the States and the United Nations' (2017) *86(1) Nordic Journal of International Law* 30 at 37–38.

62 M. O'Brien, 'The Ascension of Blue Beret Accountability: International Criminal Court Command and Superior Responsibility in Peace Operations' (2010) *15(3) Journal of Conflict and Security Law* 533 at 535.

personnel violating their obligations under the law are increasing,[63] little has been discussed regarding the UN's responsibility over these individuals. As the UN has no existing mechanism to discipline these individuals, the UN can only repatriate civilian peacekeepers, and try to persuade their home States to take legal recourse. However, as the international community has predominately focused on the military component of peacekeeping, these civilian personnel are remaining out of general consideration. However, the UN under the law has a responsibility to ensure that these civilian peacekeepers are held accountable for any breaches in their obligations, or wrongful acts committed.

Therefore, the UN and TCC/PCC will hold joint responsibility over peacekeepers actions or omission. However, each individual circumstance must be investigated to determine which body was responsible for the action or omission. To illustrate, in assessing the failure to protect in Rwanda in 1994, the UN Force Commander was commanded by the UN not to act, and therefore the failure of protection would be the responsibility of the UN. Conversely, in Juba in 2016, the Chinese Contingent disobeyed UN orders and withdrew from their position. In Juba, the State of China will bear responsibility for the omission to act.

3 Immunity of the UN

When the UN bears a portion of the legal responsibility for the conduct of peacekeepers, any form of legal remedy before the host State's domestic courts becomes limited as the UN is privileged with immunity from legal prosecution.[64] The immunity of the UN is outlined in various documents, primarily, the UN Charter; the *Convention on the Privileges and Immunities of the United Nations*; numerous Security Council resolutions; and the SOFA.[65]

The UN in the past has paid compensation to mitigate harm created by UN peace missions, however, the UN's immunity limits an individual's right to legal remedy.[66] Although the UN at times has seemed 'generous' in their

63 https://www.un.org/africarenewal/audio-main-view/new-sexual-abuse-allegations-against-un-peacekeepers-car; https://www.express.co.uk/news/world/920390/Sexual-abuse-UN-peacekeeper-accused-612-cases.

64 Burke, above note 47 at 64.

65 Model SOFA.

66 Andrew Clapham, 'Protection of Civilians under International Human Rights Law' in Haidi Willmot et al (eds), *Protection of civilians* (Oxford University Press, 2016) at 149 at 153.

ability to pay compensation,[67] they remain ambiguous about their legal obligation to actually remedy legal wrongs.[68] Even though the UN intermittently pays compensation, unfortunately this is done in limited situations as the UN does not pay compensation for any damage created "in the course of carrying out operations."[69] Thus, collateral damage or fatality by peacekeepers during a UN operation would be considered an "operational necessity"[70] and will not be compensated by the UN. For example, the UN has denied any legal responsibility with the UN Stabilization Mission in Haiti's (*MINUSTAH*) conduct in Haiti and the outbreak of cholera. Although former Secretary-General Ban Ki-Moon promised to pay compensation of $400 million to the Haiti victims, currently to date the UN has relied on the *Convention on Privileges and Immunities* in order not to pay the full amount of reparations.[71] With the FIB engaged in more offensive operations, civilian casualties have increased, however, the UN has depended on their immunity not to pay compensation to victims.[72] Furthermore, as stated in the Model MOU, the UN is to take all responsibility for any claims by third parties, whether or not the damage was created in the course of carrying out an operation, limiting individual's recourse to legal remedy against the TCC or peacekeeper.[73] Hence, even if peacekeepers are acting unofficially, and under the control of the TCCs, the UN will take all responsibility for damage created, closing all avenues to legal reparations. Thus, when peacekeepers are acting outside their official duties and committing illegal acts, all legal remedies to the victims are limited by the UN's immunity from legal disputes.

Significantly, the UN's immunity will be inherited by all bodies and individuals deemed to be organs or agents of the organisation. If UN peace missions are considered 'subsidiary organs of the UN' they will then possess the same

67 For example, in 2005 the UN Compensation Commission (UNCC) has made available $195,044,579.38 to 6 governments for distribution to 8,303 successful claimants – https://www.un.org/press/en/2005/ik486.doc.htm.

68 Conor Foley, 'What are the human rights obligations of unmiss to those sheltering on its protection sites?' (2016) 2 *Conflict Trends* 20 at 222.

69 Sheeran and Case, above note 50 at 15.

70 Ibid.

71 "But to date – almost halfway through the fund's expected three-year term – the UN Haiti Cholera Response Multi-Partner Trust Fund has only raised $8.7 million or 2.2 percent of the total – and less than half has been spent, UN figures show." – https://www.reuters.com/article/us-haiti-cholera-rights/un-criticized-for-failing-on-promise-to-help-haiti-cholera-victims-idUSKBN1I105G.

72 Willmot, Sheeran and Sharland, above note 35.

73 Model Memorandum of Understanding at Article 9.

privileges and immunities awarded to the UN.[74] Although individual contingents are considered under their national service, the overall UN peace mission is to be considered a subsidiary organ of the UN, and thus will receive immunity from victims seeking legal remedy.

Crucially, this privilege does not reside with individuals, hence, does not extend to acts or omissions that would be considered outside the performance of their official duties.[75] The UN has reiterated that the actions of 'off-duty' peacekeepers are their own and are not the actions of the UN.[76] This would include when peacekeepers are involved in sexual misconduct or any violations of the law. All actions separate to the mandate of the Security Council is to be considered the actions of 'off-duty' peacekeepers, and outside the scope of the immunity of the UN. However, under the Model MOU, the UN will bear the responsibility for all damages, whether or not the action can be deemed the action of the UN. Therefore, the UN imposes its immunity over pursuit of damages, removing all avenues to legal remedy for victims.

4 Individual Peacekeeper Accountability

4.1 *Immunity from Host State Jurisdiction*

As peacekeepers are considered to remain within their national service, they are immune from the local laws of the Host State under international law. As military personnel of a foreign State, they are privileged with immunity from legal proceedings in the host State or any transitional State. As established by the ICJ, "the conduct of individual soldiers … is to be considered as the conduct of a State organ",[77] and thus soldiers, like their home State, are immune from foreign jurisdiction. This was confirmed in the *Jurisdictional Immunities* case, where the ICJ concluded that conduct of armed forces on foreign soil, within their official duty, have immunity for acts *acta jure imperii*.[78] Expressly, this immunity is derived from the legal principle of State sovereignty that is grounded in customary international law. While foreign dignitaries and organs

74 Burke, above note 47 at 64.

75 Dieter Fleck, 'The legal status of personnel involved in United Nations peace operations' (2013) 95(891–892) *International Review of the Red Cross* 613 at 614–615.

76 Leck, above note 34 at 351.

77 *Armed Activities on the Territory of the Congo (Democractic Republic of the Congo v Uganda)*, Judgment, ICJ Reports 2005, p.168 at paragraph 213.

78 *Jurisdictional Immunities of the State*, International Court of Justice, Judgment of 3 February 2012 at paragraph 77.

of the State can be requested to leave the Host State when breaching local laws, their immunity before the host State's authorities, however, will remain.[79] Thus, as peacekeepers remain under their national service, and representatives of their State, they will maintain immunity from the host State's jurisdiction.

Although, State immunity is not absolute and has been questioned previously in the *Pinochet Case*[80] specifically regarding breaches of international law.[81] Although Pinochet contended that he enjoyed State immunity from extradition to Spain, the UK House of Lords concluded that:

> he was not acting in any capacity which gives rise to immunity ratione materiae because such actions were contrary to international law, Chile had agreed to outlaw such conduct and Chile had agreed with the other parties to the Torture Convention that all signatory states should have jurisdiction to try official torture (as defined in the Convention) even if such torture were committed in Chile.[82]

Although the House of Lord's rationale specifically applied to the Convention on Torture, as witnessed by the Court's specific analysis of the Convention to override Pinochet's immunity, these arguments can be applied to all crimes against humanity and war crimes. If we were to take a strict interpretation of the *Pinochet Case* the defence of immunity *ratione materiae* can be overturned by crimes that international law presumes to require State action, that being, crimes against humanity or specific war crimes.[83] Hence, under this interpretation of the *Pinochet Case*, unless peacekeepers have committed crimes against humanity or war crimes, their immunity within the host State jurisdiction will be upheld.

---

79 Vienna Convention on Diplomatic Relations 1961 at Article 9; As stated by the ICJ in Case Concerning United States Diplomatic and Consular Staff in Tehran (United States of America v Iran), ICJ, Judgment of 24 May 1980 at paragraph 86, that diplomatic law is self-contained, for "The rules of diplomatic law, in short, constitute a self-contained regime which, on the one hand, lays down the receiving State's obligations regarding the facilities, privileges and immunities to be accorded to diplomatic missions and, on the other, foresees their possible abuse by members of the mission and specifies the means at the disposaıof the receiving State to counter any such abuse".

80 *Regina v Bartle and the Commissioner of Police for the Metropolis and others* EX *Parte Pinochet* (*on appeal form a Divisional Court of the Quen's Bench Division*) [1998] House of Lords.

81 Ibid.

82 Ibid per judgment of Lord Browne-Wilkinson.

83 Andrea Bianchi, 'Immunity Verses Human Rights: The Pinochet Case' (1999) *10*(*2*) *European Journal of International Law* 237 at 249.

Peacekeepers' exemption from the host State's jurisdiction is reiterated in the SOFA signed between the host State and the UN. Although paragraph 6 of the Model SOFA requires peacekeepers to respect all local laws, at the same time host States waive their right to seek legal remedy when these laws are breached.[84] It is assumed by the UN that as the host State has consented to the deployment of peacekeepers, that host State will also bear the 'consequences' of the presence of those peacekeepers.[85] Although the Model SOFA has provisions for creation of a Claims Commission to deal with claims against peacekeeper conduct, no Commission has been created, and UN peace missions have generally resolved their disputes informally.[86]

The informal resolutions reached by the UN are generally confidential and not reported to the public. Moreover, these resolutions are negotiated between the UN and the Member State, rather than with the victims themselves. Therefore, the current practice of dealing with disputes is a breach of the victim's right to an effective remedy.[87] As the UN is inconsistent with their informal dispute resolution, there is no authoritative body determining the adequate remedy that should be awarded to the victims.

4.2 *Accountability under TCC/PCC Military Code*

As peacekeepers remain under the military service of their home State, they can be held accountable under their home State's military code. Regrettably, this is premised that first peacekeepers have breached a provision within their military code. For example, the Egyptian military code does not consider sexual exploitation or abuse as an offense, making it difficult to hold Egyptian peacekeepers accountable on sexual misconduct within Egyptian military courts.[88] So although peacekeepers can be held accountable under their home State's jurisdiction, that accountability is limited to a TCC's criminal code and that State's willingness to prosecute their troops.

Dissimilar to military peacekeepers, the UN police officers who are considered UN experts and are granted functional immunity, cannot be held accountable as their military counterparts. Specifically, UN police officers who are not members of the military, cannot be held legally accountable under the

84 Burke, above note 47 at 67.

85 Daphna Shraga, 'UN Peacekeeping Operations: Applicability of International Humanitarian Law and Responsibility Operatsions-Related Daamage' (2000) 94(2) *American Journal of International Law* 406 at 410.

86 Foley, above note 68 at 221.

87 ICCPR at Article 2(3).

88 https://peacekeeping.un.org/sites/default/files/egypt_fact_sheet.pdf.

military code. Remarkably, the UN still deems PCCs responsible for disciplinary actions, yet unlike military peacekeepers, the PCC will need extraterritorial criminal jurisdiction to prosecute offending police officers.[89] According to official UN reports, between 2007 and 2012 there has been 78 allegations of sexual related crimes by UNPOL, however, none have been prosecuted by their home States.[90]

In summary, although the UN contends to hold 'operational control' this does not equate to the 'effective control' test under the law. As the TCCs hold disciplinary jurisdiction and caveats over their troops, they will retain a level of legal responsibility when they interfere with UN command. Hence, under international law responsibility and accountability for peacekeepers misconduct can be held by the UN and the TCCs, jointly or individually, depending on the situation.

However, all legal remedies sought from the UN or the UN peace mission will be hindered by the organisation's immunity. Further, as individual peacekeepers are immune from the host State's jurisdiction, any accountability of peacekeeping misconduct will be beholden to the willingness of the TCCs to investigate and prosecute.

5 The Responsibility of the TCC/PCC under International Law

UN and individual peacekeeping immunity do not eliminate the TCC's responsibility and liability under international law. When a TCC has joint responsibility over a peacekeeping operation, the TCC will be responsible for actions and omissions committed. For example, if a TCC is in breach of their obligation to an individual's right to life, UN immunity will not remove the State's obligation under the law.

As such, a breach of the obligation to protect by a TCC/PCC exerting control can theoretically give rise to sanctions by the Security Council,[91] or a contentious claim in the ICJ.[92] However, Member States would be reluctant, due to political motivations, to take any action against a TCC/PCC for a breach of their obligation to protect. As evidenced, the Security Council or Member States have yet to take legal action against a TCC/PCC for failure to protect.

89 William J Durch and Michelle Ker, 'Police in UN Peacekeeping: Improving Selection, Recruitment, and Deployment' (2013) *6 Providing For Peacekeeping* at 26.

90 Ibid at 26.

91 UN Charter under Article 41.

92 *Statute of the International Court of Justice* (1945) at Article 36(2)(c).

Although, proceedings by another State is improbable, this does not remove the ability for victims to seek action against the TCC/PCC. The question of a TCC's responsibility under IHRL was questioned by the Dutch Supreme Court in *Mothers of Srebrenica v The Netherlands.*[93] In this case the foundation known as the Mothers of Srebrenica sought compensation from the Dutch government's involvement in the Bosnian peacekeeping mission, which was present during the genocide in 1995. The Court found that during the evacuation of the Bosnian refugees in July 1995, the Dutch government held joint responsibility with the UN over that operation. The Court found that as the Dutch government was involved in the decision to evacuate the refugees, and the Dutch commander organised the evacuation with the Bosnian-Serbian forces, that the Dutch State was jointly in control, and therefore, responsible. Consequently, The Netherland's was found to be in breach of their obligation under the European Convention of Human Rights, particularly, the Dutch contingent's actions denied the Bosnian males a 10% chance of not being subjected to inhumane treatment. Although the Court concluded that compensation can only be paid to the victims rather than the foundation, this is still a significant decision to peacekeeping accountability.[94]

Remarkably, the Dutch court omitted any discussion of UN immunity impeding victims seeking compensation. While it is unclear whether other domestic courts would follow the reasoning of the Dutch Court, the *Mothers of Srebrenica* case does underscore a State's responsibility in peacekeeping operations. The immunity of the UN for legal processes does not grant the same immunity to the State itself. The *Convention on the Privileges and Immunities of the UN* grants immunity to all subsidiary organs and representatives of Member States to the UN, but not to the State. As discussed earlier in this Chapter, the provision that legal disputes are dealt with by the UN is found in the SOFA signed by the host State and the UN. Interestingly, the Model SOFA specifies in Article 15:

> The United Nations peace-keeping operation, as a subsidiary organ of the United Nations, enjoys the status, privileges and immunities of the United Nations [as provided for in the present Agreement]/[in accordance with the Convention]. The provision of article II of the Convention

93 *The Mothers of Srebrenica v The Netherlands*, Supreme Court, Judgment of 19 July 2019, ECLI:NL:HR:2019:1223.

94 To read more see, Tamer Morris "State Responsibility and Accountability in UN Peacekeeping: The Case of The Mothers of Srebrenica v. The Netherlands" (2022) 29 *International Peacekeeping* 204.

> which applies to the United Nations peace-keeping operation shall also apply to the property, funds and assets of participating States used in [host country/territory] in connection with the national contingents serving in the United Nations peace-keeping operation, as provided for in paragraph 5 of the present Agreement.[95]

Although Article 15 of the Model SOFA grants immunities to the UN peace mission as a subsidiary organ it does not befit the same privilege to the TCC/PCC. As specified in Article 15, the TCC/PCC can only benefit from Article II of the Convention, that is, concerning the State's property, funds and assets.

Therefore, when a State is separately or jointly responsible for the actions of their contingents, they cannot rely on the UN's immunity for protection against legal action, specifically, any breach to their obligations under IHRL. Consequently, TCCs/PCCs may have potential responsibilities under IHRL, particularly these obligations are not limited the conduct of their troops, but as discussed in Chapter 6, may require a positive obligation to protect the human rights of civilians within their control.[96]

While TCCs/PCCs can be held liable for their violations under IHRL, a breach of the obligation to protect, as discussed in Chapter 1, does not create a legal avenue within domestic courts. As discussed in Chapter 1, comparable to Common Article 1, TCCs/PCCs are to ensure that they respect and adhere to the obligation to protect. Nevertheless, although a breach of the obligation to protect does not correlate to legal proceedings, a breach of the State's obligation under IHRL or IHL could, as seen in the Dutch courts, could lead to legal proceedings.

6 Obligation on the UN Leadership

Within customary international law there is an acknowledgement that military commanders and civilian leaders bear a level of responsibility with respect to the actions and conduct of their subordinates.[97] However, in assessing the nature of this responsibility, commentators[98] generally focus on international

95 Model SOFA at Article 15.

96 Siobhan Wills, 'The 'Responsibility to Protect' by Peace Support Forces under International Human Rights Law' (2006) *13(4) International Peacekeeping* 476 at 486.

97 Guénaël Mettraux, *The Law of Command Responsibility* (Oxford University Press, 2016) at 5.

98 Chantal Meloni, 'Command Responsibility: Mode of Liability for the Crimes of Subordinates or Separate Offence of the Superior?' (2007) *5 Journal of International*

criminal law and provisions of the Rome Statute.[99] Although command responsibility is discussed in the concept of criminal liability, it has its foundations in the concept of 'responsible command' that is codified in Additional Protocol I. Article 87 spells out the duty of commanders, specifically that commanders must prevent and suppress breaches to the Geneva Conventions,[100] and "to initiate such steps as are necessary to prevent such violations of the Conventions or this protocol, and, where appropriate, to initiate disciplinary or penal action against violations thereof."[101] Thus, not every breach of responsible command under IHL will lead to 'criminal responsibility'. For as set down in the ICTY *Mucic* case,[102] a "superior may be held criminally responsible not only for ordering, instigating or planning criminal acts carried out by his subordinates, but also for failing to take measures to prevent or repress the unlawful conduct of his subordinates."[103] However, a superior will only be responsible for peacekeepers' failure to protect "only where there exists a legal obligation to act."[104]

Although the TCCs will bear an element of the responsibility of the legal obligation of the protection of civilians, UN leadership 'commanding' those missions will also bear responsibility for duty as commanders. Specifically, UN leadership must do all that is in their control to prevent and suppress breaches of the obligation to protect. In interviews, those that considered the protection mandate a legal obligation also thought that all levels of the UN should be held accountable.[105] This responsibility was not only considered for the UN Force Commander, but all levels throughout the organisation of the UN, specifically, the Fifth Committee of the General Assembly, and the DPO were mentioned.

Even though the UN has no mechanism to discipline peacekeepers, this does not mean that they are exempt from command responsibility. Even if the TCC/PCC contradict the order of the UN, and the UN lacks "authority to control the conduct of forces in question, is still obliged to utilise all means"[106]

Criminal Justice 619; Mettraux, above note 97; Lenneke Sprik, 'Command Responsibility in Peacekeeping Missions: Normative Obligations of Protection in a Criminal Law Environment' (2017) 22(3) *Journal of Conflict and Security Law* 497.

99 Rome Statute at Articles 28(a) and (b).

100 Additional Protocol I at Article 87(1).

101 Ibid at Article 87(3).

102 Prosecutor v Delalic, Mucic, Delic and Landžo, ICTY, IT-96-21-A, 20 February 2001.

103 Ibid at paragraph 333.

104 Ibid at paragraph 334.

105 Interview with Member State on 30 January 2019; Interview with UN researcher on 28 January; Interview with Peacekeeping Researcher on 30 January 2019; Interview with UN Secretariat on 14 March 2019.

106 *Mucic et al*, ICTY, 2001.

to prevent a breach of law. An example that was cited was the Alindao attack on 15 November 2018. On 15 November, an IDP camp was attacked in CAR, where nearly 100 civilians were killed, with some being burnt alive. Although the humanitarian community blamed UN peacekeepers for lack of action,[107] only 57 peacekeepers were posted to protect the 12,000-person camp. As one researcher stated, "protection of civilians cannot be a suicide mission."[108] And so the November attacks were cited as an illustration of the lack of accountability of the UN as an institution. Throughout the literature a lack of resources becomes a main consideration when examining the reason for failure to protect.[109] Although, blame is normally placed on UN peacekeepers and the TCCs, a level of responsibility will also fall on the UN for not providing adequate resources for peacekeepers to fulfil their mandate. A classifier of the protection of civilians mandate is that peacekeepers are to protect "within their capabilities"; therefore, if they are not given adequate funding by the UN, they cannot be responsible for a failure to protect.

Moreover, it has been suggested by some participants, that the Secretary-General cannot negotiate caveats that would fundamentally undermine the overall mission.[110] By the UN allowing caveats that go against the heart of the mandate, they are aiding a contingent to breach their legal obligation to protect. Therefore, by allowing any caveat that omits the obligation to protect, the Secretary-General would be legally responsible under command responsibility.

7 Conclusion

The responsibility of peacekeepers for failure to protect will fall on the authority that has effective control. Depending on the factual circumstances, both the UN and TCC/PCC may find themselves legally responsible for a peacekeeper's failure to protect. As the UN is immune from all legal recourses, victims will be

107 https://www.amnesty.org/en/latest/press-release/2018/12/car-up-to-100-civilians-shot-and-burnt-alive-as-un-peacekeepers-leave-posts-in-alindao/#:~:text=%E2%80%9CScores%20of%20civilians%20at%20the,Response%20Adviser%20at%20Amnesty%20International.

108 Interview with UN researcher on 28 January 2019.

109 Gary Anderson, 'Preparing for the Worst Military Requirements for Hazardous Missions' in *Peace Operations*, Trends, Progress, and Prospects (Georgetown University Press, 2008) 63 at 66; Lise Morjé Howard, *UN Peacekeeping in Civil Wars* (Cambridge University Press, 2008) at 1–2.

110 Interview with UN researcher and anaylst on 28 January 2019; Interview with POC researcher on 23 January 2019.

denied any legal remedy against the UN or individual peacekeepers. Although the UN depends on the TCC/PCC to discipline their troops for any violations in the law, this is a disciplinary action rather than legal remedy for victims.

The legal obligation created by the protection of civilians mandate should be viewed comparably to the obligation created under Common Article 1 of the Geneva Conventions. Therefore, under the obligation to protect, the TCC/PCC must ensure the respect of the content of the protection obligation. This obligation would include adequately training their contingent and to prosecute peacekeepers misconduct and violation of the law.

When a TCC/PCC is exerting control over their contingent, they will not benefit from the immunity of the UN. While a breach of the obligation to protect does not give rise to legal recourse, nevertheless, a breach of the obligation to protect could incidentally violate IHL and IHRL. Consequently, a TCC/PCC's effective control over contingent can give rise to legal ramifications against the State.

Conclusion

Comparable to all Security Council Chapter VII decisions, the protection of civilians mandate has the weight of Article 25 of the UN Charter binding Member States to that decision. Subsequently, the UN, host State and TCCs/PCCs are obliged to respect and ensure the respect of the Security Council's mandate to protect civilians. As such, the Security Council's protection of civilians mandate establishes a legal obligation to protect on TCCs/PCCs, the host State and the UN. The responsibility and accountability for a failure to protect will rest on the authority that has effective control over that action or omission. Depending on the operation in question, both the UN and TCC/PCC may be legally responsible for a peacekeeper's failure to protect.

When examining the language of the Security Council, the obligation placed on UN peace missions is the protection of legal rights, particularly in connection with armed conflict and the legal status of 'civilian'. Therefore, the content of the obligation to protect comprises of existing legal obligations owed to civilians in armed conflict under the law. Particularly, the Security Council invokes the existing obligations in IHL and IHRL, placing those obligations upon the UN peace mission. From the Security Council's wording, the obligation to protect can be divided into two main categories – protection against physical violence and human rights protection. Moreover, the mandate explicitly mentions three groups of vulnerable civilians requiring 'special' protections – women, children and IDPs.

When examining the first dimension, the obligation to protect from physical violence, peacekeepers are obliged to protect civilians within the vicinity of UN bases, their person, and areas of patrol. Further, UN police officers are obliged to protect civilians within the same area from conflict-related violence, specifically sexual and gender-based violence. As peacekeepers within the current peacekeeping landscape are increasingly being considered a party to a conflict, peacekeepers are further obliged to ensure that all force is used in proportion to the direct military advantage. As peacekeepers are mandated to protect civilians, the military advantage gained must be for the protection of civilians. Therefore, peacekeepers are to ensure that an attack is proportionate to the direct protection that is anticipated. As peacekeepers are increasingly engaged in offensive operations against armed groups, peacekeepers are obliged to ensure that child soldiers are only targeted if they are taking an 'active' part in hostilities.

Regarding the dimensions of human rights protections, without clarification from the Security Council, UN peacekeepers are solely obliged to 'monitor

 | DOI:10.1163/9789004707313_010

and report' human right violations to the UN. UN peace missions will only be obliged to protect and fulfil human rights if they exert effective control over individuals. When UN peace missions exercise effective control, the obligation to protect will include the promotion and protection of those individuals' rights. In cases of detention, UN-run IDP camps, and areas of patrol, the obligation to protect will also encompass the obligation to respect, protect and fulfil individuals' human rights who are under peacekeepers' control. Specifically, as a minimum core, peacekeepers must respect, protect and fulfil individuals' rights to life, food, water, education and healthcare.

However, with the increase in protection activities there remains areas that need further clarification from the Security Council and the UN. Firstly, the Security Council needs to revise or explain the caveats to the obligation, that is, 'areas of deployment' and the consent of the host State. Particularly, for the obligation to encompass protection against the host State, the Security Council must refrain from mandating the obligation in 'assistance' of local authorities. Moreover, if the Security Council wishes for the mandate to reach beyond the vicinity of peacekeepers, they need to clarify the defined area of 'deployment'.

Secondly, with limited resources and an expanding mandate, peacekeepers are faced with prioritising their activities. The Security Council must create sufficient guidance on which group of civilians receive priority under the mandate or else peacekeepers will be forced to construct a hierarchy of protection omitting certain groups from the protection regime. Moreover, the Security Council should enforce a due diligence process to allow transparency to civilians of who decides and how decisions are made operationally.

Thirdly, in order to protect against conflict-related violence and other violent crimes, peacekeepers are engaged in detaining violent individuals. As peacekeepers are limited in operational guidance and a legal framework for detentions, they may be detaining individuals indefinitely in breach of Article 9 of the ICCPR. However, peacekeepers are current facing a dilemma, as to transfer detainees would be a breach of non-refoulement, while releasing the individual would be a breach of their obligation to protect. Without the Security Council and UN establishing operational and legal guidelines when detainees cannot be transferred to local authorities within the prescribed 72 hours, UN peace missions will be in breach of their obligations under IHRL.

Under the obligation to protect, the UN and UN command, are obliged to respect, promote and encourage compliance to the Security Council's mandate. Part of the obligation would be disallowing any national caveats that would contravene the obligation to protect, nor accept any contingent that within the UN's reasonable knowledge would not protect civilians. The reluctance of the Secretary-General in enforcing this obligation is the cost of

Member States refusing to provide troops and peace missions being unable to fulfil the required number of personnel. However, the reluctance of the Secretary-General does not negate nor eliminate the obligation placed on him by the Security Council. Further, the UN, specifically the Fifth Committee, must provide adequate resourcing and mechanisms for UN peace missions to achieve their mandate.

Although the UN is legally obliged under the mandate, individuals will be denied any legal remedy against the UN, as well as any agents and organs of the UN, due to the UN's immunity. However, although the obligation does not create a legal avenue for victims against the UN, this does not deny the existence of a legal obligation. The legal obligation created by the protection of civilians mandate should be perceived in similar fashion to the obligation created under Common Article 1 of the Geneva Conventions. That is, that the international community has a right to require respect by parties involved within the UN peace mission.

Additionally, under the obligation to protect, the TCC/PCC must ensure that their orders do not contravene the content of the protection obligation, and that their contingents are adequately trained in protection activities. Further, to ensure the respect for the obligation to protect, TCCs/PCCs are obliged to prosecute peacekeepers misconduct and violation of the law. TCCs/PCCs would be in breach of the obligation to protect, and incidentally their IHRL obligations, in tolerating impunity of their contingents. As the obligation to protect invokes existing obligations under the law, a breach of the obligation to protect must inevitably be a breach under international law.

While UN peace missions, as subsidiary organs of the UN, which benefit from the immunity of the UN, this privilege does not extend to the TCC/PCC. While a breach of the obligation to protect, will not practically give rise to a legal ramification imposed by the Security Council, consequentially a breach of the obligation to protect will also be a violation under IHL and IHRL, which *could* give rise to regional legal proceedings. Therefore, when a TCC/PCC has effective control over the contingent's action or omission, they are legally obliged to ensure the respect and fulfilment of the obligation initiated by the mandate to protect.

Appendix 1

Timeline of Protection of Civilians in Peacekeeping

Year	Date	Event
1999	22/2/99	UN Security Council first open debate on Protection of Civilians (PoC) (S/PV.3980)
	6/8/99	Secretary-General's Bulletin: Observance by United Nations Forces of International Humanitarian Law (ST/SGB/1999/13)
	30/8/99	UN Security Council Resolution 1261(1999) on Children in Armed Conflict
	8/9/99	First Secretary-General Report to the Security Council on PoC in Armed Conflict (S/1999/957)
	17/9/99	UN Security Council Resolution 1265(1999) on PoC in Armed Conflict
	22/10/99	Establishment on UNAMSIL and the first PoC mandate in UN Peace Mission (Res 1270(1999))
2000	31/10/00	Resolution 1325(2000) on Women and Peace and Security
	13/11/00	Report of the Panel on UN Peace Operations (Brahimi Report), reporting on Peacekeeping shortcomings and recommendations for operations and strategy
2001	30/3/01	First Child Protection Advisor deployed in UNAMSIL
2003	19/9/03	Security Council establishes UNMIL, and mandates the "promote and protect" of Human Rights in Resolution 1509(2003)
	19/9/03	Security Council inserts children and women protection in reference to Human Rights in Resolution 1509(2003)
2004	2/12/04	High-level Panel on the Threats, Challenges and Change on a more Secured World: Our Shared Responsibility (A/59/565)
2005	24/3/04	Report on a Strategy to Eliminate Future Sexual Exploitation and Abuse in United Nations Peacekeeping Operations (Zeid Report) (A/59/710)

 | DOI:10.1163/9789004707313_011

Year	Date	Event
2006	24/2/06	Peace Operations 2010: Reform Strategy Report by the Secretary-General
2007	15/3/07	Establishment of the Department of Field Support (DFS)
	13/4/07	Report of the Secretary-General on Strengthening the Capacity of the United Nations to Manage and Sustain Peace Operations (A/61/858)
	31/7/07	Security Council establishes UNAMID to protect civilians in Darfur, Sudan
2008	18/1/08	Publication of the United Nations Peacekeeping Operations Principles and Guidelines (Capstone Doctrine)
	22/12/08	Security Council's first explicit mention of internally displaced persons in PoC mandate in Resolution 1856(2008)
2009	30/9/09	Security Council Resolution 1888(2009) that establishes Women Protection Advisors
	5/10/09	Security Council Resolution 1889(2009) further confirming the Women Protection Advisors
	1/11/09	Independent study on Protecting Civilians in the Context of UN Peacekeeping Operations: Success, Setbacks and Remaining Challenges, commissioned by OCHA and DPKO
	1/12/09	Draft DPKO/DFS Operational Concept on the Protection of Civilians in United Nations Peacekeeping Operations, 2009, and the establishment of three tiers of protection
2010	28/5/10	Security Council insert women physical protection, in assistance of government, in Resolution 1925(2010)
	1/7/10	Security Council establishes MONUSCO to protect civilians in DRC
	23/11/10	MONUSCO with FARDC (government forces) launch operations "Protection Shield" to neutralise armed groups in South Kivu

Year	Date	Event
2011	17/3/11	Security Council authorises use of force for PoC outside Peacekeeping in Libya under Resolution 1973(2011)
	8/8/11	Security Council establishes UNMISS to protect civilians in South Sudan
2013	28/3/13	Security Council authorises the Force Intervention Brigade to 'neutralise' armed groups in the DRC in Resolution 2098(2013)
	25/4/13	Security Council inserts children and women physical protection in Resolution 2100(2013)
	28/8/13	MONUSCO peacekeeper killed by M23, during operations in support of FARDC to push M23 out of Goma
	1/10/13	MONUSCO Force Intervention Brigade being operations against M23
	15/12/13	Outbreaks of violence in Juba, South Sudan, force 30,000 civilians to seek refuge in UNMISS compounds, spontaneously creating Protection of Civilian camps
2014	4/3/14	OIOS Report on the Evaluation of the implementation and results of protection of civilians mandates in United Nations peacekeeping operations
	4/3/14	Four MONUSCO peacekeepers are injured in grenade attack by M23
	10/4/14	Security Council establishes MINUSCA to protect civilians in CAR
	22/4/14	South Sudanese Government accuse UNMISS of harbouring rebel forces in Protection of Civilian camps
	10/10/14	MINUSCA peacekeeper killed, and four injured, in ambush in Banguai
2015	10/7/15	One individual killed, and three serious injured by MINUSCA peacekeepers excessive use of force during arrest
	17/7/15	Report of the High-Level Independent Panel on UN Peace Operations (HIPPO)

Year	Date	Event
2016	11/7/16	Attacks in Juba, South Sudan, overflow to protection of civilian sites, Chinese peacekeepers abandon their post. Also, ignore calls for help by aid workers being attacked
	15/12/16	During demonstrations from 15–30 December DRC forced committed human right violations against demonstrators
2017	8/5/17	Five MINUSCA peacekeepers killed, and 10 injured, in attacks south east CAR
	1/8/17	Publication of Guidelines on the Role of United Nations Police in Protection of Civilians
	29/9/17	DRC forces violates the premises of MONUSCO in Kanaga, searching for a journalist seeking refuge
	29/11/17	Report on Improving Security of Peacekeepers (Cruz Report)
	20/12/17	First Protection of Civilians site in Melut town, South Sudan shuts down
2018		Secretary-General launches 'Action for Peacekeeping' initiative
	15/11/18	112 civilians killed in IDP camp attack in Alindao, CAR. Only 55 peacekeepers were positioned to protect the camp
	16/11/18	MONUSCO and FARDC start new operations against ADF
2019	1/1/19	UN Peace and Security Reform – DFS and DPKO combined as DPO
2020	5/05/20	The Protection of Civilians in United Nations Peacekeeping Handbook is released
	5/06/20	The Handbook for United Nations Field Missions on Preventing and Responding to Conflict-Related Sexual Violence was released
2020	22/12/20	Security Council terminates the mandate of UNAMID
2021	1/3/2021	UN Secretary-General launched Action for Peacekeeping Plus (A4P+)

Year	Date	Event
2022	15/07/22	Protests in DRC after the president of the senate, Modeste Bahati, told supporters in Goma on July 15 that MONUSCO should "pack its bags"
2023	6/2/23	MONUSCO peacekeepers fire into a crowd of civilians blocking their entrance
2023	21/06/23	Mali asks for the complete withdraw of MINUSMA. Security Council in Resolution 2690 mandates the withdraw of MINUSMA from Mali.
2023	19/12/23	Security Council in Resolution 2717 begins MONUSCO's withdraw from the DRC.

Appendix 2

Summary of Peacekeeping Missions from 1999 to April 2024

 | DOI:10.1163/9789004707313_012

UN mission name	Location	Date established	Resolution establishing mission	Replacing an existing mission	Concluding Resolution	Chapter VII mandate	Protection of civilians mandate	Protection of Human rights mandate	Variance in Mandate
United Nations Truce Supervision Organisation (UNTSO)	Middle East	14/5/48	UNSC Res 186 (1948)		On-going Mission	No	No	No	
United Nations Military Observer Group in India and Pakistan (UNMOGIP)	India and Pakistan	24/1/49	n/a		On-going Mission	No	No	No	
United Nations Peacekeeping Force in Cyprus (UNFICYP)	Cyprus	4/3/64	UNSC Res 186 (1964)		On-going Mission	No	No	No	
United Nations Disengagement Observer Force (UNDOF)	Golan, Syria	31/5/74	UNSC Res 350 (1974)		On-going Mission	No	No	No	
United Nations Interim Force in Lebanon (UNIFIL)	Lebanon	19/3/78	UNSEC Res 425 (1978)		On-going Mission	No	No	No	
United Nations Mission for the Referendum in Western Sahara (MINURSO)	Western Sahara	29/4/91	UNSC Res 690 (1991)		On-going Mission	No	No	No	
United Nations Mission in the Central African Republic (MINURCA)	CAR	27/3/98	UNSC Res 1159 (1998)		Statement by the President (S/PRST/2000/5)	No	No	No	

UN mission name	Location	Date established	Resolution establishing mission	Replacing an existing mission	Concluding Resolution	Chapter VII mandate	Protection of civilians mandate	Protection of Human rights mandate	Variance in Mandate
United Nations Interim Administration Mission in Kosovo (UNMIK)	Kosovo	10/6/99	UNSC Res 1244 (1999)		On-going Mission	No	No	No	
United Nations Mission in Sierra Leone (UNAMSIL)	Sierra Leone	22/10/99	UNSC Res 1270 (1999)	United Nations Observer Mission in Sierra Leone (UNOMSIL)	UNSC Res 1620 (2005)	Yes	Inserted in Resolution 1270 (1999) at operational paragraph 14. The protection of civilians mandated was removed in Resolution 1562(2004)	No	First protection of civilians mandate
United Nations Organization Mission in the Democratic Republic of the Congo (MONUC)	DRC	30/11/99	UNSC Res 1279 (1999)		UNSC Res 1925 (2010)	Yes	Inserted in Resolution 1291 (2000) at operational paragraph 8	Inserted in Resolution 1291 (2000) at operational paragraph 7, but not under Chapter VII	
United Nations Mission in Ethiopia and Eritrea (UNMEE)	Border of Ethiopia and Eritrea	31/7/00	UNSC Res 1312 (2000)		UNSC Res 1827 (2008)	No	No	No	

UN mission name	Location	Date established	Resolution establishing mission	Replacing an existing mission	Concluding Resolution	Chapter VII mandate	Protection of civilians mandate	Protection of Human rights mandate	Variance in Mandate
United Nations Mission of Support in East Timor (UNMISET)	East Timor	20/5/02	UNSC Res 1410 (2002)		UNSC Res 1599 (2005)	Yes	No	No	
United Nations Mission in Côte d'Ivoire (MINUCI)	Cote d'Ivoire	13/5/03	UNSC Res 1479 (2003)		UNSC Res 1527 (2004)	No	No	No	
United Nations Mission in Liberia (UNMIL)	Liberia	19/6/03	UNSC Res 1509 (2003)	United Nations Peace-building Support Office in Liberia (UNOL)	UNSC Res 2333 (2016)	Yes	Inserted in Resolution 1509 (2003) in operational paragraph 3(j). Protection mandate continued till end of Mission	Inserted in Resolution 1509 (2003) in operational paragraph 3(l)-(m). Human Rights mandate continued till the end of Mission	
United Nations Operation in Côte d'Ivoire (UNOCI)	Côte d'Ivoire	27/4/04	UNSC Res 1528 (2004)	United Nations Mission in Côte d'Ivoire (MINUCI)	UNSC Res 2284 (2016)	Yes	Inserted in Resolution 1528 (2004) at operational paragraph 6(i)	Inserted in Resolution 1528 (2004) at operational paragraph 6(n)	

UN mission name	Location	Date established	Resolution establishing mission	Replacing an existing mission	Concluding Resolution	Chapter VII mandate	Protection of civilians mandate	Protection of Human rights mandate	Variance in Mandate
United Nations Operation in Burundi (ONUB)	Burundi	21/5/04	UNSC Res 1545 (2004)		UNSC Res 1719 (2006)	Yes	No	No	
United Nations Stabilization Mission in Haiti (MINUSTAH)	Haiti	1/6/04	UNSC Res 1542 (2004)	Multinational Interim Force (IMF)	UNSC Res 2350 (2017)	Yes	Inserted in Resolution 1542 (2004) at operational paragraph 7(I)(f). Protection mandate continued until the withdrawing of troops to conclude Mission	Inserted in Resolution 1542 (2004) in operational paragraph 7(III). Human Rights mandate continued to end of Mission	
United Nations Integrated Mission in Timor-Leste (UNMIT)	East Timor	25/8/06	UNSC Res 1704 (2006)	UNOTIL	UNSC Res 2037 (2012)	No	No	No	

UN mission name	Location	Date established	Resolution establishing mission	Replacing an existing mission	Concluding Resolution	Chapter VII mandate	Protection of civilians mandate	Protection of Human rights mandate	Variance in Mandate
African Union/United Nations Hybrid operation in Darfur (UNAMID)	Sudan	31/7/07	UNSC Res 1769 (2007)	UNMIS	UNSC Res 2559 (2020)	Yes	Inserted in Resolution 1881 (2009) in operational paragraph – mandate is on-going	Inserted in Resolution 2363 (2017) at operational paragraph 15(a)(x) – mandate is on-going	
The United Nations Mission in Central African Republic and Chad (MINURCAT)	CAR and Chad	25/9/07	UNSC Res 1778 (2007)		UNSC Res 1923 (2010)	Yes	Inserted in Resolution 1778 (2007) at operational paragraph 2	Inserted in Resolution 1778 (2007) at operational paragraph 2	
United Nations Organization Stabilization Mission in the Democratic Republic of the Congo (MONUSCO)	Democratic Republic of the Congo (DRC)	1/7/10	UNSC Res 1925 (2010)	United Nations Organization Mission in the Democratic Republic of the Congo (MONUC)	On-going Mission – beginning to withdraw under UNSC Res 2717 (2023)	Yes	Inserted in Resolution 1925 (2010) at operational paragraph 12 – mandate is on-going	Inserted in Resolution 2098 (2013) in operational paragraph 12(a)(iii) – mandate is on-going	Creation of Force Intervention Brigade to 'neutralize' armed groups (Inserted in Resolution 2098 (2013) at operational paragraph 12(b) – on-going mandate)

UN mission name	Location	Date established	Resolution establishing mission	Replacing an existing mission	Concluding Resolution	Chapter VII mandate	Protection of civilians mandate	Protection of Human rights mandate	Variance in Mandate
United Nations Interim Security Force for Abyei (UNISFA)	Abyei, Sudan	27/6/11	UNSC Res 1990 (2011)		On-going Mission	Yes	Inserted in Resolution 1990 (2011) at operational paragraph 3(d) – mandate is on-going	No	
United Nations Mission in the Republic of South Sudan (UNMISS)	South Sudan	8/7/11	UNSC Res 1996 (2011)		On-going Mission	Yes	Inserted in Resolution 1996 (2011) at operational paragraph 3(b) – mandate is on-going	Inserted in Resolution 1996 (2011) at operational paragraph 3(b) – mandate is on-going	Projecting when government cannot provide security (inserted in Resolution 1996 (2011) at operational paragraph 3(b)(v)) Mandate was changed to "irrespective of the source of such violence" in Resolution 2252 (2015), which is on-going. Specific protection for Protection of

UN mission name	Location	Date established	Resolution establishing mission	Replacing an existing mission	Concluding Resolution	Chapter VII mandate	Protection of civilians mandate	Protection of Human rights mandate	Variance in Mandate
									Civilians sites (inserted in Resolution 2155 (2014) at operational paragraph 4 (a) (vi) – on-going mandate)
United Nations Supervision Mission in Syria (UNSMIS)	Syria	21/4/12	UNSC Res 2043 (2012)		N/A	No			
United Nations Multidimensional Integrated Stabilization Mission in Mali (MINUSMA)	Mali	25/4/13	UNSC Res 2100 (2013)	African-Led International Support Mission in Mali (AFISMA)	UNSC Res 2690 (2023)	Yes	Inserted in Resolution 2100 (2013) at operational paragraph 16(c) – mandate is on-going	Inserted in Resolution 2100 (2013) paragraph 16(d) – mandate is on-going	Protection of cultural sites (Inserted in Resolution 2100 (2013) at operational paragraph 16(f) – on-going mandate) Involvement in Counter-Terrorism activities (Inserted in Resolution 2364 (2017) at operational paragraph 20 (d) – on-going mandate)

UN mission name	Location	Date established	Resolution establishing mission	Replacing an existing mission	Concluding Resolution	Chapter VII mandate	Protection of civilians mandate	Protection of Human rights mandate	Variance in Mandate
United Nations Multidimensional Integrated Stabilization Mission in the Central African Republic (MINUSCA)	Central African Republic (CAR)	10/4/14	UNSC Res 2149 (2014)	African-led International Support Mission to the Central African Republic (MISCA)	On-going Mission	Yes	Inserted in Resolution 2149 (2014) at operational paragraph 30(a) – mandate is on-going	Inserted in Resolution 2149 (2014) at operational paragraph 30(e) – mandate is on-going	
United Nations for Justice Support in Haiti (MINUJUSTH)	Haiti	13/4/17	UNSC Res 2350 (2017)	MINUSTAH	UNSC Res 2466 (2019)	Yes	Inserted in Resolution 2350 (2017) at operational paragraph 13	Assistance in Human Rights monitoring in Resolution 2350 (2017) at operational paragraph 6	
United Nations Integrated Transition Assistance Mission in Sudan (UNITAMS)	Sudan	3/6/20	UNSC Res 2525 (2020)	UNAMID	On-going Mission	No			

Appendix 3

List of Questions Asked to Participants

1. Does the protection of civilians mandate create a legal obligation?
2. Who should be accountable for peacekeepers omitting protection or failure to protect?
3. When should peacekeepers use force?
4. Should peacekeepers use force for domestic violence cases?
5. Should peacekeepers use force against the host State?
6. Are there any protection activities that peacekeepers would not be permitted to use force?
7. Is there or should there be a priority of protection activities?
8. Who has 'control' over peacekeepers' actions?
9. Should there be protection outside of armed conflict?
10. What do you think is the major hindrance to protection of civilians in peacekeeping?

 | DOI:10.1163/9789004707313_013

Bibliography

International Instruments

African Charter on the Rights and Welfare of the Child (1990).

African Union Convention for the Protection and Assistance of Internally Displaced Persons in Africa.

Charter of the United Nations (1945).

Convention against Torture and Other Cruel, Inhuman or Degrading Treatment or Punishment, adopted by General Assembly resolution 39/46 of 10 December 1984.

Criminal Act 1991, Sudan.

Draft Articles on Reponsbility of States for Internationally Wrongful Acts, A/56/10.

Draft Articles on Responsibility of International Organizations.

Geneva Convention (I) Amelioration of the Condition of the Wounded and Sick in Armed Forces in the Field, Geneva, 12 August 1949.

Geneva Convention (II) Amelioration of the Condition of Wounded, Sick and Shipwrecked Members of Armed Forces at Sea, Geneva, 12 August 1949.

Geneva Convention (III) Treatment of Prisoners of War, Geneva, 12 August 1949.

Geneva Convention (IV) Relative to the Protection of Civilian Persons in Time of War, Geneva, 12 August 1949.

International Convenant on Civil and Political Rights, adopted by General Assembly resolution 200a(XXI) of 16 December 1966, entry into force 23 March 1976.

International Convenant on Economic, Social and Cultural Rights, adopted by General Assembly resolution 200A(XXI) oon 16 December 1966, entry into force 3 January 1976.

International Convention for the Protection of All Persons from Enforced Disappearance, adopted by the General Assmebly by resolution A/RES/61/177.

Loi No. 10.001 Portant Code Penal Centrafricain.

Optional Protocol to the Convention on the Rights of the Child on the Involvement of Children in Armed Conflict, A/RES/54/263 of 25 May 2000.

Protocol Additional to the Geneva Conventions of 12 August 1949 and realting to the Protection of Victims of International Armed Conflicts (Protocol I), 8 June 1977.

Protocol Additional to the Geneva Conventions of 12 August 1949 and realting to the Protection of Victims of Non-International Armed Conflicts (Protocol II), 8 June 1977.

United Nations Convention on the Rights of the Child, A/RES/44/25.

Regulations Concerning the Laws and Customs of War on the Land (Hague Regulations) 1907.

Rome Statue of the International Criminal Court, A/CONF.183.9 of 17 July 1998.

Statute of the International Court of Justice (1945).

Statute of the Special Court for Sierra Leone 2000.
The Copenhagen Process Principles and Guidelines.
Vienna Convention on Diplomatic Relations 1961.
Vienna Convention on the Law of Treaties 1969.
Worst Forms of Child Labour Convention, 1999 (No. 1).

Cases

Armed Activities on the Territory of the Congo (Democractic Republic of the Congo v Uganda), Judgment, ICJ Reports 2005, p.168.

Attorney General v Nissan (Right of UK National to Compensation for Porperty Seized by UK Forces in Cyprus; Relationship of UK Forces to Cyprus Goverment and to United Nations) [1969] UKHL 3.

Behrami and Behrami v France and *Saramati v France, Germany and Norway*, Application no 71412/01 and 78166/01, European Court of Human Rights, 2 May 2007.

Case Concerning Application of the Convention on the Prevention and Punishment of the Crime of Genocide (Bosnia and Herzegovina v Serbia and Montenegro), ICJ, 26 February 2007.

Case Concerning Military and Parmilitary Activities In and Against Nicaragua (Nicaragua v United States of America), ICJ, Judgment of 27 June 1986.

Case Concerning Questions of Interpretation and Application of the 1971 Montreal Convention Arising From the Aeria Incident at Lockerbie (Libyan Arab Jamahiriya v United Kingdom), ICJ, Judgment of 27 February 1998.

Case Concerning United States Diplomatic and Consular Staff in Tehran (United States of America v Iran), ICJ, Judgment of 24 May 1980.

Case of Al-Jedda v The United Kingdom (Application no 27021/08), European Court of Human Rights, Grand Chamber, 7 July 2011.

Case of Tagayeva and Others v Russia, Application no 26562/07 and 6 other applications, European Court of Human Rights, 13 April 2017.

Case of the S.S. Lotus (France v Turkey), PCIJ Judgment No.9, 7 September 1927.

Certain Expenses of the United Nations (Article 17, Paragraph 2, of the Charter), Advisory Opinion of 20 July 1962, ICJ Reports 1962, p.151.

Decision on the Defence Motion for Interlocutory Appeal on Jurisdiction, International Criminal Tribunal for the former Yugoslavia, Appeals Chamber Decision, 2 October 1995.

Jurisdictional Immunities of the State, International Court of Justice, Judgment of 3 February 2012.

Kaya v Turkey, Merits, App No 22535/93, ECHR 2000-III, [2000] ECHR 129, (1999) 28 EHRR 1.

Legal Consequences for States of the Continued Presence of South Africa in Namibia (South West Africa) Notwithstanding Security Council Resolution 276 (1970), Advisory Opinion of 21 June 1971, ICJ Reports 1971 p.16.

Legality of the Threat or Use of Nuclear Weapons, Advisory Opinion, ICJ Reports 1996, p 226.

Lopez Burgos v Uruguay, Saldias de Lopez (on behalf of Lopez Burgos) v Uruguay, Merits, Communication No 52/1979, UN Doc CCPR/C/13/D/52/1979, IHRL 2796 (UNHRC 1981), 29th July 1981.

Osman v The United Kingdom, Judgment, merits and just satisfaction, App no 23452/94, Case No 87/1997/871/1083, ECHR 1998-VIII, [1998] ECHR 101.

Prosecutor v Anto Furundžija, Trail Chamber Judgement, ICTY, it-95-17/1-T, 10 December 1998.

Prosecutor v Bosco Ntaganda, International Criminal Court, Pre-Trail Chamber II, NO: ICC-01/04-02/06, 9 June 2014.

Prosecutor v Dario Kordić and Mario Čerkez, International Criminal Tribunal of the former Yugoslavia, Judgment, 26 February 2001, Case No IT-95-14/2-T.

Prosecutor v Delalic, Mucic, Delic and Landžo, ICTY, IT-96-21-A, 20 February 2001.

Prosecutor v Dragoljub Kunarac, Radomir Kovac and Zoran Vukovic, ICTY, IT-96-23-T & IT-96-23/1-T, 22 February 2001.

Prosecutor v Dragomir Milošević, International Criminal Tribunal of the former Yugoslavia, Judgment, 12 December 2007, Case No IT-98-29/1-T.

Prosecutor v Issa Hassan Sesay, Morris Kallon and Augustine Gbao, Special Court for Sierra Leone, 2 March 2009, Case No SCSL-04-15-T.

Prosecutor v Kupreškić et al, International Criminal Tribunal of the former Yugoslavia, Judgment, 14 January 2000, Case No IT-95-16-T.

Prosecutor v Pavle Strugar, International Criminal Tribunal of the former Yugoslavia, Appeals decision, 17 July 2008, Case No IT-01-42-A.

Regina v Bartle and the Commissioner of Police for the Metropolis and others EX *Parte Pinochet (on appeal form a Divisional Court of the Quen's Bench Division)* [1998] House of Lords.

Reparation for Injuries Suffered in the Service of the United Nations, Advisory Opinion of April 11, 1949, ICJ.

Serdar Mohammed v Ministry of Defence [2014] EWHC 1369 (QB).

Situation in the Democractic Republic of the Congo, in the case of the Prosecutor v Thomas Lubanga Dyilo,.

International Criminal Court, Trail Chamber I, Judgment pursuant to Article 74 of the Statute, ICC-01/04-01/06, 14 March 2012.

The Mothers of Srebrenica v The Netherlands, Supreme Court, Judgment of 19 July 2019, ECLI:NL:HR:2019:1223.

The Netherlands v Hasan Nuhanović, Supreme Court of the Netherlands, First Chamber 12/03324, 6 September 2013.

The Prosecutor v Jean-Paul Akayesu, International Court Tribunal for Rwanda, ICTR-96-4-T, 2 September 1998.

The Queen on the application of Mazin Jumaa Gatteh Al-Skeini v Secretary of State for Defence [2004] EWHC 2911.

Vlastimir and Borka Bankovic, Zivana Stojanovic, Mirjana Stoimenovski, Dragana Joksimovic and Dragan Sukovic v Belgium and Other States, European Court of Human Rights, Application no. 52207/99, 12 December 2001.

UN documentation

Committee on the Elimination of Discrimination Against Women, *General Recommendation No. 30 on Women in Conflict Prevention, Conflict and Post-Conflict Situations*, 1 November 2013, UN Doc. CEDAW/C/GC/30.

Cruz, Santos, 'Improving Security of United Nations Peacekeepers: We Need to Change the Way We Are Doing Business' (United Nations, 2017).

Declaration of Shared Commitments on UN Peacekeeping Operations, Action for Peacekeeping, Secretary-General António Guterres, 16 August 2018.

Deschamps, Marie, Hassan B Jallow and Yasmin Sooka, 'Taking Action on Sexual Exploitation and Abuse by Peacekeepers: Report of an Independent Review on Sexual Exploitation and Abuse by International Peacekeeping Forces in the Central African Republic' (United Nations, 17 December 2015).

Executive Summary of the Independent Special Investigation into the Violence which Occured in Juba in 2016 and UNMISS Response.

External Review of the Functions, Structure and Capactiy of the UN Police Divison, 31 May 2016.

General Recommendations Adopted by the Committee on the Elimination of Discrimination Against Women, *General Recommendation No 19: Violecne Against Women*, Eleventh Session, 1992.

Holt, Victoria K., Glyn Taylor and Max Kelly, 'Protecting Civilians in the Context of UN Peacekeeping Operations: Success, Setbacks and Remaining Challenges' (2009) *Independent study jointly commissioned by the Department of Peacekeeping Operations and the Office for the Coordination of Humanitarian Affairs*.

Model Memorandum of Understanding between the United Nations and Participating State, Chapter 9 of UN Doc A/C.5/63/18.

Office of Internal Oversight Services, *Review of the logical frameworks underlying selected aspects of United Nations peacekeeping operations*, 28 August 2015, Assignment No IED-15-007.

Office of the High Commissioner for Human Rights, *A Report on Violations and Abuses of International Humanitarian Law in the Context of the Fighting in Juba, South Sudan, in July 2016*, January 2017.

Office of the High Commissioner for Human Rights, *CESCR General Comment No 3: The Nature of States Parties Obligations (Art 2, Para 1, of the Covenant)*, AAdopted at the Fifth Session of the Committee on Economic, Social and Cultural Rights, on 14 December 1990, UN Doc. E/1991/23.

Office of the High Commissioner for Human Rights, *CESCR General Comment No. 12: The Right to Adequate Food (Art. 11)*, Adopted at the Twentieth Session of the Committee on Economic, Social and Cultural Rights, on 12 May 1999, UN Doc. E/C.12/1999/5.

Office of the High Commissioner for Human Rights, *General Comment No 15: The Right to Water (Arts 11 and 12 of the Convenant)*, Adopted at the Twenty-ninth Session of the Committee on Economic, Social and Culture Rights, on 20 January 2003, (UN Doc. E/C.12/2002/11).

Office of the Special Representative of the Secretary-General for Children and Armed Conflict, *Working Paper No 1: The Six Grave Vioaltions Against Children During Armed Conflict: The Legal Foundation*, October 2009 (Updated November 2013).

Security Council Official Records, *1589th Meeting*, 6 October 1971, S/PV 1589.

Statemend of Karel JG van Oosterom, Permanent Representative of the Kingdom of the Netherlands to the United Nations, Security Council Open Debate: Implementation of the Note S/2017/507 – Working Methods, 6 February 2018.

Statement by Ambassador Jürgen Schulz, Permanent Mission of the Federal Republic of Germany to the United Nations, Security Council Open deabte on Reform of UN Peacekeeping: Implementation and Follow Up, 20 September 2017.

Statement by Martin Scheinin, Special Rapporteur on the Promotion and Protection of Human Rights and Fundamental Freedoms while Countering Terrorism, 65th Session of the General Assembly, Third Committee, 26 October 2010.

Statement of Ibrahim Balyan, on behalf of the Swedish Mission to the United Nations, Security Council Open Debate on Collective Action to Improve UN Peacekeeping Operations, 28 March 2018.

The United Nations General Assembly Resolution 217(III) (A Universal Declaration of Human Rights), A/RES/217(III).

United Nations High Commissione for Refugees, *The Scope of International Protection in Mass Influx*, EC/1995/SCP/CRP.3, 1995.

United Nations High Commissioner for Refugees (UNHCR), UNHCR Note on the Principle of Non-Refoulement, November 1997, available at: http://www.refworld.org/docid/438c6d972.html.

United Nations High Commissioner for Refugees, *UNHCR Guidelines on the Application in Mass Influx Situations of the Exclusion Clauses of Article 1F of the 1951 Convention relating to the Status of Refugees*, 2006.

United Nations Human Rights Committee, *General Comment No 36 (2018) on Article 6 of the International Covenant on Civil and Political Rights, on the Right to Life*, CCPR/C/GC/36.

United Nations Commissioner on Human Rights, *General Comment No 29: States of Emergency (Article 4)*, UN Doc CCPR/C/21/Rev.1/Add.11, 31 August 2001.

United Nations Department of Peace Opertions, *The Protection of Civilians in United Nations Peacekeeping Handbook*.

United Nations Department of Peacekeeping and Department of Field Support Policy (Revised) on *Formed Police United in United Nations Peacekeeping Operations* (1 March 2010).

United Nations Department of Peacekeeping Operations and Department of Field Support, *Draft DPKO/DFS Operational Concept on the Protection of Civilians in United Nations Peacekeeping Operations*, 2009.

United Nations Department of Peacekeeping Operations and Department of Field Support, *Guidelines: The Role of United Nations Police in Protection of Civilians*, Ref 2017.12.

United Nations Department of Peacekeeping Operations and Department of Field Support, *Interim Standard Operating Procedures: Detention in United Nations Peace Operations*, 25 January 2010.

United Nations Department of Peacekeeping Operations and Department of Field Support, *Policy: Authority, Command and Control in United Nations Peacekeeping Operations*, 15 February 2008.

United Nations Department of Peacekeeping Operations and Department of Field Support, *United Nations Peacekeeping Operations: Principles and Guidelines*, 2008 (Capstone Doctrine).

United Nations Department of Peacekeeping Operations and the Department of Field Support, *United Nations Police in Peacekeeping Operations and Special Political Missions*, February 2014.

United Nations Department of Peacekeeping Operations, *Handbook on United Nations Multidimensional Peacekeeping Operations*, December 2003.

United Nations Department of Peacekeeping Operations, *Second Generation Disarmament, Demobilization and Reintegration (DDR) Practices in Peace Operations: A Contribution to the New Horizon Discussion on Challenges and Opportunities for UN Peacekeeping*, 2010.

United Nations Department of Peacekeeping, *Child Protection in United Nations Peacekeeping: 2014 Review*.

United Nations Economic and Social Council, *General Comment 24 on State Obligations under the International Covenant on Economic, Social and Cultural Rights in the Context of Business Activities*, 10 August 2017, UN Doc E/C.12/GC/24.

United Nations Economic and Social Council, *Internally Displaced Persons: Report of the Representative of the Secretary-General, Mr. Francis M.Deng, submitted pursuant to Commission on Human Rights resolution 1995/57 – Compliation and analysis of legal norms*, E/CN.4/1996/52/Add.2.

United Nations General Assembly and Security Council, *Children and Armed Conflict: Report of the Secretary-General*, A/69/926-S/2015/409.

United Nations General Assembly and Security Council, *Children and Armed Conflict: Report of the Secretary-General*, UN Doc A/55/163-S/2000/712.

United Nations General Assembly and Security Council, *Children and Armed Conflict: Report of the Secretary-General*, UN Doc A/59/695-S/2005/72.

United Nations General Assembly and Security Council, *Children and Armed Conflict: Report of the Secretary-General*, UN Doc A/63/785-S/2009/158.

United Nations General Assembly and Security Council, *Human Rights Due Diligence Policy on United Nations Support to Non-United Nations Security Forces*, UN Doc A/67/775-S/2013/110.

United Nations General Assembly and Security Council, *Report of the High-level Independent Panel on Peace Operations on Uniting Our Strengths for Peace: Politics, Partnership and People*, UN Doc A/70/95-S/2015/446.

United Nations General Assembly and Security Council, *Sexual Violence in Conflict: Report of the Secretary-General*, UN Doc A/67/792-S/2013/149.

United Nations General Assembly and Security Council, *The Future of United Nations Peace Operations: Implementation of the Recommendations of the High-level Independent Panel on Peace Operations*, 17 June 2015, UN Doc A/70/357-S/2015/682 (HIPPO Report).

United Nations General Assembly and United Nations Security Council, *Responsibility to Protection: Timely and Decisive Response, Report of the Secretary-General*, UN Doc A/66/874-S/2012/578.

United Nations General Assembly Resolution 60/268 (2006).

United Nations General Assembly, *A More Secure World: Our Shared Responsibility, Report of the High-level Panel on Threats, Challenges and Change*, 2 December 2004, UN Doc A/59/565.

United Nations General Assembly, *Body of Principles for the Protection of All Persons under Any Form of Dentention of Imprisonment*, Resolution 43/173, 9 December 1988.

United Nations General Assembly, *Comprehensive Report on Strengthening th Capacity of the United Nations to Manage and Sustain Peace Operations*, UN Doc A/61/858, 13 April 2007.

United Nations General Assembly, *Disarmament, Demobilization and Reintegration: Report of the Secretary-General*, UN Doc. A/65/741.

United Nations General Assembly, *Evaluation of the Implementation and Results of Protection of Civilians Mandates in United Nations Peacekeeping Operations*, UN Doc A/68/787.

United Nations General Assembly, *Evaluation of the Implementation and results of Protection of Civilians Mandates in United Nations Peacekeeping Operations: Report of the Office of Internal Oversight Services*, UN Doc A/68/787.

United Nations General Assembly, *Model Status of Force Agreement* (SOFA), 9 October 1990, UN Doc. A/45/594.

United Nations General Assembly, *Organization of the seventy-second regular session of the General Assembly, adoption of the agenda and allocation of items: First report of the General Committee*, UN Doc A/72/250.

United Nations General Assembly, *Overview of the Financing of the United Nations Peacekeeping Operations: Budget Performance for the Period from 1 July 2004 to 30 June 2005 and Budget for the Period from 1 July 2006 to 30 June 2007, Report of the Secretary-General*, 24 February 2006, UN Doc A/60/696 (Peace Operations 2010).

United Nations General Assembly, *Report of the Secretary-General Pursuant to General Assembly Resolution 53/35: The Fall of Srebrenica*, 15 November 1999, UN Doc A/54/549.

United Nations General Assembly, *Report of the Secretary-General: Summary Study of the Experience of Derived from the Establishment and Operation of the Force*, UN Doc A/3943.

United Nations General Assembly, *Restrucuting of the United Nations Peace and Security Pillar: Report of the Secretary-General*, UN Doc A/72/525, 13 October 2017.

United Nations General Asssembly, *Promotion and Protection of the Rights of Children: Impact of Armed Conflict on Children*, UN Doc A/51/306.

United Nations Headquarters Board of Inquiry, *Board of Inquiry Report on Malakal – Executive Summary*, 5 August 2016.

United Nations High Commissioner for Refugees Emergency Handbook, "Camp Planning Standards".

United Nations Human Rights Committee, *General Comment No. 31* [80] Nature of the General Legal Obligation Imposed on States Parties to the Covenant, 26 May 2004, UN Doc: CCPR/C/21/Rev.1/Add.13.

United Nations Human Rights Concil, *Investigation by the Office of the United Nations High Commissioner for Human Rights on Libya: detailed findings*, A/HCR/31/CRP.3.

United Nations Inter-Agency Standing Committee, *Protection of Internally Displaced Persons*, Policy Paper, New York, December 1999.

United Nations Mission in South Sudan, *The State of Human Rights in the Protracted Conflict in South Sudan*, 4 December 2015.

United Nations Multidimensional Integrated Stabilization Missions in Central African Republic, *Inter-Office Memorandum: Directive on the Protection of Schools and Universities Against Military Use*, 24 December 2015, MINUSCA/OSRSG/046/2015.

United Nations Office for the Coordination of Humanitarian Affairs, *Building a Culture of Protection: 20 Years of Security Council Engagement on the Protection of Civilians*, OCHA Policy and Studies Series, May 2019.

United Nations Office for the Coordination of Humanitarian Affairs, *Guiding Principles on Internal Displacement*, 1998.

United Nations Secuirty Council Resolution 2000 (2011).

United Nations Secuirty Council Resolution 2149 (2014).

United Nations Secuirty Council, *7275th Meeting, Thursday, 9 October 2014, 10am*, UN Doc S/PV.7275.

United Nations Security Council Resolution 1001 (1995).

United Nations Security Council Resolution 1019 (1995).

United Nations Security Council Resolution 1041 (1996).

United Nations Security Council Resolution 1049 (1996).

United Nations Security Council Resolution 1173 (1998).

United Nations Security Council Resolution 1181 (1998).

United Nations Security Council Resolution 1244 (1999).

United Nations Security Council Resolution 1261 (1999).

United Nations Security Council Resolution 1265 (1999).

United Nations Security Council Resolution 1270 (1999).

United Nations Security Council Resolution 1289 (2000).

United Nations Security Council Resolution 1291 (2000).

United Nations Security Council Resolution 1314 (2000).

United Nations Security Council Resolution 1325 (2000).

United Nations Security Council Resolution 1379 (2001).

United Nations Security Council Resolution 1386 (2001).

United Nations Security Council Resolution 1410 (2002).

United Nations Security Council Resolution 143 (1960).

United Nations Security Council Resolution 1509 (2003).

United Nations Security Council Resolution 1528 (2004).

United Nations Security Council Resolution 1539 (2004).

United Nations Security Council Resolution 1540 (2004).

United Nations Security Council Resolution 1674 (2006).

United Nations Security Council Resolution 1778 (2007).

United Nations Security Council Resolution 1820 (2008).

United Nations Security Council Resolution 1856 (2008).

United Nations Security Council Resolution 1861 (2009).

United Nations Security Council Resolution 1888 (2009).

United Nations Security Council Resolution 1889 (2009).
United Nations Security Council Resolution 1894 (2009).
United Nations Security Council Resolution 1933 (2010).
United Nations Security Council Resolution 1973 (2011).
United Nations Security Council Resolution 1999 (2011).
United Nations Security Council Resolution 2003 (2011).
United Nations Security Council Resolution 2063 (2012).
United Nations Security Council Resolution 2098 (2013).
United Nations Security Council Resolution 2100 (2013).
United Nations Security Council Resolution 2113 (2014).
United Nations Security Council Resolution 2118 (2013).
United Nations Security Council Resolution 2122 (2013).
United Nations Security Council Resolution 2155 (2014).
United Nations Security Council Resolution 2156 (2014).
United Nations Security Council Resolution 2162 (2014).
United Nations Security Council Resolution 2164 (2014).
United Nations Security Council Resolution 2173 (2014).
United Nations Security Council Resolution 2175 (2014).
United Nations Security Council Resolution 2185 (2014).
United Nations Security Council Resolution 2187 (2016).
United Nations Security Council Resolution 2227 (2015).
United Nations Security Council Resolution 2277 (2016).
United Nations Security Council Resolution 2286 (2016).
United Nations Security Council Resolution 2295 (2016).
United Nations Security Council Resolution 2296 (2016).
United Nations Security Council Resolution 2301 (2016).
United Nations Security Council Resolution 2304 (2016).
United Nations Security Council Resolution 2313 (2016).
United Nations Security Council Resolution 2327 (2016).
United Nations Security Council Resolution 2363 (2017).
United Nations Security Council Resolution 2364 (2017).
United Nations Security Council Resolution 2370 (2017).
United Nations Security Council Resolution 2378 (2017).
United Nations Security Council Resolution 2382 (2017).
United Nations Security Council Resolution 2387 (2017).
United Nations Security Council Resolution 2399 (2018).
United Nations Security Council Resolution 2406 (2018).
United Nations Security Council Resolution 2409 (2018).
United Nations Security Council Resolution 2436 (2018).
United Nations Security Council Resolution 2447 (2018).

United Nations Security Council Resolution 2459 (2019).

United Nations Security Council Resolution 2474 (2019).

United Nations Security Council Resolution 2480 (2019).

United Nations Security Council Resolution 2499 (2019).

United Nations Security Council Resolution 2502 (2019).

United Nations Security Council Resolution 435 (1978).

United Nations Security Council Resolution 733 (1992).

United Nations Security Council, 8218th meeeting, Wednesday, 28 March 2018, UN Doc S/PV.8218.

United Nations Security Council, *Conflict-Related Sexual Violence: Report of the Secretary-General*, 29 March 2019, UN Doc. S/2019/280.

United Nations Security Council, *Overview of Security Council Meeting Records*, S/PV.3980 (1999).

United Nations Security Council, *Protection of Civilians in Armed Conflict,* Security Council Report: Cross-Cutting.

Report, 2010 No. 3, 29 October 2010.

United Nations Security Council, *Report of the Independant Inquiry into the Actions of the United Nations durinf the 1994 Genocide in Rwanda*, UN Doc S/1999/1257.

United Nations Security Council, *Report of the Secretary-General on Children and Armed Conflict in South Sudan*, S/2014/884.

United Nations Security Council, *Report of the Secretary-General on Children and Armed Conflict in the Central African Republic*, UN Doc S/2016/133.

United Nations Security Council, *Report of the Secretary-General on Children and Armed Conflict*, UN Doc S/2002/1299.

United Nations Security Council, *Report of the Secretary-General on Protection for Humanitarian Assistance to Refugees and Others in Conflict Situations,* UN Doc S/1998/883 (1998).

United Nations Security Council, *Report of the Secretary-General on South Sudan*, S/2015/655.

United Nations Security Council, *Report of the Secretary-General on the Protection of Civilians in Armed Conflict*, UN Doc S/2016/447.

United Nations Security Council, *Report of the Secretary-General on the Protection of Civilians in Armed Conflict*, UN Doc S/2017/414.

United Nations Security Council, *Report of the Secretary-General on the United Nations Organization Stabilization Mission in the Democratic Republic of the Congo*, S/2016/1130.

United Nations Security Council, *Report of the Secretary-General on the United Nations Organizations Stabilization Mission in the Democratic Republic of the Congo*, S/2017/206.

United Nations Security Council, *Report of the Secretary-General on United Nations Policing*, 10 November 2016, UN Doc S/2016/952.

United Nations Security Council, *Report of the Secretary-General on Women, Peace and Security*, UN Doc S/2002/1154.

United Nations Security Council, *Report of the Secretary-General Pursuant to Security Council Resolution 1820*, UN Doc S/2009/362.

United Nations Security Council, *Report of the Secretary-General to the Security Council on the Protection of Civilians in Armed Conflict*, (2001) UN Doc S/2001/331.

United Nations Security Council, *Report of the Secretary-General to the Security Council on the Protection of Civilians in Armed Conflict*, UN Doc S/1999/957.

United Nations Security Council, *Report of the Secretary-Genereal on the African Union-United Nations Hybrid Operations in Darfur*, S/2017/250.

United Nations Security Council, *Special Report of the Secretary-General on the Sudan*, UN Doc S/2011/314.

United Nations Security Council, *Women and Peace and Security: Report of the Security-General*, UN Doc S/2009/465.

United Nations, *Improving Security of United Nations Peacekeepers: We Need to Change the Way We Are Doing Business*, 19 December 2017.

United Nations, *Operation Guide to the Integrated Disarmament, Demoblilization and Reintegration Standards (IDDRS)*, 2014.

United Nations, *Operational Guide to the Integrated Disarmament, Demobilization and Reintegration Standards*, 2004.

United Nations, *Report of the Panel on United Nations Peace Operations of 21 August 2000*, UN Doc A/55/305 (Brahimi Report).

United Nations, *Report of the Preparatory Committee on the Establishment of an International Criminal Court, Addendum, Part One*, UN Doc. A/CONF.183/2/Add.1, 14 April 1998.

United Nations, *Secretary-General's Bulletin: Observance by United Nations Forces of International Humanitarian Law*, UN Doc ST/SGB/1999/13.

Newspaper Articles

Dispatches from the Field: Council Meetings in Juba and a Visit to Protection of Civilians Sites Security Council Reporter https://www.whatsinblue.org/2016/09/dispatches-from-the-field-council-meetings-in-juba-and-a-visit-to-protection-of-civilians-sites.php .

'MSF says UN failed civilians in Central African Republic attack', *Al Jazeera* 19 February 2019 2019 https://www.aljazeera.com/news/2019/02/msf-failed-civilians-central-african-republic-attack-190218075727242.html.

'Officers Had No Duty to Protect Students in Parkland Massacre, Judge Rules' (2018) https://www.nytimes.com/2018/12/18/us/parkland-shooting-lawsuit-ruling-police.html.

'South Sudan Rejects Unilateral Renewal of UNMISS Mandate', *Sudan Tribune* 6 September 2017 2017 http://www.sudantribune.com/spip.php?article63427.

'South Sudan Spells out Unresolved UN Protection Force Issues', *Reuters* 2016 https://www.reuters.com/article/us-southsudan-security-un-idUSKCN11B22H.

Literature

Abebe, A. M., 'Legal and Institutional Dimensions of Protecting and Assisting Internally Displaced Persons in Africa' (2009) 22(2) *Journal of Refugee Studies* 155.

Aitken, Harry, 'The Security Council and International Law Enforcement: A Kelsenian Perspective on Civilian Protection Peacekeeping Mandates' (2017) 22(3) *Journal of Conflict and Security Law* 395.

Allard, Kenneth, *Somalia Operations: Lessons Learned*, CCRP Publication Series (1995/2005).

Amnesty International, *Child Soldiers: Criminals or Victims?* (Amnesty International, London, 2000).

Athie, Aïssata and Sarah Taylor, *UN Peacekeeping: Where is the Gender Expertise?* <https://theglobalobservatory.org/2017/10/un-peacekeeping-where-is-the-gender-expertise/>.

Aust, H. P., 'The UN Human Rights Due Diligence Policy: An Effective Mechanism against Complicity of Peacekeeping Forces?' (2014) 20(1) *Journal of Conflict and Security Law* 1.

Begoore, Yateesh, 'Prisoner Dilemma: Ascertaining and Augmenting the Multinational NIAC Detention Regime' in *Max Planck Yearbook of United National Law Online* (United Nations, 2017) vol 20, 436.

Bellamy, Alex J. *Responsiblity to Protect: A Defense* (Oxford University Press, 2014).

Bellamy, Alex J. and Charles T. Hunt, 'Benefits of Paring down Peacekeeping Mandates Also Comes with Risks' (2019) *Global Observatory* <https://theglobalobservatory.org/2019/03/benefits-paring-down-peacekeeping-mandates-come-with-risks/>.

Bellamy, Alex J. and Paul Williams, *Understanding Peacekeeping* (Polity Press, 2nd ed, 2010).

Bellamy, Alex J. and Paul D. Williams, 'The New Politics of Protection? Côte d'Ivoire, Libya and the Responsibiity to Protect' (2011) 87(4) *International Affairs* 825.

Berdal, Mats and David H. Ucko, 'The Use of Force in UN Peacekeeping Operations' (2015) 160(1) *The RUSI Journal* 6.

Bianchi, Andrea, 'Immunity Verses Human Rights: The Pinochet Case' (1999) *10(2) European Journal of International Law* 237.

Bittner, Egon, *Aspects of Police Work* (Northeastern University Press, 1990).

Bosch, Shannon, 'Targeting and Prosecuting 'under-aged' Aged' Child Soldiers in International armed Conflicts, in Light of the International Humanitarian Law Prohibition against Civilian Direct Participation in Hostilities' (2012) *45(3) The Comparative and International Law Journal of Southern Africa* 324.

Boutellis, Arthur and Naureen Chowdhury Fink, *Waging Peace: UN Peace Operations Confronting Terrorism and Violent Extremism* (International Peace Institute, October 2016).

Bowden, Mark, 'The Protection of Civilians' in Bertrand G. Ramcharan (ed), *Human Rights Protection in the Field*, International Studies in Human Rights (Martinus Nujhoff Publishers, 2006).

Breakey, Hugh, 'Parsing Security Council Resolutions' in Vesselin Popovski and Trudy Fraser (eds), *The Security Council as Global Legislator* (Routledge, 2014).

Breakey, Hugh, 'The Protection of Civilians in Armed Conflict: Four Concepts' in Angus Francis, Vesselin Popovski and C. J. G. Sampford (eds), *Norms of Protection: Responsibility to Protect, Protection of Civilians and Their Interaction* (United Nations University Press, 2012).

Breakey, Hugh, 'The Responsibility to Protect and the Protection of Civilians in Armed Conflict: Overlap and Contrast' in Angus Francis, Vesselin Popovski and C. J. G. Sampford (eds), *Norms of Protection: Responsibility to Protect, Protection of Civilians and Their Interaction* (United Nations University Press, 2012).

Breen, Claire, 'When is a Child Not a Child? Child Soldiers in International Law' (2007) *8(2) Human Rights Review* 71.

Brodeur, Jean-Paul, *The Policing Web* (Oxford University Press, 2010).

Bruno, Charbonneau, 'Intervention in Mali: Building Peace between Peacekeeping and Counterterrorism' (2017) *35(4) Journal of Contemporary African Studies* 415.

Burke, Róisín, 'Status of Forces Deployed on UN Peacekeeping Operations: Jurisdictional Immunity' (2011) *16(1) Journal of Conflict and Secuirty Law* 63.

Busser, Mark, *Ethics, Obligation, and the Responsibility to Protect: Contesting the Global Power Relations of Accountability*, Global politics and the responsibility to protect (Routledge, 2019).

Center for Civilians in Conflict, *From Mandate to Mission: Mitigating Civilian Harm in UN Peacekeeping Operations in the DRC*, (Center for Civilians in Conflict, 2016).

Center for Civilians in Conflict, *Moving Towards Mobility: Providing Protection to Civilians Through Static Presence and Mobile Peacekeeping in South Sudan* (Center for Civilians in Conflict, 2019).

Center for Civilians in Conflict, *Protection with Less Presence: How the Peacekeeping Operation in the Democractic Republic of Congo is Attempting to Deliver Protection with Fewer Resources*, (Center for Civilians in Conflict, 2018).

Center for Civilians in Conflict, *The Primacy of Protection: Delivering on the MINUSCA Mandate in the Central African Republic*, (Center for Civilians in Conflict, 2017).

Center for Civilians in Conflict, *Under Fire: The July 2016 Violene in Juba and UN Response* (Centre for Civilians in Conflict, 2016).

Center for Civilians in Conflict, *Within and Beyond the Gates: The Protection of Civlians by the UN Mission in South Sudan*, (Center for Civilians in Conflict, 2015).

Clapham, Andrew, 'Detention by Armed Groups under International Law' (2017) *93 International Law Studies* 1.

Clapham, Andrew, 'Protection of Civilians under International Human Rights Law' in Haidi Willmot et al (eds), *Protection of Civilians* (Oxford University Press, 2016).

Crawford, Emily, *Identifying the Enemy: Civilian Participation in Armed Conflict* (Oxford University Press, 2015).

Crawford, James, *The Creation of States in International Law* (Oxford University Press, 2007).

Crossette, Barbara, 'UN Details Its Failure to Stop '95 Bosnia Massacre', *New York Times* 16 November 1999 1999 <https://www.nytimes.com/1999/11/16/world/un-details-its-failure-to-stop-95-bosnia-massacre.html>.

Daniel, C.F Donald, Taft, Patricia and Wiharta, Sharon, *Peace Operations, Trends, Progress, and Prospects* (Georgetown University Press, 2008).

David, Eric and Ola Engdahl, 'How does the Involvement of a Multinational Peacekeeping Force Affect the Classification of a Situation?' (2013) *95(891–892) International Review of the Red Cross* 659.

Davies, Sara E. and Simon Rushton, *Healing or Harming? United Nations Peacekeeping and Health* (International Peace Institute, March 2015).

de Coning, Cedric and Peter, Mateja (eds), *United Nations Peace Operations in a Changing Global Order* (Palgrave Macmillian, 2018).

de Wet, Erika, *The Chapter VII Powers of the United Nations Security Council* (Hart Publishing, 2004).

Denzin, N. and Lincoln, Y. (eds), *Strategies of Qualitative Inquiry* (SAGE Publications, 1998).

Dinstein, Yoram, *The Conduct of Hostilities under the Law of International Armed Conflict (3rd ed)* (Cambridge University Press, 2016).

Direk, Ömar Faruk, *Security Detention in International Territorial Administrations: Kosovo, East Timor and Iraq* (Brill Nijhoff, 2015).

Drahos, Peter (ed), *Regulatory Theory: Foundations and Applications* (ANU Press, 2017).

Droege, Cordula, 'Transfers of Detainees: Legal Framework, Non-refoulement and Contemporary Challenges' (2008) *90(871) International Review of the Red Cross* 669.

Droubi, Sufyan, *Resisting United Nations Security Council Resolutions* (Routledge, 2014).

Durch, William J. and Michelle Ker, 'Police in UN Peacekeeping: Improving Selection, Recruitment, and Deployment' *Providing For Peacekeeping No. 6 (International Peace Institute, November 2013)*.

Engdahl, Ola, 'The Status of Peace Operation Personnel under International Humanitarian Law' (2010) *11 Yearbook of International Humanitarian Law* 109.

Evans, Carolyn M., 'Finding Obligation: Foundation for a More Accountable Security Council' (2016) *14 New Zealand Journal of Public International Law* 129.

Fact Sheet No. 26, The Working Group on Arbitrary Detention.

Farrior, Stephanie and Brice Clagett, 'State Responsibility for Human Rights Abuses by Non-state Actors' (Paper presented at the Proceeding of the Annual Meeting (American Society of International Law), 1998).

Ferraro, Tristan, 'The Applicability and Application of International Humanitarian Law to Multinational Forces' (2014) *95(891–892) International Review of the Red Cross* 561.

Fleck, Dieter 'The Legal Status of Personnel Involved in United Nations Peace Operations' (2013) *95(891–892) International Review of the Red Cross* 613.

Foley, Conor, *UN Peacekeeping Operations and the Protection of Civilians* (Cambridge University Press, 2017).

Foley, Conor, 'What are the Human Rights Obligations of Unmiss to those Sheltering on Its Protection Sites?' (2016) *2 Conflict Trends* 20.

Fortin, Antonio, 'The Meaning of 'Protection' in the Refugee Definition' (2000) *12 International Journal of Refugee Law* 548.

Francis, Angus, Popovski, Vesselin and Sampford, C. J. G. (eds), *Norms of Protection: Responsibility to Protect, Protection of Civilians and Their Interaction* (United Nations University Press, 2012).

Fry, James D., 'The UN Security Council and the Law of Armed Conflict: Amity or Enmity?' (2006) *38(2) The George Washington International Law Review* 327.

Gade, Emily Kalah, 'The Child Soldier: The Question of Self-Defense' (2011) *10(4) Journal of Military Ethics* 323.

Gaston, Erica, 'The View from the Ground – Emerging State Practice on Individual and Unit Self-Defense' (2019) *Soldier Self-Defense Symposium* <http://opiniojuris.org/2019/05/02/soldier-self-defense-symposium-the-view-from-the-ground-emerging-state-practice-on-individual-and-unit-self-defense/>.

Gill, Terry D., 'Legal Aspects of the Transfer of Authority in UN Peace Operations' (2011) *42 Netherlands Yearbook of International Law* 37.

Gill, Terry, Fleck, Dieter, Boothby, William H. and Vanheusden, Alfons, *Leuven Manual on the International Law Applicable to Peace Operations* (Cambridge University Press, 2017).

Global Coalition to Protect Education from Attack, *Commentary on the "Guidelines for Protecting Schools and Universities from Military Use during Armed Conflict"*.

Goldberg, Elissa and Don Hubert, 'Case Study: The Security Council and the Protection of Civilians' in Rob McRae and Don Hubert (eds), *Human Security and the New Diplomacy: Protecting People, Promoting Peace* (McGrill-Queen's University Press, 2001) 223.

Goodman, Ryan, 'The Detention of Civilians in Armed Conflict' (2009) *103(1) The American Journal of International Law* 48.

Goodwin-Gill, Guy and Ilene Cohn, *Child Soldiers: The Role of Children in Armed Conflict* (Clarendon Press, 1994).

Greenbaum, Charles W., Veerman, Philip and Bacon-Shnoor, Naomi (eds), *Protection of Children during Armed Political Conflict: A Multidisciplinary Perspective* (Intersentia, 2006).

Grenfell, Katarina, 'Detention in United Nations Peace Operations' in Greogry Rose and Bruce Oswald (eds), *Detention of Non-state Actors Engaged in Hostilities* (Brill, 2016) 345.

Grenfell, Katrina, 'Perspectives on the Applicability and Application of International Humanitarian Law: the UN Context' (2013) *95(891–892) International Review of the Red Cross* 645.

Grover, Sonja, "Child Soldiers' as 'Non-combatants': The Inapplicability of the Refugee Convention Exclusion Clause' (2008) *12(1) The International Journal of Human Rights* 53.

Hamilton, Carolyn, 'Child Protection in Complex Emergencies' in Charles W. Greenbaum, Philip Veerman and Naomi Bacon-Shnoor (eds), *Protection of Children during Armed Political Conflict: A Multidisciplinary Perspective* (Intersentia, 2006).

Handeyside, Hugh, 'The Lotus Principle in ICJ Jurisprudence: Was the Ship Ever Afloat? (International Court of Justice)' (2007) *9(1) Michigan Journal of International Law* 71.

Harston, Julian, *Protection of Civilians* (Peace Operations Training Institute, Williamsburg, 2016).

Hassler, Sabine, 'R2P and the Protection Obligations of Peacekeepers' (2010) *1(1) Journal of International Humanitarian Legal Studies* 205.

Hehir, Aidan, *Hollow Norms and the Responsibility to Protect* (Springer International Publishing, 2019).

Hessbruegge, Jan Arno, *Human Rights and Personal Self-Defense in International Law* (Oxford University Press, 2017).

Hill-Cawthorne, Lawrence, *Detention in Non-International Armed Conflict* (Oxford University Press, 2016).

Hilpold, Peter, *Responsibility to Protect: A New Paradigm of International Law?* (Brill Nijhoff, 2014).

Holt, Victoria K. and Tobias C. Berkman, *The Impossible Mandate? Military Preparedness, the Responsibility to Protect and Modern Peace Operations* (2006).

Howard, Lise Morjé, *UN Peacekeeping in Civil Wars* (Cambridge University Press, 2008).

Howland, Todd, 'Peacekeeping and Conformity with Human Rights Law: How MINUSTAH Falls Short in Haiti' (2006) *13(4) International Peacekeeping* 462.

Hultman, Lisa, 'UN Peace Operations and Protection of Civilians: Cheap Talk or Norm Implementation?' (2012) *50(1) Journal of Peace Research* 59.

Human Rights Watch, *"They Burned It All": Destruction of Villages, Killings, and Sexual Violence in Unity State, South Sudan*, 2015.

Hunt, Charles T., *Protection through Policing: The Protective Role of UN Police in Peace Operations* (International Peace Institute, February 2020).

Hunt, Charles T., 'To Serve and Protect: The Role of UN Police in Protecting Civilians' (2019) *Global Observatory* <https://theglobalobservatory.org/2019/09/to-serve-and-protect-the-role-of-un-police-protecting-civilians/>.

Hunt, Charles T. and Lisa Sharland, 'Implementing R2P Through United Nations Peacekeeping Operations: Opportunities and Challenges' in Cecilia Jacob and Martin Mennecke (eds), *Implementing the Responsibility to Protect: A Future Agenda* (Routledge, 2019).

Ibreck, Rachel and Naomi Pendle, 'Community Security and Justice under United Nations Governance: Lessons from Chiefs' Court in South Sudan's Protection of Civilians Sites' (2017) *6(1) Stability: International Journal of Security and Development* 16.

Ibreck, Rachel and Naomi Pendle, *Customary Protection? Chiefs' Courts as Public Authority in UN Protection of Civilian Sites in South Sudan* (The Justice and Security Research Programme, September 2016).

International Committee of the Red Cross, *Commentaries on the Geneva Conventions* (2016).

International Committee of the Red Cross, *Commentary on the First Geneva Convention: Convention (I) for the Amelioration of the Condition of the Wounded and Sick in Armed Forces in the Field* (*Commentaries on the 1949 Geneva Conventions*) (Cambridge University Press, 2016).

International Committee of the Red Cross, 'ICRC Protection Policy' (2009) *90(871) International Review of the Red Cross* 751.

International Committee of the Red Cross, *Internal Displacement in Armed Conflict: Facing up to the Challenges* (November 2009).

International Committee of the Red Cross, *Internment in Armed Conflict: Basic Rules and Chanllenges*, Opinion Paper, November 2014.

International Committee of the Red Cross, *Professional Standards for Protection Work: Carried out by Humanitarian and Human Rights Actors in Armed Conflict and Other Siutations of Violence* (ICRC, Geneva, 2013).

International Committee of the Red Cross, *Strengthening Protection in War: A Search for Professional Standards* Sylvie Giossi Caverzasio (ed), (Genenva, Switzerland, 1996–2000).

International Committee of the Red Cross, *Study on Customary Interantional Humanitarian Law (Customary IHL Database)*.

International Labour Organization, *Worst Forms of Child Labour Recommendation 190*, 1999 (No.190).

International Organization for Migration, *We Leave We Are Killed: Lessons Learned from South Sudan Protection of Civilians Sites 2013–2016*, 2016.

Ipsen, Knut, 'Combatants and Non-combatants' in Michael Bothe (ed), *The Handbook of International Humanitarian Law, 3rd Edition* (Oxford University Press, 2013).

Jacob, Cecilia and Mennecke, Martin (eds), *Implementing the Responsibility to Protect: A Future Agenda* (Routledge, 2019).

Jacques, Mélanie, *Armed Conflict and Displacement: The Protection of Refugees and Displaced Person under International Humanitarian Law* (Cambridge University Press, 2012).

Jain, N., 'A Separate Law for Peacekeepers: The Clash between the Security Council and the International Criminal Court' (2005) *16(2) European Journal of International Law* 239.

Jones, Trevor and Trevor Newburn, *Private Security and Public Policing* (Clarendon Press-Oxford University Press, 1998).

Kabano, Jacques, 'The Criminal Responsibility of Child Soldier under International Criminal Law, Case Study: Northern Uganda and Democratic Republic of Congo (DRC)' (2016) *2(2) E-Journal of Law* 15.

Kargbo, Franklyn Bai, 'International Peacekeeping and Child Soldiers: Problems of Security and Rebuilding' (2004) *3(3) Cornell International Law Journal* 485.

Karlsrud, John, 'The UN at War: Examining the Consequences of Peace-enforcement Mandates for the UN Peacekeeping Operations in the CAR, the DRC and Mali' (2015) *36(1) Third World Quarterly* 40.

Karlsrud, John, 'Towards UN Counter-Terrorism Operations?' (2017) *38(6) Third World Quarterly* 1215.

Kayode, Sijuade Sunday, "Intervention Brigade' for the Congo; A Precedent for UN Peace Enforcement?' (2014) *10(38) Uluslararasi Hukuk ve Politika* 99.

Kessing, Peter Vedel, 'Security Detention in UN Peace Operations' in Kjetil Mujezinović Larsen, Camila Guldahl Cooper and Gro Nystuen (eds), *Searching for a 'Principle of Humanity' in International Humanitarian Law* (Cambridge University Press, 2013) 272.

Khali, Mona Ali, 'Legal Aspects of the Use of Force by Unitd Nations Peacekeepers for the Protection of Civilians' in Haidi Willmot et al (eds), *Protection of Civilians* (Oxford University Press, 2016).

Kolb, Andreas S., *The UN Security Council Members' Responsibility to Protect A Legal Analysis*, Beiträge zum ausländischen öffentlichen Recht und Völkerrecht,

Veröffentlichungen des Max-Planck-Instituts für ausländisches öffentliches Recht und Völkerrecht, 274 (Springer Berlin Heidelberg, 2018).

Krippendorff, Klaus, 'Content Analysis' in Neil J. Salkind (ed), *Encyclopedia of Reserach Design* (SAGE Publications, 2010).

Kuleza, Joanna, *Due Diligence in International Law*, Queen Mary Studies in International Law (Brill Nijhoff, 2016).

Kurth, Michael E., 'The *Lubanga* Case of the International Criminal Court: A Critical Analysis of the Trial Chamger's Findings on Issues of Active Use, Age, and Gravity' (2013) *5 Goettingen Journal of International Law* 431.

Labuda, Patryk I., *With or against the State? Reconciling the Protection of Civilians and Host-State Support in UN Peacekeeping* (International Peace Institute, May 2020).

Lamont, Carina and Emma Skeppström, *The United Nations at War in the DRC?: Legal aspects of the Intervention Brigade* (Defence Analysis, Totalförsvarets forskningsinstitut (FOI), 2013).

Lamp, Nicholas and Dana Trif, 'United Nations Peacekeeping Forces and the Protection of Civilians in Armed Conflict' (2009) *47 Hertie School of Governance – Working papers*.

Larsen, Kjetil Mujezinović, Cooper, Camila Guldahl and Nystuen, Gro (eds), *Searching for a 'Principle of Humanity' in International Humanitarian Law* (Cambridge University Press, 2013).

Lauterpacht, Hersch, *Recognition in International Law* (Cambridge University Press, 1947).

Leck, Christopher, 'International Responsibility in United Nations Peacekeeping Operations: Command and Control Arrangements and the Attribution of Conduct' (2009) *10 Melbourne Journal of International Law* 346.

Levine, Daniel H., *Peacekeeper Impartiality: Standards, Processes, and Operations* (Center for International and Security Studies in Maryland, April 2010) < https://drum.lib.umd.edu/items/49740ad1-d296-40db-a463-412ea6b38926 >.

Lovell, David W. and Primoratz, Igor (eds), *Protecting Civilians During Violent Conflict: Theoretical and Practical Issues for the 21st Century* (Ashgate Publishing Limited, 2012).

Lubell, Noam, 'Challenges in Applying Human Rights Law to Armed Conflict' (2010) *87(860) International Review of the Red Cross* 737.

Malan, Mark, 'Disarming and Demobilising Child Soldiers: The Underlying Challenges' (2000) *9(5/6) African Security Review*.

Malan, Mark and Charles T. Hunt, *Between a Rock and a Hard Placel: The UN and the Protection of Civilians in South Sudan* (Institute for Security Studies, 2014).

Mamiya, Ralph, 'A History and Conceptual Development of the Protection of Civilians' in Haidi Willmot et al (eds), *Protection of Civilians* (Oxford University Press, 2016).

Månsson, Katarina, 'Integration of Human Rights in Peace Operations: Is there an Ideal Model?' (2006) 13(4) *International Peacekeeping* 547.

Månsson, Katarina, 'Use of Force and Civlian Protection: Peace Operations in the Congo' (2005) 12(4) *International Peacekeeping* 503.

Maus, Sylvia, 'Jus Post Bellum a la United Nations? Human Rights, UN Peace Operations, and the Creation of International Law' (2014) 32(4) *Wisconsin International Law Journal* 675.

McRae, Rob and Hubert, Don (eds), *Human Security and the New Diplomacy: Protecting People, Promoting Peace* (McGrill-Queen's University Press, 2001) 223.

Mégret, Frédéric, 'Between R2P and the ICC: "Robust Peacekeeping" and the Quest for Civilian Protection' (2015) *26 Criminal Law Forum* 101.

Mégret, Frédéric and Florian Hoffman, 'The UN as a Human Rights Violator? Some Reflections on the United Nations Changing Human Rights Responsibilities' (2003) *25 Human Rights Quarterly* 314.

Meloni, Chantal, 'Command Responsibility: Mode of Liability for the Crimes of Subordinates or Separate Offence of the Superior?' (2007) *5 Journal of International Criminal Justice* 619.

Melzer, Nils, *Interpretive Guidance on the Notion of Direct Participation in Hostilities Under International Humanitarian Law*, International Committee of the Red Cross, Reference Paper, 2009.

Mettraux, Guénaël, *The Law of Command Responsibility* (Oxford University Press, 2016).

Milanovic, Marko, *Extraterritorial Application of Human Rights Treaties : Law, Principles and Policy* (Oxford University Press, 2011).

Miller, Anthony J., 'Legal Aspects of Stopping Sexual Exploitation and Abuse in UN Peacekeeping Operations' (2006) *39 Cornell International Law Journal* 71.

Ministry of Foreign Affairs of Denmark, Legal Department, 'The Copenhagen Processions – The Handling of Detainees in International Military Operations' (2007) *46 Mil L and L War Rev* 363.

Morjane, Kamel, 'The Protection of Refugees and Displaced Persons' in Bertrand G. Ramcharan (ed), *Human Rights Protection in the Field*, International Studies in Human Rights (Martinus Nijhoff Publishers, 2006) 79.

Morris, Tamer 'State Responsibility and Accountability in UN Peacekeeping: The Case of the Mothers of Srebrenica v. The Netherlands' (2022) 29(2) *International Peacekeeping* 204.

Müller, Lars, 'The Force Intervention Brigade – United Nations Forces beyond the Fine Line between Peacekeeping and Peace Enforcement' (2015) 20(3) *Journal of Conflict and Secuirty Law* 359.

Murphy, Ray, 'The United Nations Mission in South Sudan and the Protection of Civilians' (2017) 22(3) *Journal of Conflict and Security Law* 367.

Murphy, Ray, 'United Nations Military Operations and International Humanitarian Law: What Rules Apply to Peacekeepers?' (2003) *14(2) Criminal Law Forum* 153.

Murray, Daragh (ed), *Practitioners' Guide to Human Rights Law in Armed Conflict* (Oxford University Press, 2017).

Nadin, Peter, *The Use of Force in UN Peacekeeping* (Routledge, 2018).

Naert, Frederik, 'The Legal Framework and Main Categories of Detainees' (2006) *45 Military Law and Law War Review* 51.

Nasu, Hitoshi, *International Law on Peacekeeping: A Study of Article 40 of the UN Charter* (Martinus Nijhoff Publishers, 2009).

Nasu, Hitoshi, 'Operationalizing the Responsibility to Protect in the Context of Civilian Protection by UN Peacekeepers' (2011) *18(4) International Peacekeeping* 364.

Nasu, Hitoshi, 'Peacekeeping, Civilian Protection Mandates and the Responsibility to Protect' in Angus Francis, Vesselin Popovski and C. J. G. Sampford (eds), *Norms of Protection: Responsibility to Protect, Protection of Civilians and their Interaction* (United Nations University Press, 2012).

Nasu, Hitoshi, 'The Protection of Civilians from Violence and the Effects of Attacks in International Humanitarian Law' in David W. Lovell and Igor Primoratz (eds), *Protecting Civilians During Violent Conflict: Theoretical and Practical Issues for the 21st Century* (Ashgate Publishing Limited, 2012) 65.

Nicholson, Joanna, 'Is Targeting Naked Child Soldiers a War Crime?' (2016) *16(1) International Criminal Law Review* 134.

Nolkaemper, André, 'Failures to Protect' in International Law' in Marc Weller (ed), *The Oxford Handbook of the Use of Force in International Law*, Oxford Handbooks in Law (Oxford University Press, 2015).

O'Brien, M., 'The Ascension of Blue Beret Accountability: International Criminal Court Command and Superior Responsibility in Peace Operations' (2010) *15(3) Journal of Conflict and Security Law* 533.

Öberg, Marko Divac, 'The Legal Effects of Resolutions of the UN Security Council and General Assembly in the Jurisprudence of the ICJ' (2005) *16(5) European Journal of International Law* 879.

Odello, M., 'Tackling Criminal Acts in Peacekeeping Operations: The Accountability of Peacekeepers' (2010) *15(2) Journal of Conflict and Security Law* 347.

Okimoto, Keiichiro, 'Violations of International Humanitarian Law by United Nations Forces and their Legal Consequences' (2003) *6 Yearbook of International Humanitarian Law* 199.

Oraá, Jaime, *Human Rights in States of Emergency in International Law*, Oxford Monographs in International Law (Clarendon Press, 1992).

Osiatyński, Wiktor, 'The Historical Development of Human Rights' in Scott Sheeran and Nigel Rodley (eds), *Routledge Handbook of International Human Rights Law* (Taylor and Francis, 2014).

Osland, Kari M., 'UN Policing: The Security-Trust Challenge' in Cedric de Coning and Mateja Peter (eds), *United Nations Peace Operations in a Changing Global Order* (Palgrave Macmillian, 2018).

Oswald, Bruce, 'Detention by United Nations Peacekeepers: Searching for Definition and Categorisation' (2011) *15(1–2) Journal of International Peacekeeping* 118.

Oswald, Bruce, 'Detention in Military Operations: Some Military, Political and Legal Aspects' (2007) *46 Military Law and Law War Review* 341.

Oswald, Bruce, 'Some Controversies of Detention in Multinational Operations and the Contributions of the Copenhagen Principles' (2014) *95(891–892) International Review of the Red Cross* 707.

Oswald, Bruce Ossie, 'The Law on Military Occupation: Answering the Challenges of Detention during Contemporary Peace Operations?' (2007) *8(2) Melbourne Journal of International Law* 311.

Oxfam, *The Role of UN Peacekeeping Missions in the Protection of Civilians*, Oxfam Policy Compendium Note (July 2012).

Pacholska, M., '(Il)legality of Killing Peacekeepers: The Crime of Attacking Peacekeepers in the Jurisprudence of International Criminal Tribunals' (2015) *13(1) Journal of International Criminal Justice* 43.

Palchetti, Paolo, 'The Allocation of Responsibility for Internationally Wrongful Acts Committed in the Course of Multinational Operations' (2013) *95(891–892) International Review of the Red Cross* 727.

Pejic, Jelena, 'Procedural Principles and Safeguards for Internment/Administrative Detention in Armed Conflict and other Situations of Violence' (2010) *87(858) International Review of the Red Cross*.

Penny, Christopher K., "Drop that or I'll Shoot ... Maybe': International Law and the Use of Deadly Force to Defend Property in UN Peace Operations' (2007) *14(3) International Peacekeeping* 353.

Perova, Natalia, 'Disentangling 'Effective Control' Test for the Purpose of Attribution of the Conduct of UN Peacekeepers to the States and the United Nations' (2017) *86(1) Nordic Journal of International Law* 30.

Phuong, Catherine, *The International Protection of Internally Displaced Persons* (Cambridge University Press, 2004).

Plattner, Denise, 'Protection of Children in International Humanitarian Law' (1984) *24 International Review of the Red Cross* 140.

Ramcharan, Bertrand G. (ed), *Human Rights Protection in the Field*, International Studies in Human Rights (Martinus Nijhoff Publishers, 2006).

Report of the High-Level International Conference on the Protection of Civilians, *The Kigali Principles on the Protection of Civilians* (Kigali, Rwanda, 28–29 May 2015).

Rodenhäuser, Tilman, 'Strengthening IHL protecting Persons Deprived of their Liberty: Main Aspects of the Consultations and Discussions Since 2011' (2016) *98(903) International Review of the Red Cross* 941.

Ronzitti, Natalino, 'The Expanding Law of Self-Defence' (2006) *11(3) Journal of Conventional Weapons Destruction* 343.

Rose, Greogry and Oswald, Bruce (eds), *Detention of Non-state Actors Engaged in Hostilities* (Brill, 2016).

Rosen, David, *Armies of the Young: Child Soldiers in War and Terrorism* (Rutgers University Press, 2005).

Rowe, Peter, *The Imact of Human Rights Law on Armed Forces* (Cambridge University Press, 2006).

Saul, Ben, *Defining Terrorism in International Law* (Oxford University Press, 2006).

Schütte, Robert, *Civilian Protection in Armed Conflicts: Evolution, Challenges and Implementation* (Springer VS, 2013).

Sebastián, Sofia, 'The Role of Police in UN Peace Operations' *Civilians in Conflict Policy Brief volume 3* (September 2015).

Sebastián, Sofia and Aditi Gorur, *UN Peacekeeping and Host-State Consent: How Missions Navigate Relationships with Governments* (Stimson Center, 2017).

Security Council Reporter, *Security Council Action Under Chapter VII: Myths and Realities*, Speacil Research Report, 23 June 2008.

Sheeran, Scott, 'The Use of Force in United Nations Peacekeeping Operations' in Marc Weller (ed), *The Oxford Handbook of the Use of Force in International Law* (Oxford University Press, 2015).

Sheeran, Scott and Catherine Bevilacqua, 'The UN Security Council and International Human Rights Obligations: Towards a Theory of Contrainst and Derogation' in Scott Sheeran and Nigel Rodley (eds), *Routledge Handbook of International Human Rights Law* (Taylor and Francis, 2014) 371.

Sheeran, Scott and Catherine Kent, 'Protection of Civilians, Responsibility to Protect, and Humanitarian Intervention' in Haidi Willmot et al (eds), *Protection of Civilians* (Oxford University Press, 2016) 29.

Sheeran, Scott and Stephanie Case, *The Intervention Brigade: Legal Issues for the UN in the Democractic Republic of the Congo* (International Peace Institute, 2014).

Sheeran, Scott and Rodley, Nigel (eds), *Routledge Handbook of International Human Rights Law* (Taylor and Francis, 2014).

Shelton, Dinah (ed), *The Oxford Handbook of International Human Rights Law* (Oxford University Press, 2013).

Shotton, Anna, 'A Strategy to Address Sexual Exploitation and Abuse by United Nations Peacekeeping Personnel' (2006) *39 Cornell International Law Journal* 97.

Shraga, Daphna, 'The Secretary-General's Bulletin on the Observance by United Nations Forces of International Humanitarian Law–A Decade Later' (2009) *39 Israel Yearbook on Human Rights* 357.

Shraga, Daphna, 'UN Peacekeeping Operations: Applicability of International Humanitarian Law and Responsibility Operatsions-Related Daamage' (2000) *94*(2) *American Journal of International Law* 406.

Shue, Henry, *Basic Rights* (Princeton University Press, 1980).

Simm, Gabrielle, 'Regulating Sex in Peace Operations' in Peter Drahos (ed), *Regulatory Theory: Foundations and Applications* (ANU Press, 2017).

Sinha, G. Alex, 'Child Soldiers as Super-privileged Combatants' (2013) *17*(*4*) *The International Journal of Human Rights* 584.

Sivakumaran, Sandesh, *The Law of Non-international Armed Conflict* (Oxford University Press, 2012).

Sloan, James, 'Peacekeepers under Fire: Prosecuting the RUF for Attacks against the UN Assistance Mission in Sierra Leone' (2010) 9(2) *The Law and Practice of International Courts and Tribunals* 243.

Sprik, Lenneke, 'Command Responsibility in Peacekeeping Missions: Normative Obligations of Protection in a Criminal Law Environment' (2017) 22(3) *Journal of Conflict and Security Law* 497.

Stamnes, Eli, *The United Nations Mission in the Republic of South Sudan (UNMISS): Protecting Civilians in a Volatile Environment* (Norwegian Institute of International Affairs, 2015).

Stephens, Dale, 'The Lawful use of Force by Peacekeeping Forces: the Tactical Imperative' (2005) *12*(2) *International Peacekeeping* 157.

Stern, Jenna, *Establishing Safety and Security at Protection of Civilians Sites* (Stimson Center, September 2015).

Strauss, Anselm and Juliet Cobin, 'Grounded Theory Methodology' in N Denzin and Y Lincoln (eds), *Strategies of Qualitative Inquiry* (SAGE Publications, 1998).

Talmon, Stefan, *Recognition of Governments in International Law* (Oxford University Press, 2001).

Tardy, Thierry, 'A Critique of Robust Peacekeeping in Contemporary Peace Operations' (2011) *18*(2) *International Peacekeeping* 152.

Tardy, Thierry, 'The Reluctant Peacekeeper: France and the Use of Force in Peace Operations' (2014) *37*(*5*) *Journal of Strategic Studies* 770.

Tardy, Thierry, 'The UN and the Use of Force: A Marriage Against Nature' (2007) *38*(*1*) *Security Dialogue* 49.

Thompson, Alexandra, 'After the Rwanda Genocide the UN Promised 'Never again' – Now It's Time For Them To Take Action Against ISIS', *Forbes* 20 April 2017 2017 <https://www.forbes.com/sites/realspin/2017/04/20/after-the-rwandan-genocide-the-un-promised-never-again-now-its-time-for-them-to-take-action-against-isis/#45226b641424>.

Tripodi, Paolo, 'Peacekeepers, Moral Autonomy and the Use of Force' (2006) 5(3) *Journal of Military Ethics* 214.

Tsagourias, Nicholas, 'Consent, Neutrality/Impartiality and the Use of Foce in Peacekeeping: Their Constitutional Dimension' (2007) 11(3) *Journal of Conflict and Security Law* 465.

Uddin, Md Kamal, 'Human Rights Violations by UN Peacekeepers' (2014) 25(1) *Security and Human Rights* 130.

UNMISS, *UNMISS Urges Parties to Deescalate Tensions and Lift Movement Restrictions* <https://unmiss.unmissions.org/sites/default/files/160712_unmiss_urges_parties_to_deescalate_tensions_and_lift_movement_restrictions.pdf>.

Urgent South Sudan Consultations Security Council Reporter <https://www.whatsinblue.org/2016/07/urgent-south-sudan-consultations.php>.

Van Der Vyver, Johan D., 'Sovereignty' in Dinah Shelton (ed), *The Oxford Handbook of International Human Rights Law* (Oxford University Press, 2013).

von Einsiedel, Sebastian and Louise Bosetti, 'Realizing the UN's Protection Promise: A Central Challenge for the Next Secretary-General' (2016) 8(4) *Global Responsibility to Protect* 366.

Weller, Marc (ed), *The Oxford Handbook of the Use of Force in International Law* (Oxford University Press, 2015).

Whittle, Devon, 'Peacekeeing in Conflict: The Intervention Brigade, MONUSCO, and the Application of International Humanitarian Law to United Nations Forces' (2015) 46(3) *Georgetown Journal of International Law* 837.

Williamson, Jamie A., 'Protection of Civilians under International Humanitarian Law' in Haidi Willmot et al (eds), *Protection of Civilians* (Oxford University Press, 2016).

Williamson, K., Gupta, P., Gillespie, L. A., Shannon, H., and Landis, D., *The Impact of Protection Interventions on Unaccompanies and Separated Children in Humanitarian Crises* (Humanitarian Evidence Programme, Oxford, 2017).

Willmot, Haidi and Ralph Mamiya, 'Mandated to Protect: Security Council Practice on the Protection of Civilians' in Marc Weller (ed), *The Oxford Handbook of the Use of Force in International Law* (Oxford University Press, 2015).

Willmot, Haidi and Scott Sheeran, 'The Protection of Civilians Mandate in UN Peacekeeping Operations: Reconciling Protection Concepts and Practices' (2013) 95(891/892) *International Review of the Red Cross* 517.

Willmot, Haidi, Sheeran, Scott and Sharland, Lisa, *Safety and Security Challenges in UN Peace Operations* (International Peace Institute, 2015).

Willmot, Haidi, Mamiya, Ralph, Sheeran, Scott and Weller, Marc (eds), *Protection of Civilians* (Oxford University Press, 2016).

Wills, Siobhán, 'Continuing Impunity of Peacekeepers: The Need for a Convention' (2013) 4(1) *Journal of International Humanitarian Legal Studies* 47.

Wills, Siobhán, *Protecting Civilians: The Obligations of Peacekeepers* (Oxford University Press, 2009).

Wills, Siobhán, 'The 'Responsibility to Protect' by Peace Support Forces under International Human Rights Law' (2006) 13(4) *International Peacekeeping* 476.

Wills, Siobhán, 'Use of Deadly Force by Peacekeepers Operating Outside of Armed Conflict Situations: What Laws Apply?' (2018) 40(3) *Human Rights Quarterly* 663.

Wynn-Pope, Phoebe, *Perceptions about Protection of Civilians: A Survey of Practitioners* (Australian Civil-Military Centre; Oxfam, 2014).

Young, Katharine G., 'The Minimum Core of Economic and Social Rights: A Concept in Search of Content' (2008) 117 *Yale International Law Journal* 113.

Zwanenburg, Marten, 'International Humanitarian Law Interoperability in Multinational Operations' (2013) 95(891–892) *International Review of the Red Cross* 681.

Index